This outstanding edited volume, gathering contributions from top specialists, brings EU migration law and EU criminal law in conversation with each other, delivering a thorough and topical exploration of the (ab)uses of criminal justice mechanisms for migration enforcement purposes, combining legal-doctrinal, theoretical, and socio-legal insights. It makes a critical contribution to ongoing debates, pushing the limits of "crimmigration" research in key ways that will remain influential for years to come.

Violeta Moreno-Lax, *Professor, ICREA-Universitat de Barcelona & Queen Mary University of London*

This insightful and thought-provoking edited volume critically examines the intersection of criminal justice and immigration control in the EU. Offering a compelling analysis of crimmigration, it highlights its profound legal, ethical, and human rights implications. A must-read for scholars, policymakers, and anyone concerned with justice, migration, and fundamental rights.

Anne Weyembergh, *Professor and Vice-Rector of Université libre de Bruxelles (ULB) for External Relations and Development Cooperation*

In many parts of the world, not least in the European Union, criminal law is increasingly used as an additional tool to regulate and govern migration. The contributors to this volume explore the many facets of this policy development and offer a cogently critical account from an interdisciplinary perspective.

Bruno De Witte, *Professor of European Law, Maastricht University*

Intertwining Criminal Justice and Immigration Control in the EU

This book offers a contemporary understanding of the state of the art of "crimmigration" with a focus on the European Union and challenges this paradigm of intersecting criminal justice and immigration control.

The contributions to this book explore the conceptual and philosophical underpinnings of EU and national policies intertwining criminal and migration law, as well as their practical use (and abuse). They analyse migration control through criminal law from multidisciplinary and interdisciplinary perspectives, incorporating insights from law, philosophy, and criminology. The book revisits fundamental questions on the suitability of criminal law to regulate and govern migration and provides insights as to whether and how the law should be amended to limit the negative consequences of the criminalisation of migration. The authors critique the key legal challenges crimmigration poses in terms of legality, fundamental rights, and rule of law adherence. Finally, this volume outlines, through concrete examples, how criminalisation of migration translates into the emergence of hostile environments for migrants and those who assist them.

This book will be of interest to criminologists, sociologists, legal scholars, and all those engaged in studies on migration and the European Union.

Niovi Vavoula is Associate Professor and Chair in Cyber Policy at the University of Luxembourg. Her research interests involve EU immigration law, particularly the intersection of migration law and technology and criminalisation of migration, as well as IT law, with an emphasis on the regulation of cyberspace, AI, and data protection.

Evangelia (Lilian) Tsourdi is Professor and Jean Monnet Chair in European Migration Law and Governance at the Law Faculty of Maastricht University.

Valsamis Mitsilegas is Professor of European and Global Law and Dean of the School of Law and Social Justice at the University of Liverpool. He is the author of 11 books and over 150 articles and chapters in the fields of European and transnational criminal law, migration law, security, human rights, and the rule of law.

Routledge Studies in Criminal Justice, Borders and Citizenship

Globalizing forces have had a profound impact on the nature of contemporary criminal justice and law more generally. This is evident in the increasing salience of borders and mobility in the production of illegality and social exclusion. *Routledge Studies in Criminal Justice, Borders and Citizenship* showcases contemporary studies that connect criminological scholarship to migration studies and explore the intellectual resonances between the two. It provides an opportunity to reflect on the theoretical and methodological challenges posed by mass mobility and its control. By doing that, it charts an intellectual space and establishes a theoretical tradition within criminology to house scholars of immigration control, race, and citizenship including those who traditionally publish *either* in general criminological *or* in anthropological, sociological, refugee studies, human rights and other publications.

Edited by
Prof José A. Brandariz
ECRIM, University of A Coruña
Prof Maggy S Y Lee
The University of Hong Kong
Katja Franko
University of Oslo

Border Frictions
Gender, Generation and Technology on the Frontline
Karine Côté-Boucher

Policing Mobility Regimes
Frontex and the Production of the European Borderscape
Giuseppe Campesi

Gendered Labour, Everyday Security and Migration
An Examination of Domestic Work and Domestic Workers' Experiences in Singapore and Hong Kong
Shih Joo Tan

Intertwining Criminal Justice and Immigration Control in the EU
Edited by Niovi Vavoula, Evangelia (Lilian) Tsourdi and Valsamis Mitsilegas

The Refugee Abyss
Hyab Yohannes

For more information about this series, please visit: https://www.routledge.com/criminology/series/CJBC

Intertwining Criminal Justice and Immigration Control in the EU

Edited by Niovi Vavoula,
Evangelia (Lilian) Tsourdi
and Valsamis Mitsilegas

Routledge
Taylor & Francis Group
LONDON AND NEW YORK

First published 2026
by Routledge
4 Park Square, Milton Park, Abingdon, Oxon OX14 4RN

and by Routledge
605 Third Avenue, New York, NY 10158

Routledge is an imprint of the Taylor & Francis Group, an informa business

British Library Cataloguing-in-Publication Data
A catalogue record for this book is available from the British Library

ISBN: 978-1-032-45730-7 (hbk)
ISBN: 978-1-032-45731-4 (pbk)
ISBN: 978-1-003-37844-0 (ebk)

DOI: 10.4324/9781003378440

Typeset in [Sabon]
by Apex CoVantage, LLC

Contents

Acknowledgements

We embarked on this journey of collaboration, reflection, research, and scientific exchanges on the intertwinement of criminal justice with immigration control in early 2020. We had three important milestones in this process. An exploratory workshop on our joint research themes took place in the Brussels Hub of Maastricht University in October 2021. We are extremely grateful for funding support for this workshop through Maastricht University's "Globalisation and Law Network" funded under the Sectorplan Social Sciences and Humanities of Dutch Universities. This helped us debate early drafts and dialogue on evolving research. Next, we held an authors' workshop at Queen Mary University of London in April 2023, where we exchanged expert commentary on fully developed research and finetuned content. The (B)orders Centre financially supported these authors' workshop. Finally, in March 2024, we held a debate panel at Maastricht University, where we brought in conversation authors of the volume with expert colleagues in the field to jointly reflect on the research themes. The Jean Monnet Chair in EU Migration Law and Governance that Evangelia (Lilian) Tsourdi holds at the Faculty of Law of Maastricht event supported the latter event.

We are grateful to all our colleagues who accompanied us in this journey. Firstly, our authors, for their intellectual insights, our stimulating scientific dialogues, their diligence, and their patience. Next, we would like to acknowledge intellectual exchanges with several "Globalisation and Law Network" members—especially its coordinator, Mariolina Eliantonio—and Johannes Keiler. We are equally indebted to Tom Sutton and Vanshinka Chaudhary from Routledge, who have enthusiastically embraced this project from its inception, for their support, professionalism, kind encouragement, and patience. We are also thankful to our team of research assistants, who ensured the technical quality of the contributions, and, notably, Giacomo Zamperi (University of Luxembourg) and Marianna Hu (University of Maastricht and EUI). We would also like to thank Elke Hundhausen from the Maastricht University Law Faculty events team for superb and diligent support in realising the Maastricht-based events.

Niovi Vavoula would like to acknowledge the financial support for the research and coordination activities for this volume by the (B)orders Centre of Queen Mary University of London—QMUL (Department of Law). She is indebted to her former colleagues at QMUL for their enthusiastic support, stimulating intellectual contributions, and practical support—particularly Prof. Violeta Moreno-Lax, Inaugural Director of the (B)orders Centre. She is also grateful to her family, partner, and friends for their unwavering support throughout her professional endeavours. Last, but certainly not least, she is very grateful to Lilian and Valsamis for the excellent collaboration; working with amazing colleagues is always a tremendous pleasure.

Evangelia (Lilian) Tsourdi would like to acknowledge financial support for the research and coordination activities for this volume from a European Research Council Starting Grant EU Grant Agreement 101165167, PI Lilian Tsourdi), a VENI programme grant (project Nr. VI.Veni.191R.040, PI: Evangelia (Lilian) Tsourdi) funded by the Dutch Research Council (NWO) and the "Globalisation and Law Network" funded under the Sectorplan Social Sciences and Humanities of Dutch Universities. She is also indebted more broadly to the scientific community at the Law Faculty of Maastricht University, its Globalisation and Law Network, and its Maastricht Centre for European Law, for stimulating and supportive research environments. She is especially grateful to Bruno De Witte for his mentorship and continuous encouragement during the development of this research line. A debt of gratitude is owed to her loved ones, and especially to her husband, Frederik, for kind support throughout the lengthy process of the development of this volume, and to her son Alexander for bringing joy and necessary distraction. And, of course, she is exceptionally indebted to Niovi and Valsamis for embarking together on this ambitious journey and for constant and stimulating dialogues on the scientific content.

Valsamis Mitsilegas extends his thanks to Niovi Vavoula and Evangelia (Lilian) Tsourdi for the cooperation, enthusiasm, drive, and their intellectual contribution to the volume.

Luxembourg, Maastricht, and Liverpool
January 2025

Contributors

Francesca Cancellaro

Francesca Cancellaro is a criminal lawyer specialised in fundamental rights of individuals and NGOs. Partner lawyer of the European Center for Constitutional and Human Rights (ECCHR), she received her PhD from the University of Bologna. She is defence attorney in the Kinsa case.

Galina Cornelisse

Dr Galina Cornelisse is Professor of Courts and Transnational Justice at the Law Faculty of the Vrije Universiteit Amsterdam in the Netherlands. Her work focuses on access to justice for those who have traditionally been excluded from justice on account of the territoriality of the global political system. Her interest in access to justice, protection of fundamental rights, and equality also drives her work as Adjudicating Commissioner for the Netherlands Institute for Human Rights.

Maja Grundler

Maja Grundler is a lecturer at Northumbria Law School. She holds a PhD in law from Queen Mary University of London and is the co-founder and co-chair of the Human Trafficking Research Network. Maja's research focuses on the intersection of refugee law and irregular migration, human trafficking, and migrant smuggling.

Johannes Keiler

Johannes Keiler is Assistant Professor of Criminal Law in the Department of Criminal Law and Criminology at Maastricht University (The Netherlands). His research focuses on various aspects of substantive criminal law, as well as comparative and European criminal law. He currently lectures on subjects including comparative criminal law and Dutch substantive criminal law.

Marta Minetti

Dr Marta Minetti is Lecturer in Law at Goldsmiths, University of London, where she teaches immigration law, criminal law, and advanced criminal law. Her research focuses on the legislative contrast to irregular migration and humanitarian assistance in Italy, its relationship with the expansion of the populist rhetoric in the legislative field, and the incompatibilities with the cardinal principles of the rule of law.

Valsamis Mitsilegas

Valsamis Mitsilegas is Professor of European and Global Law and Dean of the School of Law and Social Justice at the University of Liverpool. He is the author of 11 books and over 150 articles and chapters in the fields of European and transnational criminal law, migration law, security, human rights, and the rule of law.

Flavia Patanè

Flavia Patanè is a PhD candidate at Maastricht University. Her research examines the interplay between criminal law, criminological perspectives, and international refugee law, with a particular focus on human smuggling. She explores the legal and policy frameworks governing migration control in the EU and their implications for human rights and criminal justice systems.

Alessandro Spena

Alessandro Spena is Professor of Criminal Law at the University of Palermo; Senior Visiting Fellow at the Nathanson Centre on Transnational Human Rights, Crime and Security (York University, Toronto—2012); Jemolo Fellow at Nuffield College (Oxford University—2013); and Senior Visiting Fellow at Max Planck Institute for the Study of Crime, Security and Law, Freiburg i.Br. (2024). Main subjects: corruption, hate speech, crimmigration, rights, and criminal responsibility.

Evangelia (Lilian) Tsourdi

Evangelia (Lilian) Tsourdi is Professor and Jean Monnet Chair in European Migration Law and Governance at the Law Faculty of Maastricht University.

Niovi Vavoula

Dr Niovi Vavoula is Associate Professor and Chair in Cyber Policy at the University of Luxembourg. Her research interests involve EU immigration law, particularly the intersection of migration law and technology and criminalisation of migration as well as IT law, with an emphasis on the regulation of cyberspace, AI, and data protection.

Stefano Zirulia

Stefano Zirulia is Associate Professor of Criminal Law at the University of Milan. His main area of research is in the relationship between criminal law and fundamental rights, with a special focus, inter alia, on immigration criminal law.

Series Editor's Introduction

José A. Brandariz

Routledge Studies in Criminal Justice, Borders and Citizenship showcases contemporary studies that connect criminological scholarship to migration studies and explores the intellectual resonances between the two. It provides an opportunity to reflect on the theoretical and methodological challenges posed by mass mobility and its control. Inaugurated in 2013, the series sets out the cutting edge of scholarship in the field of border criminology and related disciplines.

The EU Pact on Migration and Asylum, which was passed in May 2024 and is expected to be fully implemented by mid-2026, is a critical legal and policy milestone whose implications are going to be widely felt for years to come. Although the pact is largely focused on asylum policies, it will have a significant impact on every dimension of European migration policy. In addition, it will be further developed in the coming years, leading to new legal arrangements, such as the reframed Return Directive. Criminalisation of migration policies will also be profoundly altered by the EU Pact and its legal and policy developments. In this specific field, academic and political conversations in Europe have been mainly focused on migrant smuggling and the facilitation of irregular migration. In fact, the expected reform of these offences has sparked intense debates in recent years across Europe.

Vavoula, Tsourdi, and Mitsilegas' new collection, *Intertwining Criminal Justice and Immigration Control in the EU*, squarely addresses these debates. It gathers an impressive collection of contributions exploring current manifestations of crimmigration law in Europe, that is, the increasing interrelation of criminal law and immigration law in curbing irregular migration and governing the lives of non-citizens. The collection examines emerging issues in this field and provides cutting-edge, theoretically sophisticated approaches to the criminalisation of migration. Although it is particularly focused on the southern European jurisdictions, such as Greece and Italy, which have been turned into the "ground zero" of migration control innovation, this collection also provides compelling explorations on crimmigration practices in countries far from the EU's external borders, such as Germany and the Netherlands, as well as the UK. All in all, *Intertwining Criminal Justice and Immigration Control in the EU* is a path-breaking collection anticipating the research questions that will call the attention of crimmigration scholars in the coming future.

1 Intertwining Criminal Justice and Immigration Control in the EU

Theoretical, Interdisciplinary, and Practical Perspectives

*Niovi Vavoula and Evangelia (Lilian) Tsourdi**

1.1 Introduction

The introductory chapter sheds light on the evolving criminalisation of migration, or "crimmigration" and its consequences, with a focus on the European Union (EU) context. Crimmigration broadly encompasses the entire arsenal of coercive measures stemming from the criminal justice system and currently available for immigration enforcement. This continuum of preventive and repressive measures includes detention, preventive policing, deportation of migrants convicted of criminal offences,[1] and the creation of an array of criminal offences for non-compliance with immigration legislation.

The chapter first conceptualises the criminalisation of migration with reference to its theoretical underpinnings at the intersection of law, criminology, and philosophy (Section 1.2) before critiquing its origin and evolution (Section 1.3). We then scrutinise three different facets through which crimmigration manifests: The use of substantive criminal law to regulate the presence of migrants (Section 1.4), the banalisation of detention (Section 1.5), and the transplantation of surveillance tools to manage migration (Section 1.6). This scrutiny highlights key legal challenges crimmigration poses, in terms of legality, fundamental rights, and rule of law adherence. Our analysis mobilises and juxtaposes existing studies in criminology, philosophy of law, and criminal and migration law—including previous works of the co-editors—with original findings and arguments from the various contributions to this volume. The chapter concludes with overarching observations, paving the way for the volume's original contributions (Section 1.7).

* This research was supported by a European Research Council Starting Grant (EU Grant Agreement 101165167, PI Lilian Tsourdi).

DOI: 10.4324/9781003378440-1

1.2 Conceptualising the Criminalisation of Migration

Recent decades have witnessed the growing transplantation of criminal law strategies to pre-empt and manage migration. To refer to this convergence of criminal and migration law in 2006, Juliette Stumpf coined the term "crimmigration".[2] Focusing on the United States (US), Stumpf stressed that the division between criminal law and migration law "has grown indistinct" to the extent that "the merger of the two areas in both substance and procedure has created parallel systems in which immigration law and the criminal justice system are merely nominally separate".[3] Stumpf's observation about the intertwining of migration and criminal law was not entirely novel. Since the early 2000s, several American scholars had already pinpointed and described at least parts of this trend.[4] For example, as early as in 2003, Teresa Miller referred to a "dynamic process by which both systems converge at points to create a new system of social control that draws from both immigration and criminal justice".[5] Nevertheless, by coining the term crimmigration for this phenomenon, Stumpf attracted growing scholarly attention and contributed to launching a new field of study.

Although it originated in the US, crimmigration is now transnational and well-established in different regions, such as Europe[6] and Australia.[7] It refers to criminal law mechanisms and imagery being heavily relied upon as part of a political strategy for managing migration flows.[8] As a framework, it has proven to be particularly useful for understanding the contemporary forms of immigration control and the various ways it is both shaped by and shapes the criminal justice system.[9] As Leanne Weber and Jude McCulloch stress: "[the concept of crimmigration] provides a powerful and systematic framework for the examination of punitive practices such as criminal deportation, immigration detention and migration policing, and is particularly useful in framing analyses of how immigration controls are enforced".[10]

At its most basic, criminalisation of migration describes the convergence of two bodies of law: Criminal law and procedure, with immigration law and procedure, in the context of public authorities' responses to irregular migration. This is notwithstanding the fact that these are traditionally two clearly distinct legal spheres, with little doctrinal or theoretical overlap, each pursuing its own objectives and underpinned by different principles. Thus, at first sight, it might seem curious that these two domains are becoming increasingly alike, "because criminal law seems a distant cousin to immigration law".[11] Indeed, while criminal law concerns the harm caused by individuals to other individuals or society, immigration law deals with questions regarding the admissibility and status of foreigners within the national territory. That said, the two areas share certain common features. For example, they both pertain to the relationship between individuals and the state, they wield government power over the physical liberty of individuals, and they operate as gatekeepers, in the sense of determining who belongs to a given society and who does not.[12] As Stumpf notes:

> [B]oth criminal and immigration law are, at their core, systems of inclusion and exclusion. They are similarly designed to determine whether and how to include individuals as members of society or exclude them from it. Both create insiders and outsiders. Both are designed to create categories of people.[13]

At the same time, the two fields are separate, given that criminal law is concerned with internal security (thus looking inwards), the moral borders of society, and censuring substantial wrongdoing, while migration law concentrates more on external security and territorial borders.[14] This is reflected in early court decisions on immigration matters. As early as 1893, in *Fong Yue Ting v United States*, the US Supreme Court stressed that immigration powers are rooted in international law and linked to concerns over foreign affairs.[15] Criminal law and procedure were thought to be the territory of prosecutors, criminal defence attorneys, and judges who oversee criminal prosecutions. Importantly, the two fields have distinct outcomes: Criminal enforcement may lead to exclusion in the form of imprisonment, whereas exclusion in the context of immigration enforcement means refusing entry to, or removal from, national territory. In the migration field, exclusion further translates into the denial of basic substantive and procedural rights, for example, through the application of fast-track procedures to asylum applicants arriving irregularly at the borders, even while those individuals remain fully subject to the criminal law, including its procedural safeguards.

The dissolution of the boundaries between criminal and immigration law is a bi-directional process, whereby criminal law has started to incorporate elements of immigration law and *vice versa* due to a "gravitational pull" on each other.[16] To understand the origins of crimmigration, Stumpf identified a change in societal perceptions of irregular migrants, who are increasingly perceived as criminals, likely to commit future crimes because of their history of entering the country without authorisation.[17] There also exists a discursive link between migration and terrorism.[18] In the EU, under a security-oriented approach, refugees and migrants are redefined as a security threat to state sovereignty and to the internal security of the Schengen borderless area.[19]

In an attempt to explain the motive behind this change of perception, crimmigration has been tied to "membership theory", according to which individual rights and privileges should be restricted to members of the social contract between the government and the people, with other individuals excluded.[20] Membership theory provides decision-makers with justification for using criminal law to regulate as a means of exclusion, with only the harshest elements of each area of law incorporated into the crimmigration regime. Though framed differently, both criminal law and migration law are preoccupied with questions about belonging and exclusion; the former assumes membership and the latter assumes non-membership. More recently, criminalisation of migration has been conceptualised as creating a "paradox of exclusion". While migrants are constructed as criminal populations who must accordingly be subject to criminal justice mechanisms to be isolated from the rest of the society, once constructed as criminals, migrants enter a terrain that traditionally operates pursuant to a logic of inclusivity and equality.[21] For example, this is reflected in the strong constitutional protections and procedural rights that criminal defendants hold.

At the heart of criminalisation of migration lies the expression of the penal power of the state against foreigners through various coercive tools, including deportation, detention, and *stricto sensu* criminalisation. Criminalisation may be viewed in the broader context of state efforts to control global mobility, instead of viewing mobility as intrinsic to human nature. In a "culture of control", as David Garland has eloquently put it, there is growing societal motivation for the identification, segregation, and incapacitation of certain classes of people perceived as "the dangerous other",[22] with migrants and refugees falling within this realm of risky individuals. In a "risky society", the criminalisation of migration, thus, satisfies the need of the state to reaffirm its legitimacy and sovereignty, ultimately preventing migration, minimise the "supply" of risky migrants, and remove those who are not deterred.

However, this is not the sole theoretical lens through which to understand how drastically and rapidly criminal justice institutions are reconfigured and the significance of this process for contemporary penal power. Criminalisation must be viewed in parallel with the development of other theoretical frameworks, such as the adaptation of "new penology"[23] and "enemy penology".[24] As pointed out by Weber and McCulloch,[25] the crimmigration lens highlights the *how* of immigration control; it sheds light on the mechanisms and processes of immigration and border control, while also drawing attention to its exclusionary effects. The new penology lens highlights the *why* of immigration control and elucidates the underlying sociopolitical and sociocultural drivers of increased migration management. Migration, mobility, and individuals on the move are framed as potential risks that need monitoring in order to avert security or national identity-related threats. As for enemy penology, this theoretical framework explains the *when* of immigration control. A risk-based approach (and language) justifies the use of various proactive and preventive measures, state control, and penal power to identify potential threats at the earliest stage possible, before the commission of any criminal offences or the breach of any laws. Practices of risk assessments and profiling to identify the dangerous other are inextricably linked to a preventive approach. Crimmigration is also closely linked to the rise in anti-immigrant rhetoric, solidifying the ideological construction of large groups of foreigners as "illegal" with the moral stigma and negative connotations that accompany that term. This brings to the fore broader questions beyond the how, why, and when of criminalisation of migration management, on the intertwinement of criminal justice with immigration control. In this context, questions of race, citizenship, gender, and neo-colonial relations of power are also pertinent.

1.3 The Evolving Criminalisation of Migration

Criminalisation of migration started approximately 40 years ago. Until the 1980s, citizens and foreigners were largely punished alike for the commission of criminal offences. Furthermore, immigration law intersected with criminal law only in cases where entry into national territory was denied to individuals with a criminal history. Therefore, in the first centuries of the existence of the US, the criminal background of a foreigner could impact whether they could enter the country, but it generally did not justify expelling those already settled.[26] Irregular migration and unauthorised entry were not punishable criminal offences; the official response to irregular entry was usually deportation, not prosecution, and foreigners who perpetrated criminal offences after entering a country were not to be deported. When resident foreigners committed crimes, the criminal justice system, not deportation, addressed the conduct, assigning sentences and other forms of punishment as used against citizens.[27]

In the mid-1980s, the stark separation between criminal law and immigration law shifted quickly and drastically. In the US, the "war on drugs" inspired legislation–the Anti-Drug Abuse Act of 1988[28]–that, among other changes, created a category of grounds of deportation based on a variety of crimes, irrespective of when they were committed, and rendered many long-term resident foreigners vulnerable to deportation. Simultaneously, the US took a key step towards making crime-based deportation grounds unassailable, as almost all avenues for relief from deportation based on criminal grounds were taken away through two legal acts: The Antiterrorism and Effective Death Penalty Act of 1996,[29] and the Illegal Immigration Reform and Immigration Responsibility Act of 1996.[30] Thus, progressively, a foreigner with criminal charges began to face possible immigration penalties, and nowadays, it has become increasingly difficult to distinguish where the criminal justice system ends and the immigration process begins. Furthermore, unlawful entry, which had long been a crime in the US, but was rarely enforced through the criminal justice system, was increasingly the ground for prosecution, becoming the largest category of federal criminal prosecutions.[31] Creating an impenetrable border with Mexico became the flagship of immigration control, resulting in the assignment of federal law enforcement officers to the border.

This two-way street between migration and criminal enforcement has also evolved in Europe, where "immigration control is used to achieve security objectives, while security and crime governance methods are being used to conduct border and immigration controls".[32] Crimmigration law emerged along two interrelated levels; at the EU level and the Schengen Area, and within individual Member States.[33] The abolition of internal border controls in the Schengen Area was coupled with heightened concerns about the connection between immigration and organised crime and their links to internal security, which could affect the economic stability and the welfare capacities of the EU Member States, leading to a securitisation of migration trend in the EU. The links between internal security, organised crime, and immigration control became more apparent in the early 1990s, when the EU powers governing migration and border control expanded via legislation that adopted substantive criminal law provisions, characterising conduct associated with irregular migration flows as criminal as well as sanctionable for the violation of immigration-related provisions. As we analyse below, the adoption of legal instruments on combatting trafficking in human beings is a prime example in that respect.[34]

Human smuggling, or in more neutral EU terms, the facilitation of unauthorised entry, transit, or residence, is (for now) regulated by a dual legislative framework (the "Facilitators' Package"). The package is comprised of a brief Directive that defines "facilitation of unauthorised entry, transit and residence"[35] and a complementary Framework Decision, which confirms that the conduct defined in the Directive is to be treated as a criminal offence and punishable by effective, proportionate, and dissuasive criminal penalties, and imposes specific high levels of sanctions only when certain aggravating circumstances occur.[36] This set of legal instruments is completed by the Employers' Sanctions Directive (Directive 2009/52/EC), which imposes duties on employers of irregular migrants and provides for sanctions in case of non-compliance, or if they infringe the prohibition on employing "illegally staying third-country nationals". Whereas the focus of these instruments is individuals who act as facilitators or intermediaries of irregular migration in a broad sense, any violations of immigration law by irregular migrants themselves are not dealt with by EU law, but, as we explain below, by national law.

The concept of crimmigration has thus sought to address the growing merger of these two fields, whereby the immigration process has grown to resemble the criminal process, and the powers of immigration and criminal law enforcement agencies have become almost indistinguishable. There are different facets of crimmigration, both at substantive and at procedural levels.[37] First, immigration and criminal laws increasingly overlap. This overlap is witnessed in the expansion of criminal grounds that justify deportation of foreigners who are deemed to be risky from national territory, the overall banalisation of detention (typically a criminal law instrument),[38] and in the elevation of a growing number of immigration law violations to the status of criminal offences with penalties ranging from fines to imprisonment. A second trend concerns the increasing resemblance of immigration enforcement and criminal law enforcement, in terms of mandate, powers, and the tools used to exert control, including physical control, over individuals. Police agencies and even military actors are increasingly involved in controlling migration and enforcing immigration laws, for example, through stop and search powers and the performance of street identity checks.

Third, the procedural aspects of prosecuting immigration violations have taken on many of the trademarks of criminal procedure without, however, a corresponding transfer of the procedural protections that are integral to the criminal justice system.[39] The imprint of the administrative law paradigm on immigration procedures is reflected in the position of the judge reviewing executive decision-making. The scope and intensity of judicial review differ significantly from criminal law cases, as evidenced by recognising extensive administrative leeway and limited checks and balances. Nowhere is this facet better reflected than in the jurisprudence of the European Court of Human Rights (ECtHR), which, in *Maaouia v France*, opined that immigration procedures are not covered by the human right to a fair trial enshrined in Article 6 of the European Convention of Human Rights (ECHR), as these procedures do "not entail any determination of civil rights or obligations or of a criminal charge".

In the next sections, we scrutinise more closely these three different faces of crimmigration, that is, the use of substantive criminal law to regulate the presence of migrants; the banalisation of detention; and the transplantation of surveillance tools to manage migration. To do so, we draw from the fields of criminology, philosophy of law, and criminal and migration law, while weaving in original findings and arguments from the various contributions to this volume.

1.4 Crimmigration as the Use of Substantive Criminal Law to Regulate the Presence of Migrants

The contamination of immigration law with measures that traditionally fall within the realm of criminal law has progressively established a hybrid "criminal-type" system of immigration control, whereby criminal law lends enforcement agencies and tools to administrative law, and provides a variety of sanctioning options.[40] A prominent manifestation of criminalisation of migration lies in the worldwide proliferation of crimes based on conduct related to migration, such as irregular entry, and subsequently imposing adverse criminal law consequences as sanctions for such conduct, as well as the increasing enforcement of those crimes. Increased criminalisation stems from the framing of irregular migration as a criminal problem instead of an administrative one.[41] This coincides with a rather narrow view of crimmigration, which concerns the use of substantive criminal law to regulate migration through the creation of immigration-related criminal offences and the imposition of criminal sanctions for these offences, which may be combined with immigration-related consequences, such as deportation.

Various studies have mapped the extent to which different states impose criminal sanctions for irregular entry. Overall, around 124 countries treat irregular entry as a criminal offence, punishable by a wide range of sanctions, including deportation, fines, community service, or imprisonment.[42] The length of imprisonment varies from several months to 15 years, depending on the circumstances of the entry. Most countries prescribe stricter punishment if irregular migrants were armed, used or threatened to use force, or caused damage to private property in the course of irregular entry. In some jurisdictions, irregular entry by a group entails harsher punishment than irregular border crossing by an individual. The countries that only impose civil or administrative penalties include Angola, Argentina, Australia, Brazil, Colombia, the Czech Republic, Ecuador, Mexico, Peru, Portugal, Slovakia, Spain, Turkey, Venezuela, and Vietnam. Even in these countries, however, criminal sanctions may apply in the presence of aggravating circumstances. In line with the 1951 Refugee Convention, undocumented entrants are often exempted from penalties when they are seeking asylum or are otherwise entitled to international protection.[43]

In Europe, the assignation of criminal penalties to violations of immigration rules has taken place at national and EU levels. The EU Agency for Fundamental Rights (FRA) has found that in almost all EU Member States, irregular entry and stay are directly criminalised, often punishable with custodial sentences.[44] In particular, legislation in 17 EU Member States punishes irregular entry with imprisonment and/or a fine. Eight EU Member States punish it with a fine only, although in aggravated circumstances, the punishment may still be imprisonment. Malta, Portugal, and Spain do not punish irregular entry with a fine or imprisonment, but return procedures are immediately initiated. Similarly, legislation 25 EU Member States punishes irregular stay, with ten applying a fine and/or imprisonment and 15 a fine only. Such sanctions are in addition to the coercive measures that may be taken to ensure the removal of the person from the territory. For irregular entry and stay, fines can be up to €10,000 (Italy). For irregular entry, the maximum length of imprisonment ranges from one month in Croatia and three months in Belgium to five years in Bulgaria. For irregular stay, it ranges from 60 days in Croatia to three years in Cyprus.

The breadth of immigration offences is striking, as states enact various norms criminalising conduct ancillary to irregular migration, such as use, or even mere possession, of forged immigration documents. The example of the United Kingdom (UK) is illustrative in this respect. Immigration crimes were introduced in the Immigration Act 1971, but between 1999 and 2016, Parliament added no fewer than 89 new types of immigration offences to the 70 that had been introduced between 1905 and 1998 concerning not only foreigners but also other actors involved in migration.[45] Entering without documents (previously an administrative violation) is now a strict liability offence and the most prosecuted immigration offence.[46] Notwithstanding the widespread criminalisation, the majority of enforcement actions against third parties and migrants have been undertaken through civil penalties and removals rather than criminal prosecution, reflecting the primarily symbolic and deterrent purpose of criminalisation. Criminalisation in the UK has expanded through the Nationality and Borders Act 2022, according to which merely entering the UK without permission (irregular entry) or—even more worryingly—overstaying a visa has been made a criminal offence punishable by up to four years in prison. This broad criminalisation has rightly raised significant concerns about its compatibility with Article 31 of the Refugee Convention and the potential of *en masse* prosecutions of asylum seekers, putting significant pressure on the UK criminal justice system.

The normative foundations of criminalising irregular entry and stay have been subject to criticism. Alessandro Spena has considered criminalisation an abuse of criminal law, as it puts a ban on certain groups of persons, rather than their individual conduct (actions or omissions), in a way that a principled criminal law should not do.[47] Furthermore, he argued that criminalisation constitutes a perversion of the criminal law, whereby "criminal norms are (unjustifiably) used as means to attain extra-penal aims". This type of criminalisation also disregards basic principles of criminal law, such as the requirements of the harm principle and culpability.[48] In this volume, Spena frames criminalisation of migration in terms of hatred and hate speech. He highlights the antithesis between the existence of crimmigration principles and norms and the fight against hate speech, which inevitably affects the credibility of the political message sent through both.[49] In his view, crimmigration contributes and nourishes hostile sociopolitical media narratives and "seals them with the formal authority of the state and provides them with new arguments of a legal-bureaucratic nature". As a result, "illegal" migrants are made "criminal strangers, marked with a foreignness/extraneousness/Otherness that is no longer only national, but also criminal", "deviant subjects" whose "social stigmatisation finds in criminal law a reason, an argument, additional to those found in migration law".[50]

At EU level, criminalisation has translated into the adoption of various substantive criminal law measures by the EU legislature, which are concerned with the criminalisation of acts relating to irregular migration, such as human smuggling.[51] That said, and notwithstanding the treatment of many violations of national immigration law, such as irregular entry, as criminal offences in the majority of EU Member States, EU law has not assigned criminal sanctions to the conduct of irregular migrants as such. Rather, the law has centred on targeting individuals who broadly facilitate, in one way or another, irregular migration, based on a broader process of securitisation of migration. As a result, criminal law is primarily aimed at treating conduct associated with migration flows as criminal offences, with sanctions for violating the relevant provisions. In particular, the phenomena of trafficking human beings and facilitation of unauthorised entry, transit, or stay are viewed as global security threats and as part and parcel of the threat of transnational organised crime.[52] As a response, the EU legislature has adopted various legal instruments aimed at combating these phenomena.

With regard to trafficking of human beings, EU legislation first emerged with the adoption of Framework Decision 2002/629/JHA.[53] The latter was adopted in the aftermath of the 2000 United Nations (UN) Convention on

Transnational Organized Crime (Palermo Convention),[54] which includes two Protocols, one on human trafficking (Trafficking Protocol)[55] and one on human smuggling (Smuggling Protocol).[56] The fact that this Protocol was attached to a Convention on organised crime supported claims that human trafficking was simply a form of organised crime that ought to be fought through the use of criminal law.[57] This security-oriented approach and the establishment of a link with irregular migration resulted in a framework decision that took a strictly punitive approach.[58] Council Directive 2004/81/EC on short-term residence permits for victims of trafficking affords some protection for the victims of human trafficking, though limited in terms of both time and substance. This instrument remains applicable to date.[59]

A slight re-balancing towards a more protection-oriented approach was achieved with the adoption of Directive 2011/36/EU, which was hybrid in nature, as it contained both substantive criminal law measures and provisions on the rights of victims.[60] However, a number of the victims' provisions "continue to be framed in whole or in part under a logic of prosecutorial efficiency",[61] and a number of concepts, such as "abuse of power", "abuse of a position of vulnerability", and "forced labour", were either vaguely defined or not defined at all.[62] The reform of the Anti-Trafficking Directive via Directive 2024/1712[63] resulted in more explicit links with migration, but without sufficient protection. In particular, the Directive does not effectively promote access to safe reporting for individuals without documentation at risk of exploitation, or access to residence permits, or to regularisation.[64]

The Facilitators' Package is a rather old set of EU legal instruments to regulate the facilitation of unauthorised entry, transit, or residence which creates a very broad scope for criminalisation. As Johannes Keiler rightly observes in this volume, the Directive distinguishes between the facilitation of illegal entry and transit, and the facilitation of residence of irregular migrants.[65] For assistance provided to migrants with regard to illegal entry and transit, no financial gain is required for liability, whereas for assistance for illegal stay, financial gain is a constitutive requirement for liability.[66] Therefore, with regard to the facilitation of illegal entry, by dispensing with the condition that a financial or other material benefit occurs, the EU legal framework contravenes the UN Smuggling Protocol, which explicitly requires obtaining a financial or other material benefit as a constituent element of liability for migrant smuggling.[67] Criminalisation can cover any form of assistance to enter or transit the territory of an EU Member State, including humanitarian assistance towards refugees and migrants, which may include a range of activities such as search and rescue (SAR) at sea, providing shelter to asylum seekers, or transporting them after their rescue to a place of safety.[68] A "humanitarian exception" is optional;[69] thus, its protective scope is dependent upon national implementation. Only seven Member States' legislation includes provisions specifically exempting from punishment conduct relating to facilitation for humanitarian assistance.[70]

This broad scope of criminalisation has resulted in a number of high-profile cases, such as the prosecution of Carola Rackete in Italy for bringing migrants to Italian shores through rescue ships that had been banned from docking at ports,[71] or the case in Greece concerning more than ten members of the NGO Emergency Response Centre International, who face charges for migrant smuggling, espionage, and membership in a criminal organisation.[72] Criminalisation of those assisting migrants, on the other hand, is underpinned by the notion that solidarity is exclusively due to citizens or residence permit holders. Pro-migrant mobilisations initiated by citizens or civil society actors are framed as practices of "inclusive solidarity" that aim to renegotiate societal structures and overcome forms of social exclusion at the national level.[73] They challenge citizenship as a bounded legal category based on national identity in *lieu* of active or performative citizenship, and their criminalisation redefines the relationship between the citizen and the state.[74]

Politicisation of migration is an important factor in the intertwinement of immigration with criminal law.[75] In certain Member States, such as Italy, the motivation to alienate the "dangerous other" may be influenced by "penal populism", understood as "the use, for political purposes, of diffused punitive instances and as an expressive political orientation guided by consensus obtained through the promise of quick, exemplary, and definite intervention for the reassuring of the citizens against a perceived common threat".[76] Penal populism is seen as an inevitable product of the intersection of democratic politics and criminality, as political elites seek to satisfy the (perceived) demand of citizens for punitive policies. Employing criminal law in this context is symbolic rather than substantive, exemplified by low and discretionary enforcement. As such, it fails to live up to its promise of control, stemming from protecting the public against crime, and ultimately lacks ethical underpinnings.[77] As Marta Minetti highlights in this volume, the influence of populism in Italy has led to the "distortion of the preventive and rehabilitative aim of criminal law", with significant impact on the fundamental rights of migrants, where SAR operations are hindered as well as the rule of law, ultimately threatening the democratic foundations of the society.[78]

The trend of criminalising migration has extended to the criminalisation and prosecution of human smuggling in a rather sweeping manner, including cases of "self-smuggling". As Flavia Patanè analyses in this volume, national authorities take a "formalistic approach in which agency of migrants annihilates their status as asylum seekers and exposes them to different levels of criminalisation".[79] As a result, the fact that smuggled individuals may be both "objects" and "agents" in their journey is not accounted for, making the Facilitators' Package, as implemented at national level, unsuitable and ineffective for tackling smuggling.[80]

As part of a package of legislative measures aimed at "countering migrant smuggling", in November 2023, the Commission put forward a proposal aimed to replace the Facilitators' Package with a Directive laying down minimum rules to prevent and counter the facilitation of unauthorised entry, transit, and stay in the EU.[81] As Valsamis Mitsilegas highlights in this volume, the focus of the proposal remains primarily preventive, aiming to prevent access of migrants and refugees to EU territory, which is evident not least from the very title of the proposed legal instrument ("to prevent and counter the facilitation").[82] Furthermore, profit again does not feature as one of the constituent elements of the baseline offence. Only Recital 7 of the Preamble mentions that third-country nationals should not become criminally liable for having been subject to such criminal offences. The same recital states that it is not the purpose of the proposed Directive to criminalise assistance provided to family members, humanitarian assistance, or the support of basic human needs provided to third-country nationals in compliance with legal obligations. Otherwise, mitigating circumstances are strictly limited to cooperation with state authorities, thus maintaining a securitised emphasis on criminalisation and disregarding humanitarian motives.[83]

The timing of the proposal is particularly interesting in light of the preliminary reference before the Court of Justice of the EU (CJEU) in the *Kinsa* case, which directly questions the compatibility with the EU Charter of Fundamental Rights of the criminalisation of the facilitation of unauthorised entry in EU law on a non-profit-making basis without exclusion of humanitarian assistance.[84] As Stefano Zirulia and Francesca Cancellaro explore in this volume, criminalisation of humanitarian assistance violates the principle of proportionality.[85] In their view, the limitation placed on fundamental rights is not justified by the benefits criminalisation intends to obtain, particularly because it "affects rescue and humanitarian conduct, leading to the sacrifice of the most important personal interests in the name of a counter-interest, that of the integrity of borders, which is clearly of a lower rank".[86]

Whereas both trafficking and smuggling constitute criminal offences, smuggled persons are not perceived as equally vulnerable and in need of protection; such status is reserved only to trafficked persons, even though the distinction between trafficking and smuggling is often very blurry.[87] In this volume, Maja Grundler calls for a nuanced approach towards trafficked and smuggled persons' vulnerability as comprised of inherent, situational, and consequential aspects to inform irregular migrants' treatment as victims of crime.[88] EU law employs a restrictive view, failing to acknowledge that irregular migrants are re-victimised, not just by traffickers and smugglers but also by the state and that the latter and its actions -may thus be a source of vulnerability.[89]

Another strand of criminalisation measures has been linked with the wider trend of immigration control privatisation, whereby states increasingly co-opt the private sector to assist in immigration control and to prevent irregular movement or stay.[90] Criminalisation, in this context, targets employers of irregular migrants by providing for sanctions if they fail to comply with a series of imposed duties or if they infringe the prohibition on employing "illegally staying third-country nationals".[91] The Directive also contains important protective elements to redress injustices against migrants in an irregular situation, such as exploitative conditions, and to promote access to justice, for example, to claim outstanding wages. However, the logic of the Employers Sanctions Directive displays a paradoxical approach, whereby both the employers and irregular migrants are simultaneously viewed as allies of the state, co-opted in conducting immigration control duties (for employers), and assisting in fighting employment exploitation (for irregular migrants), and as targets, viewing employment in the EU as a pull factor for irregular migration.[92]

At the same time, the EU's involvement in crimmigration is not only direct, through criminalisation of violations of immigration law, but also *indirect*, through the limitations placed on Member States' power to criminalise by the case law of the CJEU. Irregular entry and stay constitute criminal offences in all EU Member States and trigger a deportation procedure. This brings to the fore questions about the compatibility of these procedures with the EU legal instrument that regulates the standards and procedures applicable to persons subject to a return decision, Directive 2008/115/EC (the Return Directive).[93] The Directive obliges Member State authorities to issue a return decision in every case where an irregular migrant is detected on national territory. Through a series of judgements, starting with the cases of *El Dridi* and *Achughbabian*, the CJEU has imposed significant limits on the Member States' powers to enforce criminal law provisions, primarily on the imposition of penalties of imprisonment, prioritising the effectiveness of the Directive over the enforcement of crimmigration laws.[94] Nonetheless, the imposition of fines,[95] or even custodial penalties for repeat offenders[96] or where the person is non-returnable,[97] is not excluded.

As this section has stressed, the use of substantive criminal law to regulate the presence of migrants and other actors relating to their migration is extensive, multifaceted, dynamic, and remains a highly controversial field for research.

1.5 Crimmigration as Banalisation of Detention

Detention corresponds to a "singular blending" of the criminal and migration law areas[98] and is a ubiquitous part of crimmigration enforcement. Detention of asylum seekers pending the determination of their claim, and of irregular migrants pending their eventual removal, shares the key features of pre-trial detention and imprisonment. It entails total control over the physical liberty of the detainee and solidifies their exclusion from society. At the same time, detention challenges the right to liberty of a person, recognised in Article 5 of the ECHR and Article 9 of the International Covenant on Civil and Political Rights (ICCPR) as well as Article 6 of the EU Charter of Fundamental Rights.

Australia operates a severe and punitive immigration detention system, whereby detention is mandatory, indefinite, without distinction between adults, children, or asylum seekers.[99] In the US, a series of statutes has developed groups of foreigners who must be subjected to mandatory detention in a way that has stripped immigration officers of their discretionary power to decide whether to detain them or to release them on bond. The US immigration detention system is legally classified as civil, rather than criminal, and therefore non-punitive. This means that many constitutional protections available under criminal law are missing from the system; immigrants can be detained indefinitely, there is no federal right to legal representation for detainees, and most immigrants are not entitled to government-appointed lawyers, greatly reducing their prospects of winning their cases.[100] At the same time, immigration detention mimics the criminal incarceration system and holds detained individuals in punitive, prison-like conditions.[101] Within immigration detention centres, there are increasing reports of civil and human rights abuses, including preventable deaths in custody, but significant fragmentation of responsibility and accountability among the agencies managing the immigration detention system is also experienced.

At European level, the use of detention in migration management is not *per se* a recent novelty; Article 5(1)(f) of the ECHR allows "the lawful arrest or detention of a person against whom action is being taken with a view to deportation or extradition". According to ECtHR case law, legislation authorising detention should satisfy general principles of legal certainty, including being accessible, precise, and foreseeable in its application to avoid the risk of arbitrariness.[102] What is new, though, is that the significant increase in migration rates in the last two decades has altered the practical impact of detention.[103] Specifically, migration detention has shifted from being an instrument to facilitate dealing with individual cases of uncertain migratory status to being an avenue to massive and indiscriminate incarceration of migrants as a form of penalisation.[104]

Consequently, the meaning of detention has changed, as the more it is banalised, the less effective it becomes as a means of migration management. Yet, the systematic reliance on detention seems to be anchored in certain collateral effects beyond its (very limited) capacity to contribute to migrants' identification and expulsion. These are its deterrent effect, incapacitation, and expression of moral resentment, even though these effects pertain more closely to criminal sanctions.[105] Detention of irregular immigrants identifies foreigners as already criminal until proven otherwise. Detention in prison-like conditions also solidifies ideas of migrants as threats to the economic prosperity, social cohesion, and even physical security of the citizens.[106]

Under EU law, Member States typically apply immigration detention in three contexts: Upon arrival to prevent entry into their territory; during asylum procedures (Asylum Procedures Directive),[107] including Dublin transfer procedures;[108] and to carry out return procedures (in accordance with the Return Directive).[109] The discretion of the administration is not unfettered. The relevant instruments establish limited detention grounds and do not allow for the indiscriminate use of detention, for example, merely because a third-country national has requested asylum or because they are subjected to a return procedure.[110] They also foresee a number of guarantees, such as the right to an effective remedy. In addition, the instruments make the deprivation of liberty subject to the principles of necessity and proportionality, emphasising the need for an individual assessment of each case. Nevertheless, in practice, Member States do not always live up to these standards, and detention has been increasingly used as a deterrent in certain contexts, such as in border locations.

The provisions of various instruments under the New Pact on Migration, which are already in force but will become applicable in the spring of 2026, are likely to enhance this trend. Screening,[111] border asylum processing,[112] and border return procedures[113] are meant to make up a new seamless process at the EU's external borders. The new regulations also contemplate that those undergoing screening and border procedures may be deprived of their liberty during the processing. In addition, the reformed Reception Conditions Directive establishes a new detention ground relating to non-respect of restrictions on freedom of movement by the applicant, while there continues to be a risk of absconding,[114] further expanding the scope of detention.

While the instruments clarify that the full array of guarantees continues to apply in the border context, there are a number of concerns. First, vulnerable individuals are not automatically exempted from border procedures, even if there are additional safeguards established in their case.[115] Therefore, the regulations contemplate potentially imposing restrictions on freedom of movement or depriving vulnerable applicants, such as families with minor children, of their liberty. The potential detention of vulnerable groups was a controversial point in the political debate and a stumbling block in the finalisation of the negotiations. Relatedly, there is abundant case law placing significant restrictions on the detention of vulnerable applicants, especially minors.[116]

An additional concern in this context is that Member States might mischaracterise regimes that deprive applicants of their liberty as merely imposing restrictions on freedom of movement. The example of the transit zones in Hungary illustrates this. In a reference for a preliminary ruling scrutinising the conditions within the transit zones, the CJEU found multiple violations of the substantive asylum and return *acquis*, and specifically of detention standards, due to the arbitrary deprivation of liberty.[117] The Hungarian Government, however, contended that the regime in the transit zones did not amount to deprivation of liberty.

When it comes to the new rules, the difficulty could derive from the fact that the difference between restriction of freedom of movement and deprivation of liberty is one of degree, and not nature or substance. According to settled case law, determining whether someone is deprived of their liberty depends on their concrete situation and factors like the type, duration, effects, and implementation of the measure.[118] Thus, an individual examination of the execution of each national regime will be necessary to conclude if it actually amounts to deprivation of liberty, regardless of what the official national designation for the scheme might be. Current practice raises concerns as to the potential expansion of a generalised use of deprivation of liberty in border areas.

These concerns are compounded by the fact that, currently, migrant detention centres mimic prison conditions and fail to meet basic human rights protections, putting into question the legitimacy and justification of these sites of confinement. Whereas detaining migrants in centres resembling carceral facilities has solidified an understanding of migration as a security issue, the CJEU has ruled that conditions in detention facilities must not be prison-like if they are to qualify as specialised detention facilities.[119] The CJEU has also opined that detention should comply with specific safeguards, such as existence of a legal basis, clarity, predictability, accessibility, and protection against arbitrariness; it must be necessary and proportionate; it must be ordered in a formal decision; and it must entail judicial review.[120] It should be imposed only as a last resort when there are no available non-custodial alternatives.[121] Mary Bosworth and Marion Vannier have also challenged the legality of the maximum detention period, noting that whereas in the UK problems arise from the absence of a statutory upper time limit to detention, in France due process and other humanitarian concerns are raised due to the short time for which foreign nationals may be held before deportation.[122]

1.6 Crimmigration as Immigration Enforcement Mirroring Criminal Law Enforcement

Another manifestation of crimmigration is through the similarities of immigration enforcement with criminal law enforcement and the transplantation of criminal enforcement tools and mechanisms for the purpose of controlling migration flows. Here, rather than criminalising migration-related conduct, emphasis is placed on the deployment of similar techniques to those of criminal law enforcement to discover and prevent the entry of irregular migrants and refugees and to exercise control over them. These powers entail stop and search, conducting identity checks, arrest for administrative violations of migration laws, such as unlawful presence, interrogation of foreigners to discover information relevant to those violations, and authority to administratively detain and transport non-citizens in order to exclude or expel them.[123]

For example, in the US, the appearance and powers of the two immigration enforcement agencies, that is, the Immigration and Customs Enforcement and the US Customs and Border Protection, are hardly distinguishable from those of a criminal law enforcement organisation, marking a shift from the administrative nature of immigration enforcement to criminal law enforcement.[124] Exemplary of that shift is also that the responsibility of border control is bestowed on the Department of Homeland Security. Similarly, in other countries, such as France, it is police forces that are entrusted with immigration-related powers.

At the heart of immigration enforcement are its criminal security and crime governance methods that are being used to conduct border and immigration controls. However, here the scope of enforcement powers is often extended beyond foreigners to cover more broadly people on the move, such as travellers. This aspect of crimmigration entails the widespread deployment of automated surveillance techniques and networks. Key examples in this respect are the digital tracking of the movements of foreigners through fingerprinting and the operation of highly sophisticated databases to detect criminal and migration-related irregularities and to monitor movement, by collecting and storing vast amounts of personal data on travellers, migrants, and those who have had contact with the immigration and criminal justice system.[125]

The deployment of surveillance towers and drones to patrol borders and the recent burst of interest in artificial intelligence (AI) systems, such as algorithmic profiling, are also symptomatic of this crimmigration aspect, whereby new technologies, particularly the most controversial ones have been (and are still being) "tested" on migrants and refugees or otherwise legitimised in immigration management.[126] These surveillance networks are progressively transnational, combining information from public and private data sources, such as air carriers. They also enable controlling migration at a wide range of different locations and by a wide range of actors, at the actual border, at external sites, and inside national territories.

Processing of personal data is contingent not on a criminal conviction or immigration proceedings but merely on whether the individual has encountered a national agency that administers the database, which can be for either administrative or law enforcement purposes. As a result, databases collect and retain large amounts of information about people, such as travellers or border crossers (including their possible associations with other individuals, such as visa sponsors), without basis for suspicion of criminal or immigration violations. The records of foreigners are stored in large databases, which construe profiles that render them "manageable" and "controllable" and able to assess, or even predict, the degree of risk of criminal, terrorist, or migration-related activity they may pose. This assessment is grounded on a default suspicion that foreigners may be potential terrorists, criminals, irregular migrants, or bogus asylum seekers.[127]

These surveillance networks thus manifest a novel understanding of risk thinking and social exclusion.[128] Dennis Broeders and James Hampshire refer instead to the use of digital "social sorting" mechanisms,[129] which categorise individuals to enable differentiated treatment by degrees of riskiness. The first category consists of black-listed individuals who are to be excluded, such as undesirable foreigners recorded in the EU Schengen Information System (SIS) or in the US executive orders on travel bans (Protecting the Nation from Foreign Terrorist Entry into the United States orders). The second category, "grey-listing", refers to individuals who are subject to risk profiling, as in the case of advanced passenger information (API) and passenger name records

(PNRs). Finally, "green listing" equates to facilitated inclusion, as in the case of the "desirables" or the "registered travellers" who can pass, unsupervised, through e-borders after an initial check and screening at time of registration. By fast-tracking the border crossing of wanted individuals, more resources can be reallocated to potentially riskier ones.

However, processing of personal data as a crimmigration technique is not reserved solely for foreigners; as we analyse in our chapter in this volume, administrative surveillance can be further extended to civil society organisations (CSOs) assisting asylum seekers and migrants on the ground.[130] In Greece, the two registries for migration-related CSOs and their members have significantly shrunk the operational space for their activities in the country. This has been achieved through increased bureaucracy marked by tight deadlines, consecutive legal reforms creating confusion, and legal uncertainty as to the registration requirements, which are particularly extensive and cumbersome.[131] As we argue in our chapter, this hostile environment poses challenges to national constitutional law and fundamental rights, including freedom of association and personal data protection, and raises broader questions about the compatibility with rule of law.[132]

A final, more recent example of this type of crimmigration practice is the transformation of the asylum system in Europe into a site for social control, in which punitive and disciplinary elements intersect with humanitarian concerns.[133] In this volume, Galina Cornelisse explores explicit punitive sanctions against migrants who the state portrays as "difficult", "troublesome", or "less deserving".[134] These sanctions do not follow ordinary criminal law procedures, either because they violate the fundamental principles inherent in those procedures or because they remain administrative in nature, if only formally.[135] Cornelisse draws from relevant practice in the Netherlands, analyses the limitations of fundamental rights and constitutional guarantees to challenge this practice, and reflects on the potential of engaging with questions of global redistributive justice instead in order to address the root causes, which she connects with the regulation of global mobility more broadly.[136]

The EU's New Pact on Migration and Asylum instruments also reflect this trend. One target is asylum seekers who conduct secondary movements, that is, asylum seekers who move between EU Member States, seeking to choose their asylum country within the EU, which is not permitted according to EU asylum rules. Those "troublesome" asylum seekers, who conduct secondary movements, will face penalties that will affect their asylum procedures and their reception conditions: Their asylum applications will be rejected as implicitly withdrawn, and they will face, at least, reduction in their reception conditions.[137] Another example of punitive treatment under the pact is the subjection to mandatory border processing—which foresees fewer guarantees than "in-territory processing"—for asylum seekers coming from countries with "low recognition rates".[138] EU law defines this category as asylum seekers who come from countries that have a recognition rate at first instance of 20% or lower, according to the latest available yearly union-wide average Eurostat data, unless there has been a significant change of circumstances, or the applicant comes from a group for which this recognition rate is not representative (for example LGBTQI+ applicants).[139]

1.7 Conclusion

Although the links between criminal and immigration law are not new, the forceful and persisting intertwinement of the two policy domains is the product of the past 40 years. Crimmigration has essentially transformed both fields, as well as border control and internal policing more broadly. The merging is so strong and extensive that it is hard to untangle its interwoven threads. This chapter has provided an overview of the theoretical underpinnings, the origins, and the various formations of crimmigration. Governments have increasingly employed criminal enforcement tools, such as surveillance and detention, in response to unwanted mobility, and territorial exclusion has become a common response to criminal behaviour. In turn, criminalisation has expanded to penalise various violations of administrative law not only by the foreigners themselves, but also involving other actors, including individuals providing assistance to migrants. Overall, crimmigration fosters the expansion of state power, without, however, the commensurate transfer of due process protections for individuals from the criminal sphere into the immigration sphere, while human rights protection standards are significantly watered down. The balance has shifted so much in favour of criminal justice that change has become not just desirable, but necessary.

In view of the fast-evolving regulatory framework, the emergence of (often inconsistent) national case law, as well as law enforcement practices at the margins of legality and the rule of law, closer attention to the highly dynamic nature of crimmigration is needed. The contributions to this book explore the conceptual and philosophical underpinnings of EU and national policies intertwining criminal and migration law, as well as their practical use (and abuse) and its impact on the protection of fundamental rights of migrants and the rule of law. The contributions revisit fundamental questions on the suitability of criminal law to regulate and govern migration and provide insights as to whether and how the law should be amended to limit the negative consequences of the criminalisation of migration. The contributions outline, through concrete examples, how criminalisation of migration translates into the emergence of hostile environments for migrants and those who assist them. They analyse migration control through criminal law from multidisciplinary and interdisciplinary perspectives, incorporating insights from law, philosophy, and criminology, providing a contemporary understanding of the state of the art of 'crimmigration', and ultimately challenging this paradigm of intersecting criminal justice and immigration control.

Notes

1 Sarah Turnbull and Ines Hasselberg, 'From Prison to Detention: The Carceral Trajectories of Foreign National Prisoners in the United Kingdom' (2016) 19 Punishment & Society 135.
2 Juliette Stumpf, 'The Crimmigration Crisis: Immigrants, Crime, and Sovereign Power' (2006) 56 American University Law Review 367.
3 Stumpf (n 2) 376.
4 Daniel Kanstroom, 'Criminalizing the Undocumented: Ironic Boundaries of the Post-September 11th "Pale of Law"' (2004) 29 North Carolina Journal of International Law and Commercial Regulation 639; Stephen Legomsky, 'The Ethnic and Religious Profiling of Noncitizens: National Security and International Human Rights' (2005) 25 Boston College Third World Law Journal 161; Michael Welch, 'Quiet Constructions in the War on Terror: Subjecting Asylum Seekers to Unnecessary Detention' (2004) 31 Social Justice 113.
5 Teresa Miller, 'Citizenship and Severity: Recent Immigration Reforms and the New Penology' (2003) 17 Georgetown Immigration Law Journal 611, 618.
6 Valsamis Mitsilegas, *The Criminalisation of Migration in Europe—Challenges for Human Rights and the Rule of Law* (Springer 2014); Elspeth Guild and Paul Minderhoud, *Immigration and Criminal Law in the European Union: The Legal Measures and Social Consequences of Criminal Law in Member States on Trafficking and Smuggling in Human Beings* (Brill | Nijhoff 2006).
7 Peter Billings, *Crimmigration in Australia: Law, Politics, and Society* (Routledge 2019).
8 Luisa Marin and Alessandro Spena, 'Introduction: The Criminalization of Migration and European (Dis)Integration' (2016) 18 European Journal of Migration and Law 147.
9 Jelmer Brouwer, 'Detection, Detention, Deportation: Criminal Justice and Migration Control Through the Lens of Crimmigration' (Ph.D. Thesis, Leiden University 2020) 5.
10 Leanne Weber and Jude McCulloch, 'Penal Power and Border Control: Which Thesis? Sovereignty, Governmentality, or the Pre-Emptive State?' (2019) 21 Punishment & Society 496 (emphasis present in the original).
11 Stumpf (n 2) 379.
12 Brouwer (n 9).
13 Stumpf (n 2) 379.
14 Katja Franko Ass, 'The Ordered and the Bordered Society: Migration Control, Citizenship, and the Northern Penal State' in Katja Franko Ass and Mary Bosworth (eds), *The Borders of Punishment: Migration, Citizenship, and Social Exclusion* (OUP 2013).
15 US Supreme Court *Fong Yue Ting v. United States* [1893] 149 US 698.
16 Stephen Legomsky, 'The New Path of Immigration Law: Asymmetric Incorporation of Criminal Justice Norms' (2007) 64 Washington and Lee Law Review 469.
17 Stumpf (n 2) 395.
18 Elspeth Guild, 'Terrorism and Migration Law' in Ben Saul (ed), *Research Handbook on International Law and Terrorism* (2nd edn, Edward Elgar 2018).
19 For example, see Didier Bigo, 'Security and Immigration: Toward a Critique of the Governmentality of Unease' (2002) 27 Alternatives 63.
20 Stumpf (n 2).
21 For a slightly different view see Rottem Rosenberg Rubins, 'Crimmigration and the "Paradox of Exclusion"' (2022) 42 Oxford Journal of Legal Studies 266, 277.
22 David Garland, *Culture of Control* (Chicago UP 2001).
23 Mary Bosworth and Mhairi Guild, 'Governing Through Migration Control: Security and Citizenship in Britain' (2008) 48 British Journal of Criminology 703.

24 Susanne Krasmann, 'The Enemy on the Border: Critique of a Programme in Favour of a Preventive State' (2007) 9 Punishment and Society 30.
25 Weber and McCulloch (n 10).
26 Juliette Stumpf, 'Crimmigration—Encountering the Leviathan' in Sharon Pickering and Julie Ham (eds), *Routledge Handbook on Crime and International Migration* (Routledge 2017) 238.
27 Daniel Kanstroom, 'Reaping the Harvest: The Long, Complicated, Crucial Rhetorical Struggle over Deportation' (2007) 39 Connecticut Law Review 1911.
28 US Congress Public Law 100–690 *Anti-Drug Abuse Act* [1988].
29 US Congress Public Law 104–32 *Antiterrorism and Effective Death Penalty Act* [1996].
30 US Congress Public Law 104–208 *Omnibus Consolidated Appropriations Act of* [1997].
31 Jennifer Chacón, 'Managing Migration Through Crime' (2009) 109 Columbia Law Review 135.
32 Mitsilegas (n 6) 29.
33 Valsamis Mitsilegas, Jörg Monar and Wyn Rees, *The European Union and Internal Security: Guardian of the People* (Palgrave Macmillan 2003).
34 See Directive 2011/36/EU of 5 April 2011 on preventing and combating trafficking in human beings and protecting its victims, and replacing Council Framework Decision 2002/629/JHA [2011] OJ L101/1 and Council Directive 2004/81/EC of 29 April 2004 on the residence permit issues to third-country nationals who are victims of trafficking in human beings or who have been the subject of an action to facilitate illegal migration, who cooperate with the competent authorities [2004] OJ L261/19, that grant (conditional) residence permits rights to victims of trafficking.
35 Proposal for a Directive laying down minimum rules to prevent and counter the facilitation of unauthorised entry, transit, and stay in the Union, and replacing Council Directive 2002/90/EC and Council Framework Decision 2002/946 JHA, article 1.
36 Council Framework Decision 2002/946/JHA of 28 November 2002 on strengthening of the penal framework to prevent the facilitation of unauthorised entry, transit and residence, Article 1.
37 Stumpf (n 2).
38 Thus, inducing fear to migrants who may refuse to use public services, endure labour exploitation, and avoid public spaces, resulting in social exclusion and interrupted integration. Adam Goodman, *The Deportation Machine: America's Long History of Expelling Immigrants* (Princeton UP 2020). This trend of immigrationisation of criminal law entails migration control-related consequences being attached to criminal convictions, see Chacón (n 31). The revocation of a residence permit or citizenship deprivation are other examples of the use of administrative law as a response to the commission of criminal offences by migrants, see David Moffette, 'Governing Immigration Through Probation: The Displacement of Borderwork and the Assessment of Desirability in Spain' (2014) 45 Security Dialogue 262; in other words, criminal convictions increasingly result in regular migrants being deprived of their legal status and in their subsequent removability. See, e.g., various contributions in the special issue 'The Challenge of Detention to Refugee Protection' (2016) 35 Refugee Survey Quarterly co-edited by Philippe De Bruycker and Evangelia (Lilian) Tsourdi.
39 Legomsky (n 16).
40 Gian Luigi Gatta, Valsamis Mitsilegas and Stefano Zirulia, *Controlling Immigration Through Criminal Law—European and Comparative Perspectives on 'Crimmigration'* (Hart 2021).
41 Juliette Stumpf, 'Crimmigration—Encountering the Leviathan' in Pickering and Ham (n 26).

42 The Law Library of Congress, *Criminalization of Illegal Entry Around the World* (The Law Library of Congress, 2019).
43 Convention Relating to the Status of Refugees [1951], article 31.
44 For an overview, see European Union Agency for Fundamental Rights (FRA), *Criminalisation of Migrants in an Irregular Situation and of Persons Engaging with Them* (Self-Published 2014). Also see Joana Parkin, *The Criminalisation of Migration in Europe: A State of the Art of the Academic Literature and Research* (CEPS, No 61, 2013); Mark Provera, *The Criminalisation of Irregular Migration in the European Union* (CEPS, No 80, 2015).
45 Ana Aliverti, *Immigration Offences: Trends in Legislation and Criminal and Civil Enforcement* (Migration Observatory 2016).
46 Ana Aliverti, 'Making People Criminal: The Role of the Criminal Law in Immigration Enforcement' (2012) 16 Theoretical Criminology 417.
47 Alessandro Spena, '*Iniuria Migrandi*: Criminalization of Immigrants and the Basic Principles of the Criminal Law' (2014) 8 Criminal Law and Philosophy 835.
48 Ana Aliverti, *Crimes of Mobility: Criminal Law and the Regulation of Immigration* (Routledge 2013).
49 See Chapter 5 of this volume.
50 See Chapter 5 of this volume.
51 It must be noted that criminalisation encompasses a broader set of characteristics, such as the integration of criminal law processes into immigration control; the integration of immigration law into the sphere of criminal law (such as the expulsion of migrants convicted of particular crimes); the prioritisation of resources towards deportation of migrants akin to a criminal enforcement approach; the adoption of criminal law enforcement strategies (such as detention). See Legomsky (n 16); Stumpf (n 2). For the EU law context, see Mitsilegas (n 6).
52 Mitsilegas (n 6) 48.
53 Council Framework Decision 2002/629/JHA (n 35). For an analysis of the Framework Decision, see Tom Obokata, 'EU Council Framework Decision on Combating Trafficking in Human Beings: A Critical Appraisal' (2003) 40 Common Market Law Review 917.
54 UN Convention on Transnational Organized Crime [2003].
55 Protocol to Prevent, Suppress and Punish Trafficking in Persons Especially Women and Children, supplementing the United Nations Convention against Transnational Organized Crime [2003].
56 Protocol against the Smuggling of Migrants by Land, Sea and Air, supplementing the United Nations Convention against Transnational Organized Crime [2004].
57 Carolina Villacampa Estiarte, 'The European Directive on Preventing and Combating Trafficking in Human Beings and the Victim-Centric Treatment of this Criminal Phenomenon' (2012) 2 European Criminal Law Review 291, 300. Also see Anne Gallagher, *The International Law of Human Trafficking* (CUP 2011) 71; Valsamis Mitsilegas, 'Immigration Control in an Era of Globalization: Deflecting Foreigners, Weakening Citizens, Strengthening the State' (2012) 19 Indiana Journal of Global Legal Studies 3.
58 Villacampa Estiarte (n 57) 299–300.
59 Council Directive 2004/81/EC (n 34). For an analysis, see Niovi Vavoula, 'The Criminalisation of Irregular Migration Under EU Law: An Evolving Human-Rights Centred Legal Framework?' in Valsamis Mitsilegas, Maria Bergström and Teresa Quintel (eds.) *Research Handbook on EU Criminal Law* (2nd edn, Edward Elgar 2024).
60 Council Directive 2011/36/EU (n 34).
61 Mitsilegas (n 6) 51.

62 Elisavet Symeonidou-Kastanidou, 'Directive 2011/36/EU on Combating Trafficking in Human Beings: Fundamental Choices and Problems of Implementation' (2017) 7 New Journal of European Criminal Law 465, 471–73.
63 Directive 2024/1712 of 13 June 2024 amending Directive 2011/36/EU on preventing and combating trafficking in human beings and protecting its victims [2024] OJ 1712/2024.
64 Giacomo Manca, 'Op-Ed: Revising the EU Anti-Trafficking Directive: An Opportunity to Strengthen the Rights of Trafficked Persons' (*ECRE*, 15 December 2023) <https://ecre.org/revising-the-eu-anti-trafficking-revising-the-eu-anti-trafficking-directive-an-opportunity-to-strengthen-the-rights-of-trafficked-persons-an-opportunity-to-strengthen-the-rights-of-trafficked-person/> accessed 16 January 2025, as all the hyperlinks included in this chapter.
65 See Chapter 2 of this volume.
66 See Chapter 2 of this volume.
67 This is confirmed by the UNODC, which, as per the protocol, "does not seek and cannot be used as the legal basis for the prosecution of humanitarian actors". See UNODC, *Legislative Guide for the Implementation of the United Nations Convention Against Transnational Organized Crime and the Protocols Thereto* (UNODC 2004) 24. For an analysis on further differences between the international and EU legal framework, see Chiara Maria Ricci, 'Criminalising Solidarity? Smugglers, Migrants and Rescuers in the Reform of the "Facilitators' Package"' in Valsamis Mitsilegas, Violeta Moreno-Lax and Niovi Vavoula (eds), *Securitising Asylum Flows—Deflection, Criminalisation and Challenges for Human Rights* (Brill | Nijhoff 2020).
68 For an analysis see Sergio Carrera and others, *Policing Humanitarianism—EU Policies Against Human Smuggling and Their Impact on Civil Society* (Hart 2019).
69 Article 1 para 2.
70 European Commission, 'Staff Working Document—REFIT Evaluation of the EU Legal Framework Against Facilitation of Unauthorised Entry, Transit and Residence' (2017) 117 final, 14.
71 For the judgement, see <https://www.giurisprudenzapenale.com/wp-content/uploads/2020/02/Cass-6626-2020.pdf>. For an analysis, see Zara Freudenberg and others, 'The Island of Hope in a Sea of Misery—the Italian Court of Cassation's Unequivocal Stance on the Right to Disembark' (*Verfassungsblog*, 10 March 2020) <https://verfassungsblog.de/the-island-of-hope-in-a-sea-of-misery/>.
72 ECRE, 'Greece: Criminalisation of Rescuers, Death for People on the Move, Impunity for Vigilantes, States Persist with Dublin Take-Back Requests Despite Risks and Deficiencies' (*ECRE*, 29 October 2021) <https://ecre.org/greece-criminalisation-of-rescuers-death-for-people-on-the-move-impunity-for-vigilantes-states-persist-with-dublin-take-back-requests-despite-risks-and-deficiencies/>.
73 Helge Schwiertz and Helen Schwenken, *Inclusive Solidarity and Citizenship Along Migratory Routes in Europe and the Americas* (Routledge 2022); Maurizio Ambrosini, 'Humanitarian Help and Refugees: De-Bordering Solidarity as a Contentious Issue' (2022) 22 Journal of Immigration and Refugee Studies 517.
74 Janina Pescinski, 'Mountain Patrols at the Franco-Italian Border: Performing Solidarity, Dissent and Citizenship' in Donatella Della Porta and Elias Steinhilper (eds), *Contentious Migrant Solidarity Shrinking Spaces and Civil Society Contestation* (Routledge 2021).
75 Evangelia (Lilian) Tsourdi, 'Asylum in the EU: One of the Many Faces of Rule of Law Backsliding?' (2021) 17 European Constitutional Law Review 471.
76 John Pratt, *Penal Populism* (Routledge 2007); see Marta Minetti, 'The Facilitators Package, Penal Populism and the Rule of Law: Lessons from Italy' (2020) 11 New Journal of European Criminal Law 335.

77 For example, see the work of Ana Aliverti in this context, e.g., Ana Aliverti, 'Exploring the Function of Criminal Law in the Policing of Foreigners: The Decision to Prosecute Immigration-Related Offences' (2012) 21 Social & Legal Studies 511.
78 See Chapter 9 of this volume.
79 See Chapter 6 of this volume.
80 See Chapter 6 of this volume.
81 European Commission (n 70).
82 See Chapter 10 of this volume.
83 See Chapter 10 of this volume.
84 Case C 460/23 Kinsa [2023] ECLI:EU:C:2023:784. The case was formerly named as Kinshasa. Request for a preliminary ruling from the Tribunale di Bologna (Italy) lodged on 21 July 2023.
85 See Chapter 3 of this volume.
86 See Chapter 3 of this volume.
87 See Chapter 4 of this volume.
88 See Chapter 4 of this volume.
89 See Chapter 4 of this volume.
90 This trend is fleshed out in the imposition of sanctions to carriers transporting undocumented travellers. See Sophie Scholten, *The Privatisation of Immigration Control Through Carrier Sanctions—the Role of Private Transport Companies in Dutch and British Immigration Control* (Brill | Nijhoff 2015). For a broader problematisation, see Mary Bosworth and Lucia Zedner, *Privatising Border Control—Law at the Limits of the Sovereign State* (OUP 2022).
91 Directive 2009/52/EC of 18 June 2009 providing for minimum standards on sanctions and measures against employers of illegally staying third-country nationals [2009] OJ L168/24 (hereinafter Employers Sanctions Directive).
92 Mitsilegas (n 6).
93 Directive 2008/115/EC of 16 December 2008 on common standards and procedures in Member States for returning illegally staying third-country nationals [2008] OJ L348/98 (hereinafter Return Directive).
94 For an analysis on the relevant case law examining the imposition of limits to criminalisation, see Niovi Vavoula, 'Criminalisation of Irregular Migration in the EU: The Impact of *El Dridi*' in Valsamis Mitsilegas, Alberto di Martino and Leandro Mancano (eds), *The Impact of European Union Law on National Criminal Law Challenges and Constraints to Individual Liability in the Member States* (Hart 2019); Niovi Vavoula, 'The Interplay Between EU Immigration Law and National Criminal Law—the Case of the Return Directive' in Valsamis Mitsilegas, Maria Bergström and Theodore Konstantinides (eds), *Research Handbook on EU Criminal Law* (1st edn, Edward Elgar 2016); Madalina Moraru, Galina Cornelisse and Philippe De Bruycker (eds), *Law and Judicial Dialogue on the Return of Irregular Migrants from the European Union* (Hart 2022).
95 Case C-430/11 *Criminal Proceedings Against Md Sagor* ECLI:EU:C:2012:777.
96 Case C-290/14 *Criminal Proceedings Against Skerdjan Celaj* ECLI:EU:C:2015:640.
97 Case C-294/16 PPU *JZ v. Prokuratura Rejonowa Łódź—Śródmieście* ECLI:EU:C:2016:610.
98 Stumpf (n 26) 242.
99 Global Detention Project, *Immigration Detention in Australia: Turning Arbitrary Detention into a Global Brand* (Global Detention Project 2022).
100 Altaf Saadi and others, 'Understanding US Immigration Detention: Reaffirming Rights and Addressing Social-Structural Determinants of Health' (2020) 22 Health Human Rights 187.

101 Jamie Longazel, Jake Berman and Benjamin Fleury-Steiner, 'The Pains of Immigrant Imprisonment' (2016) 10 Sociology Compass 989.
102 ECtHR *Sadaykov v Bulgaria* [2007] 75157/01.
103 Mary Bosworth, *Inside Immigration Detention* (OUP 2014).
104 Marin and Spena (n 8) 148.
105 Arjen Leerkes and Dennis Broeders, 'A Case of Mixed Motives? Formal and Informal Functions of Administrative Immigration Detention' (2010) 50 British Journal of Criminology 830.
106 Mary Bosworth, 'Immigration Detention in Britain', in Maggy Lee (ed), *Human Trafficking* (Willan 2007) 171.
107 Directive 2013/32/EU of 26 June 2013 on common procedures for granting and withdrawing international protection (recast) [2013] OJ L180/60 (hereinafter Asylum Procedures Directive).
108 Regulation (EU) 604/2013 of 26 June 2013 establishing the criteria and mechanisms for determining the Member States responsible for examining an application for international protection lodged in one of the Member States by a third-country national or a stateless person [2013] OJ L180.
109 Directive 2008/115/EC (n 93).
110 Galina Cornelisse, *Immigration Detention and Human Rights—Rethinking Territorial Sovereignty* (Brill | Nijhoff 2010).
111 Regulation (EU) 2024/1356 of 14 May 2024 introducing the screening of third-country nationals at the external borders and amending Regulations (EC) No 767/2008, (EU) 2017/2226, (EU) 2018/1240 and (EU) 2019/817, [2024] OJ 2024/1356.
112 Regulation (EU) 2024/1348 of 14 May 2024 establishing a common procedure for international protection in the Union and repealing Directive 2013/32/EU, [2024] OJ 2024/1348.
113 Regulation (EU) 2024/1349 of 14 May 2024 establishing a return border procedure, and amending Regulation (EU) 2021/1148, [2024] OJ 2024/1349.
114 Directive 2024/1346 of 14 May 2024 laying down standards for the reception of applicants for international protection [2024] OJ L2024/1346, article 10 para 4(c).
115 Regulation (EU) (n 113), Article 53.
116 See, e.g., ECtHR, *Mubilanzila Mayeka and Kaniki Mitunga v. Belgium* [2006] 13178/03, ECtHR, *Popov v. France* [2012] 39472/07 and 39474/07, as well as HRC, General Comment 35, CCPR/C/GC/35, 2014, para 18 and HRC, D and *E v Australia*, Comm 1050/2002, para 7(2); and HRC, *Jalloh v Netherlands*, Comm 794/1998, paras 8(2) and 8(3). See also, Evangelia (Lilian) Tsourdi, 'Alternatives to Immigration Detention: Shaping Control Standards and Judicial Interaction in an Heterarchy' in Madalina Moraru, Galina Cornelisse and Philippe De Bruycker (eds), *Law and Judicial Dialogue on the Return of Irregular Migrants from the European Union* (Hart 2020) 167–91.
117 See, Joined Cases C-924/19 and C-925/19 *FMS and Others v Országos Idegenrendészeti Főigazgatóság Dél-alföldi Regionális Igazgatóság* [2020] ECLI:EU:C:2020:367; and Evangelia (Lilian) Tsourdi, 'Asylum in the EU: One of the Many Faces of Rule of Law Backsliding?' (2021) 17 European Constitutional Law Review (2021) 471–97.
118 ECtHR, *Austin and Others v the United Kingdom* [2012] 39692/09, 40713/09 and 41008/09, para 57. See also ECtHR *Guzzardi v Italy* [1980] 7367/76, paras 92–93; ECtHR, *Medvedyev and Others v France* [2010] 3394/03, para 73.
119 Joined Cases C-473/13 and C-514/13 *Adala Bero v Regierungspräsidium Kassel, Ettayebi Bouzalmate v Kreisverwaltung Kleve* [2014] OJ C315/22.
120 Case C-528/15 *Al Chodor and Others* [2017] ECLI:EU:C:2017:213; Joined Cases C-924/19 and C-925/19 (n 117).

121 See for analysis Tsourdi (n 116) 167–90.
122 Mary Bosworth and Marion Vannier, 'Blurred lines: Detaining Asylum Seekers in Britain and France' (2019) 56 Journal of Sociology 53.
123 Juliette Stumpf, 'Two Profiles of Crimmigration Law: Criminal Deportation and Illegal Migration' in Francis Pakes (ed), *Globalisation and the Challenge to Criminology* (Routledge 2013); Leanne Weber, *Policing Noncitizens* (Routledge 2013).
124 Stumpf (n 2) 387.
125 Katja Franko Aas, '"Crimmigrant" Bodies and Bona Fide Travelers: Surveillance, Citizenship and Global Governance' (2011) 15 Theoretical Criminology 331.
126 Niovi Vavoula, *Immigration and Privacy in the Law of the EU: The Case of Information Systems* (Brill | Nijhoff 2022).
127 Valsamis Mitsilegas, 'Security Versus Justice: The Individualisation of Security and the Erosion of Citizenship and Fundamental Rights' in Barbara Hudson and Synnove Ugelvik (eds), *Justice and Security in the 21st Century. Risks, Rights and the Rule of Law* (Routledge 2012).
128 Thomas Gammetoft-Hansen, *Filtering Out the Risky Migrant: Migration Control, Risk Theory, and the EU* (Akademiet for Migrationsstudier i Danmark, Aalborg Universitet 2006).
129 Dennis Broeders and James Hampshire, 'Dreaming of Seamless Borders: ICTs and the Pre-Emptive Governance of Mobility in Europe' (2013) 39 Journal of Ethnic and Migration Studies 1201.
130 See Chapter 7 of this volume.
131 See Chapter 7 of this volume.
132 See Chapter 7 of this volume.
133 Isabelle Leroy, 'Migrant Reception Centres and Coercive Social Control: Rule by Legal Uncertainty?' [2024] Social & Legal Studies 1; Ivana Acocella and Margherita Turchi, 'The Reception System for Asylum Seekers and Refugees in Italy: A Case of a New Total Institution?' (2020) 2 Österreichisches Jahrbuch Für Soziale Arbeit 73; Lorenzo Gabrielli, Blanca Garcés-Mascareñas and Olatz Ribera-Almandoz, 'Between Discipline and Neglect: The Regulation of Asylum Accommodation in Spain' (2022) 35 Journal of Refugee Studies 262.
134 See Chapter 8 of this volume.
135 See Chapter 8 of this volume.
136 See Chapter 8 of this volume.
137 See, respectively, Regulation (EU) 2024/1348 (n 114), Article 41 para 1(f) in combination with Regulation (EU) 2024/1351 of 14 May 2024 on asylum and migration management, amending Regulations (EU) 2021/1147 and (EU) 2021/1060 and repealing Regulation (EU) No 604/2013, OJ 2024/1351, 22 May 2024 (hereafter: Asylum and Migration Management Regulation), Article 36 para 3 for procedural sanctions, as well as Asylum and Migration Management Regulation, Article 18 in combination with Directive (EU) 2024/1346 (n 116), Article 21 for sanctions pertaining to reception conditions.
138 Asylum Procedures Regulation, article 45.
139 Asylum Procedures Regulation, article 45.

Bibliography

Aas KF, '"Crimmigrant" Bodies and Bona Fide Travelers: Surveillance, Citizenship and Global Governance' (2011) 15 Theoretical Criminology 331.

Acocella I and Turchi M, 'The Reception System for Asylum Seekers and Refugees in Italy: A Case of a New Total Institution?' (2020) 2 Österreichisches Jahrbuch Für Soziale Arbeit 73.

Aliverti A, 'Exploring the Function of Criminal Law in the Policing of Foreigners: The Decision to Prosecute Immigration-Related Offences' (2012) 21 Social & Legal Studies 511.

Aliverti A, 'Making People Criminal: The Role of the Criminal Law in Immigration Enforcement' (2012) 16 Theoretical Criminology 417.

Aliverti A, *Crimes of Mobility: Criminal Law and the Regulation of Immigration* (Routledge 2013).

Aliverti A, *Immigration Offences: Trends in Legislation and Criminal and Civil Enforcement* (Migration Observatory 2016).

Ambrosini M, 'Humanitarian Help and Refugees: De-Bordering Solidarity as a Contentious Issue' (2022) 22 Journal of Immigration and Refugee Studies 517.

Ass KF, 'The Ordered and the Bordered Society: Migration Control, Citizenship, and the Northern Penal State' in Ass KF and Bosworth M (eds), *The Borders of Punishment: Migration, Citizenship, and Social Exclusion* (OUP 2013).

Bigo D, 'Security and Immigration: Toward a Critique of the Governmentality of Unease' (2002) 27 Alternatives 63.

Billings P, *Crimmigration in Australia: Law, Politics, and Society* (Routledge 2019).

Bosworth M, 'Immigration Detention in Britain', in Lee M (ed), *Human Trafficking* (Willan 2007).

Bosworth M, *Inside Immigration Detention* (OUP 2014).

Bosworth M and Guild M, 'Governing Through Migration Control: Security and Citizenship in Britain' (2008) 48 British Journal of Criminology 703.

Bosworth M and Vannier M, 'Blurred Lines: Detaining Asylum Seekers in Britain and France' (2019) 56 Journal of Sociology 53.

Bosworth M and Zedner L, *Privatising Border Control—Law at the Limits of the Sovereign State* (OUP 2022).

Broeders D and Hampshire J, 'Dreaming of Seamless Borders: ICTs and the Pre-Emptive Governance of Mobility in Europe' (2013) 39 Journal of Ethnic and Migration Studies 1201.

Brouwer J, 'Detection, Detention, Deportation: Criminal Justice and Migration Control Through the Lens of Crimmigration' (Ph.D. Thesis, Leiden University 2020).

Carrera S and others, *Policing Humanitarianism—EU Policies Against Human Smuggling and Their Impact on Civil Society* (Hart 2019).

Chacón J, 'Managing Migration Through Crime' (2009) 109 Columbia Law Review 135.

Cornelisse G, *Immigration Detention and Human Rights—Rethinking Territorial Sovereignty* (Brill | Nijhoff 2010).

De Bruycker P and Tsourdi E, 'The Challenge of Detention to Refugee Protection—Special Issue' (2016) 35 Refugee Survey Quarterly.

European Union Agency for Fundamental Rights (FRA), *Criminalisation of Migrants in an Irregular Situation and of Persons Engaging with Them* (Self-Published 2014).

Gabrielli L, Garcés-Mascareñas B and Ribera-Almandoz O, 'Between Discipline and Neglect: The Regulation of Asylum Accommodation in Spain' (2022) 35 Journal of Refugee Studies 262.

Gallagher A, *The International Law of Human Trafficking* (CUP 2011).

Gammetoft-Hansen T, *Filtering Out the Risky Migrant: Migration Control, Risk Theory, and the EU* (Akademiet for Migrationsstudier i Danmark, Aalborg Universitet 2006).

Garland G, *Culture of Control* (Chicago UP 2001).

Gatta GL, Mitsilegas V and Zirulia S, *Controlling Immigration Through Criminal Law—European and Comparative Perspectives on 'Crimmigration'* (Hart 2021).

Global Detention Project, *Immigration Detention in Australia: Turning Arbitrary Detention into a Global Brand* (Global Detention Project 2022).

Goodman A, *The Deportation Machine: America's Long History of Expelling Immigrants* (Princeton UP 2020).
Guild E, 'Terrorism and Migration Law' in Saul B (ed), *Research Handbook on International Law and Terrorism* (2nd edn, Edward Elgar 2018).
Guild E and Minderhoud P, *Immigration and Criminal Law in the European Union: The Legal Measures and Social Consequences of Criminal Law in Member States on Trafficking and Smuggling in Human Beings* (Brill | Nijhoff 2006).
Kanstroom D, 'Criminalizing the Undocumented: Ironic Boundaries of the Post-September 11th "Pale of Law"' (2004) 29 North Carolina Journal of International Law and Commercial Regulation 639.
Kanstroom D, 'Reaping the Harvest: The Long, Complicated, Crucial Rhetorical Struggle over Deportation' (2007) 39 Connecticut Law Review 1911.
Krasmann S, 'The Enemy on the Border: Critique of a Programme in Favour of a Preventive State' (2007) 9 Punishment and Society 30.
Leerkes A and Broeders D, 'A Case of Mixed Motives? Formal and Informal Functions of Administrative Immigration Detention' (2010) 50 British Journal of Criminology 830.
Legomsky S, 'The Ethnic and Religious Profiling of Noncitizens: National Security and International Human Rights' (2005) 25 Boston College Third World Law Journal 161.
Legomsky S, 'The New Path of Immigration Law: Asymmetric Incorporation of Criminal Justice Norms' (2007) 64 Washington and Lee Law Review 469.
Leroy I, 'Migrant Reception Centres and Coercive Social Control: Rule by Legal Uncertainty?' [2024] Social & Legal Studies 1.
Longazel J, Berman J and Fleury-Steiner B, 'The Pains of Immigrant Imprisonment' (2016) 10 Sociology Compass 989.
Marin L and Spena A, 'Introduction: The Criminalization of Migration and European (Dis)Integration' (2016) 18 European Journal of Migration and Law 147.
Miller T, 'Citizenship and Severity: Recent Immigration Reforms and the New Penology' (2003) 17 Georgetown Immigration Law Journal 611.
Minetti M, 'The Facilitators Package, Penal Populism and the Rule of Law: Lessons from Italy' (2020) 11 New Journal of European Criminal Law 335.
Mitsilegas V, 'Immigration Control in an Era of Globalization: Deflecting Foreigners, Weakening Citizens, Strengthening the State' (2012) 19 Indiana Journal of Global Legal Studies 3.
Mitsilegas V, 'Security Versus Justice: The Individualisation of Security and the Erosion of Citizenship and Fundamental Rights' in Hudson B and Ugelvik S (eds), *Justice and Security in the 21st Century. Risks, Rights, and the Rule of Law* (Routledge 2012).
Mitsilegas V, *The Criminalisation of Migration in Europe—Challenges for Human Rights and the Rule of Law* (Springer 2014).
Mitsilegas V, Monar J and Rees W, *The European Union and Internal Security: Guardian of the People* (Palgrave Macmillan 2003).
Moffette D, 'Governing Immigration Through Probation: The Displacement of Borderwork and the Assessment of Desirability in Spain' (2014) 45 Security Dialogue 262.
Moraru M, Cornelisse G and De Bruycker P (eds), *Law and Judicial Dialogue on the Return of Irregular Migrants from the European Union* (Hart 2022).
Obokata T, 'EU Council Framework Decision on Combating Trafficking in Human Beings: A Critical Appraisal' (2003) 40 Common Market Law Review 917.
Parkin J, *The Criminalisation of Migration in Europe: A State of the Art of the Academic Literature and Research* (CEPS, No 61, 2013).

Pescinski J, 'Mountain Patrols at the Franco-Italian Border: Performing Solidarity, Dissent and Citizenship' in Della Porta D and Steinhilper E (eds), *Contentious Migrant Solidarity Shrinking Spaces and Civil Society Contestation* (Routledge 2021).

Pratt J, *Penal Populism* (Routledge 2007).

Provera M, *The Criminalisation of Irregular Migration in the European Union* (CEPS, No 80, 2015).

Ricci CH, 'Criminalising Solidarity? Smugglers, Migrants and Rescuers in the Reform of the "Facilitators' Package"' in Mitsilegas V, Moreno-Lax V and Vavoula N (eds), *Securitising Asylum Flows—Deflection, Criminalisation and Challenges for Human Rights* (Brill | Nijhoff 2020).

Rosenberg Rubins R, 'Crimmigration and the "Paradox of Exclusion"' (2022) 42 Oxford Journal of Legal Studies 266.

Saadi A and others, 'Understanding US Immigration Detention: Reaffirming Rights and Addressing Social-Structural Determinants of Health' (2020) 22 Health Human Rights 187.

Scholten S, *The Privatisation of Immigration Control Through Carrier Sanctions—The Role of Private Transport Companies in Dutch and British Immigration Control* (Brill | Nijhoff 2015).

Schwiertz H and Schwenken H, *Inclusive Solidarity and Citizenship Along Migratory Routes in Europe and the Americas* (Routledge 2022).

Spena A, '*Iniuria Migrandi*: Criminalization of Immigrants and the Basic Principles of the Criminal Law' (2014) 8 Criminal Law and Philosophy 835.

Stumpf J, 'The Crimmigration Crisis: Immigrants, Crime, and Sovereign Power' (2006) 56 American University Law Review 367.

Stumpf J, 'Two Profiles of Crimmigration Law: Criminal Deportation and Illegal Migration' in Pakes F (ed), *Globalisation and the Challenge to Criminology* (Routledge 2013).

Stumpf J, 'Crimmigration—Encountering the Leviathan' in Pickering S and Ham J (eds), *Routledge Handbook on Crime and International Migration* (Routledge 2017).

Symeonidou-Kastanidou E, 'Directive 2011/36/EU on Combating Trafficking in Human Beings: Fundamental Choices and Problems of Implementation' (2017) 7 New Journal of European Criminal Law 465.

The Law Library of Congress, *Criminalization of Illegal Entry Around the World* (The Law Library of Congress 2019).

Tsourdi E, 'Alternatives to Immigration Detention: Shaping Control Standards and Judicial Interaction in an Heterarchy' in Moraru M, Cornelisse G and De Bruycker P (eds), *Law and Judicial Dialogue on the Return of Irregular Migrants from the European Union* (Hart 2020).

Tsourdi E, 'Asylum in the EU: One of the Many Faces of Rule of Law Backsliding?' (2021) 17 European Constitutional Law Review 471.

Turnbull S and Hasselberg I, 'From Prison to Detention: The Carceral Trajectories of Foreign National Prisoners in the United Kingdom' (2016) 19 Punishment & Society 135.

Vavoula N, 'The Interplay Between EU Immigration Law and National Criminal Law—the Case of the Return Directive' in Mitsilegas V, Bergström M and Konstantinides T (eds), *Research Handbook on EU Criminal Law* (1st edn, Edward Elgar 2016).

Vavoula N, 'Criminalisation of Irregular Migration in the EU: The Impact of *El Dridi*' in Valsamis Mitsilegas, di Martino A and Mancano L (eds), *The Impact of European Union Law on National Criminal Law Challenges and Constraints to Individual Liability in the Member States* (Hart 2019).

Vavoula N, *Immigration and Privacy in the Law of the EU: The Case of Information Systems* (Brill | Nijhoff 2022).
Vavoula N, 'The Criminalisation of Irregular Migration Under EU Law: An Evolving Human-Rights Centred Legal Framework?' in Mitsilegas V, Bergström M and Quintel T (eds) *Research Handbook on EU Criminal Law* (2nd edn, Edward Elgar 2024).
Villacampa Estiarte C, 'The European Directive on Preventing and Combating Trafficking in Human Beings and the Victim-Centric Treatment of This Criminal Phenomenon' (2012) 2 European Criminal Law Review 291.
Weber L, *Policing Noncitizens* (Routledge 2013).
Weber L and McCulloch J, 'Penal Power and Border Control: Which Thesis? Sovereignty, Governmentality, or the Pre-Emptive State?' (2019) 21 Punishment & Society 496.
Welch M, 'Quiet Constructions in the War on Terror: Subjecting Asylum Seekers to Unnecessary Detention' (2004) 31 Social Justice 113.

2 The EU's Facilitators' Package—in the Twilight of Fighting Organised Crime and the (Over)criminalisation of Solidarity

A Comparative Evaluation

Johannes Keiler

2.1 Introduction

Global migration constitutes an enormous challenge for both the EU and national legislators who wish to regulate and control it.[1] Driven forward by the increasing politicisation and securitisation of migration, several states have adopted restrictive and draconian migration policies in recent years. A prime example of such restrictive policies is the increasing use of criminal law to combat irregular migration. Many of these measures have a preventive focus aiming to stop irregular migration before it occurs.[2] These preventive laws and measures target non-citizens, that is, outsiders who are often perceived as presumptively untrustworthy and potentially dangerous.[3]

The trend of (over-)criminalisation of migration is also clearly visible and has become interwoven with the fight against human smuggling. Fighting and preventing migrant smuggling are at the centre of the European Union's approach to migration management.[4] The core objective of the EU's multidisciplinary policy framework is to "disrupt the business model of criminal organizations that put migrant lives at risk and threaten our societies' security".[5] Human smuggling is thus depicted as a highly profitable, serious crime, perpetrated by ruthless criminal networks, which also threatens security in the Area of Freedom, Security and Justice.[6]

This chapter analyses the offence of human smuggling from a European and national perspective. It first scrutinises the EU legal framework on human smuggling and highlights problematic elements and inherent shortcomings. Subsequently, the implementation of the EU legal framework and the approach to human smuggling adopted by two domestic criminal justice systems, that is, Germany and the Netherlands, is analysed. The approach to human smuggling adopted by these two central European states has thus far not been investigated in depth, as the existing literature on the topic has primarily focused on countries located on the periphery of the EU, that is,

DOI: 10.4324/9781003378440-2

countries with an external border.[7] This provides insights into the current scope of liability of human smuggling and furthermore demonstrates the impact of the shortcomings of the EU legal framework on national law. Based on this analysis, this chapter proceeds to discuss a recent Commission reform proposal and outlines and debates different ways in which the offence of human smuggling could be reformed.

2.2 The EU Approach to Human Smuggling—the Facilitators' Package

The EU's common legal framework to tackle migrant smuggling stems from the pre-Lisbon era and was created more than 20 years ago in 2002. The EU's response was influenced by, among other things, the Dover tragedy of 2000, in which 58 Chinese nationals lost their lives in a sealed lorry container. Soon after this incident, France submitted a proposal to criminalise human smuggling, which formed the basis for the further legislative process.[8] The framework consists of two complementary legal instruments, a Directive and a Framework Decision, commonly referred to as the Facilitators' Package.[9] Directive 2002/90 of 28 November 2002, defining the facilitation of unauthorised entry, transit, and residence,[10] sets out the prohibited conduct. Framework Decision 2002/946 of 28 November 2002, on the strengthening of the penal framework to prevent the facilitation of unauthorised entry, transit, and residence,[11] obliges Member States to ensure that the proscribed conduct is punishable by effective, proportionate, and dissuasive criminal penalties.

The Directive makes a distinction between the facilitation of illegal entry and transit and the facilitation of residence of irregular migrants. Pursuant to Article 1(a) of Dir. 2002/90, intentionally assisting a person who is not a national of a Member State to enter, or transit across, the territory of a Member State in breach of the laws of the state concerned on the entry or transit of aliens ought to give rise to criminal liability. Furthermore, according to Article 1(b), any person who, for financial gain, intentionally assists a person who is not a national of a Member State to reside within the territory of a Member State in breach of the laws of the State concerned on the residence of aliens must incur criminal liability.

The Directive thus draws a distinction between assistance provided to migrants with regard to illegal entry and transit, for which no financial gain is required, and assistance for illegal stay of a migrant, for which financial gain is a constitutive requirement for liability. With regard to the facilitation of illegal entry, the EU legal framework thus goes further than the corresponding international framework of the UN Migrant Smuggling Protocol,[12] which explicitly requires obtaining a financial or other material benefit as a constituent element of liability for migrant smuggling.[13] The explicit inclusion of a profit requirement in the UN Smuggling Protocol seeks to ensure that the main thrust of the offence is tackling organised crime, which is generally motivated by profit.[14] Considering that the EU legislator also conceives migrant smuggling as a highly profitable crime carried out by (ruthless) organised criminal networks that strive for profit maximisation, it seems puzzling that EU law does not contain a profit requirement.[15]

This also leads to over-criminalisation, as any form of assistance provided to migrants, even when not for financial gain, may give rise to criminal liability. The purported reasons brought forward by the European Commission for the exclusion of a profit requirement in the EU legal framework are primarily efficiency-related. A financial benefit requirement would hamper the investigation and prosecution of this crime, as financial flows are hard to trace, and the generation of profit may be hard to prove in practice, so the argument runs.[16] From a normative as well as practical perspective, none of these arguments is, however, fully convincing.[17] It can be doubted that the inclusion of a profit requirement (tied to the fault element of the offence) would really constitute such a formidable obstacle to the application of the offence and, furthermore, while efficiency may certainly be one factor shaping the contours of criminalisation, this ought to be balanced against fundamental principles of criminal law, such as *ultima ratio,* proportionality, and legal certainty.[18]

Be that as it may, the fact that Article 1(a) can lead to legislative overreach due to the absence of a profit requirement is implicitly acknowledged by the Directive itself. As any form of assistance may give rise to criminal liability, conduct of those who act out of solidarity with migrants or out of humanitarian reasons may trigger criminal liability. The antidotal measure to the broad scope of liability created by Article 1(a) is enshrined in Article 1(2), which *allows* Member States to not impose sanctions where assistance to illegal entry is provided for humanitarian purposes. However, this clause is only optional and does not oblige Member States to exempt humanitarian actors from liability. Furthermore, the wording of the provision suggests that Article 1(2) does not require implementation into national law, but, rather, allows Member States and national courts to exempt humanitarian conduct from liability based on national law and practice. In any case, Article 1(2) also fails to specify which conduct should qualify as humanitarian assistance and for what reasons. This leaves Member States with a very broad margin of appreciation to decide which conduct should give rise to liability and which not. Accordingly, only few Member States have made use of Article 1(2) in domestic law, and even where they have, the exemption is often narrowly construed, so that some forms of humanitarian aid can still be prosecuted.[19]

Article 2 of the Directive subsequently further expands the scope of liability to also cover instigation, complicity, and attempted offences. This assures that attempted assistance to illegal entry or residence as well as aiding someone who (attempts to) aid the illegal entry or residence of a migrant will also give rise to criminal liability. As the prohibited conduct need not be successful, this creates an inchoate form of liability for smuggling, underlining the preventive or even precautionary nature of the offence.[20] What is more, the obligation to criminalise instigation of assistance to enter, transit, or reside on the territory of a Member State *de facto* amounts to an obligation to criminalise also the migrant who invokes the help of a smuggler to reach his/her destination of choice.

The inherent vagueness of the Directive may furthermore lead to frictions with the principle of legality.[21] This principle is, *inter alia*, enshrined in Article 49 of the EU Charter of Fundamental Rights (CFR), and requires that criminal norms are drafted as clearly and precisely as possible so that citizens can determine in advance which conduct will give rise to criminal liability and which will not.[22] In addition, the broad scope of liability created causes frictions with the principle of proportionality enshrined in Article 52 of the CFR. The criminalisation of any form of (attempted) assistance to illegal entry/residence in order to tackle human smuggling seems disproportionate and rides roughshod over the fundamental rights of the accused and of the migrants themselves.[23]

2.2.1 *Normative and Theoretical Foundations of the EU Framework on Human Smuggling*

2.2.2.1 *Normative Foundations*

In addition to the overbroad scope of human smuggling created by EU law, the legal framework also rests on problematic normative and theoretical foundations.[24] The Directive embodies an instrumental use of criminal law while failing to include sufficient safeguards that would protect the interests and fundamental (human) rights of those being smuggled. Here, one can again detect a fundamental difference between the UN and the EU legal frameworks on migrant smuggling, as the UN Smuggling Protocol states clearly in Article 2 that the underlying goal, next to combating human smuggling, is the protection of the dignity and rights of smuggled migrants. This raises questions regarding the underlying goal as well as the legal interest protected by the EU legal framework on human smuggling.[25] The fact that Directive 2002/90 casts human smuggling in terms of facilitation or aiding of illegal migration can be considered telling in this context.[26] In legal doctrine, complicity is often conceptualised as a form of derivative liability.[27] This means that participation is generally not a crime in itself, but only becomes so in connection with the offence committed by the perpetrator. Thus, aiding often denotes an ancillary action to the primary wrong committed by the perpetrator. Consequently, as European law conceives human smuggling as a form of complicity to illegal migration, this suggests that the primary wrong which the legal framework seeks to address is irregular entry or stay, and thus irregular migration.[28] Accordingly, EU law seems to see the smuggled foreigner as a co-author in the crime of the smuggler.[29]

Such an approach may form an impediment to the right of asylum and furthermore marginalises the state's duty to protect migrants from human rights violations linked to smuggling.[30] Accordingly, this conceptualisation, combined with the ongoing securitisation of migration, has the effect that the interests of migrants, such as the protection of their fundamental human rights and dignity, take a back seat. Instead, controlling mobility by securing borders and protecting the administrative immigration apparatus (i.e., the prerogative of states to decide who has the right to entry) become the main protected interests. Through this, the selective exclusion of those who are deemed not to belong becomes a consequence of the EU legal framework.[31]

2.2.2.2 *Theoretical Conceptualisation of Human Smuggling*

As already mentioned, central to the criminalisation of human smuggling in EU law is the underlying theoretical assumption that human smuggling is a business, primarily committed by organised criminal networks that, by hook or by crook, seek profit maximisation. However, this begs the question of whether human smuggling is indeed always, or at least primarily, a product of organised crime.[32]

In any case, linked to the organised crime rationale is the assumption that human smuggling is primarily a profit-driven business. While this is certainly true in some cases, the focus on smuggling as a business enterprise obscures the fact that some individuals who are involved in the facilitation of irregular entry do so for altruistic reasons and receive little or no compensation.[33] In fact, it has also been shown that asylum seekers and labour migrants can be key players in the facilitation of irregular migration, either on their own behalf, on behalf of their families, or in order to reunite with family members at their European destination.[34] Hence, the conception of smuggling as a business obscures and misjudges the role that personal networks and social non-profit actors can play in the migration process. Furthermore, the focus on financial gain and the business model of human smuggling creates a deceptively simple distinction between smugglers and humanitarians, where the former act out of financial self-interest and the latter out of purely altruistic reasons.[35]

All this arguably shows that the European legal framework currently lacks a solid theoretical or normative foundation.[36] In combination with the vagueness and breadth of the offence definitions in Directive 2002/90, this creates problems with regard to the protection of fundamental rights and the rule of law and undermines the legitimacy of the European human smuggling framework.[37]

2.3 The National Level—Human Smuggling in Domestic Criminal Law

2.3.1 *Introduction*

The aforementioned deficiencies in the EU human smuggling framework are also visible on a national level, where the outlined uncertainties and expansive tendencies may produce far-reaching punitive effects. One problematic aspect of the Facilitators' Package, which has contributed to this development, is its failure to define key terms, such as (humanitarian) assistance, profit, and facilitation.

In particular, as the concept of facilitation is an abstract one, a large variety of forms of conduct may satisfy this requirement. As mentioned above, this leads to a situation where not only smugglers stricto senso but also migrants themselves[38] and their families–as well as NGOs, other organisations, and individuals that provide humanitarian assistance, basic social services, and fundamental human rights to migrants—may become targets of criminal sanctions.[39]

The effects of this broad scope of liability on NGOs, civil society actors, and individuals have been well-documented by now.[40] For instance, one research identified 49 cases of investigation and prosecution in 11 Member States between 2015 and 2018.[41] Citizens have, *inter alia*, been charged for trying to smuggle out family members from Greece or for housing irregular migrants, and NGOs have been classified as criminal organisations.[42] The most blatant cases of criminalisation of humanitarian assistance have, however, occurred with regard to SAR operations at sea, where migrants often find themselves in a life-threatening situation when they try to cross the sea in overcrowded, unstable, and unseaworthy vessels.[43] In this context, however, international law[44] generally imposes a duty on coastal states and shipmasters to render assistance to persons in distress and to bring them to a place of safety.[45] Imposing criminal liability on rescuers for facilitating irregular migration, thus, is in direct contradiction to duties imposed by international law. Such conduct is clearly not wrongful and must not give rise to liability. On the contrary, several European states, such as Germany and the Netherlands, have easy rescue statutes incorporated into their criminal codes that criminalise failure to rescue people from (mortal) danger.[46] The European Commission has acknowledged this and, in a non-binding communication, made it clear that "humanitarian assistance that is mandated by law cannot and should not be criminalised" and that this was, in particular, the case for SAR operations at sea.[47] Still, ample examples exist where SAR has led to criminal liability; it remains to be seen if states will heed the Commission's guidance.[48]

In any case, to shed more light on how human smuggling is defined, how key elements are interpreted, and which problems arise in national law, this contribution will now take a closer look at how human smuggling offences have been implemented in Germany and the Netherlands. This will also provide us with valuable insights regarding the functioning and repercussions of the Facilitators' Package in domestic criminal justice systems. A comparison of these two jurisdictions will, furthermore, reveal how human smuggling offences are applied in these central European countries and whether humanitarian activities have been subsumed also outside situations of SAR.

2.3.2 *A Comparison of Human Smuggling in Germany and the Netherlands*

2.3.2.1 *Mapping the Contours of the Legal Frameworks*

Germany and the Netherlands have adopted different approaches to human smuggling. This is linked to the fact that while, similar to the situation in Italy[49] and other EU Member States,[50] irregular stay and entry constitute a criminal offence in Germany,[51] at first sight, this does not seem to be the case in the Netherlands. However, an exception exists with regard to foreigners against whom an entry ban has been imposed or who have been declared undesirable foreign nationals pursuant to Article 197 of the Dutch Criminal Code (DCC).[52] Through the mechanism of an imposed entry ban, illegal stay is thus also criminalised in the Netherlands. German law also contains a separate offence in § 96 Residence Act (RA) that aims to tackle human smuggling as a form of organised crime, which is not the case in the Dutch system. Relevant legal provisions for the criminalisation of facilitation of illegal entry, transit, and residence in Germany are §§ 95, 96, and 97 RA.

In Dutch criminal law, human smuggling is enshrined in Article 197a DCC. Facilitation of irregular entry is criminalised by Article 197a (1), while facilitation of irregular stay is covered by 197a (2) DCC.[53] As will become clear below, in both countries, profit is not a constituent element for illegal entry but is with regard to illegal stay. Article 197a of the DCC independently criminalises accessorial conduct and thereby does away with the requirement of a derivative link between the conduct of the perpetrator and the accessory. Article 197a DCC makes it an offence to (1) provide assistance to another to obtain entry to or transit through the Netherlands or another Member State of the European Union,. . ., or to provide that person with the opportunity, means, or information enabling them to do so, while knowing or having serious reason to suspect that such entry or transit is unlawful; or (2) for profit, to assist another in acquiring residence in the Netherlands or another Member State of the European Union,. . ., or to provide that person with the opportunity, means, or information enabling them to do so, while knowing or having serious reason to suspect that such residence is unlawful.

Due to the fact that irregular entry or residence is itself an offence in Germany, facilitation of irregular entry or stay can lead to criminal liability via two avenues, while in the Netherlands only Article 197a of the DCC is applicable. As mentioned above, in German law, § 95 RA imposes criminal liability on foreigners who enter[54] or reside illegally in Germany as a basic offence. This may, for instance, be the case where the foreigner enters or resides in Germany without being in possession of a recognised and valid passport[55] or a valid residence title pursuant to § 4 RA.[56] Thus, these offences are predicated on administrative immigration law.[57] Furnishing or using false or incomplete information to procure a residence title or a suspension of deportation for oneself or another is prohibited by § 95 (2) Nr. 2 RA.[58] Residence titles obtained by threat, bribery, collusion, or furnishing incorrect or incomplete information are also considered illegal pursuant to § 95 (6) RA.[59]

In Dutch law, the requirement that the entry or stay was unlawful makes a similar link to administrative migration rules and covers similar variations of irregularity. Unlawful in this context means without any subjective right or license. The term is, however, interpreted broadly in case law. For example, a residence title or permit that was obtained under false pretences will amount to unlawful stay, and the same applies to visas that were obtained on the basis of fake invitations or guaranties.[60] A legal stay (e.g., on a tourist visa) can become unlawful if the foreigner takes up employment in violation of immigration rules.[61] However, even the fact that someone legally stays in the Netherlands need not negate the unlawfulness of his/her transit through the Netherlands. In a pertinent decision, the defendant had helped several minors who were staying legally in the Netherlands pending their asylum procedure to reunite with family in Italy. He provided the help as a friend and did not receive any reimbursement for his services. The Supreme Court upheld the decision of the Court of Appeal that the transit was unlawful, as the conduct of the asylum seekers made it impossible for the Dutch authorities to take a decision in the pending asylum procedure. Any other conclusion would negate the purpose of Article 197a of the DCC, the argument went.[62]

Moreover, the fact that a foreigner can invoke Article 31 of the Refugee Convention will not remove unlawfulness and will lead to liability for the facilitation of entry or transit where the foreigner used another person's passport to enter or transit the Netherlands.[63] Even the fact that an application for asylum by the irregular migrant would presumably be successful does not remove the unlawfulness of the entry or stay.[64]

A similar stance exists in Germany, where despite the fact that § 95 (5) RA provides that Article 31 (1) of the Refugee Convention remains unaffected, this does not mean that smuggling asylum seekers will not lead to criminal liability. The German Supreme Court has established that while refugees can rely on the Refugee Convention and will not be punished for irregular entry, this is not the case for the smuggler, as refugee status is conceived as merely a personal exemption from punishment, which will not remove the unlawfulness of the offence.[65] Accordingly, assisting asylum seekers may lead to criminal liability in both countries. Considering that refugees may often have no other option than to invoke the help of others to reach their destination, this can be considered problematic, as it severely curtails possibilities to rely on the right to asylum and may cause frictions with the principle of non-refoulement. This may be the case when participation in the smuggling process adversely affects asylum claims, and as a result, migrants are returned to a country where they would face torture, cruel, inhuman, or degrading treatment or punishment, or other irreparable harm.[66]

2.3.2.2 *Protected Legal Interest*

§§ 95, 96, and 97 RA aim to protect the administrative control function of the immigration process.[67] Moreover, some of the aggravating circumstances outlined in §§ 96 (2) and 97 RA also protect the interests of the migrant, such as his life and limb and his human dignity. In any case, the focus on protecting the administrative immigration process corresponds to § 1 (1) RA, which holds that "this Act serves to manage and limit the influx of foreigners into the Federal Republic of Germany. ..."

This corresponds largely to the situation in the Netherlands, where, according to the explanatory memorandum to the implementation of the Facilitators' Package, the prohibition of human smuggling serves to protect the interests of the state by ensuring that within its territory only people permitted to reside do so.[68] In other words, it serves to protect the state's policies to tackle illegal stay, which may endanger the Treasury.[69] Furthermore, also in the Netherlands, aggravated circumstances outlined in Article 197a of the DCC protect some fundamental interests of migrants, such as life and limb.

From the above, it can be concluded that in both Germany and the Netherlands, human smuggling offences are closely tied to administrative immigration rules and essentially punish violations of formal entry or residence requirements. Interests of the state, such as protecting sovereignty by managing migration and controlling borders, seem to be driving factors underlying domestic human smuggling offences. The interests of the migrants can matter as well but appear to take a more ancillary role.

2.3.2.3 The Scope of Facilitation

The notion of facilitation is, in both countries, interpreted broadly and can cover any conduct that furthered or made the irregular stay or entry easier. The provided aid does not need to be a *conditio sine qua non* for the irregular entry or stay, but any conduct that objectively fosters or facilitates the prohibited conduct will lead to liability for aiding.[70]

Intentionally inducing or aiding a person to unlawfully enter or reside in Germany or the Netherlands—by, for instance, providing housing, subsistence, or transportation to irregular migrants—can thus lead to criminal liability.[71] Hence, for instance, letting rooms or apartments to irregular migrants will generally qualify as assistance to irregular residence, provided the necessary mens rea can be established. Furthermore, providing information with regard to crossing the border, falsified passports and documents, as well as sham marriages,[72] or transporting, accompanying, or guiding people across the border, etc., may qualify as aid.[73] In the Netherlands, providing assistance to organise a sham marriage constitutes assistance to irregular residence even if the sham marriage subsequently does not take place.[74] Furthermore, intentionally assisting someone with filing an application for a residence permit based on false facts will also qualify as assistance to irregular stay in the Netherlands.[75] The same will be the case with regard to driving irregular migrants to their place of work in order to make this work possible (in this case prostitution).[76]

If no irregular entry takes place or the inducement was unsuccessful, liability for attempted aid is still possible.[77] Assistance needs to be provided intentionally in both countries.[78] However, according to Dutch law, the intent does not need to cover the element that the entry or residency was irregular, while in Germany, the defendant must act with intent in the form of *dolus eventualis* regarding the irregularity of the entrance or stay.[79]

In Dutch law, pursuant to Article 197a of the DCC, the person who provides assistance to irregular entry, transit, or stay needs to know or have serious reason to suspect that the entry, stay, etc., is unlawful. Knowing in this case requires intent, including conditional intent,[80] and "serious reasons to suspect" refers to negligence.[81] With regard to conditional intent, it will be sufficient to establish that the defendant accepted the considerable risk that the foreigner enters or resides in the Netherlands irregularly. This means that landlords have, under certain circumstances, a duty to investigate what the immigration status of their tenants is. In a pertinent case, the District Court held that the defendant should have sought information as to whether the persons to whom he was letting required a residence permit in the Netherlands. By failing to do so, he had accepted the considerable risk that the tenants' stay was irregular.[82]

With regard to negligence, gross carelessness is required. This was not the case in a situation in which a landlord was aware of the fact that the tenant had lodged an asylum application but had not asked for his passport and had simply assumed that he would register with the municipality. Under these circumstances, the defendant had, according to the Supreme Court, no serious reason to suspect that the tenant stayed irregularly in the Netherlands.[83] With regard to negligence as to the irregular status of the foreigner, no general duty to investigate seems to be imposed on property owners. However, culpable or feigned naiveté may lead to liability. In a pertinent decision, the defendant let rooms to foreigners for several months without a written rental contract. The Court in The Hague held that the defendant had acted with gross negligence, considering the fact that he knew that he was letting rooms for a longer period of time to foreigners who did not speak Dutch and communicated in broken English. Therefore, he should have made enquiries regarding the residence status of his tenants.[84]

2.3.2.3.1 HUMANITARIAN ASSISTANCE

The broad definition of assistance outlined above raises questions with regard to assistance provided by humanitarian actors or assistance consisting of neutral, socially adequate conduct. In German law, this question arises in the context of § 95 as well as § 96 RA.[85] With regard to the former, the general rules on participation enshrined in §§ 26 and 27 of the German Criminal Code (GCC) apply.[86] Profit is thus not a requirement for criminal liability. How far this also covers humanitarian assistance, or neutral or socially adequate conduct is not entirely clear.[87] Some scholars have argued that conduct that seeks to ensure the mere humane existence of the offender ought not lead to liability, but only conduct that seeks to maintain the irregular stay, such as hiding the offender from the authorities, ought to trigger liability.[88] The District Court Landshut, for instance, rejected liability for the facilitation of irregular stay in a case where the defendant lived in cohabitation with her partner who had resided irregularly in Germany for several years. The court held that the defendant's conduct was socially adequate, as she had not acted out of self-centred financial motives nor to prevent prosecution or deportation.[89]

Cases of religious sanctuary provided by the church to prevent the deportation of irregular migrants are also controversial. In a pertinent decision, the Higher Regional Court of Bavaria confirmed the acquittal of a monk who had provided sanctuary to a man from Gaza. The court argued that the man had initially resided legally in Germany during the processing of his asylum request. Due to this, no underlying legal offence existed that the monk had aided. After the negative asylum decision had been taken, the continued provision of food and shelter by the monk was classified as a failure to stop the provision of sanctuary. As no legal duty to act, however, rested on the monk, liability for aiding illegal stay could not be imposed on this basis either.[90]

The decision of the Higher Regional Court of Bavaria can be considered exceptional and does not apply to situations where foreigners are deliberately hidden from the authorities or where deportation is intentionally foiled. Other occasions of religious sanctuary have been considered to constitute facilitation of stay.[91] The Higher Regional Court of Hamm quashed, for instance, the acquittal of a priest who had provided lodging and small amounts of money to a Turkish/Kurdish mother and her two daughters, holding that humanitarian assistance can lead to an acquittal for facilitation of stay only in exceptional circumstances. This will only be the case in acute emergency situations and if the aid does not exceed what is necessary in the case at hand, which will generally be short-term measures.[92]

This narrow exemption of humanitarian assistance from liability seems to correspond to the approach adopted by Dutch law, where humanitarian assistance can currently only be excluded from liability in case a general defence, such as necessity or duress, can be invoked. The Supreme Court has explicitly mentioned this possibility in two cases in which a claim of humanitarian assistance was rejected. In one case, the defendant organised the journey of two persons from Uganda to the Netherlands by, *inter alia*, sending them money and procuring falsified passports and visas. The defence had argued that the defendant had acted under duress, as the two persons were family members. The Supreme Court, however, upheld the conviction of the Court of Appeal, which had held that duress required an (external) psychological pressure of such a nature that the defendant could not and should not have resisted it. These requirements were not fulfilled, as it was not established that no other alternatives existed to help the smuggled persons, and they were not in an acute life-threatening situation that forced the defendant to act as he did.[93]

In another Supreme Court decision, the defendant had brought two Eritrean nationals from Italy to the Netherlands. Considering the humanitarian situation in Eritrea, the defence relied on the justification of necessity. The Supreme Court confirmed again that humanitarian aid in the context of Article 197a of the DCC can be invoked as a justification/excuse. The defence of necessity applies in situations of actual danger to legal interests, which can only be averted by infringing the less valuable interest. Considering the legislative history of Article 197a of the DCC, the Supreme Court found that a justification may be invoked if the humanitarian assistance is provided to foreigners for purely altruistic reasons and where it is reasonable to assume that they find themselves in a life—or security—threatening situation and cannot escape this situation by any other means than entering the Netherlands irregularly.[94] Considering the fact that the foreigners travelled from Italy (a safe country) to the Netherlands, the court denied the existence of an emergency situation and also doubted that no other ways to help their escape than irregularly entering the Netherlands had been available.[95]

Next to assisting the irregular entry or stay of migrants pursuant to § 95 RA in conjunction with the general rules on participation, liability may, in Germany, also arise for the aggravated offence of smuggling enshrined in § 96 RA. Predicated on the basic offence of § 95, § 96 (1)[96] and (2)[97] RA list several aggravating circumstances and make it an offence to incite or assist another person to irregularly enter or reside in Germany, as outlined in § 96 (1) Nr. 1 or 2 RA. Thus, only the forms of illegal entry or stay outlined in the article can lead to liability pursuant to § 96 RA.[98]

§ 96 RA is designed to tackle human smuggling as a form of organised crime and creates an independent offence of facilitation of illegal entry and residence.[99] If the requirements of § 96 RA are fulfilled, aiding and abetting is punished as a form of perpetration. The sentence range available for aiding and facilitation was, considering the mandatory mitigation of punishment enshrined in § 27(2) GCC, considered too low to cover the increased wrongfulness of the conduct if committed by organised and profit-driven smuggling networks.[100]

In spite of the fact that § 96 RA elevates facilitation to a form of perpetration, the general rules of participation, including the derivative nature of complicity, still apply.[101] As a result, § 96 RA has a tripartite structure. It requires (1) an intentional and wrongful main offence pursuant to § 95 RA committed by the smuggled person; (2) incitement or facilitation by the smuggler; and (3) fulfilment of one of the criteria of smuggling mentioned in § 96 RA.[102]

With regard to (3), the distinction between entry and residence offences as a basis for the smuggling offence of § 96 RA is important, as it influences the smuggling criteria (Schleusermerkmale) that need to be proven. In order for liability for illegal entry to arise, the offender needs to (1) receive an advantage[103] or the promise of an advantage in return or (2) act repeatedly[104] or for the benefit of several foreigners.[105] With regard to the facilitation of illegal residence, the perpetrator needs to receive a pecuniary advantage or the promise of a pecuniary advantage in return.

The underlying main offence needs to be committed intentionally and wrongfully.[106] The requirement of intentional conduct can lead to difficulties in case of illegal entry of minors.[107] If the smuggled person does not act intentionally or wrongfully, no liability for smuggling pursuant to § 96 RA can be imposed. The liability of the smuggler thus hinges on the intentional and unlawful offences committed by the smuggled person.[108]

The smuggler needs to incite or aid the commission of the unlawful offence. Incitement means inducing someone to enter or reside in Germany irregularly, as may, for instance, be the case if people are recruited for irregular employment, which includes prostitution.[109] As outlined above, aiding includes any conduct that objectively furthered the commission of the offence.

Furthermore, it is also possible to aid the facilitation of irregular entry pursuant to § 27 GCC[110] in conjunction with § 96 RA. For example, a promise to assist can already qualify as aid, which broadens the scope of liability considerably and may criminalise the smuggled foreigners themselves.

In a pertinent case, the defendant had agreed with smugglers to bring him from Turkey to Greece for a price of 2000 euros. The smuggling process was organised in such a way that the large group of migrants travelling to Greece was split into smaller groups, and one man acted as a contact person for each group. The defendant promised the smugglers to act as the contact person for two women and their four children aged one to seven. The defendant kept his promise and helped with the transport of their luggage and provided them with food and water while they were waiting for the crossing. The women paid for the food and water, and he received no further financial gain for his help. During the crossing to Greece, disaster struck, and the two women and their children drowned. The Supreme Court found that the promise to function as a contact person amounted to aid and upheld the conviction for aiding the facilitation of irregular entry, causing the death of another, resulting in a prison sentence of one year and six months.[111] However, it may be questioned here if the defendant really furthered the wrongful conduct of the smugglers or rather acted out of solidarity and humanity to his fellow travel companions. Furthermore, the fact that § 96 RA aims to tackle organised crime also sits uncomfortably with imposing liability on a smuggled foreigner.[112]

In any case, due to the fact that German law does not provide for an explicit exemption of humanitarian conduct, the problem of criminalising humanitarian assistance resurfaces in the context of § 96 RA. After all, humanitarian actors and organisations provide aid intentionally while being aware of the irregular status of the people they help.[113] The situation for humanitarian actors is also not helped by the fact that the Residence Act makes financial profit only a *necessary* element of the offence of facilitation of stay. This is because § 95 RA does not contain any profit requirement at all, and § 96 RA requires in case of irregular entry that the smuggler receives or is promised an advantage, or alternatively, acts repeatedly or in favour of several migrants.[114] Hence, only for the facilitation of stay is it necessary that the smuggler receives a pecuniary advantage or the promise of a pecuniary advantage in return. This corresponds to the situation in the Netherlands, where the profit requirement for illegal entry was removed during the implementation of Directive 2002/90. As the Directive did not contain a profit requirement for the facilitation of entry, it was argued that maintaining it was not in line with the EU legal framework and would, furthermore, undermine the effective application of human smuggling.[115]

2.3.2.4 Profit

The profit requirement is defined broadly in both countries. According to German law, pecuniary advantage or profit pursuant to § 96 (1) Nr. 2 RA is any positive development of the smugglers financial situation. The profit does not need to be unlawful but must be causally connected to the aid provided to the migrant. Any form of *profit* will suffice, which means that the requirement will not be satisfied in case of payments to merely cover the cost of the provided assistance (e.g., costs of transportation).[116] The offender needs to receive or be promised the financial benefit for him or herself. Accordingly, an enrichment of third parties will not satisfy this requirement. In a pertinent decision, the Supreme Court ruled that in a case where the defendant had aided the operation of a smuggling network which smuggled people via Germany to Canada in exchange for being reunited with her mother and brother in Germany (where she lawfully resided), the profit requirement was not fulfilled. This was due to the fact that not the defendant but rather her mother and brother were to profit from the service of the smuggling network.[117]

The definition of profit under Dutch law closely resembles that of the UN Smuggling Protocol, as any direct or indirect financial or other material advantage will suffice.[118] There is no *de minimis* threshold for the profit requirement in Dutch law. Thus, similar to German law, anything that leads to a favourable economic situation will suffice. Accordingly, receiving a rent of 100 euros for a room will satisfy the requirement.[119] Furthermore, in a pertinent case, the defendants had provided lodging to a Chinese citizen who worked as a nanny and also carried out other chores which arose in the context of the restaurant that the defendants ran. For her work, the nanny received between 900 and 1300 euros per month. The court held that the profit requirement was satisfied if the defendant's aim was enrichment and that it was not necessary that this resulted in a monetary advantage nor that the envisaged advantage materialised.[120] By illegally employing the nanny, they, according to the court, saved employer and payroll taxes, were able to work longer in their restaurant, and therefore gained an economic advantage.[121]

2.3.2.5 Concluding Remarks

It becomes apparent from the foregoing that the scope of criminal liability for facilitation of irregular entry and stay is broad under Dutch and German law. Profit is not a constituent element for all variants of human smuggling but only with regard to the facilitation of stay. The profit requirement is interpreted broadly and covers any economic benefit. In addition, neither country provides for an explicit exemption of humanitarian assistance. The exact borders of criminal liability in this context thus remain unclear, which may have a chilling effect on those who act out of humanitarian reasons.[122] In case law, a strict stance towards invoking humanitarian assistance in the form of a general defence seems to be followed. Only in emergency situations (possibly due to idealistic reasons) and only when no other possibilities are available may a general defence be applicable.[123]

Admittedly, the profit requirement in the context of facilitation of stay may offer some protection for those who offer support to migrants who already reside in the country. However, in German law, this only applies to liability pursuant to § 96 RA, leaving the possibility of liability for aiding the offence of the migrant pursuant to § 95 RA untouched.[124] In Dutch law, the fact that negligence as to the irregular status of the migrant is sufficient for liability for the facilitation of stay increases the risk for landlords and property owners to incur criminal liability for letting to foreigners. This may have a chilling effect, as landlords may be wary about letting to non-EU citizens, which will make it increasingly difficult for them to find lodging. Moreover, both countries criminalise the smuggling of refugees and do not provide for exemptions in case of self-smuggling or when assistance is provided to family members, and the facilitation of irregular entry or stay, therefore, has ties to the right to family life.

2.4 Reforming Human Smuggling Legislation

As discussed above, the European human smuggling framework suffers from various shortcomings. Its normative, and conceptual foundations are shaky. While its alleged goal is to target ruthless organised smuggling networks, in practice, the broad concept of facilitation of entry or stay criminalises a wide variety of conduct, which lacks a link to the harm threatened by organised crime. The foregoing comparison of national law seems to confirm this picture.

The inherent vagueness and breadth of the European human smuggling framework are, thus, also visible in domestic law, which causes frictions with the principle of legality. Furthermore, it creates the possibility for states to deploy human smuggling offences as a preventive tool in the context of migration management.

The current state of affairs may, therefore, be considered problematic with regard to legal certainty, the protection of fundamental rights, and the rule of law. The crucial question that, therefore, arises is how the situation can be improved.

The European Commission has recently conceded that the current EU legal framework on human smuggling is in need of modernisation and has tabled a proposal to replace the Facilitators' Package.[125] While the proposal, as further discussed below, contains important improvements, it fails to acknowledge the complexities of migrant smuggling or the interests of migrants.[126] Furthermore, it insufficiently addresses the persistent fundamental rights and rule of law concerns in relation to the criminalisation of human smuggling.[127]

2.4.1 The Theoretical Conceptualisation of Human Smuggling

Any reform of human smuggling ought to be based on an empirically grounded conception of the phenomenon to ensure effective regulation and to prevent over-criminalisation. Just like the current legal framework outlined above, the proposal links human smuggling to the fight against organised crime.[128] A first question that should accordingly be addressed is whether human smuggling is indeed an offence that is primarily committed by organised and structured groups, or rather by other, looser social structures. This will help to clarify the structure of the criminal process and behaviour the law seeks to address and the archetypal perpetrator the offence targets. However, this is admittedly not an easy task, as the concept of organised crime is amorphous, which raises the question of what may empirically as well as normatively be considered organised crime.[129]

In any case, in spite of a large and growing literature on the topic, the definition of human smuggling remains contested.[130] Social scientists have, for instance, severely criticised the organised crime rationale of human smuggling.[131] It seems certainly not necessary to have large organisations involved in human smuggling. Such organisations may be involved in some instances, but it seems likely that human smuggling is also frequently carried out by socially embedded networks rather than hierarchical and rule-bound organisations.[132]

The degree of involvement of organised networks in the smuggling process may arguably also vary depending on the chosen smuggling route. Different smuggling routes have different characteristics and vary in terms of complexity of the required action, which determines the applied modus operandi.[133] These peculiarities may in turn influence the involvement of organised criminal groups in the smuggling process.[134] Generally, however, it seems that human smuggling is less frequently organised by kingpins and that the organisations involved are less hierarchical, permanent, and clear-cut than usually assumed.[135]

Thus, there is reason to doubt that human smuggling is primarily carried out by mafia-like criminal organisations.[136] Instead, empirical evidence points more towards loosely cast networks, so that "migrant smuggling operations appear to be organised along a primarily horizontal structure of intermediaries that interface with each other".[137] Research, therefore, shows a more complex and nuanced picture of human smuggling, which challenges the simple yet popular narrative of cold-blooded smuggling networks that must be stopped, whatever the costs.[138] Some data also suggests that many human smugglers are "in fact independent operators, often working on behalf of friends and family members, or who are migrants themselves trying to reach a destination";[139] a view that is partially confirmed by German and Dutch case law, as discussed above. Accordingly, framing human smuggling as an instance and key activity of organised crime and smugglers as ruthless criminals who threaten national security seems therefore overly simplistic.[140]

Similar objections can be raised against framing human smuggling as a business revolving around financial gain.[141] This conceptualisation overlooks that migrants may have other motives to use the service provided by smugglers and that people involved in smuggling do not necessarily do so for business reasons. This conception, for instance, neglects the fact that family members, churches, and NGOs may also be involved in helping people cross borders.

The conceptualisation of smuggling as organised crime or business also creates a simplistic picture of the smuggling process, where migrants are often seen as mere passive actors. Yet, often human smuggling appears to be a much more complex and diverse process.[142] Unfortunately, the current proposal fails to take into account the "nuanced realities of migration".[143] The choice of legal basis—i.e., Article 83(2) of the Treaty on the Functioning of the European Union (TFEU), which does not mention organised crime—also casts doubt on this alleged rationale.[144]

Nevertheless, currently effective laws still extend the stigma of organised crime and ruthless business practices by proxy to the smuggled migrants, making them part of the problem as they choose to engage in illegal practices. This is also evidenced by the fact that migrants who help to steer boats or navigate to reach safety are often held liable for being part of the criminal organisation.[145] In any case, framing human smuggling as an organised crime phenomenon is arguably a clear example of the securitisation of migration[146] that shapes (supra)national responses to human smuggling and helps to justify the broad scope of liability as well as the introduction of other punitive immigration measures.[147] This also helps to obscure the fact that the absence of safe and legal channels to access the EU is one of the factors that contributes to increasing human smuggling.[148]

2.4.2 *Profit as an Element of Human Smuggling?*

To improve the current state of affairs, the proposal for a new Directive, as has also long been suggested in literature, foresees the introduction of a profit requirement for both irregular entry and stay. According to Article 3(1)(a) of the proposal, liability for human smuggling would require that the smuggler requests, receives or accepts, directly or indirectly, a financial or material benefit, or a promise thereof, or carries out the conduct in order to obtain such benefit.[149] Profit would, however, not be required for facilitation where there is a high likelihood of causing serious harm to a person pursuant to Article 3(1)(b). Thus, while at least at first sight, a profit requirement may generally seem like an advancement compared to the current situation; profit would not be required for all instances of human smuggling, which could still lead to misapplication of the law.

In any case, if human smuggling is perceived as an instance of organised crime, then the inclusion of a profit requirement makes sense. However, if, as suggested above, fighting organised crime is not the primary rationale of human smuggling offences, a profit requirement becomes less convincing. In addition, it can be questioned whether such a requirement can at all function as a sufficient restraint to the current sweeping scope of the Facilitators' Package. Due to this inherent vagueness, much will depend on the exact contours of the profit requirement. What qualifies as a financial or material benefit, and how will profit be defined in this context? Will any form of profit, as is the case in the Netherlands, suffice, or is it necessary that the profit exceeded a certain threshold and can, therefore, be considered unjust? The question then, however, becomes where to draw the line. How to categorise, for instance, donations to relief organisations that aid migrants? Will cost recovery qualify as profit or is the requirement only fulfilled once the amount received exceeds the current market price of the provided service? As outlined above, in Germany, the enrichment need not be unjust, yet mere cost recovery will not satisfy the profit requirement. In Austria, however, it has, in the context of licensed taxi drivers, been held that charging a regular fare will not amount to unjust enrichment.[150] Generally, a more nuanced profit requirement is to be preferred; however, this may necessitate determining, in every case, what amounts to an adequate reimbursement for the service provided. This would require a case-by-case approach by the courts, which may lead to uncertainty.

In addition to these definitional difficulties, a profit requirement seems inadequate from a normative and conceptual perspective. A profit requirement gives the impression that blameworthy and non-blameworthy conduct can be easily distinguished by a "single guiding motivation" captured by the profit-making requirement.[151] This ignores the fact that many of those involved in the complex endeavour of facilitation of irregular entry do so out of unselfish reasons and convictions and receive no or hardly any reward for their contribution.[152] Furthermore, it gives the impression that altruistic acts can never involve any element of gain. Historically, this distinction is, however, not supported. During World War II, "smugglers" helped Jews and other people persecuted by the Nazi regime flee to Switzerland, some of them for financial reimbursement.[153] Likewise, "smugglers" who helped people to flee the German Democratic Republic also often asked money for their services.[154] These examples show that humanitarian acts and financial gain can coexist. Furthermore, they raise questions with regard to the practice of countries, such as Germany and the Netherlands, of imposing liability for human smuggling on those who help migrants to flee from countries where their life or freedom was endangered and who can rely on Article 31 of the Refugee Convention. The risk of incurring criminal liability in such instances may, furthermore, have a chilling effect on humanitarians and refugee advocates.

2.4.3 *Exempting Humanitarian Assistance from Liability*

The binary distinction created by a profit requirement seems, therefore, insufficient to distinguish between wrongful or reprehensible, and humanitarian forms of smuggling. For this reason, it has also been suggested that a reform of the human smuggling framework ought to include the introduction of an obligatory exemption of humanitarian assistance.[155] Yet, the Commission proposal does not include such a humanitarian exception. Nevertheless, Recital 7 of the Preamble states that it is not the purpose of the Directive to (1) hold migrants liable for being smuggled, nor to criminalise (2) assistance provided to family members or (3) humanitarian assistance or the support of basic human needs provided to third-country nationals in compliance with legal obligations. Yet, this does not seem to go far enough, as it can be questioned whether a preambular provision can provide sufficient protection for humanitarian actors under national law.[156]

This is particularly so, as the proposal in Article 3(1)(b) also aims to criminalise assistance of irregular entry or stay in cases where a high likelihood of causing serious harm to a person exists. When this will be the case remains, however, unclear, causing frictions with the demands of legal certainty and raising concerns that the provision may be applied to continue the criminalisation of humanitarian assistance, especially during SAR operations.[157]

The inclusion of a binding humanitarian exemption would, therefore, have been preferable. Yet, such a clause would still require careful definition to ensure legal certainty and equal application in domestic law. What qualifies as humanitarian assistance and for which reasons? Would, for instance, family members also be able to invoke the exception? In this sense, the situations outlined in the Preamble of the proposed Directive (i.e., assistance to family members, humanitarian assistance, or support of basic human needs in compliance with legal obligations) can constitute a starting point for debate, but the exact contours should be further defined to clarify what conduct will fall outside the scope of the offence. Will, for instance, liability for human smuggling also be excluded where assistance was provided to migrants whose fundamental human rights are threatened, which may result in serious harm?[158] And what about situations where migrants find themselves in a more generic situation of need, falling short of serious imminent risks to life and limb or fundamental human rights?

In any case, while the inclusion of a binding and clearly defined exemption would constitute an improvement, casting humanitarian assistance in terms of an exemption would not bar the initiation of criminal investigations and proceedings and would put the burden of invoking the exemption on humanitarian actors.[159] Furthermore, enshrining humanitarian assistance as an exemption may still provide a convenient basis for law enforcement authorities to deploy other modalities of policing humanitarianism.[160]

Thus, while the proposed anti-smuggling Directive represents an important development in addressing migrant smuggling in the EU, it simultaneously perpetuates some of the shortcomings of the Facilitators' Package. From a human rights perspective, a better solution would, therefore, require more radical and advanced reforms.[161] The following section hopes to contribute to this discussion.

2.4.4 *Rethinking Human Smuggling*

The starting point of such a revision of human smuggling offences should be a clearly defined legal interest that the offence seeks to protect. In addition, the offence should reflect the complex and multifaceted realities of migration.[162] As outlined above, human smuggling is a very diverse and complex process, which need not involve organised crime. The focus on fighting organised crime should, therefore, not constitute the normative foundation of the offence. A broader, more socially embedded conception of human smuggling seems preferable. This better reflects the intricate dynamics of migration as well as empirical findings and creates room for taking into account the migrants' agency in the smuggling process and the protection of their fundamental rights. It allows acknowledging the vulnerability of migrants to exploitation, mistreatment, and violation of dignity and fundamental rights linked to the process or consequences of being smuggled, and helps to balance crime control interests with human rights.[163]

Therefore, two interests should form the normative foundation of human smuggling. The first is derived from general principles of Union law and takes into account the interests of the migrant. According to the European CFR, the Union is founded on the indivisible, universal values of human dignity, freedom, equality, and solidarity; it is based on the principles of democracy and the rule of law.[164] Any future legislation needs to respect the values protected by the CFR and, in particular, the inviolability of human dignity (Article 1), the right to life (Article 2) and physical integrity (Article 3), the prohibition of torture and inhuman or degrading treatment or punishment (Article 4), the right to family and private life (Article 7), the right to asylum (Article 18), the right to non-discrimination (Article 21), and the principle of legality (Article 49).[165]

Accordingly, a crucial role should be given to the notion of human dignity and the protection of fundamental rights of the migrant.[166] As will be further explained below, adding such a human rights perspective has crucial implications for the scope of the offence. In addition, as in Dutch and German law, it seems generally accepted that the offence of human smuggling aims to protect the sovereignty interests of the EU and the Member States in controlling their borders, as well as to uphold immigration rules and procedures. The latter interest is, however, problematic in light of the *ultima ratio* principle and the principle of proportionality, as it remains questionable whether the protection of migration rules cannot be sufficiently achieved by administrative law and whether the use of sweeping criminal rules is proportionate to that end.[167] Therefore, this interest alone cannot justify the criminalisation of human smuggling.[168] Only by combining the states' interest regarding irregular movement with the interest of protecting the rights and wellbeing of the persons concerned does the application of criminal law seem justified.[169]

The different elements of the offence of human smuggling should align with and work towards the end of safeguarding the legal interests protected by the offence, so that the principle of legality also exerts influence on the offence definition. It requires the legislator to clearly define offences and the penalties that they attract. This means that an individual must, based on the wording of the provision and with the help of the case law of the courts, be able to determine which acts will make the perpetrator criminally liable.[170] The current offence definition of facilitation of irregular entry or stay is, as outlined above, broad and over-inclusive and does not allow actors who act out of humanitarian reasons or solidarity to migrants to determine, with sufficient precision and in advance, what conduct will trigger criminal liability. The offence of human smuggling ought, therefore, to clearly delineate the offence elements that, if fulfilled, will trigger liability. The Commission proposal addresses some of these shortcomings by distinguishing two variants of aiding and one of instigating irregular entry or stay (Article 3) as well as several aggravated criminal offences (Article 4). However, the potential scope of liability remains broad, and the focus remains on prevention and migration management.[171] Furthermore, it fails to sufficiently take into account the interests of migrants and the complex dynamics of migration.[172]

Arguably, the smuggling offence should thus not be couched in terms of assistance or facilitation of entry and stay, as these terms are notoriously vague and significantly contribute to the current breadth of the offence. To circumscribe the scope of the offence from the outset, it seems, therefore, preferable to use the term human smuggling. To respect and protect the interests of the people smuggled, the crime should not exclusively be defined by the irregularity of the entrance or stay but should also take into account the motivation of the smuggler.[173] The latter can find expression in the fault element of the offence. This seems crucial to draw a distinction between wrongful and humanitarian smugglers. This allows the notion of human dignity of migrants to fulfil a guiding function. Wrongful smuggling arguably manifests in circumstances where migrants are deprived of their human dignity and treated as commodities or objects and not as subjects with an inherent worth.[174] Human smuggling should, therefore, focus on acts where the smuggler enables someone to cross a border irregularly and in so doing intentionally or recklessly subjects that person to inhumane or degrading treatment or endangers their life or physical integrity.[175] When human smuggling amounts to inhumane or degrading treatment will depend on the specific situation at hand. Factors such as the exact manner of transportation, the conditions of life, travel, or housing that migrants are exposed to, the fee charged, the duration of the treatment, and its physical or mental effects—combined with individual characteristics of the person, such as age, health, and sex—may therefore play a role.[176]

Such a narrowly defined offence of human smuggling would, from the outset, exclude liability for humanitarian assistance and only criminalise conduct that creates a risk of harm for the underlying protected legal interests, that is, the human dignity of migrants and the control of the border. At the same time, it would make clear that the offence does not target conduct motivated by humanitarian considerations or acts of solidarity with migrants. Conduct that aims at securing a humane existence, such as providing food and shelter or other basic human needs, can thus never lead to criminal liability. Similarly, conduct motivated by close family relationships and aiming to secure the right to family life can, as it will generally not be aimed at or carried out with intent to jeopardise the human dignity of migrants, fall outside the scope of human smuggling. However, from a doctrinal perspective, exempting family members from liability on the basis of their status alone remains difficult to justify.

Integrating human dignity and the protection of fundamental rights as a protected legal interest not only works to protect the rights of people who aid migrants, but arguably also leads to an exclusion of liability for those who have been smuggled, that is, the migrants. They should not be considered as *aiders* in their own irregular entry. For optimal legal certainty, the redrafted offence should, like the UN Smuggling Protocol, include an explicit exemption for this form of self-smuggling instead of a mere preambular provision, as in the current proposal.

Creating an offence of human smuggling along the lines outlined above would create a clearly defined offence built on a solid normative foundation. It makes clear that protecting migrants' fundamental rights and human dignity forms a key interest to be protected by the offence. The demarcation of punishable wrongful human smuggling and permissible behaviour would thereby become clearer and more foreseeable. Furthermore, it would make clear that the law supports solidarity and humanitarian activities, which may remove some of the chilling effects that the current offence of human smuggling has on humanitarian actors.[177]

2.5 Conclusion

The EU legal framework on human smuggling, enshrined in the Facilitators' Package, allows for the criminalisation of a broad range of behaviours and has been utilised by states to prevent and control migrant flows towards their territory. However, the offence rests on shaky normative and theoretical foundations.

The breadth of the offence, combined with a lack of clearly defined protected legal interests, has also led to over-criminalisation by allowing the conduct of humanitarian actors to be subsumed under the offence of human smuggling. This has had a significant impact on the humanitarian work of NGOs and individuals, most visible in the context of SAR operations in the Mediterranean Seas. The impacts of the Facilitators' Package are also visible beyond the European sea borders. This chapter investigated the implementation of the Facilitators' Package in two central European countries, namely Germany and the Netherlands. The analysis has shown that the scope of liability created by the offence of human smuggling in these two countries is broad and can also target humanitarian conduct. The Commission, however, has recently tabled a proposal that seeks to address some of the shortcomings of the Facilitators' Package.

Against this background, this chapter analysed the proposal, submitting that it fails to fully address fundamental rights and rule of law concerns,[178] and outlined possible ways in which the over-inclusive scope of the human smuggling framework may be circumscribed. It has been argued that the inclusion of a profit requirement in combination with a mandatory humanitarian exemption in the legal framework may remedy some, but not all, of the far-reaching effects caused by the current state of affairs. The chapter therefore proposed to carefully redraft the offence of human smuggling in such a way that the specific offence elements are aligned with and support the protection of the underlying protected legal interests. This would give rise to a clearly circumscribed offence definition, which would create legal certainty.

In any case, it should be kept in mind that the use of criminal law in the context of migration control remains problematic. While the offence of human smuggling may serve to protect important legal interests, it is crucial that the primary thrust of the offence is aimed at the wrongful conduct of the smuggler and does not lead, by proxy, to the criminalisation of permissible and even desirable humanitarian assistance or irregular migration per se.

Notes

1 Katja Franko, *Globalization & Crime* (Sage 2020) 30.

2 Valsamis Mitsilegas, 'The Criminalisation of Migration in the Law of the European Union—Challenging the Preventive Paradigm' in Gian Luigi Gatta, Valsamis Mitsilegas and Stefano Zirulia (eds), *Controlling Immigration Through Criminal Law* (Hart Publishing 2021) 25–45. See also Lina Vosyliute and Carmine Conte, 'Crackdown on NGOs and Volunteers Helping Refugees and Other Migrants' Resoma Report (2019); Valsamis Mitsilegas, 'The Normative Foundations of the Criminalization of Human Smuggling: Exploring the Fault Lines Between European and International Law' (2019) 10 New Journal of European Criminal Law 68.

3 Franko (n 1) 79 et seq. See also Andrew Ashworth and Lucia Zedner, *Preventive Justice* (OUP 2014) 225 et seq. and Alessandro Spena, 'The Double-Deviant Identity of the Mass-Foreigner and the Lack of Authority of the Crimigrationist State' (2019) 22 New Criminal Law Review 301.

4 European Commission, 'A Renewed EU Action Plan Against Migrant Smuggling (2021–2025)' COM (2021) 591 final, which builds on: European Commission, 'EU Action Plan Against Migrant Smuggling' (2015–2020), COM (2015) 285 final and EU Commission, 'Roadmap to EU Action Plan Against Migrant Smuggling' (2021–2025) Ref. Ares(2021)1557057. See also Stefano Zirulia, 'Is that a Smuggler?' in Gatta, Mitsilegas and Zirulia (n 2) 235; Sergio Carrera and others, *Policing Humanitarianism* (Hart Publishing 2020) 1, 24 et seq. and Sergio Carrera, Jennifer Allsopp and Lina Vosyliute, 'Policing the Mobility Society: The Effects of EU Anti-Migration Smuggling Policies on Humanitarianism' (2018) 4 International Journal of Migration and Border Studies 237.

5 European Commission, 'Guidance on the Implementation of EU Rules on Definition and Prevention of the Facilitation of Unauthorised Entry, Transit and Residence', Com (2020) 6470 final, p. 1. Similarly European Commission, 'A Renewed EU Action Plan Against Migrant Smuggling' (2021–2025), Com (2021) 591 final, p. 1, 2, 8, 10, 22 and European Commission, 'EU Action Plan Against Migrant Smuggling' (2015–2020), Com (2015) 285 final, p. 2.

6 European Commission, 'A Renewed EU Action Plan Against Migrant Smuggling' (2021–2025), Com (2021) 591 final, p. 1. Similarly European Commission, 'EU Action Plan Against Migrant Smuggling' (2015–2020), Com (2015) 285 final, p. 1. European Commission, 'Roadmap to EU Action Plan Against Migrant Smuggling' (2021–2025) Ref. Ares(2021)1557057. See also Europol, 'European Migrant Smuggling Centre—5th Annual Report' (2021). Similarly Enrico Fassi, 'The EU, Migration and Global Justice. Policy Narratives of Human Smuggling and Their Normative Implications' (2020) 1 Rivista Trimestrale di scienza dell'aministrazione 1–30.

7 For example, Marta Minetti, 'The Facilitators Package, Penal Populism and the Rule of Law: Lessons from Italy' (2020) 11 New Journal of European Criminal Law 335; Alessandro Spena, 'Migrant Smuggling: A Normative and Phenomenological View from Italy' in Vincenzo Militello and Alessandro Spena, *Between Criminalization and Protection. The Italian Way of Dealing with Migrant Smuggling and Trafficking Within the European and International Context* (Brill 2019) 5–54; Jennifer Allsopp, Lina Vosyliūtė and Stephanie Brenda Smialowski, 'Picking "Low Hanging Fruit" While the Orchard Burns: The Costs of Policing Humanitarian Actors in Italy and Greece as a Strategy to Prevent Migrant Smuggling' (2021) 27 European Journal on Criminal Policy and Research 65; Eugenio Cusumano and Matteo Villa, 'From "Angels" to "Vice Smugglers": The Criminalization of Sea Rescue NGOs in Italy' (2021) 27 European Journal of Criminal Policy and Research 23.

8 Ilse van Liempt and Stephanie Sersli, 'State Responses and Migrant Experiences with Human Smuggling: A Reality Check' [2013] Antipode, 1036 et seq.

9 André Klip, *European Criminal Law* (Intersentia 2021) 244.

10 Council Directive 2002/90/EC of 28 November 2002 defining the facilitation of unauthorised entry, transit and residence [2002] OJ L328/17.

11 Council Framework Decision 2002/946/JHA of 28 November 2002 on the strengthening of the penal framework to prevent the facilitation of unauthorised entry, transit and residence [2002] OJ L328/1.

12 Protocol against the Smuggling of Migrants by Land, Sea and Air, Supplementing the United Nations Convention against Transnational Crime (adopted 15 November 2000, entered into force 28 January 2004) 2241 UNTS 480.

13 See Smuggling Protocol (n 12) article 6; UNODC, 'The Concept of Financial or Other Material Benefit in the Smuggling of Migrants Protocol' Issue Paper (2017).

14 Mitsilegas (n 2) 34 et seq. See also UNDOC, 'The Concept of Financial or Other Material Benefit in the Smuggling of Migrants Protocol' Issue Paper (2017) iii, xi.

15 Mitsilegas (n 2) 79.
16 Mitsilegas (n 2) 29 et seq.
17 Mitsilegas (n 2) 29 et seq. Mitsilegas (n 2) 79 et seq. See also Zirulia (n 4) 252 et seq.
18 Mitsilegas (n 2) 29 et seq. In a recent proposal the Commission also seems to have changed its mind regarding the necessity and practicality of a profit requirement. See further section 2.4.
19 Resoma Report 2019, Sergio Carrera and others, *Fit for Purpose? The Facilitation Directive and the Criminalisation of Humanitarian Assistance to Irregular Migrants: 2018 Update* (CEPS 2019) 11.
20 Mitsilegas (n 2) 29 et seq.; Mitsilegas (n 2) 68.
21 Especially in case a Member State chooses to implement the Directive verbatim.
22 Generally see Christina Peristeridou, *The Principle of Legality in European Criminal Law* (Intersentia 2015); Case C-308/06 *Intertanko* [2008] ECLI:EU:C:2008:312, para 71; Case C 194/14 *AC Treuhand vs Commission* [2015] ECLI:EU:C:2015:717, para 40; Case C 102/16 *Vaditrans* [2017] ECLI:EU:C:2017:1012, para 51.
23 Zirulia (n 4) 263. See also Case C-460/23, Kinshasa: Request for a preliminary ruling from the Tribunale di Bologna (Italy) lodged on 21 July 2023—Criminal proceedings against OB, OJ C, C/338, 25.09.2023, p. 12.
24 Mitsilegas (n 2) 25–45.
25 Mitsilegas (n 2) 25–45.
26 Alessandro Spena, 'Human Smuggling and Irregular Immigration in the EU: From Complicity to Exploitation?' in Sergio Carrera and Elspeth Guild (eds), *Irregular Migration, Trafficking and Smuggling of Human Beings—Policy Dilemmas in the EU* (CEPS 2016) 37; Alessandro Spena (n 7) 47 et seq.
27 Johannes Keiler, *Actus Reus and Participation in European Criminal Law* (Intersentia 2013) 153–67.
28 Mitsilegas (n 2) 81.
29 Spena (n 7) 42 et seq.
30 Kinga Janik, 'A Human Rights Approach to Extremely Vulnerable People: Challenges and Feasibility in Assessing Smuggled Migrants' in Valsamis Mitsilegas, Violeta Moreno-Lax and Niovi Vavoula (eds), *Securitising Asylum Flows* (Brill 2020) 57–78.
31 Scott Watson, 'The Criminalization of Human and Humanitarian Smuggling' (2015) 1 Migration, Mobility, & Displacement 39–53 at 49.
32 See section 2.4.1.
33 Watson (n 31) 43.
34 Luigi Achilli and Gabriella Sanchez, 'What Does it Mean to Disrupt the Business Models of People Smugglers?' Policy Briefs, Issue (2017/09), Migration Policy Centre <https://hdl.handle.net/1814/46165>.
35 Watson (n 31) 42 et seq. See also Yvon Dandurand and Jessica Jahn, 'The Failing International Legal Framework on Migrant Smuggling and Human Trafficking' in J Winterdyk and J Jones (eds), *The Palgrave International Handbook of Human Trafficking* (Palgrave 2019) 783–800.
36 Mitsilegas (n 2) 25–45; Mitsilegas (n 2) 68–85.
37 Similarly, Marc Provera, 'The Criminalization of Irregular Migration in the European Union' (February 2015) CEPS Paper in Liberty and Security No 80.
38 Flavia Patané and others, 'Asylum-Seekers Prosecuted for Human Smuggling: A Case Study of Scafisti in Italy' (2020) 39 Refugee Survey Quarterly 123–52.
39 Allsopp, Vosyliūtė and Smialowski (n 7).
40 Carrera and others (n 4) 1, 24 et seq.; Carrera, Allsopp and Vosyliute (n 4) 237, Zirulia (n 4) 242 et seq.; Vosyliute and Conte (n 2); Carrera and others (n 19);

Chiara Maria Ricci, 'Criminalising Solidarity? Smugglers, Migrants and Rescuers in the Reform of the Facilitators' Package' in Valsamis Mitsilegas, Violeta Moreno-Lax and Niovi Vavoula (eds), *Securing Asylum Flows* (Brill 2020) 36 et seq.

41 Lina Vosyliute and Carmine Conte, 'Crackdown on NGOs and Volunteers Helping Refugees and Other Migrants' (June 2019) Final Synthetic Report. See also FRA, 'June 2023 Update—Search and Rescue Operations in the Mediterranean and Fundamental Rights' (2023) <https://fra.europa.eu/en/publication/2023/2023-update-ngo-ships-sar-activities> accessed 1 March 2024.

42 Vosyliute and Conte (n 41) 26–31. See also Paul Kirby, 'Greek Trial of 24 Rescuers Who Saved Migrants in Med Begins' *BBC News* (10 January 2023).

43 Allsopp, Vosyliūtė and Smialowski (n 7). See also note 40, 41.

44 The UN Convention on the law of the sea (UNCLOS, 1982), the International Convention for the safety of life at sea (Conv SOLAS, 1974) and the International Convention on Maritime search and rescue (Conv SAR, 1979).

45 Zirulia (n 4) 242 et seq.

46 Dutch Criminal Code, article 450; German Criminal Code, § 323c.

47 EU Commission guidance on the implementation of EU rules on definition and prevention of the facilitation of unauthorised entry, transit and residence, C(2020) 6470 final.

48 See scholarship note 43.

49 Spena (n 7) 11 et seq.; Minetti (n 7) 335.

50 For an overview see FRA, 'Criminalisation of Migrants in an Irregular Situation and of Persons Engaging with Them—Annex' (2014) <https://fra.europa.eu/sites/default/files/fra_uploads/fra-2014-criminalisation-of-migrants-annex-0_en.pdf>.

51 See Residence Act § 95.

52 See HR 01.12.2020, ECLI:NL:HR:2020:1893. Kai Lindenberg in *Tekst & Commentaar Strafrecht* (Kluwer 2022), commentaar op art. 197 Sr, at point 8e.

53 The subsections (3)–(7) of Article 197a contain aggravating circumstances such as when the conduct is committed by civil servants or when the smuggling caused sever bodily injuries, endangered the life or caused the death of the smuggled person.

54 Residence Act § 95 (1) Nr. 3.

55 § 95 (1) Nr. 1 of the Residence Act prohibits residence without a valid passport, while Nr. 2 prohibits residence without a valid title in case: (1) he or she is legally required to leave the federal territory; (2) he or she has not been granted a period for departure or this has expired; and (3) his or her deportation has not been suspended.

56 Residence titles are: a visa pursuant to section 6 (1), no 1 and (3), a temporary residence permit (section 7), an EU Blue Card (section 18b (2)), an ICT Card (section 19), a Mobile ICT Card (section 19b), a permanent settlement permit (section 9) or an EU long-term residence permit (section 9a).

57 Jan Gericke in *Münchener Kommentar zum StGB* (Verlag C.H. Beck 4. Auflage 2022) AufenthG § 95, Mn 2.

58 The maximum punishment in this case is three years.

59 The proscribed punishment ranges from one to three years imprisonment or a fine.

60 Lindenberg (n 52), commentaar op art 197a Sr, at point 10f; Rechtbank Zwolle, ECLI:NL:RBZWO:1999:AB8934 and HR 31.5.2016, NJ 2016, 270.

61 HR 19.1.2010, NJ 2010, 280; Rechtbank Zutphen 17.3.2009, ECLI:NL:RBZUT:2009:BH6262.

62 HR 9.3.2010, NJ 2010, 530.

63 HR 02.12.2014, ECLI:NL:HR:2014:3488.

64 Rechtbank Noord-Nederland, 12.04.2022, ECLI:NL:RBNNE:2022:1198.

65 BGH 26.2.2015, NJW-Spezial 2015, 281; BGH 4.5.2017, NStZ 2018, 286.

66 Claire Brolan, 'An Analysis of the Human Smuggling Trade and the Protocol Against the Smuggling of Migrants by Land, Air and Sea (2000) from a Refugee Protection Perspective' [2000] International Journal of Refugee Law 592.

67 Gericke (n 57) AufenthG § 96, Mn 1; Carina Stephan in Jan Bergmann and Klaus Dienelt (eds), *Ausländerrecht* (14. Auflage, Verlag C.H. Beck 2022) § 95 Mn 5. Ute Hohoff in Winfried Kluth and Andreas Heusch (eds), *BeckOK Ausländerrecht* (35. Edition, Verlag C.H. Beck 2022) § 95 Mn 1.
68 Kamerstukken II 2003/04, 2003/04, 29291, 3, p. 2.
69 HR 9 februari 2016, NJ 2016/143. See also Lindenberg (n 60) commentaar op art. 197a Sr, at point 5.
70 BGH 2.9.2009, NStZ 2010, 171. See also the annotation by Andreas Mosbacher in NStZ 2010, 457. For Dutch law see: Lindenberg (n 60) commentaar op art. 197a Sr, at point 10 b.
71 For a pertinent Dutch case see: Rechtbank Zwolle-Lelystad ECLI:NL:RBZLY:2008:BG5546. See also the parliamentary debate in Kamerstukken II 1995/96, 24269, 5, p. 9.
72 Facilitation of irregular stay will also be assumed in case of procurement of or entering into a sham marriage. In the latter case, the partner can be held liable as perpetrator or aider of § 95 (2) Nr. 2 RA, depending on whether or not (s)he provided incorrect information to the authorities. See Gericke (n 57) AufenthG § 95, Mn 112 et seq.; Stephan (n 67) § 95 Mn 104 et seq.; Hohoff (n 67) § 95 Mn 95.
73 Gericke (n 57) AufenthG § 96, Mn 14 et seq.; Carina Stephan in Jan Bergmann and Klaus Dienelt (eds), *Ausländerrecht* (14. Auflage, Verlag C.H. Beck 2022) § 96 Mn 9 et seq.
74 Gerechtshof Arnhem-Leeuwarden ECLI:NL:GHARL:2018:3742. See also: HR 7.4.1998, NJ 1998, 558. Similarly: HR 01.09.2020, ECLI:NL:HR:2020:1348, NJB 2020/2097.
75 HR 31.05.2016, NJ 2016, 270.
76 HR 26.09.2006, ECLI:NL:2006:AY8857, NJ 2006, 541.
77 BGH 6.6.2012, NJW 2012, 2821. For Dutch law see: Rechtbank Rotterdam 27.11.2014, ECLI:NL:RBROT:2014:9778; Gerechtshof Den Haag, 09.05.2014, ECLI:NL:GHDHA: 2014:97978. For liability for preparatory conduct to human smuggling see: Rechtbank Rotterdam 03.06.2022, ECLI:NL:RBROT:2022:4376.
78 Lindenberg (n 60) article 197a Sr, at point 9. For Germany see: Hohoff (n 67) § 95 Mn 11et seq. and 96 Mn. 10–14.
79 Lindenberg (n 60) commentaar op art. 197a Sr, at point 9. For Germany see: Ute Hohoff in Winfried Kluth and Andreas Heusch (eds), *BeckOK Ausländerrecht* (35 edn, Verlag C.H. Beck 2022) § 96 Mn. 10–14.
80 HR 13.04.2010, NJ 2010, 233.
81 Lindenberg (n 60) commentaar op art. 197a Sr, at point 9b, A.J. Machielse in *Noyon/Langemeijer/Remmelink Strafrecht* (Kluwer 2018), commentaar op art 197a Sr, aant 5.
82 Gerechtshof 's Gravenhage ECLI:NL:GHSGR:2008:BD3374. Similar: HR 13.04.2010, NJ 2010, 233.
83 HR 8.11.2011, ECLI:NL:HR:2011:BQ8629.
84 Gerechtshof Den Haag, ECLI:NL:GHDHA:2019:2096. Similar: Rechtbank Alkmaar, ECLI:NL:RBALK:2008:BC7327.
85 Eg BGH 28.4.2015, NJW 2015, 2276. See also: Lukas Semmelmayer, 'Keine Strafbarkeit des Transportes ukrainischer Kriegsflüchtlinge', [2022] UKuR 116.
86 Gericke (n 57) AufenthG § 95, Mn 12, 48, 58; Stephan (n 67) § 95 Mn 16.
87 Hohoff (n 67) § 95 Mn 26. See also: Jens Lehmann, 'Ärztliche Hilfe für "Illegale": eine Straftat nach dem Aufenthaltsgesetz' [2008] ZAR 24.
88 Heine/Weißer in *Schönke/Schröder Strafgesetzbuch*, (30. Auflage 2019) § 27 Mn 16. Hohoff (n 67) § 95 Mn 26. See also: Lehmann, (n 87) 24.
89 LG Landshut 24.6.2008, NStZ 2009, 61.
90 BayOblG 25.2.2022, NStZ 2022, 486.
91 Hohoff (n 67) § 95 Mn 26; Stephan (n 67) § 95 Mn 44; Gericke (n 57) AufenthG § 95, Mn 12, 48, 58. See also: OLG München, 3.5.2018, NJW 2018, 3041.

92 OLG Hamm 01.06.2010, BeckRS 2010, 16651.
93 HR 16.05.2017, NJ 2017, 367.
94 HR 30.10.2018, ECLI:NL:HR:2018:2005.
95 HR 30.10.2018, ECLI:NL:HR:2018:2005 at 2.4.1. See also: Gerechtshof Arnhem-Leeuwarden, 03-05-2016, ECLI:NL:GHARL:2016:3504.
96 The maximum punishment proscribed by § 96 (1) RA is five years.
97 § 96 (2) RA further lists several aggravating circumstances, such as when the offender makes a living out of smuggling (*gewerbsmäßig*) (Nr. 1), acts as part of a gang (Nr. 2), carries a firearm (Nr. 3) or other weapon (Nr. 4), or subjects the smuggled persons to potentially fatal, inhumane, or humiliating treatment or a risk of serious harm to their health (Nr. 5). In this case, the maximum punishment ranges from six months to ten years.
98 These are: irregular entry without a valid passport or residence title, or in contravention of an entry ban (Nr. 1); irregular residence without a valid passport or residence permit if the smuggled person is (1) enforceably required to leave the federal territory; (2) he or she has not been granted a period for departure or this has expired; and (3) his or her deportation has not been suspended. The same will be the case with regard to unauthorised employment by people possessing a Schengen Visa and furnishing or using false or incomplete information in order to procure a residence title or a suspension of deportation for themselves or for another. See Gericke (n 57) AufenthG § 96, Mn 12, 21. Stephan (n 73) § 96 Mn 8.
99 Gericke (n 57) AufenthG § 96, Mn 2, 9. Stephan (n 73) § 96 Mn 2.
100 Gericke (n 57) AufenthG § 96, Mn 2; Stephan (n 73) § 96 Mn 2–8.
101 BGH 24.10.2018, NJW 2018, 3658. Gericke (n 57) AufenthG § 96, Mn 3.
102 Joachim Kretschmer, 'Schleuserkriminalität—§§ 96 und 97 AufenthG im Überblick anhand aktueller Rechtsprechung' [2019] ZAR 263 et seq., Gericke (n 57) AufenthG § 96; Stephan (n 73) § 96.
103 Advantage pursuant to § 96 (1)(a) RA covers any material or immaterial benefit for the smuggler. Humanitarian assistance rendered for purely altruistic reasons will generally not fulfil this requirement. Gericke (n 57) AufenthG § 96, Mn 18 et seq, 24. Stephan (n 73) § 96 Mn 15 et seq.
104 Repeatedly means having committed at least one other instance that qualifies as smuggling.
105 Which means at least two immigrants, see BGH 11.7.2003, NStZ 2004, 45.
106 This means that the smuggled person must have intentionally entered or resided irregularly in Germany and that this conduct cannot be justified.
107 See BGH 24.10.2018, NStZ 2019, 2831, where it was held that the intention of minors to enter Germany irregularly needs to be carefully established, as considering their age and cognitive development, it can be doubtful whether they were aware of being smuggled and acted intentionally with regard to their irregular entry.
108 See also BGH 6.10.2021, NStZ 2022, 239.
109 Gericke (n 57) AufenthG § 96, Mn 14, 22.
110 The general rules on participation.
111 BGH 14.11.2019, NStZ-RR 2020, 184.
112 See also Joachim Kretschmer, 'Rechtsprechung zum Migrationsstrafrecht' [2021] NStZ 83, 90.
113 Kretschmer (n 102).
114 Gericke (n 57) AufenthG § 96, Mn 18 et seq, 24. Stephan (n 73) § 96 Mn 15 et seq.
115 Kamerstukken II 2003/04, 29291, 3, p. 5 et seq. See also Machielse (n 81) commentaar op art. 197a Sr, aant 4 and HR 16.05.2017, NJ 2017/367.
116 Gericke (n 57) AufenthG § 96, Mn 24 et seq. Stephan (n 73) § 96 Mn 17 et seq.
117 BGH 12.12.2017, NStZ 2018, 447.

118 Kamerstuken II 2003/04, 29291, 7, p. 4. Lindenberg (n 60), commentaar op art. 197a Sr, at point 10a, Machielse (n 81) commentaar op art 197a Sr, aant 4.
119 Gerechtshof s-Gravenhage, 06.06.2008, ECLI:NL:GHSGR:2008:BD3374.
120 Rechtbank Amsterdam, 18.03.2021, ECLI:NL:RBAMS:2021:1159. See also: HR 12.11.2012, NJ 2012/672.
121 Similar: Rechtbank Amsterdam, 21.01.2022, ECLI:NL:RBAMS:2022:1691.
122 See generally Carrera and others (n 4); Carrera, Allsopp and Vosyliute (n 4) 237.
123 Yet, the opportunity principle applied in the Netherlands may help to filter out clear cases of humanitarian assistance by religious and other non-profit actors.
124 Kretschmer (n 102) 268.
125 Proposal for a Directive laying down minimum rules to prevent and counter the facilitation of unauthorised entry, transit, and stay in the Union, and replacing Council Directive 2002/90/EC and Council Framework Decision 2002/946 JHA, COM (2023) 755 final, Brussels, 28.11.2023.
126 Gabriella Sanchez, Luigi Achilli and Federico Alagna, 'The EU's New Counter-Smuggling Directive Proposal: Persisting Challenges and Recommendations Towards Implementation' RSC, Policy Brief 2024/01, Migration Policy Centre <https://hdl.handle.net/1814/76397> 6.
127 Valsamis Mitsilegas, 'Reforming the EU "Facilitators' Package": The New Commission Proposal in the Light of the Kinshasa Litigation' (2024) 15 New Journal of European Criminal Law 3, 10.
128 Proposal for a Directive laying down minimum rules to prevent and counter the facilitation of unauthorised entry, transit, and stay in the Union (n 125) 1, 2.
129 Tanya Wyatt, Daan van Uhm and Angus Nurse, 'Differentiating Criminal Networks in the Illegal Wildlife Trade: Organized, Corporate and Disorganized Crime' (2020) 23 Trends in Organized Crime 350–66.
130 Theodore Baird and Ilse van Liempt, 'Scrutinising the Double Disadvantage: Knowledge Production in the Messy Field of Migrant Smuggling' (2016) 42 Journal of Ethnic and Migration Studies 400–417.
131 Paolo Campana, 'The Market for Human Smuggling into Europe: A Macro Perspective' (2017) 11 Policing 448–456; Gabriella Sanchez, 'Beyond the Matrix of Oppression: Reframing Human Smuggling Through Instersectionally-Informed Approaches' (2017) Theoretical Criminology 46–56; Gabriella Sanchez, 'Critical Perspectives on Clandestine Migration Facilitation: An Overview of Migrant Smuggling Research' (2017) Journal of Migration and Human Security 9–27; Paolo Campana, 'Human Smuggling: Structure and Mechanisms' (2020) 49 Crime and Justice 471–519.
132 Ilse van Liempt, *Navigating Borders—Inside Perspectives on the Process of Human Smuggling in the Netherlands* (Amsterdam UP 2007) 45.
133 Spena (n 7) 11 et seq.
134 For the situation in Italy Spena (n 7) 12 et seq.
135 van Liempt (n 132) 45; Sheldon Zhang, Gabriella Sanchez and Luigi Achilli, 'Crimes of Solidarity in Mobility: Alternative Views on Migrant Smuggling' (2018) 676 The Annals of the American Academy 6–15 and the empirical articles in the special issue in this volume of The Annals.
136 Paolo Campana, 'The Market for Human Smuggling into Europe: A Macro Perspective' (2017) 11 Policing 448–56; Sanchez (n 131) 46–56; Ferruccio Pastore, Paola Monzini and Giuseppe Sciortino, 'Schengen's Soft Underbelly? Irregular Migration and Human Smuggling Across Land and Sea Borders to Italy' (2006) 44 International Migration 95–116; Zhang, Sanchez and Achilli (n 135) 6–15 and the empirical articles in the special issue in this volume of The Annals.
137 European Commission, 'A Study on Smuggling of Migrants, Final Report' (2015) 48. See also Campana (n 131); Joris van Wijk, 'Luanda—Holanda: Irregular Migration from Angola to the Netherlands' [2008] International Migration 1.

138 Allsopp, Vosyliūtė and Smialowski (n 7) 72.
139 Gabriella Sanchez, 'Five Misconceptions About Migrant Smuggling' Policy Briefs, 2018/07, Migration Policy Centre <http://hdl.handle.net/1814/54964> 1; Gabriella Sanchez and Luigi Achilli, 'Critical Insights on Irregular Migration Facilitation: Global Perspectives' (Florence: European University Institute 2019) <https://cadmus.eui.eu/handle/1814/62384>.
140 Sanchez (n 131) 9–27. Dandurand and Jahn (n 35) 783–800. See also Federico Alagna and Gabriella Sanchez, 'The Persisting Challenges of the New European Commission's Smuggling Directive Proposal' (*Border Criminologies*, 2024) <https://blogs.law.ox.ac.uk/border-criminologies-blog/blog-post/2024/01/persisting-challenges-new-european-commissions> accessed 28 February 2024.
141 See Proposal for a Directive laying down minimum rules to prevent and counter the facilitation of unauthorised entry, transit, and stay in the Union (n 125) 1.
142 van Liempt and Sersli (n 8); Allsopp, Vosyliūtė and Smialowski (n 7) 72.
143 Sanchez, Achilli and Alagna (n 126) 6.
144 Mitsilegas (n 127) 10.
145 Patané and others (n 38); see also From Sea to Prison, 'The Criminalization of Boat Drivers in Italy' <https://fromseatoprison.info/> accessed 1 March 2024.
146 Joanna Parkin, 'The Criminalisation of Migration in Europe' (2013) CEPS Research Paper No 61, 6.
147 Parkin (n 146) 6 et seq.; see also Sanchez (n 131) 46–56, 53.
148 I thank Niovi Vavoula for pointing this out.
149 Proposal for a Directive laying down minimum rules to prevent and counter the facilitation of unauthorised entry, transit, and stay in the Union (n 125) Article 3 para 1(a).
150 See VfGH 22.02.2016, G531/2015ua and OGH 28.09.2015, 11Os125/15i. This will, however, only be the case if the conduct in question remains confined to mere transport and does not amount to general facilitation of irregular entry. OGH 11.10.2017 13 Os 84/17b.
151 Watson (n 31) 42 et seq.
152 Watson (n 31) 42 et seq.
153 Milena Holzgang, 'Schlepperei versus humanitäre Fluchthilfe: Bereicherungsabsicht als Differenzkriterium?' (2018) 2 Zeitschrift für Flüchtlingsforschung 193–230, 198.
154 Christian Jakob, 'Hier Held, dort Verbrecher' *TAZ* <https://taz.de/Fluchthelfer-und-Schlepper/!5029223/>. See also Rachel Landry, 'The "Humanitarian Smuggling" of Refugees. Criminal Offence or Moral Obligation?' (2016) Refugee Studies Centre (RSC), Working Paper Series No 119 8, 16.
155 See also Zirulia (n 4) 258; Ricci (n 40) 52 et seq.; Sergio Carrera and others, 'Fit for Purpose? The Facilitation Directive and the Criminalisation of Humanitarian Assistance to Irregular Migrants' (LIBE 2016) 64.
156 Mitsilegas (n 127) 10.
157 Mitsilegas (n 127) 10.
158 See also Landry (n 154) 13 et seq. Landry inter alia argues that the prohibition of torture, inhumane and degrading treatment, slavery and servitude as well as the right to liberty and security, the right to a fair trial or the right to family life may be protected through the exemption.
159 Ricci (n 40) 52 et seq.
160 Generally Carrera and others (n 4).
161 See also Sanchez, Achilli and Alagna (n 126) 6.
162 Sanchez, Achilli and Alagna (n 126) 6.
163 Janik (n 30) 57–78. Tom Obokata, 'Smuggling of Human Beings from a Human Rights Perspective: Obligations of Non-State and State Actors Under

International Human Rights Law' (2005) 17 International Journal of Refugee Law 394–415, 399 et seq and 414 et seq.
164 See Preamble of European Charter of Fundamental Rights, OJ C 364/9.
165 Similarly: Proposal for a Directive laying down minimum rules to prevent and counter the facilitation of unauthorised entry, transit, and stay in the Union (n 125) 10.
166 Generally Obokata (n 163) 394–415, 414 et seq. See also Mitsilegas (n 2) 34; Zirulia (n 4) 256 et seq.; Janik (n 30) 57–78.
167 See also note 23.
168 See also Alessandro Spena, 'A Just Criminalization of Irregular Immigration Is it Possible?' (2017) 11 Criminal Law and Philosophy 351–73.
169 Janik (n 30) 62.
170 CJEU C-308/06 *Intertanko* (n 22), para 71, *AC Treuhand vs Commission* (n 22), C 194/14, para 40, C 102/16 *Vaditrans* (n 22), para 51.
171 Mitsilegas (n 127) 10.
172 Sanchez, Achilli and Alagna (n 126) 6.
173 Watson (n 31) 43.
174 See Holzgang (n 153) 222 et seq.
175 For similar suggestions based on exploiting the vulnerability of migrants, see Zirulia (n 4) 259. For a reform proposal based on harm and risk of harm, see Landry (n 154).
176 Similarly Janik (n 30) 57–78.
177 Zirulia (n 4) 259.
178 Mitsilegas (n 127) 10.

Bibliography

Achilli L and Sanchez G, 'What Does It Mean to Disrupt the Business Models of People Smugglers?' (2017) European University Institute, Policy Brief.

Allsopp J, Vosyliūtė L and Smialowski SB, 'Picking "Low Hanging Fruit" While the Orchard Burns: The Costs of Policing Humanitarian Actors in Italy and Greece as Strategy to Prevent Migrant Smuggling' (2021) 27 European Journal on Criminal Policy and Research 65.

Ashworth A and Zedner L, *Preventive Justice* (OUP 2014).

Baird T and van Liempt I, 'Scrutinising the Double Disadvantage: Knowledge Production in the Messy Field of Migrant Smuggling' (2016) 42 Journal of Ethnic and Migration Studies 400–417.

Brolan C, 'An Analysis of the Human Smuggling Trade and the Protocol Against the Smuggling of Migrants by Land, Air and Sea (2000) from a Refugee Protection Perspective' (2000) 14 International Journal of Refugee Law 561.

Campana P, 'The Market for Human Smuggling into Europe: A Macro Perspective' (2017) 11 Policing 448–456.

Campana P, 'Human Smuggling: Structure and Mechanisms' (2020) 49 Crime and Justice 471–519.

Carrera S, Allsopp J and Vosyliūtė L, 'Policing the Mobility Society: The Effects of EU Anti-Migration Smuggling Policies on Humanitarianism' (2018) 4 International Journal of Migration and Border Studies 236–276.

Carrera S and others, 'Fit for Purpose? The Facilitation Directive and the Criminalisation of Humanitarian Assistance to Irregular Migrants' (Study requested by LIBE Committee, European Parliament, 2016).

Carrera S and others, *Fit for Purpose? The Facilitation Directive and the Criminalisation of Humanitarian Assistance to Irregular Migrants: 2018 Update* (CEPS 2019).

Carrera S and others, *Policing Humanitarianism—EU Policies Against Human Smuggling and Their Impact on Civil Society* (Hart Publishing 2019).

Cusumano E and Villa M, 'From "Angels" to "Vice Smugglers": The Criminalization of Sea Rescue NGOs in Italy' (2021) 27 European Journal of Criminal Policy and Research 23.

Dandurand Y and Jahn J, 'The Failing International Legal Framework on Migrant Smuggling and Human Trafficking' in Winterdyk J and Jones J (eds), *The Palgrave International Handbook of Human Trafficking* (Palgrave 2019).

Fassi E, 'The EU, Migration and Global Justice. Policy Narratives of Human Smuggling and Their Normative Implications' (2020) 1 Rivista Trimestrale di scienza dell'amministrazione 1–30.

Franko K, *Globalization & Crime* (Sage 2020).

Holzgang M, 'Schlepperei versus humanitäre Fluchthilfe: Bereicherungsabsicht als Differenzkriterium?' (2018) 2 Zeitschrift für Flüchtlingsforschung 193–230.

Janik K, 'A Human Rights Approach to Extremely Vulnerable People: Challenges and Feasibility in Assessing Smuggled Migrants' in Mitsilegas V, Moreno-Lax V and Vavoula N (eds), *Securitising Asylum Flows* (Brill 2020).

Keiler J, *Actus reus and participation in European Criminal Law* (Intersentia 2013).

Klip A, *European Criminal Law* (Intersentia 2021).

Landry R, 'The "Humanitarian Smuggling" of Refugees. Criminal Offence or Moral Obligation?' (2016) Oxford Refugee Centre, Working Paper Series No 119.

Minetti M, 'The Facilitators Package, Penal Populism and the Rule of Law: Lessons from Italy' (2020) 11 New Journal of European Criminal Law 335.

Mitsilegas V, 'The Normative Foundations of the Criminalization of Human Smuggling: Exploring the Fault Lines Between European and International Law' (2019) 10 New Journal of European Criminal Law 68.

Mitsilegas V, 'The Criminalisation of Migration in the Law of the European Union—Challenging the Preventive Paradigm' in Gatta GL, Mitsilegas V and Zirulia S (eds), *Controlling Immigration Through Criminal Law* (Hart Publishing 2021).

Mitsilegas V, 'Reforming the EU "Facilitators' Package": The New Commission Proposal in the Light of the Kinshasa Litigation' (2024) 15 New Journal of European Criminal Law 3.

Obokata T, 'Smuggling of Human Beings from a Human Rights Perspective: Obligations of Non-State and State Actors Under International Human Rights Law' (2005) 17 International Journal of Refugee Law 394–415.

Parkin J, *The Criminalisation of Migration in Europe* (CEPS, No 6, 2013).

Pastore F, Monzini P and Sciortino G, 'Schengen's Soft Underbelly? Irregular Migration and Human Smuggling Across Land and Sea Borders to Italy' (2006) 44 International Migration 95–119.

Patané F and others, 'Asylum-Seekers Prosecuted for Human Smuggling: A Case Study of Scafisti in Italy' (2020) 39 Refugee Survey Quarterly 123.

Peristeridou C, *The Principle of Legality in European Criminal Law* (Intersentia 2015).

Provera M, *The Criminalization of Irregular Migration in the European Union* (CEPS, No 80, 2015).

Ricci CM, 'Criminalising Solidarity? Smugglers, Migrants and Rescuers in the Reform of the Facilitators' Package' in Mitsilegas V, Moreno-Lax V and Vavoula N (eds), *Securitising Asylum Flows* (Brill 2020).

Sanchez G, 'Beyond the Matrix of Oppression: Reframing Human Smuggling Through Instersectionally-Informed Approaches' (2017) 21 Theoretical Criminology 46–56.

Sanchez G, 'Critical Perspectives on Clandestine Migration Facilitation: An Overview of Migrant Smuggling Research' (2017) 5 Journal of Migration and Human Security 9–27.

Sanchez G, Achilli L and Alagna F, 'The EU's New Counter-Smuggling Directive Proposal: Persisting Challenges and Recommendations Towards Implementation' (2024) European Policy Institute, Policy Brief.
Spena A, 'Human Smuggling and Irregular Immigration in the EU: From Complicity to Exploitation?', in Carrera S and Guild E (eds), *Irregular Migration, Trafficking and Smuggling of Human Beings—Policy Dilemmas in the EU* (CEPS 2016).
Spena A, 'A Just Criminalization of Irregular Immigration: Is It Possible?' (2017) 11 Criminal law and Philosophy 351–373.
Spena A, 'Migrant Smuggling: A Normative and Phenomenological View from Italy' in Militello V and Spena A (eds), *Between Criminalization and Protection. The Italian Way of Dealing with Migrant Smuggling and Trafficking Within the European and International Context* (Brill 2019).
Spena A, 'The Double-Deviant Identity of the Mass-Foreigner and the Lack of Authority of the Crimigrationist State' (2019) 22 New Criminal Law Review 301.
Van Liempt I, *Navigating Borders—Inside Perspectives on the Process of Human Smuggling in the Netherlands* (Amsterdam UP 2007).
Van Liempt I and Sersli S, 'State Responses and Migrant Experiences with Human Smuggling: A Reality Check' (2013) 45 Antipode 1029–1046.
van Wijk J, 'Luanda—Holanda: Irregular Migration from Angola to the Netherlands' (2008) International Migration 1.
Vosyliute L and Conte C, 'Crackdown on NGOs and Volunteers Helping Refugees and Other Migrants' Resoma Report (2019).
Vosyliute L and Conte C, 'Crackdown on NGOs and Volunteers Helping Refugees and Other Migrants' Final Synthetic Report (2019).
Watson S, 'The Criminalization of Human and Humanitarian Smuggling' (2015) 1 Migration, Mobility, & Displacement 39–53.
Wyatt T, van Uhm D and Nurse A, 'Differentiating Criminal Networks in the Illegal Wildlife Trade: Organized, Corporate and Disorganized Crime' (2020) 23 Trends in Organized Crime 350–366.
Zhang SX, Sanchez GE and Achilli L, 'Crimes of Solidarity in Mobility: Alternative Views on Migrant Smuggling' (2018) 676 The Annals of the American Academy 6–15.
Zirulia S, 'Is that a Smuggler?' in Gatta GL, Mitsilegas V and Zirulia S (eds), *Controlling Immigration Through Criminal Law* (Hart Publishing 2021).

3 Building Limits to the Over-Criminalisation of Facilitating Irregular Migration

The *Kinsa* Case

Francesca Cancellaro and Stefano Zirulia[*]

3.1 Introduction

On 27 August 2019, Mrs. E.K., of Congolese origin, was arrested at Bologna airport on charges of facilitating irregular immigration, for having attempted to introduce her daughter and another minor girl into Italian territory by exhibiting false passports. Indeed, the offence laid down in Article 12, para 1 of the Italian Consolidated Text on Immigration (hereinafter, in the Chapter, *t.u. imm.*) criminalises anyone who performs acts aimed at procuring the irregular entry of foreigners, even if the entry does not take place.[1] As the offence was aggravated by the use of false documents and an international transport service (according to Article 12, para 3(d), *t.u. imm.*), E.K. risked being sentenced to between 5 and 15 years' imprisonment. The subsequent developments of this case are of paramount importance for criminal immigration law at both national and European levels, with regard to the problem of over-criminalisation of facilitating the irregular entry of third-country nationals into the EU space.[2]

First, in late 2020, the Criminal Court of Bologna suspended the trial against E.K. and raised a question of constitutional legitimacy in relation to the proportionality of the custodial penalty provided for the aggravated offence. In Judgement n 63 of 2022, the Constitutional Court held that the sentence of 5–15 years' imprisonment was disproportionate and, therefore, removed the aggravating circumstances of the use of false documents and international transport services from the Italian system. As a result of this ruling, E.K. risked being convicted of the same offence in a non-aggravated form, which carries a sentence of between one and five years' imprisonment.

Then, on 17 July 2023, the Tribunal of Bologna again suspended the trial against E.K., this time in order to refer to the Court of Justice of the European Union (CJEU) questions on the validity and interpretation of

* Although this chapter is based on shared reflections, Sections 2, 3 and 6 have been written by Stefano Zirulia, while Section 4 has been written by Francesca Cancellaro. Sections 1, 5, 7 and 8 are co-authored.

DOI: 10.4324/9781003378440-3

both the Facilitators' Package[3] and the Italian legislation implementing it. As the woman had, in the meantime, applied for asylum, her name must remain anonymous, so the case was renamed "Kinshasa" (the Capital of Congo), and subsequently "Kinsa", while the defendant's initials have been reworded O.B.[4] The judgement has been released on the 3rd of June 2025.

The aim of this chapter is to explore the two aspects of the proportionality assessment underlying the *Kinsa* case: The proportionality of the penalty, which the Italian Constitutional Court addressed; and the proportionality of criminalisation, which was at the heart of the question for preliminary ruling referred to the CJEU. Both these aspects are crucial for the European debate on the limits to legislative discretion in the fight against smuggling of migrants, a debate that is particularly topical given that the European Commission recently put forward a proposal to reform the Facilitators' Package.

The following section examines the *E.K.* case, where the Italian Constitutional Court ruled on the disproportionate nature of punishment provided for by the Italian legislation on facilitating illegal immigration. The third section dwells on the relevance of this domestic judgement at the European level. In the fourth section, the attention shifts to the pending preliminary reference to the CJEU, where the case was first renamed *Kinshasa* and subsequently *Kinsa*. The fifth section addresses the implications of the *Kinsa* case on the European Commission's proposal to reform the Facilitators' Package. The sixth and the seventh sections provides an assessment on the Opinion of Advocate General de la Tour and with the Court of Justice's judgment on *Kinsa* respectively. Finally, the eighth section is dedicated to concluding remarks.

3.2 The Italian Constitutional Court's Ruling in the *E.K.* Case

The case of *E.K.* brought to the attention of the Italian Constitutional Court for the first time the problem of the *disproportion by excess* of the penalties provided for the Italian crime of facilitating irregular entry.

The principle of proportionality of criminal penalties is not expressly provided by the Italian Constitution. However, according to a consolidated jurisprudence, it can be drawn from a joint reading of the principles of equality-reasonableness (Article 3 of the Constitution) and the re-educative purpose of punishment (Article 27).[5] The underlying idea is that an unreasonable penalty, insofar as it is disproportionate to the severity of the offence, cannot even aspire to foster the resocialisation of the convicted person, representing, rather, a further unjust evil that is added to that caused by the offence. In the *E.K.* case, in its judgement No. 63 of 2022, the Constitutional Court declared the illegitimacy of the aggravating circumstances of the use of forged documents and international transport services, provided for by Article 12, para 3(d), finding them in contrast with the principle of proportionality of the penalty.[6] In the following, the reasoning of the court will be illustrated, focusing on the most interesting aspects from the perspective of their repercussions at the European level.

The judgement dwells first on the legal interest (*Rechtsgut*) protected by the basic offence of facilitating irregular entry (Article 12, para 1, *t.u. imm.*), adopted by the Italian legislator in implementation of the Facilitators' Package. This interest is described in terms of "orderly management of migration flows", that is, a legal asset that is merely "instrumental" to the protection of other interests that are likely to be compromised by uncontrolled immigration, such as the labour market, the sustainability of the social security system, and public order and safety.[7] The criminal sanction is, therefore, envisaged to function for the protection not of the smuggled migrants, but of a public interest, traceable to the exercise of the state function of protecting the territory from undesirable migration flows.

That said with regard to the basic offence, the Constitutional Court reached different conclusions on the apparatus of aggravating circumstances provided for in Article 12, paras 3, 3-bis, and 3-ter. Some of them are recognised by the court as having the function of protecting, in addition to national borders, the fundamental rights of irregular foreigners transported, who are often in a state of need:[8] This category of circumstances includes those based on exposing migrants to danger to life or limb (Article 12, para 3(b)); on subjecting migrants to inhuman or degrading treatment (para 3(c)); and on the purpose of exploitation, by means of conduct very close to trafficking in persons (para 3-bis(a)). Other aggravated hypotheses, the court further adds, appear to evoke "scenarios of involvement of criminal organisations active in the international trafficking of migrants": Such are the circumstances based on the presence of five or more foreigners; or of three or more facilitators in complicity; or of the availability of weapons (para 3(a), para (d), para (e)). In conclusion, the aforementioned aggravating circumstances respond to the need to offer a more vigorous criminal response to criminal phenomena more serious than plain facilitation, either because of the infringement of some fundamental rights of migrants, or because of the greater dangers of organised trafficking activities.

The Constitutional Court then turns to the two aggravating circumstances that are the subject of the constitutional assessment. Although they give rise to an increase in sentence identical, or similar, to that provided for the aforementioned aggravating circumstances, neither appears to be based on a similar, reasonable justification. In fact, the use of international transport services is a safe way of transferring foreign nationals, which certainly does not endanger their fundamental rights, nor does it generate particular difficulties for investigators.[9] With regard to the use of forged documents, the court acknowledges that this is a particularly insidious way of carrying out the offence with respect to border protection, but notes that the penalty provided for is much higher than that provided for general offences of document forgery in Italian law.[10]

These arguments are sufficient, in the Constitutional Court's view, to conclude that the aggravating circumstances under consideration result in penalty increases without reasonable justification and as such are contrary to the prohibition of disproportionate sentences. Nonetheless, the court goes on to develop particularly significant arguments aimed at further reinforcing the ruling that the two aggravating circumstances are illegitimate under the principle of proportionality of penalties.

According to the court, the Italian legislation on facilitating irregular immigration appears, on the whole, consistent with the distinction between what the court defines as two different "criminological types": Article 12 para 1 punishes "individual" or "altruistic" facilitation, where the undocumented foreigner is a "beneficiary" of the unlawful conduct; Article 12 para 3 and para 3-bis punish, more seriously, "international trafficking in migrants", consisting of an organised activity, for profit, in which the foreigner is a "victim". This distinction, the court observes, is reflected in the supranational instruments concerning the fight against migrant smuggling: On the one hand, the Facilitators' Package, which, in the words of the court, "aims to strike at both phenomena (with respect to the objective of controlling migratory flows within, in particular, the Schengen Area), but calibrates its obligations of criminalisation and punishment separately for the two types of conduct, reserving the obligation to adopt severe custodial penalties only to those attributable to international migrant smuggling";[11] on the other hand, the Palermo Protocol of 2000, which "only targets the phenomenon of international smuggling of migrants, mostly managed by large criminal organisations that make huge profits from this activity".

Thus, in this generally consistent regulatory context, the aggravating circumstances under scrutiny constitute a disharmonious element, since they require the national court to apply the penalties calibrated for international migrant smuggling also to situations more in keeping with contexts of individual and altruistic facilitation. This, the court concludes, is what would "emblematically"[12] happen in the case of the defendant E.K., if the aggravating circumstances of the use of false documents and international transport services were to apply.

On the basis of the arguments set out above, the judgement finds there is no reasonable justification for the significant increase in the penalty provided for in Article 12 para 3(d) and, therefore, declares the two aggravating circumstances illegitimate under the Italian legal system. Following the Constitutional Court's judgment, the trial against E.K. was resumed for the basic offence, without aggravating circumstances, which the court had removed from the Italian system with retroactive effect.

3.3 The Disproportionate Nature of Penalties for Facilitating Irregular Immigration: Profiles of Cross-Fertilisation between Constitutional Law and European Union Law

The principle of proportionality of penalties is recognised, at the European level, both by Article 49 para 3 of the EU Charter of Fundamental Rights (hereinafter the Charter), according to which "the penalties imposed must not be disproportionate to the offence"; and by secondary legislation containing criminalisation obligations, whenever Member States are called upon to provide for criminal penalties that are "effective, proportionate and dissuasive".[13] As to the Facilitators' Package, the principle is mentioned by Article

1 of the Framework Decision and Article 3 of the Directive. The prohibition of providing for and applying excessively disproportionate penalties therefore affects, equally, the European legislator, when adopting secondary legislation (essentially Directives) in criminal matters; the national legislators, when implementing those Directives; and the national courts, when applying the penalties provided for by the domestic transposing legislation.[14]

In terms of content, the principle under consideration entails, first, the obligation to provide for penalties that correspond, in type and extent, to the seriousness of the offence; and second, the obligation to take into account the specific circumstances of each concrete case when quantifying the penalty.[15] From this standpoint, the proportionality *of the penalty* is "retrospective", as it looks at an offence committed in the past. Instead, as will be illustrated below when addressing the question for preliminary ruling raised to the CJEU, the proportionality *of the offence* is definitely "prospective", as it focuses on the functional and finalistic profiles of the offence and is, in this sense, directed towards the future. In other words, while assessing the proportionality of the penalty means checking the consistency between a certain offence and the penalty provided for its perpetrators; assessing the proportionality of the offence consists of verifying whether the chosen means (the criminalisation of that course of conduct) is fit for the purpose of reaching a certain end (such as protecting some private or public interest). Although this distinction between the two notions of proportionality has been clearly conceptualised by legal scholarship,[16] one has the impression that the Court of Justice sometimes tends to conflate them.

Indeed, the CJEU has already had occasion to declare the illegitimacy of sanctions, and other national restrictive measures of a criminal or otherwise punitive nature, on the grounds of their *excessive* scope and/or impact on individuals. For example, the court found that some pecuniary sanctions provided by Austrian labour law for the purpose of social protection of posted workers constituted a disproportional limitation to the right to provide services under Article 56 of the Treaty on the Functioning of the European Union (TFEU), as they (1) amounted to several million euros; (2) could not fall below a predefined amount even in case of non-particularly serious violations; and (3) were convertible into custodial sanctions in the event of non-payment.[17] A few months later, the court put forward similar arguments in a judgement that found the same Austrian labour law incompatible with the requirement of proportionality of penalties provided by Article 20 of Directive 2014/67/EU on the enforcement of the legislation on the posting of workers.[18] More recently, the court found incompatible with Article 49(3) of the Charter the minimum penalty of five years' imprisonment under Bulgarian law for all cases of unauthorised use of a mark in the course of trade, holding that this minimum limit did not allow the national judicial authority to impose a penalty not exceeding the gravity of the offence established in each case.[19]

However, as already mentioned, the CJEU rulings on proportionality have so far swung, not always clearly, between prospective and retrospective proportionality. The court is, in fact, used to carrying out the proportionality test by referring almost indistinguishably to the two principles: Both when it enunciates the general principles on which the decision is based, referring cumulatively to Articles 52 para 1 and 49 para 3 of the Charter, and when it possibly detects profiles of illegitimacy.[20]

The development of the Italian constitutional jurisprudence on the (retrospective) proportionality of the penalty, along the lines traced by other higher courts,[21] offers arguments that the CJEU could take up in order to decide future cases where proportionality is at stake. This influence should not be looked upon as an oddity, bearing in mind that Article 52 para 4 obliges the interpretation of the provisions of the Charter, including therefore Article 49 para 3, to take into account the corresponding principles that can be found in the "constitutional traditions common to the Member States".

Over time, the Italian Constitutional Court has aligned itself with the Anglo-Saxon doctrine, which distinguishes between two different ways of assessing the proportionality of the penalty, labelled as "ordinal" and "cardinal" scaling of punishment, respectively:[22] The former addresses the question of "how severely crimes should be punished relative to each other", while the latter addresses "what overall levels of onerousness should be chosen to anchor the system of penalties".[23] Put differently, ordinal proportionality is a *relative* judgement. It is aimed at verifying the *internal coherence* of the system of penalties, by checking whether similar offences, in terms of their seriousness, correspond to similar penalties, in terms of their severity (and whether different offences correspond to different penalties). Cardinal proportionality, for its part, is an *absolute* judgement, aimed at verifying whether the severity of the penalty is *per se* consistent with the seriousness of the offence for which it is provided. In order to prevent this latter judgement from encroaching on legislative discretion, it is considered that it should be limited to a *negative* assessment, that is, whether the penalty is not manifestly disproportionate to the gravity of the offence.[24]

The constitutional judgement in *E.K.* offers an example of the application of both criteria under consideration. The unlawfulness of the aggravating circumstance of the *use of international transport services* is based on the cardinal criterion: The Constitutional Court notes that this circumstance, in fact, does not entail any additional harm to justify the substantial increase in the penalty; on the contrary, it is a course of conduct of low seriousness, because, unlike clandestine journeys, it does not involve any specific danger for the transported alien. The unlawfulness of the aggravating circumstance of the use of forged documents, for its part, is based on the ordinal criterion, in that the court highlights the disparity in treatment compared with the penalties provided for by the Italian legal system for other offences of forgery.

Turning now to the European legal system, the same criteria to assess retrospective proportionality could also guide the CJEU in assessing the proportionality of the penalties provided for by both the Facilitators' Package and the national implementing legislation. With reference to the former, the only indication provided by the EU legislator is that of maximum sentences of no less than eight years in the case of conduct carried out for "profit", provided that there is, as a further condition, the presence of a "criminal organisation" or of a "danger to life" for the migrants.[25] At first glance, this provision does not look disproportionate from a cardinal point of view, given that it relates to situations involving, according to reasonable evaluations on a statistical basis, actual *migrant smuggling*. However, one could question its reasonability from an ordinal point of view, given that, with regard to the more serious offence of human trafficking, Member States are obliged to provide a maximum penalty of at least five years of imprisonment.[26]

Further critical profiles might be found within national criminal law provisions implementing the Facilitators' Package, whenever they provide for penalties which are even harsher than those imposed by the Package. This is the case in Italy, where, after a recent reform introduced by the far-right government, which took power in October 2022, the occurrence of the aggravating circumstances considered by the Framework decision (danger for life and financial gain purpose) would carry a penalty of up to 24 years of imprisonment.[27] At this point, it should be highlighted that national courts could order the disapplication of the national provision, insofar as it is necessary in order to ensure that the penalty treatment is proportionate to the gravity of the offence, since the prohibition of disproportionate penalties has direct effect.[28] Although the Directive in fact provides for minimum standards, this obviously does not mean that national legislators are free to set the sentencing limits at their own discretion, without taking into account the fundamental criminological distinction, drawn by the Italian Constitutional Court, between occasional facilitators and organised traffickers.

Consider, again, the Italian case. The maximum penalty for facilitating irregular entry that results in a danger to the life (or even just the physical integrity) of migrants is currently up to 16 years' imprisonment.[29] The same punishment applies when the case involves five or more migrants or three or more accomplices in complicity.[30] If the purpose of financial gain is also established, as already mentioned above, the maximum sentence is 24 years' imprisonment. These provisions are liable to be declared invalid due to their disproportionality, both from an ordinal point of view, as they do not find comparison in supranational instruments or in other national norms; and from a cardinal point of view, since those based on the mere numbers of migrants and accomplices do not necessarily reveal situations of exploitation distinctive of migrant smuggling.

3.4 From the Disproportionality of the Penalty to the Disproportionality of the Offence: The Evolution of the *E.K.* Case in *Kinsa*

Following the Constitutional Court's ruling, the trial against E.K. resumed before a different judge of the Court of Bologna.[31] At the request of the defence, the judge once again suspended the trial, this time in order to refer a question to the CJEU for a preliminary ruling under Article 267 of the TFEU.[32] Two questions were put to the judges in Luxembourg. The first concerned the compatibility between the principle of proportionality in Article 52 para 1 of the Charter, read in conjunction with a series of rights provided for in the same Charter (see below), and the scope of the Facilitators' Package obligation to criminalise the facilitation of illegal entry in any Member State. The Italian judge argued that, in so far as the Package lays down the obligation to criminalise any course of conduct which intentionally facilitates irregular entry, without providing for the obligation to recognise a cause of justification for humanitarian conduct, it may in fact jeopardise a number of fundamental rights protected by the Charter, pertaining both to migrants and to those who facilitate them for humanitarian purposes. The second question concerned the compatibility between, again, the Charter, and the Italian legislation which transposes the Facilitators' Package into domestic law, criminalising any form of facilitation and providing for a cause of exclusion of liability only for humanitarian conduct carried out in Italy in favour of foreigners *already present* in the national territory (thus excluding from its scope the humanitarian help provided before and during the crossing of the Italian borders).

3.4.1 The Prospective Proportionality Test: Overview

What comes to the fore in this case, therefore, is not an issue of lack of proportionality of the penalty (or, as seen above, retrospective proportionality) but rather one of lack of proportionality of the offence (or prospective proportionality). In fact, the CJEU was asked to assess whether the "all-encompassing" criminalisation of facilitating irregular entry is compatible with the principle of proportionality under Article 52 para 1 of the Charter, which sets the conditions for the justified limitation of the fundamental rights prescribed therein. Although Article 52 para 1 is not specifically dedicated to criminal law (unlike Article 49 para 3, which concerns the proportionality of the criminal sanction or retrospective proportionality), its scope undoubtedly includes criminal law, insofar as the latter, by criminalising a certain conduct, introduces limitations to one or more rights provided for by the Charter.

This statement will become clearer as soon as we examine the proportionality of the criminalisation of facilitating irregular immigration. Before doing so, however, we shall briefly recall the steps in which, according to well-established doctrine[33] transposed by CJEU case law,[34] the judgement of proportionality is articulated. First, it has to be assessed whether, by means of some kind of state intervention, such as the criminalisation of certain conduct, there has been a limitation of any of the fundamental rights provided by the Charter. Second, whether that limitation complies with the four sub-tests into which the prospective proportionality review is traditionally divided: Legitimacy of the protected counter-interest (*legitimate goal*); appropriateness of the measure to realise it (*suitability*); necessity of the interference (*necessity*); and proportionality in the strict sense (*proportionality stricto sensu*).[35]

3.4.2 *Prospective Proportionality and the Criminalisation of Facilitating Irregular Immigration*

Following the above mentioned test, and thus starting by the assessment of a limitation of the fundamental rights provided by the Charter, there is no doubt that the criminalisation of facilitating irregular entry entails, first of all, a limitation to the rights *of those who assist irregular migrants*, namely the right to personal liberty (Article 6 of the Charter) and the right to property (Article 17), which are compressed by the application of custodial or pecuniary penalties, respectively. Moreover, a limitation of fundamental rights *of irregular migrants* is possible, such as the right to life (Article 2 of the Charter), to physical integrity (Article 3), to seek asylum (Article 18), as well as to family life and the rights of the child (Articles 7 and 24), to the extent that the criminalisation produces a *chilling effect* on the conduct that serves to protect those rights. Indeed, the risk of being subjected to severe criminal sanctions, and even before being subjected to investigation, possible preventive measures and criminal trial, can generate a psychological counter-push to humanitarian conduct, such as rescuing migrants in danger, helping asylum seekers to reach a safe country, or assisting family members, including minors, in order to preserve or re-establish family unity. This *chilling effect* argument has already been extensively used by constitutional and supranational courts to assess the proportionality of restrictions of fundamental rights, such as freedom of expression.[36]

Once the rights affected by criminalisation have been identified, the four-step proportionality test can be carried out. Starting with the interests protected by criminalisation, the Facilitators' Package identifies them in both the fight against migrant smuggling and border protection *per se*.[37] There is no doubt that these are both *legitimate interests*, deserving of protection and falling within the competence of the Union. However, given the notable differences between them (in terms of the kind of harm resulting from their violation), the provision of the same criminal measures to protect them produces, as we shall see below, inconsistencies with regard to the second step of the proportionality assessment, that of suitability.

At first sight, the criminalisation of all forms of facilitating irregular entry fulfils the *suitability* requirement, since it makes it possible to target both occasional conduct, which at most offends the integrity of borders, and organised smuggling of migrants. However, it must be borne in mind that the judgement of suitability also includes that of the *effectiveness* of the intervention. In this regard, it is clear that targeting any form of aiding and abetting could result in an ineffective response, as it is dispersive of the limited resources available to the law enforcement apparatus, resources that, instead of being concentrated on the most serious forms of migrant smuggling, are spread over a variety of conduct of heterogeneous gravity. From this angle, the two aims pursued by the Facilitators' Package come into conflict and, therefore, at least with respect to the aim of effectively tackling migrant smuggling, the instrument could fail the suitability test.[38]

The CJEU has already considered the *ineffectiveness* of a criminal offence in the field of immigration law in terms of *illegitimacy* of the measure itself. In the well-known *El Dridi* case,[39] in fact, the court held that the application of a custodial sanction to a foreigner who failed to comply with an order to leave the territory[40] frustrated the objective of the so-called Return Directive,[41] namely the rapid repatriation of illegal aliens, because it, in fact, delayed their removal from the territory until after the end of the sentence. The same judgement of invalidity could now reach, *mutatis mutandis*, the Facilitators' Package, insofar its overbroad criminalisation would limit fundamental rights without any benefit in terms of enhanced crackdown on migrant smuggling. Upstream of the problem, as already pointed out, is the choice by the European legislator to use the same criminal measures to protect two different interests, without modulating the punitive measures according to the criminological types they are intended to strike, as instead recommended by the Italian Constitutional Court in *E.K.*

Even if the suitability test was deemed to have been passed, the question would be whether criminalisation is *necessary* to achieve the purpose, that is, whether there are no other equally effective measures from which a lesser sacrifice of fundamental rights would result. From this point of view, the criminalisation of facilitating irregular entry is more difficult to attack, as the use of administrative law may be effective in some areas (such as, e.g., carrier sanctions),[42] but would certainly have less of a deterrent effect on occasional conduct or organised crime. Moreover, the provision of an offence with a narrower scope (e.g., limited to conduct carried out for profit) would certainly be less effective with respect to the objective of strengthening the protection of external borders as much as possible.[43]

Seriously problematic, finally, is the lawfulness of the rules in the light of *proportionality in the strict sense*, which requires the legislator to reasonably balance conflicting interests. The question here is whether the limitation on the aforementioned fundamental rights is justified by the benefits intended to be obtained through the criminalisation. The answer looks undeniably negative. Indeed, it seems almost impossible to argue that the objective of protecting the borders, that is, an interest belonging to the state in the exercise of its institutional functions, can *alone* justify the limitation of individual rights of the highest rank. The problem is evident, first, with respect to the personal liberty of the accused persons: Given that the irregular entry of an individual foreigner represents a mere administrative violation, or, at most in some jurisdictions, a minor criminal offence, linking the imprisonment penalty to the conduct of those who assist in this regard appears to be a choice devoid of any reasonable justification. The problem is even more evident, second, with respect to the fundamental rights of undocumented foreigners: The criminalisation of facilitation *per se*, without any element capable of restricting liability to actual migrant smuggling, inevitably affects rescue and humanitarian conduct, leading to the sacrifice of the most important personal interests in the name of a counter-interest, that of the integrity of borders, which is clearly of a lower rank.

It this respect, regional courts have already affirmed that border protection must give way to the right to life and physical integrity. For example, the European Court of Human Rights (hereinafter, in this chapter, ECtHR), the rulings of which form an integral part of Strasbourg law, which in turn is an interpretative parameter of the Charter, found a violation of Article 2 of the European Convention on Human Rights (ECHR) with regard to the violation of positive obligations to protect the life of a migrant who died while trying to cross a river at the border between Serbia and Hungary.[44] Similarly, it is common ground that border protection cannot jeopardise the right to seek asylum and must instead be reasonably balanced with it, given that asylum seekers are necessarily, at least in certain moments, undocumented aliens. In this sense, one may recall, for example, the Strasbourg case law on the prohibition of refoulement of boat migrants found in international waters,[45] as well as the judgement of the CJEU in the case *Commission v Hungary* (2021), which declared the Hungarian crime of assisting at the borders foreigners who do not qualify for refugee *status*, incompatible with Articles 8 para 2 and 22 para 1 of the Procedures Directive (2013/32/EU), as well as Article 10 para 4 of the Reception Directive (2013/33/EU).[46]

Finally, numerous rulings have re-balanced border protection with the right to family unity, sometimes sanctioning the precedence accorded by states to the former. In a case where the ECtHR considered the penalty imposed for facilitating the irregular entry of a family member to be lawful under Article 8 of the ECHR, the Strasbourg judges took into account, for the purposes of the proportionality assessment, the fact that the applicant had benefited from an "exclusion from punishment" ("*dispense de peine*", Articles 132–59 of the French Criminal Code) precisely because of the altruistic nature of his conduct.[47] In the light of what has been observed, it seems correct to conclude that neither the Facilitators' Package, nor, by extension, the national criminal laws implementing it, satisfy the proportionality test in the strict sense, since they are evidently centred on the logic of *absolute border protection*, which ends up sacrificing the essential core of fundamental rights recognised by the Charter.

Returning to the preliminary reference in the *Kinsa* case, the CJEU could have in principle either, found the European and national rules incompatible with Article 52 para 1 of the Charter, thus declaring them invalid; or alternatively could have adopted an interpretative ruling excluding from the scope of the criminalisation any conduct qualifying as rescue, humanitarian assistance, or support to a family member. The latter solution would have been similar, *mutatis mutandis,* to the one adopted by the Supreme Court of Canada in the *Appulonappa* case,[48] which deemed incompatible with the right to personal liberty of defendants[49] the criminalisation with severe prison sentences of mere aid to irregular entry, even when provided on a non-profit and unorganised basis.[50] Against this background, the Canadian Court considered it inappropriate to merely delete the incriminating provision, given the gap in border protection that this would have created, and decided to declare it "not applicable" to the three categories of conduct in respect of which it was disproportionate, namely humanitarian aid to undocumented foreigners, mutual aid between asylum seekers, and assistance between family members.[51] As we will see below (para. 7) the CJEU followed a somehow similar approach, although tailoring it to the specific case's context, i.e. that of family relations between adults and children under their effective care.

3.5 The Relevance of the *Kinsa* Case for the Commission's Proposal to Reform the Facilitators' Package

In November 2023, the European Commission released a proposal for a new Directive on the criminalisation of facilitating irregular migration, which would replace the Facilitators' Package.[52] It is hard to doubt that the proposal was prompted precisely by the preliminary referral in the *Kinsa* case, considering that the Commission itself had, in the past, deemed it unnecessary to reform the Facilitators' Package;[53] that the proposal came out just a few months after the order for a preliminary referral; and that it is devoid of impact assessment, an exceptional circumstance that suggests that it was hastily drafted.[54]

Article 3 para 1 of the Directive proposed by the Commission obliges Member States to criminalise intentional assistance for the entry, transit, or residence of undocumented aliens provided that (1) such assistance is given for financial or other material gain or (2) there is a serious risk of endangering a person. Thus, in contrast to the current Facilitators' Package, the obligation to incriminate does not simply address the conduct of intentionally helping an alien to enter, transit, or stay; it additionally requires that one of the conditions—(1) or (2)—is fulfilled. However, the Commission's proposal does not provide for a cause of exclusion of liability for those who facilitate entry, transit, or residence for rescue or humanitarian purposes, or for assistance between family members. The Commission, therefore, has not only failed to consider the recommendation from numerous scholars and research centres to provide for a *mandatory* humanitarian clause,[55] it has even taken a step backwards compared to the Facilitators' Package, which at least had provided the *option* for states to introduce such a provision. In response to such criticisms, the Commission would probably reply that the problem of over-criminalisation has been solved, in the proposal, by narrowing the scope of criminalisation under the aforementioned conditions (1) and (2), that is by providing as elements of the offense either the purpose of financial gain or the danger for foreigners.[56]

This reply, however, would not be satisfactory for several reasons. First, Member States would remain free to introduce more extensive criminal laws, or to leave in place the existing ones, based on the Facilitators' Package. Therefore, only providing facilitators with an effective "humanitarian defence" could avoid the risk of criminalising activities such as rescuing migrants in distress or assisting asylum seekers and family members. Second, the specifications in (1) and (2) are not, by themselves, sufficient to avoid criminalising activities aimed at protecting the fundamental rights of migrants. One might think, for example, of legal assistance to asylum seekers, carried out for legitimate remuneration; of a small boat carrying out humanitarian activities that rescues several dozens of migrants found in distress, thus endangering its own crew; of a shepherd accompanying a foreigner through a dangerous mountain path to prevent him from getting lost. Some of these activities might fall under the defence of necessity, but it must be borne in mind that states have different disciplines on the justification of necessity, and that in any case, the existence of justification would have to be ascertained in a trial, resulting in a chilling effect on any activity that consists of providing assistance to foreigners. For all these reasons, the overreaching scope of the Facilitators' Package, in the sense clarified above,[57] may indeed be inherited by the new directive, unless amendments are adopted. This would be either for the EU legislator, in the formulation of criminalisation obligations in conformity with the fundamental rights provided by the Charter, or at least for the national legislators, in the transposition phase of the proposed Directive.[58]

The proposed Facilitation Directive includes detailed provisions on penalties (Article 6). From this point of view, the proposal could be assessed under the lens of the principle of the proportionality of punishment, provided for in Article 49 para 3 of the Charter. On this subject, the judgement in the *Kinsa* case cannot have any influence, because it deals with the different question of the proportionality of the offence under Article 52 para 1 of the Charter. However, the considerations made above with respect to the relevance of the constitutional traditions of the Member States for the interpretation of the Charter[59] could be emphasised to interpret Article 49(3) in light of the criteria of cardinal and ordinal proportionality. For example, the provision of a maximum term of custody of no less than ten years for facilitating the irregular entry of unaccompanied minors (Article 6 para 3 of the proposal) could be deemed incompatible with the principle of proportionality in the ordinal sense, given that this is the same penalty required for the more serious offence of trafficking in human beings committed against minors (Article 4 para 2(a) Directive 2011/36/EU). Or, on the level of cardinal proportionality, one could question the consistency between the penalty of ten years' imprisonment and the seriousness of the offence of facilitating irregular entry by endangering the foreigner through gross negligence (as provided, again, by Article 6 para 3 of the proposal), given that situations of mere unintentional danger can also occasionally characterise humanitarian conduct, as already mentioned.

3.6 The Advocate General's Opinion on *Kinsa* (and the Missing Proportionality *Stricto Sensu*)

On 7 November 2024, Advocate General De La Tour delivered his opinion on the *Kinsa* case.[60] First, the opinion admits that the obligation of incrimination under Article 1(1)(a) of the Facilitation Directive encompasses any form of assistance, including that performed by the parent for the benefit of the undocumented child. The argument goes even further, recognising that, with Article 1(1)(a) of the Directive,

> the EU legislature did indeed intend to define a general infringement, covering all actions intended to facilitate unauthorised entry into the territory of a Member State, including where such acts are committed

> disinterestedly, out of altruism, compassion or solidarity, for humanitarian reasons or because of the existence of family ties.[61]

This is the first time, as far as we know, that an institutional act explicitly recognises that European law is formulated in order to punish all forms of assistance to the entry of an undocumented migrant, without any constraint for Member States to recognise, as an exempting factor, possible altruistic, compassionate, or humanitarian purposes of the agent.

The second conclusion states that the Directive is valid under the principles of both legality and proportionality. As to legality, the Advocate General emphasises that European instruments of harmonisation, given their nature as minimum standards, do not have to meet the same degree of precision required of criminal law rules that directly impose responsibility on individuals. The Advocate General argues that the proportionality test is satisfied because the broad notion of "assisting", laid down in Article 1(1)(a) of the Directive, is *appropriate* to achieve its intended purpose, namely protecting European borders against (any) irregular entry;[62] and *necessary* for the same purpose, making it possible to repress even sham acts of solidarity, which, in reality, have other purposes, including exploitation.[63] At this point, however, the opinion moves directly into examining the proportionality *of the penalty* (retrospective proportionality). In so doing, it misses the fourth, and final, assessment concerning the proportionality *of the offence* (prospective proportionality): That is, proportionality in the strict sense. As a result, the opinion omits to address some of the arguments that, as examined above, were paramount to the request for a preliminary ruling. Perhaps the Advocate General's choice to focus exclusively on Article 49 of the Charter, instead of 52(1), has also contributed to this shortcoming.

The Advocate General's third, and final, conclusion somehow revives prospective proportionality, although solely with respect to domestic criminal law implementing the Facilitators' Package. The opinion indeed states that the principle of proportionality *precludes* a national criminal law that does not allow a domestic court to differentiate, in terms of punishability or at least of sentencing, a parent who has facilitated the entry of a minor child, for humanitarian or necessity reasons, from a person whose actions are motivated solely by profit. Interestingly, such a conclusion is not limited to the family context but extends

> to the possibility of exonerating from criminal liability persons whom are shown to have acted disinterestedly, out of altruism, compassion or solidarity, for humanitarian reasons or because of family ties, or of adapting the system of penalties applicable to them.[64]

3.7 The Court of Justice's judgment restores the "prospective proportionality" test under Article 52(1) of the Charter

On June 3rd, 2025, The Grand Chamber of the Court of Justice delivered its judgment on the *Kinsa* case.

Firstly, Luxembourg judges reformulated the questions raised by the Tribunal, tailoring them to the specific case, and thus focusing solely on the criminal liability of those who enter irregularly with a minor under their care, rather than more generally on the issue of responsibility for solidarity or humanitarian assistance.

Secondly, the Court ruled out what both the Tribunal and the Advocate General considered to be an indisputable premise, namely that the Facilitators' package's scope also includes facilitating the entry of minors in one's custody. In this respect, the Court pointed out that EU law must be interpreted in line with the Charter of Fundamental Rights, so that, among the various possible interpretations, it is the one that guarantees its legitimacy (and therefore its validity) that has to be chosen. On these premises, the Court stated that the European concept of facilitating illegal immigration, despite being formulated in a very broad manner by Article 1 of Directive 2002/90/EC, must be understood as not including facilitation carried out in favour of minors under custody of the facilitator: as the Court clearly stated, "A contrary interpretation of that provision would entail a particularly serious interference with the right to respect for family life and the rights of the child, enshrined, respectively, in Articles 7 and 24 of the Charter, to such an extent that it would undermine the essence of those fundamental rights, within the meaning of Article 52(1) of the Charter" (§52).

With regard to the national legislation implementing the Facilitators Package, the Court stated that, for the same reasons, i.e. in order not to jeopardize the essence of Articles 7 and 24 of the Charter, Member States are precluded from criminalising the person who irregularly cross a border together with a child under his/her effective care; and that, where necessary, the national court has the power to disapply domestic law on the grounds of incompatibility with the Charter. This statement is of paramount importance, as European criminal law rules are generally minimum standards, leaving Member States free to punish a wider range of conduct. The exclusion of facilitating between family members from the scope of Directive 2002/90/EC would not therefore automatically have entailed a prohibition on Member States punishing such conduct, if the Court didn't rule on this latter point explicitly.

In addition to the right to family life and the rights of minors, the Court also based its ruling on the right to seek asylum. Since the defendant in the Italian proceedings applied for asylum, she cannot be subject to criminal penalties either on account of her own unauthorised entry into Italian territory, as prescribed by Article 31 of the Geneva Convention; or on account of the fact that, at the time of that entry, she was accompanied by her daughter and her niece, over whom she exercises actual care. In this regard, the Court recalls that: the fight against migrant smuggling cannot be carried out in a manner that prejudices the right to asylum (Article 6 of Framework Decision 2002/946/JHA and Article 4 of the Schengen Borders Code); an asylum seeker cannot be considered irregular until their application has been rejected at first instance (judgment of 16 November 2021, C-821/2019, *Commission v Hungary*); and, finally, Member States should ensure that, in the context of the reception of applicants for international protection, the principles of the best interests of the child and family unity are fully respected (Directive 2011/95/EU, Directive 2013/33).

For the first time the Court has reviewed the legitimacy of European and national criminal laws under the proportionality test set out in Article 52(1) of the Charter, in conjunction with the substantive rights, provided for in the Charter itself, which were relevant in the specific case. This represents an important precedent both for litigation relating to the discipline of migrant smuggling, the scope of which could be further reduced by emphasising other substantive rights provided by the Charter, and more generally for determining the limits on the criminalisation choices made by legislators.

3.8 Conclusion

Examining the *Kinsa* case allows us to place the criminalisation of facilitating irregular immigration under the lens of the principle of proportionality *as a whole*, including both retrospective and prospective proportionality, thus deploying all the limiting potentialities of this principle in respect to states' punitive power. From this perspective, the Charter is a powerful instrument because, unlike many national constitutions, it codifies both aspects of proportionality within two provisions that have the same legal value as the treaties: Article 49 para 3 and Article 52 para 1.

The *Kinsa* litigation is also remarkable because of its procedural developments, which saw first a passage before the Italian Constitutional Court and then a preliminary reference before the Court of Justice. Although the two proceedings concern, as extensively illustrated, two different aspects of proportionality, nevertheless what the Italian Constitutional Court has affirmed, in particular with reference to the necessary adherence of the normative datum to the empirical reality that it aims to regulate, has been implicitly taken into account by the Court of Justice when assessing whether the European legislator has made sound use of its discretion in its choices of criminalisation.

Finally, *Kinsa* is forward-looking in that it is part of a legislative process (indeed, it was probably its prompter) aimed at reforming, after more than 20 years, the European legislation on facilitating irregular immigration. This is perhaps a once-in-a-lifetime opportunity to transform into binding legal principles what legal scholarship has been asserting for years: Namely, that the current framework is excessively broad, unfairly punitive of altruistic conduct, and dysfunctional with respect to the repression of the most serious forms of trafficking, which are the only courses of conduct truly detrimental to people's fundamental rights.

Notes

1 For an extensive critical analysis of the Italian discipline for combating the facilitation of irregular migration, see Alessandro Spena, 'Migrant Smuggling: A Normative and Phenomenological View from Italy' in Vincenzo Militello and Alessandro Spena (eds), *Between Criminalization and Protection. The Italian Way of Dealing*

with Migrant Smuggling and Trafficking Within the European and International Context (Brill | Nijhoff 2019); for an up-to-date overview of Italian policies ascribable to the conceptual category of 'crimmigration', see Giulia Mentasti, 'The Criminalisation of Migration in Italy: Current Tendencies in the Light of EU Law' (2022) 13 New Journal of European Criminal Law 502–25.

2 For an overview and critical analysis on this context, see Sergio Carrera and others, *Policing Humanitarianism. EU Policies Against Human Smuggling and Their Impact on Civil Society* (Hart 2020); Maria Chiara Ricci, 'Criminalising Solidarity? Smugglers, Migrants and Rescuers in the Reform of the "Facilitators' Package"' in Valsamis Mitsilegas, Violeta Moreno-Lax and Niovi Vavoula (eds), *Securitising Asylum Flows* (Brill | Nijhoff 2020); Amnesty International 'Punishing Compassion: Solidarity on Trial in Fortress Europe' Research Briefing, EUR 01/1828/2020 (March 2020) <https://www.amnesty.org/en/documents/eur01/1828/2020/en/> accessed 10 September 2024, as all the hyperlinks included in this Chapter; Jennifer Allsopp, Lina Vosyliūtė and Stephanie Brenda Smialowski, 'Picking "Low-Hanging Fruit" While the Orchard Burns: The Costs of Policing Humanitarian Actors in Italy and Greece as a Strategy to Prevent Migrant Smuggling' (2021) 27 European Journal on Criminal Policy and Research 65; Stefano Zirulia, 'Is That a Smuggler?' in Gian Luigi Gatta, Valsamis Mitsilegas and Stefano Zirulia (eds), *Controlling Immigration Through Criminal Law. European and Comparative Perspectives on "Crimmigration"* (Hart 2021).

3 The expression "Facilitators Package" is commonly used to indicate the European discipline that obliges Member States to adopt criminal measures to combat the facilitation of irregular entry, contained in the Council Directive 2002/90/EC of 28 November 2002 defining the facilitation of unauthorised entry, transit, and residence [2002] OJ L328/4, and in the Council Framework Decision 2002/946/JHA of 28 November 2002 on the strengthening of the penal framework to prevent the facilitation of unauthorised entry, transit, and residence [2002] OJ L328/1 (adopted jointly according to the double-text technique used until 2005, when it was common opinion that directives, as first-pillar instruments, could not impose criminalisation obligations). For an overview of European and international regulations on the criminalisation of migrant smuggling (the latter provided by the UN Palermo Convention 2000), see Andreas Schloenhardt, 'Smuggling of Migrants and Refugees' in Cathryn Costello, Michelle Foster and Jane McAdam (eds), *The Oxford Handbook of International Refugee Law* (OUP 2021).

4 See Case C 460/23 Kinsa [2023] ECLI:EU:C:2023:784. The case was formerly named as "Kinshasa".

5 Case C 460/23 Kinsa [2023] ECLI:EU:C:2023:784, Court of Bologna, Order of 1 December 2020. The order of the Court is available at <https://www.sistemapenale.it/pdf_contenuti/1607288715_tribunale-bologna-questione-legittimita-costituzionale-art-12-tu-immigrazione.pdf>.

6 Case C 460/23 Kinsa [2023] ECLI:EU:C:2023:784, Constitutional Court, Judgment 63 of 8 February 2022, ECLI:IT:COST:2022:63. For an extensive commentary, see Alessandro Spena, 'Favoreggiamento dell'immigrazione irregolare vs. traffico di migranti: una dicotomia rilevante nell'interpretazione dell'art. 12 TUI? (Ragionando su Corte Cost. 63/2022)' [2022] Diritto, immigrazione e cittadinanza 238–67.

7 See, in the Judgment of the Constitutional Court (n 6), the section titled "Considerato in diritto" (*Conclusions on points of law*) para 4(2).

8 See the section titled "Considerato in diritto" (n 7) para 4(3).

9 See the section titled "Considerato in diritto" (n 7) para 4(4)(1).

10 See the section titled "Considerato in diritto" (n 7) para 4(4)(2).

11 The reference made by the Court is to article 1 para 3 of Council Framework Decision 2002/946/JHA (n 3).

12 See the section titled "Considerato in diritto" (n 7) para 4(3) para 4(5).

13 See, e.g., Article 9 of Council Directive 2019/713 of 17 April 2019 on combating fraud and counterfeiting of non-cash means of payment [2019] OJ L123/18; article 15 of Council Directive 2017/541 of 15 March 2017 on combating terrorism [2017] OJ L88/6; article 4 of Council Directive 2011/36 of 5 April 2011 on preventing and combating trafficking in human beings and protecting its victims [2011] OJ L101/1.

14 For the distinction between "legislative proportionality" and "proportionality in adjudication", and for the different stages at which the principle of proportionality applies, see Emmanouil Billis, 'The Typology of Proportionality' in Emmanouil Billis, Nandor Knust and Jon Petter Rui (eds), *Proportionality in Crime Control and Criminal Justice* (Hart 2021); For a commentary, see Valsamis Mitsilegas and Emmanouil Billis, 'Article 49—Principles of Legality and Proportionality of Criminal Offences and Penalties' in Steve Peers and others (eds), *The EU Charter of Fundamental Rights—a Commentary* (2nd edn, Hart 2022).

15 See, *verbatim*, Case C-384/17 Dooel Uvoz-Izvoz Skopje Link Logistic N&N v Budapest Rendőrfőkapitánya [2018] ECLI:EU:C:2018:810, Judgment of the Fifth Chamber, para 45.

16 See, e.g., Petter Asp, 'Two Notions of Proportionality' in Kimmi Nuotio (ed), *Festschrift in Honour of Raimo Lathi* (Helsinki University 2007); Antony Duff, 'Proportionality and the Criminal Law: Proportionality of What to What?' in Billis, Knust and Rui (eds) (n 14).

17 Joined Cases C-64, C-140, C-146 and C-148/18 *Zoran Maksimovic and Others v Bezirkshauptmannschaft Murtal and Finanzpolizei* [2019] ECLI:EU:C:2019:723, Judgment of the Sixth Chamber, paras 42–48.

18 Case C-645/18 NE v Bezirkshauptmannschaft Hartberg-Fürstenfeld and Finanzpolizei [2019] ECLI:EU:C:2019:1108, paras 36–41.

19 Case C-655/21 G. ST. T. (Proportionnalité de la peine en cas de contrefaçon) [2023] ECLI:EU:C:2023:791, paras 81–85.

20 In this respect, see all the above-mentioned judgements: Joined Cases C-64, C-140, C-146, and C-148/18 *Maksimovic* (n 17), para 39: "the severity of the penalty must be commensurate with the seriousness of the offence. In particular, the administrative or punitive measures permitted under national legislation must not go beyond what is necessary in order to attain the objectives legitimately pursued by that legislation"; Case C-655/21 *G. ST.T.* (n 19), para 65: "the punitive measures permitted under national legislation must not go beyond what is necessary in order to attain the objectives legitimately pursued by that legislation. The severity of the sanctions must be commensurate with the seriousness of the infringements for which they are imposed, in particular by ensuring a genuinely deterrent effect, while not going beyond what is necessary to attain that objective"; Case C-645/18 *NE* (n 18), paras 39–40 "*une réglementation telle que celle au principal n'apparaît pas en adéquation avec la gravité des violations sanctionnées.... Par ailleurs, la mise en œuvre effective des obligations dont le non-respect est sanctionné par une telle réglementation pourrait être assurée par des mesures moins restrictives*". For the overlap between the two kinds of proportionality, see also Case C-384/17 *Link Logistic* (n 15), para 42: "The severity of a penalty must thus correspond to the seriousness of the offence concerned, that requirement following both from Article 52 para 1 of the Charter and from the principle of proportionality of penalties in Article 49 para 3 of the Charter". For a clearer distinction between the two assessments, see Joined Cases C-497 and C498/15 *Euro-Team Kft. and Spirál-Gép Kft v Budapest Rendőrfőkapitánya* [2017] ECLI:EU:C:2017:229, paras 40–42; Case C-501/14 EL-EM-2001 Ltd v Nemzeti Adó- és Vámhivatal Dél-alföldi Regionális Vám- és Pénzügyőri Főigazgatósága [2016] ECLI:EU:C:2016:777.

21 Although there is a general deference of the constitutional courts to respect the legislature's discretion in quantifying punishments, there is no lack of significant case law that attributes a constitutional basis, and thus the nature of a limit to the power of punishment, to the prohibition of disproportionate punishments: with reference, in particular, to the US and Canadian legal systems, see, respectively, the seminal cases *Weems v United States* 217 U.S. 349 (1910) and *R. v Smith (Edward Dewey)*, (1987) 1 SCR 1045 (Supreme Court of Canada), which ushered in a jurisprudential trend that is still valid today.

22 For an accurate overview, see Andrew von Hirsch and Andrew Ashworth, 'Criteria for Proportionality: A Review' in Andrew von Hirsch and Andrew Ashworth (eds), *Proportionate Sentencing. Exploring the Principle* (OUP 2005).

23 Von Hirsch and Ashworth (n 22) 138.

24 See Andrew Ashworth, *Sentencing and Criminal Justice* (4th edn, CUP 2012), who argues, giving the example of imprisonment for three years for a purely pecuniary offence such as theft, "there surely is such a thing as utter disproportionality, even if there is no such thing as absolute proportionality" (120). For a recent and comprehensive analysis, aimed at elaborating, starting (also) from the Italian constitutional jurisprudence, the contents and the applicative scope of the prohibition to impose excessively disproportionate punishments, see Francesco Viganò, *La proporzionalità della pena. Profili di diritto penale e costituzionale* (Giappichelli 2021).

25 Article 1 para 3 of Council Framework Decision 2002/946/JHA (n 3).

26 Article 4 para 1 of Council Directive 2011/36/EU of 5 April 2011 on preventing and combating trafficking in human beings and protecting its victims, and replacing Council Framework Decision 2002/629/JHA [2011] OJ L101/1, the article is on the problematic issue of the distinction between migrant smuggling and trafficking in human beings, which cannot be dealt with here, see, among the many, Anne Gallagher and Fiona David, *The International Law of Migrant Smuggling* (CUP 2014); James Hathaway, 'The Human Rights Quagmire of "Human Trafficking"' [2008] Virginia Journal of International Law 1–59.

27 Legislative Decree *Consolidated Act of Provisions Concerning Immigration and the Condition of Third Country Nationals* n 286 of 25 July 1998 (Italian Consolidated Text on Immigration—t.u. imm.), article 12 para 3(b) and 3-ter (b).

28 In this sense, Case C-205/20 Bezirkshauptmannschaft Hartberg-Fürstenfeld (Effet direct) [2022] ECLI:EU:C:2022:168, expressly overruling the earlier judgment Case C-384/17 *Link Logistic* (n 15), para 29 and 44.

29 Italian Consolidated Text on Immigration—t.u. imm. (n 27), article 12 para 3(b).

30 Italian Consolidated Text on Immigration—t.u. imm. (n 27), article 12, paras 3(a) and (d), respectively.

31 With the aggravating circumstances having ceased to exist, jurisdiction has changed from the previous three-judge panel to a single judge due to the lesser seriousness of the offence.

32 For references to the relevant judicial acts, see Footnote 4. For first commentaries to the issues referred to the CJEU, see Valsamis Mitsilegas, 'Reforming the EU "Facilitators Package": The New Commission Proposal in the Light of the Kinshasa Litigation' (*University of Liverpool School of Law and Social Justice Blog*, 12 February 2024) <https://www.liverpool.ac.uk/law/blog/reforming-the-eu-facilitators-package/>; Cathryn Costello and Stefano Zirulia, 'Pushing Back. How to Limit Overcriminalisation of Assistance to Those in Need of Protection' (*Verfassungsblog*, 29 February 2024) <https://verfassungsblog.de/pushing-back/>; Lorenzo Bernardini, 'Il *delit de solidarité* davanti alla Corte di Giustizia: il caso *Kinshasa* come *game changer* per le politiche migratorie europee' [2024] Diritto, immigrazione e cittadinanza 1–25.

33 Duff (n 16) 34–35; Robert Alexy, 'Constitutional Rights, Proportionality, and Argumentation' in Jan Sieckmann (ed), *Proportionality, Balancing, and Rights.*

Robert Alexy's Theory of Constitutional Rights (Springer 2021) 2; Ralf Poscher, 'Proportionality and the Bindingness of Fundamental Rights' in Billis, Knust and Rui (eds) (n 14).

34 See, albeit in the different matter of television rights, Case C-283/11 *Sky Österreich GmbH v Österreichischer Rundfunk* [2013] ECLI:EU:C:2013:28, paras 48–50: "In accordance with Article 52 para 1 of the Charter, any limitation on the exercise of the rights and freedoms recognised by the Charter must be provided for by law and respect the essence of those rights and freedoms and, in compliance with the principle of proportionality, must be necessary and actually meet objectives of general interest recognised by the European Union or the need to protect the rights and freedoms of others . . . 50. In so far as it concerns the proportionality of the interference found to exist, the Court recalls that, according to settled case-law, the principle of proportionality requires that measures adopted by European Union institutions do not exceed the limits of what is appropriate and necessary in order to attain the objectives legitimately pursued by the legislation in question; when there is a choice between several appropriate measures recourse must be had to the least onerous, and the disadvantages caused must not be disproportionate to the aims pursued". The proportionality test has also been articulated in the same terms by other judgements, although without necessarily referring to Article 52 para 1 of the Charter, see Case C-210/10 Márton Urbán v Vám- és Pénzügyőrség Észak-alföldi Regionális Parancsnoksága [2012] ECLI:EU:C:2012:64, para 24; Joined Cases C-379 and C-380/08 *Raffinerie Mediterranee (ERG) SpA, and others* [2010] ECLI:EU:C:2010:127.

35 The test articulated by the Court of Justice corresponds to well-established theorisations on the subject: see Duff (n 16), *Proportionality and the Criminal Law* 34–35; Alexy (n 33) 2. These authors prefer a test based on three steps, but simply because they incorporate the first test ("legitimate goal") into the last one ("proportionality in the strict sense"). Apart from that, there is no substantive difference between their assessment of proportionality and the four sub-tests scheme adopted by the Court.

36 For a framing and initial systematisation of the *chilling effect* theory, see Columbia Law Review Association, 'Notes: The Chilling Effect in Constitutional Law' (1969) 69 Columbia Law Review 808; Monica Youn, 'The Chilling Effect and the Problem of Private Action' (2013) 66 Vanderbilt Law Review 1473, 1474–95. With regard to the relevance assigned to the chilling effect in the jurisprudence of the European Court of Human Rights on freedom of expression, see Rónán Ó Fathaigh, 'Article 10 and the Chilling Effect Principle' [2013] European Human Rights Law Review 304. For a recent in-depth analysis aimed at enhancing the chilling effect theory on the level of limits to criminalisation choices, see Nicola Recchia, *Il principio di proporzionalità nel diritto penale. Scelte di criminalizzazione e ingerenza nei diritti fondamentali* (Giappichelli 2020) 251–317.

37 Both objectives are mentioned by the 'Facilitators' Package' in particular in the Preamble of Council Directive 2002/90/EC (n 3), at para 2 "measures should be taken to combat the aiding of illegal immigration both in connection with unauthorised crossing of the border in the strict sense and for the purpose of sustaining networks which exploit human beings". For an examination of the problem of the plurality and heterogeneity of the objectives pursued by the 'Facilitators Package', see Ricci (n 2) 41–43.

38 For the place of the judgement of effectiveness in the framework of the judgement of the suitability of the measure, see Duff (n 16) 41.

39 Case C-61/11 PPU *Hassen El Dridi, alias Karim Soufi* [2011] ECLI:EU:C:2011:268.

40 Such a penalty was, at that time, provided in Italian Consolidated Text on Immigration—t.u. imm. (n 27), by Article 14 para (5-ter), which sanctioned by imprisonment of up to four years the non-compliance with the order of expulsion

from the Italian territory issued by the public security authority against the irregular foreigner.

41 Council Directive 2008/115/EC of 16 December 2008 on common standards and procedures in Member States for returning illegally staying third-country nationals [2008] OJ L348/98.

42 With regard to the mechanism of imposing administrative sanctions on private carriers who transport illegal aliens due to their failure to check passengers' documents, see. Theodore Baird, 'Carrier Sanctions in Europe: A Comparison of Trends in 10 Countries, in European Journal of Migration and Law' (2017) 19 European Journal of Migration and Law 307.

43 See Spena (n 1) 44, who frames the main function of these penalisation obligations in the fight against irregular immigration; the same opinion is expressed by Valsamis Mitsilegas, 'The Criminalisation of Migration in the Law of the European Union. Challenging the Preventive Paradigm' in Gatta, Mitsilegas and Zirulia (eds) (n 2) 29.

44 *Alhowais v Hungary* [2023] ECLI:CE:ECHR:2023:0202JUD005943517, paras 133–45.

45 *Hirsi Jamaa and Others v Italy* [2012] ECLI:CE:ECHR:2012:0223JUD002776509.

46 Case C-821/19 *European Commission v Hungary* [2021] ECLI:EU:C:2021:930.

47 *Mallah v France* [2011] ECLI:CE:ECHR:2011:1110JUD002968108, para 40.

48 *R. v Appulonappa* (2015) SCC 50 (Supreme Court of Canada). For a commentary, see David Moffette and Nevena Aksin, 'Fighting Human Smuggling or Criminalising Refugees? Regimes of Justification in and around *R v Appulonappa*' (2018) 33 Canadian Journal of Law and Society 21–40. The case concerned approximately 70 ethnic Tamils from Sri Lanka on board a ship, fleeing civil war and therefore intending to seek asylum. The passengers had paid between USD 30 and 40,000, and the Canadian authorities believed that the captain of the ship and three crew members were trusted associates of the criminal organisation that had organised the trafficking.

49 The parameter of legitimacy was Section 7 of the *Canadian Charter of Rights and Freedoms*, incorporated into Part I of the Canadian Constitution of 1982.

50 Immigration and Refugee Protection Act (Statues of Canada 2001) Section 117(1) was headed "Organising entry into Canada" and worded as follows: "No person shall knowingly organise, induce, aid or abet the coming into Canada of one or more persons who are not in possession of a visa, passport or other document required by this act". Sections 177(2) and (3) set out the imprisonment and monetary penalties. Section 121(1)(c), headed "Aggravating factors", provided that the purpose of profit, irrespective of its actual realisation, should be taken into account in the commensuration of the sentence. In 2012, thus subsequent to the events in question, Section 117 was amended by the Protecting Canada's Immigration System Act (Statutes of Canada 2012) Section 41(1) and 41(4). Thus, the provision on the basis of which the appellants had been convicted on appeal was no longer in force at the time of the constitutionality judgement.

51 See the judgement *R. v Appulonappa* (2015) (n 48) paras 84–85: "The extent of the inconsistency that has been proven is the overbreadth of section 117 in relation to three categories of conduct: (1) humanitarian aid to undocumented entrants, (2) mutual aid amongst asylum-seekers, and (3) assistance to family entering without the required documents. . . . I conclude that the preferable remedy is to read down section 117 as not applicable to persons who give humanitarian, mutual or family assistance".

52 Commission, 'Proposal for a Directive of the European Parliament and of the Council laying down minimum rules to prevent and counter the facilitation of unauthorised entry, transit and stay in the Union, and replacing Council Directive 2002/90/EC and Council Framework Decision 2002/946 JHA' COM (18 November 2023) 755 final.

53 See Commission, 'Refit evaluation of the EU legal framework against facilitation of unauthorised entry, transit and residence: the Facilitators Package' SWD (22 March 2017) 117 final.
54 Commission, Explanatory Memorandum in the 'Proposal for a Directive of the European Parliament and of the Council' (n 52) 10 "The proposal is exceptionally presented without an accompanying impact assessment".
55 See, e.g., Sergio Carrera and others, *Fit for Purpose? The Facilitation Directive and the Criminalisation of Humanitarian Assistance to Irregular Migrants: 2018 Update* (CEPS 2019) <https://www.europarl.europa.eu/thinktank/en/document/IPOL_STU(2018)608838>; Zirulia (n 2).
56 See the Preamble in the 'Proposal for a Directive of the European Parliament and of the Council' (n 52) para 7:

> It is appropriate to provide for criminal liability where there is a link to a financial or material benefit, or where migrants are highly likely to be subjected to serious harm. These elements will usually not be fulfilled when it comes to assistance among family members or the provision of humanitarian assistance or the support of basic human needs.

57 See Section 3.4.
58 For directions in this regard, see Mitsilegas (n 32); Costello and Zirulia (n 32).
59 See Section 3.3.
60 Case C-460/23 *Kinsa*—Opinion of Advocate General Richard de la Tour delivered on 7 November 2024 ECLI:EU:C:2024:941.
61 Case C-460/23 *Kinsa*—Opinion of Advocate General Richard de la Tour delivered on 7 November 2024 ECLI:EU:C:2024:941, para 46.
62 Case C-460/23 *Kinsa*—Opinion of Advocate General Richard de la Tour delivered on 7 November 2024 ECLI:EU:C:2024:941, paras 78–79.
63 Case C-460/23 *Kinsa*—Opinion of Advocate General Richard de la Tour delivered on 7 November 2024 ECLI:EU:C:2024:941, paras 80–84.
64 Case C-460/23 *Kinsa*—Opinion of Advocate General Richard de la Tour delivered on 7 November 2024 ECLI:EU:C:2024:941, para 115.

Bibliography

Alexy R, 'Constitutional Rights, Proportionality, and Argumentation' in Sieckmann J (ed), *Proportionality, Balancing, and Rights. Robert Alexy's Theory of Constitutional Rights* (Springer 2021).

Allsopp J, Vosyliūtė L and Smialowski SB, 'Picking "Low-Hanging Fruit" While the Orchard Burns: The Costs of Policing Humanitarian Actors in Italy and Greece as a Strategy to Prevent Migrant Smuggling' (2021) 27 European Journal on Criminal Policy and Research 65.

Amnesty International, *Punishing Compassion: Solidarity on Trial in Fortress Europe* (Self-Published 2020).

Ashworth A, *Sentencing and Criminal Justice* (4th edn, CUP 2012).

Asp P, 'Two Notions of Proportionality' in Nuotio K (ed), *Festschrift in Honour of Raimo Lathi* (Helsinki University 2007).

Baird T, 'Carrier Sanctions in Europe: A Comparison of Trends in 10 Countries, in European Journal of Migration and Law' (2017) 19 European Journal of Migration and Law 307.

Bernardini L, 'Il *delit de solidarité* davanti alla Corte di Giustizia: il caso *Kinshasa* come *game changer* per le politiche migratorie europee' (2024) 1 Diritto, immigrazione e cittadinanza 1.

Billis E, 'The Typology of Proportionality' in Billis E, Knust N and Rui JP (eds), *Proportionality in Crime Control and Criminal Justice* (Hart 2021).

Carrera S and others, *Policing Humanitarianism: EU Policies Against Human Smuggling and Their Impact on Civil Society* (Hart 2019).

Carrera S and others, *Fit for Purpose? The Facilitation Directive and the Criminalisation of Humanitarian Assistance to Irregular Migrants: 2018 Update* (CEPS 2019).

Columbia Law Review Association, 'Notes: The Chilling Effect in Constitutional Law' (1969) 69 Columbia Law Review 808.

Duff A, 'Proportionality and the Criminal Law: Proportionality of What to What?' in Billis E, Knust N and Rui JP (eds), *Proportionality in Crime Control and Criminal Justice* (Hart 2021).

Fathaigh RÓ, 'Article 10 and the Chilling Effect Principle' (2013) European Human Rights Law Review 304.

Gallagher A and David F, *The International Law of Migrant Smuggling* (CUP 2014).

Hathaway J, 'The Human Rights Quagmire of "Human Trafficking"' (2008) 49 Virginia Journal of International Law 1.

Mentasti G, 'The Criminalisation of Migration in Italy: Current Tendencies in the Light of EU Law' (2022) 13 New Journal of European Criminal Law 502.

Mitsilegas V, 'The Criminalisation of Migration in the Law of the European Union. Challenging the Preventive Paradigm' in Gatta GL, Mitsilegas V and Zirulia S (eds), *Controlling Immigration Through Criminal Law. European and Comparative Perspectives on "Crimmigration"* (Hart 2021).

Mitsilegas V and Billis E, 'Article 49—Principles of Legality and Proportionality of Criminal Offences and Penalties' in Peers S and others (eds), *The EU Charter of Fundamental Rights—a Commentary* (2nd edn, Hart 2022).

Moffette D and Aksin N, 'Fighting Human Smuggling or Criminalising Refugees? Regimes of Justification in and Around *R v. Appulonappa*' (2018) 33 Canadian Journal of Law and Society 21.

Poscher R, 'Proportionality and the Bindingness of Fundamental Rights' in Billis E, Knust N and Rui JP (eds), *Proportionality in Crime Control and Criminal Justice* (Hart 2021).

Recchia N, *Il principio di proporzionalità nel diritto penale. Scelte di criminalizzazione e ingerenza nei diritti fondamentali* (Giappichelli 2020).

Ricci MC, 'Criminalising Solidarity? Smugglers, Migrants and Rescuers in the Reform of the "Facilitators' Package"' in Mitsilegas V, Moreno-Lax V and Vavoula N (eds), *Securitising Asylum Flows* (Brill | Nijhoff 2020).

Schloenhardt A, 'Smuggling of Migrants and Refugees' in Costello C, Foster M and McAdam J (eds), *The Oxford Handbook of International Refugee Law* (OUP 2021).

Spena A, 'Migrant Smuggling: A Normative and Phenomenological View from Italy' in Militello V and Spena A (eds), *Between Criminalization and Protection. The Italian Way of Dealing with Migrant Smuggling and Trafficking Within the European and International Context* (Brill | Nijhoff 2019).

Spena A, 'Favoreggiamento dell'immigrazione irregolare vs. traffico di migranti: una dicotomia rilevante nell'interpretazione dell'art. 12 TUI? (Ragionando su Corte Cost. 63/2022)' (2022) 3 Diritto, immigrazione e cittadinanza 239.

Viganò F, *La proporzionalità della pena. Profili di diritto penale e costituzionale* (Giappichelli 2021).

Von Hirsch A and Ashworth A, 'Criteria for Proportionality: A Review' in Von Hirsch A and Ashworth A (eds), *Proportionate Sentencing. Exploring the Principle* (OUP 2005).

Youn M, 'The Chilling Effect and the Problem of Private Action' (2013) 66 Vanderbilt Law Review 1473.

Zirulia S, 'Is that a Smuggler?' in Gatta GL, Mitsilegas V and Zirulia S (eds), *Controlling Immigration Through Criminal Law. European and Comparative Perspectives on "Crimmigration"* (Hart 2021).

4 Who Is the "Vulnerable" Victim? Trafficked and Smuggled Persons as Victims of Crime under EU Law

Maja Grundler

4.1 Introduction

Victims of crime are entitled to special protection under EU law, including rights related to compensation, mutual recognition of protection orders, and rights during criminal proceedings.[1] For the purposes of EU law, a victim is "a natural person who has suffered harm, including physical, mental, or emotional harm or economic loss which was directly caused by a criminal offence" and the category of victim also includes "family members of a person whose death was directly caused by a criminal offence and who have suffered harm as a result of that person's death".[2]

Although there is a common definition of "victim" under EU law, some victims of crime benefit from more protections than others. Indeed, EU law has developed specific instruments providing particular types of assistance and protection for certain groups of victims.[3] Trafficked persons are such a group, and as a result, they benefit from the protection of both the Trafficking Directive[4] and the Residence Permit Directive.[5] While the provisions of the Residence Permit Directive *may* also be extended to smuggled persons, EU law does not foresee special protection tailored to the needs of this group of irregular migrants. Although it is questionable whether smuggling—or rather facilitation of irregular entry—should be dealt with under criminal law at all, and it has been argued that administrative law would be the more appropriate legal framework,[6] the fact remains that both trafficking in human beings and facilitation of unauthorised entry are criminal offences related to irregular migration under EU law. Yet, the victims of both practices are treated very differently and, as Letschert and Rijken note, "the attention for specific groups of victims might generate a hierarchy between groups of victims and fragmentation of the rights given".[7]

This chapter examines the hierarchy between trafficked and smuggled persons as victims of crime under EU law. While not all trafficked persons enter the EU irregularly,[8] the chapter focuses on trafficked and smuggled persons as irregular migrants in order to comment on why EU law differentiates between the two groups and whether this differential treatment is justified. I use the term "irregular migrants" in full recognition of the fact that this irregularity

DOI: 10.4324/9781003378440-4

is "a condition that is *produced* through various processes of (ir)regularization",[9] rather than a status inherent to or chosen by the relevant individuals.

The chapter begins by analysing the definitions of the offences of trafficking and smuggling (or facilitation of unauthorised entry for the purpose of EU law), and the assumptions these produce about the victims of both crimes. It then outlines how the protection of trafficked and smuggled persons as victims of crime differs under EU law. Against this background, the chapter outlines trafficked and smuggled persons' experiences during migration to show that, based on those experiences, differentiating between the two groups is unprincipled. The chapter then explores which victims are seen as vulnerable and, therefore, in need of special protection under the relevant EU legal instruments. It draws on vulnerability theory to show that EU law's understanding of vulnerability is limited. The chapter offers a more comprehensive account of trafficked and smuggled persons' vulnerability, with a focus on state-produced vulnerability. Finally, it shows how EU law's limited understanding of trafficked and smuggled persons' vulnerability leads to secondary and repeat victimisation of irregular migrants. The chapter closes with the observation that framing some victims as more worthy of protection than others helps the EU to justify its migration policies.

4.2 Trafficking in Human Beings and Facilitation of Unauthorised Entry

4.2.1 Defining Trafficking and Smuggling

Trafficking in human beings and facilitation of unauthorised entry are both crimes under EU law. Much like their international law counterparts, the EU law definitions of trafficking and smuggling (or facilitation of unauthorised entry) create a binary distinction between the two practices and, by extension, between the victims of both offences. Indeed, the definitions introduce certain assumptions about trafficked and smuggled persons, which, in turn, have effects on the protection offered to the two groups.

Trafficking in human beings is defined in the EU Trafficking Directive as

> [t]he recruitment, transportation, transfer, harbouring or reception of persons, including the exchange or transfer of control over those persons, by means of the threat or use of force or other forms of coercion, of abduction, of fraud, of deception, of the abuse of power or of a position of vulnerability or of the giving or receiving of payments or benefits to achieve the consent of a person having control over another person, for the purpose of exploitation.[10]

The Directive goes on to state that

> [e]xploitation shall include, as a minimum, the exploitation of the prostitution of others or other forms of sexual exploitation, forced labour

> or services, including begging, slavery or practices similar to slavery, servitude, or the exploitation of criminal activities, or the removal of organs, or the exploitation of surrogacy, of forced marriage, or of illegal adoption.[11]

Thus, the EU law definition is almost identical to the international law definition in the UN Trafficking Protocol,[12] though EU law adds "the exchange or transfer of control over . . . persons"[13] to the actions constituting trafficking, as well as "begging", "the exploitation of criminal activities", and the "exploitation of surrogacy, of forced marriage, or of illegal adoption" to the list of the examples of exploitation.[14]

The EU law definition of facilitation of unauthorised entry, on the other hand, is substantially different from its international law counterpart, the UN Smuggling Protocol's definition of "smuggling of migrants". While the latter defines smuggling of migrants as "the procurement, in order to obtain, directly or indirectly, a financial or other material benefit, of the illegal entry of a person into a State Party of which the person is not a national or a permanent resident",[15] EU law omits the financial gain criterion. The Facilitation Directive calls on Member States to adopt appropriate sanctions on

> any person who intentionally assists a person who is not a national of a Member State to enter, or transit across, the territory of a Member State in breach of the laws of the State concerned on the entry or transit of aliens.[16]

It is worth noting that, in 2023, the European Commission presented a proposal for a recast Facilitation Directive, which, if adopted, would align EU law more closely with international law by requiring that an individual facilitating irregular entry or stay "requests, receives or accepts, directly or indirectly, a financial or material benefit",[17] though the proposal is problematic for other reasons.[18]

The effects of this discrepancy between the international and the current EU law definitions of smuggling have been discussed in detail elsewhere.[19] The purpose of the next subsection is to compare the EU law definitions of trafficking and smuggling and to analyse the assumptions EU law makes about the victims of each of these crimes.

4.2.2 *Assumptions About Trafficked and Smuggled Persons*

The definitions of "trafficking in persons" and "smuggling of migrants" are criminal law definitions seeking to define offences and thus they focus on the actions and intentions of perpetrators. However, in drawing a distinction between traffickers and smugglers, the definitions also automatically create a binary between trafficked persons and smuggled persons. What is more, they introduce assumptions about these two groups, which shape states' responses towards them.

Several differences are immediately apparent when comparing the definition of trafficking to that of smuggling (or facilitation of unauthorised entry). First, as opposed to the trafficking definition, the smuggling definition does not contain a "means element",[20] that is, a reference to "threat or use of force", etc., as is mentioned in the trafficking definition. Since, in the trafficking definition, the means element gives the impression that trafficked persons have been forced, coerced, or deceived into migrating, its absence in the smuggling definition introduces the assumption that smuggled persons embark on their journeys voluntarily.

This forced/voluntary binary is also connected to assumptions about the gender of trafficked and smuggled persons and related notions of agency. The Trafficking Directive's definition of human trafficking is adapted from that of the UN Trafficking Protocol, whose full title—"Protocol to Prevent, Suppress and Punish Trafficking in Persons, Especially Women and Children"—fuels the idea that trafficked persons are more likely to be female than male. As Buckland notes, there is a "preconception that smuggled 'criminals' are men, while trafficked 'victims' are women".[21] This "victim" narrative, in turn, paints trafficked women as "inherently passive, action-less and incapable of making choices".[22] The trafficked woman is imagined as an "ideal victim",[23] "innocent, helpless, not complicit in the offence and [with] no personal direct or indirect connections to the crimes or their perpetrators".[24] This " 'ideal victim' bias", in turn, "means that other victims are overlooked".[25] First, the focus on female "victims" of trafficking has the effect of excluding trafficked men from the protective scope of the trafficking legal framework.[26] Second, based on the construction of a "victim" as a (female) trafficked person, smuggled persons are not perceived as "victims" and are, therefore, assumed not to be in need of protection.

This is also reflected in the fact that the smuggling definition makes no reference to exploitation, save perhaps financial exploitation of the smuggled person paying the smuggler.[27] Gallagher argues that since the smuggling definition "remove[s] the 'exploitation' element from the concept of migrant smuggling", it "shift[s] the focus of the definition on to the action of migrant smuggling rather than its impact on those who are smuggled".[28] While the trafficking definition does not reveal much about trafficked persons' experiences either, it does show that, besides deception, coercion, etc., harm in the form of "use of force" and (possibly) exploitation can be part of the trafficking experience. In contrast, by not mentioning similar elements, the smuggling definition seems to suggest that smuggled persons do not experience any harm. It should be noted that the proposal for a recast Facilitation Directive does also criminalise facilitation of entry or stay where "there is a high likelihood of causing serious harm to a person",[29] thus admitting that smuggled persons, too, may experience harm. Yet, this fact is used only to (over-)criminalise the relevant conduct,[30] not to assist smuggled persons as victims of crime. Indeed, smuggling is considered to be a "victimless crime" or, alternatively, it is not the smuggled person, but the state that person enters irregularly, which is considered to be the "victim" of smuggling.[31]

In summary, the definitions of "trafficking in persons" and "smuggling of migrants" and their interplay create two main assumptions: That trafficked persons are forced into trafficking, while smuggled persons migrate voluntarily, and that the former experience harm in the process and therefore need protection, while the latter do not experience harm and thus need not be protected. Thus, criminal law constructs a binary between trafficked persons as "victims" and smuggled persons as "illegals" who are considered less deserving of protection and support than trafficked victims because of their original motive—their decision to choose to migrate illegally".[32] As a result, states respond very differently to trafficked persons versus smuggled persons with regard to the protection extended. As the following sections will show, trafficked persons are perceived as being in need of special protection, while smuggled persons are not as easily perceived as victims in need of assistance.

4.3 Trafficked Persons as Victims of Crime

While the Trafficking Directive's definition of trafficking in human beings differs only slightly from the corresponding international law definition, its provisions on the protection of trafficked persons are more generous than those of its international law counterpart. Indeed, while the Trafficking Protocol "does not impose binding identification, assistance and protection obligations",[33] the Trafficking Directive contains a requirement to identify victims, and once there is "a reasonable-grounds indication for believing" that a person has been trafficked, an entitlement to assistance is triggered, which must "not [be] made conditional on the victim's willingness to cooperate in the criminal investigation".[34] The assistance foreseen includes

> at least standards of living capable of ensuring victims' subsistence through measures such as the provision of appropriate and safe accommodation and material assistance, as well as necessary medical treatment including psychological assistance, counselling and information, and translation and interpretation services where appropriate.[35]

The Directive also makes provision for "victims with special needs", stating that Member States "shall attend" to such victims where their special needs "derive, in particular, from whether they are pregnant, their health, a disability, a mental or psychological disorder they have, or a serious form of psychological, physical or sexual violence they have suffered".[36] Further, the Directive specifies that Member States shall provide access to legal counselling and legal representation—including for the purpose of claiming compensation—free of charge in cases where the trafficked person in question does not have sufficient means.[37] It also states that trafficked persons must have access to asylum procedures.[38] Finally, the Directive puts in place special protection for child victims of trafficking, such as supporting them in their "physical and psycho-social recovery", which includes providing access to education.[39]

In addition, trafficked persons have rights under the Residence Permit Directive. Member States "*shall* apply this Directive to the third-country nationals who are, or have been victims of offences related to the trafficking in human beings".[40] Thus, trafficked persons are entitled to a recovery and reflection period, during which they cannot be removed from the territory.[41] After the expiry of the reflection period, Member States "shall consider" issuing trafficked persons with residence permits, but only where they intend to cooperate in the criminal investigation and have severed all ties with their traffickers.[42] These residence permits come with additional entitlements, for example, access to "necessary" medical care for trafficked persons with special needs (and insufficient resources), "such as pregnant women, the disabled or victims of sexual violence or other forms of violence".[43] Residence permits lead to access to the labour market, to vocational training and to education, though it is up to individual Member States to define the rules for access.[44]

Overall, a number of procedural and substantive rights derive from the status of "victim of trafficking". While these rights are certainly "limited in terms of both time and substance",[45] trafficking "victims" are clearly seen as being in need of special assistance and support.

4.4 Smuggled Persons as Victims of Crime?

Smuggled persons, meanwhile, are not conceived of as needing similar levels of support. The Facilitation Directive, which defines the crime of facilitation of unauthorised entry and stay, and its accompanying Framework Decision do not contain any provisions on protection for the "victims" of the relevant offences.[46] The same is true of the proposal for a recast Facilitation Directive.[47] However, Member States "*may* apply" the Residence Permit Directive to "third-country nationals who have been the subject of an action to facilitate illegal immigration".[48] The wording of this provision, however, suggests that smuggled persons are not "victims", like trafficked persons, but merely the "subjects" of criminal conduct.

Nevertheless, the victim protection provisions of the Residence Permit Directive *may* be applied to smuggled persons, so that they, too, may be able to benefit from, *inter alia*, a recovery and reflection period, medical treatment (but only where the individual concerned has insufficient means and special needs), as well as access to the labour market (the conditions and procedures for this are defined by Member States).[49] It must be kept in mind, however, that the main purpose of the Residence Permit Directive is not to protect irregular migrants, but to "combat illegal immigration"[50] and to incentivise irregular migrants to cooperate in criminal proceedings against those who facilitate such migration.[51]

Overall, as Gallagher and David have noted, "the status of 'smuggled migrant' has not been elevated to a legal category to which any special or additional rights are attached".[52] Even though both trafficking and smuggling are crimes under international and EU law, trafficked persons are perceived as victims of crime who need (admittedly limited) assistance measures, while smuggled persons are not normally perceived as "victims", a status which instead may be extended to them on a discretionary basis if they are perceived to be useful in criminal proceedings.

At the same time, the fact that the Residence Permit Directive's provisions may be extended to smuggled persons raises the question of whether they, too, should be perceived and treated as victims of crime, not on a discretionary basis, but as a matter of course. The next section compares trafficked and smuggled persons' experiences to examine whether drawing a distinction between the two groups is justified and whether, like trafficked persons, smuggled persons can satisfy the Victim Protection Directive's definition of "victim of crime".[53]

4.5 Trafficked and Smuggled Persons' Experiences: Challenging Assumptions

As evident from the discussion above, being identified as either a trafficked or a smuggled person has real consequences in terms of protection, assistance, and the right to remain in the territory of the state a person was trafficked or smuggled into. Yet, the relevant EU legal instruments (and indeed their international law counterparts) engage with trafficked and smuggled persons' experiences only selectively and in order to reinforce the distinction between the two, rather than depicting the complexities of trafficking and smuggling. This section seeks to challenge the assumption that trafficked persons are forced migrants in need of protection, whereas smuggled persons are voluntary migrants not in need of protection. It does so by contrasting the legal framing of trafficked and smuggled persons with their *actual* experiences, focusing on their inability to take safe and legal migration routes and their resulting experiences during irregular migration.

Trafficked and smuggled persons are often, literally, in the same boat when travelling irregularly. Indeed, "smugglers and traffickers often adopt the same routes and transportation".[54] This is because extraterritorial border controls prevent irregular migrants from travelling to states of destination legally and safely.[55] The fact that the vast majority of asylum seekers who come to the EU, many of whom are later recognised as refugees, have to rely on the services of smugglers to reach EU territory points to the fact that, in many instances, neither the departure nor the means of transport was chosen freely.[56] Thus, traffickers and smugglers use the same routes and means of transportation, because travelling regularly is difficult.

Without a visa, it is almost impossible to travel by regular transport. Visa requirements and carrier sanctions "have driven asylum flows underground, 'irregularizing' movement towards the EU, and leaving protection seekers with no alternative but to rely on smuggling services (or fall prey to traffickers) to reach safety".[57] Both trafficked and smuggled persons are likely to travel irregularly, not because they wish to do so, but because regular migration pathways are closed to them. In light of this, it is difficult to uphold the claim that relying on smugglers is voluntary while trafficking is coerced. Irregular migrants are forced to rely on traffickers and smugglers, because these facilitators are their best hope of making it to their destination alive.[58]

As a result of their similar modes of travel, trafficked and smuggled persons' experiences during their migratory journeys are also very much alike. The UNHCR Trafficking Guidelines provide a useful summary of possible experiences in the trafficking context. These can include "abduction, incarceration, rape, sexual enslavement, enforced prostitution, forced labour, removal of organs, physical beatings, starvation [and] the deprivation of medical treatment".[59] While some of these harms may be inferred from the trafficking definition, UNHCR provides a more comprehensive picture of trafficked persons' experiences.

This is the case even more so for smuggled persons, whose experiences of harm are almost entirely omitted in anti-smuggling legislation. Indeed, UNHCR also provides an overview of the experiences of smuggled persons. Types of harm encountered by this group on the journey to Europe include "abuse and violence by smugglers", as well as kidnappings, "sexual violence and torture", and forced labour.[60] Stoyanova notes that being smuggled "can involve truly traumatic experiences, including physical violence, rape, loss of family members, etc., and can be even more traumatic than being deceived and forced to migrate to the EU for the purpose of exploitation".[61] Further, once smuggled persons reach the country of destination, they may continue to experience harm. Whereas "trafficking [is] considered an ongoing and relational process that violate[s] rights", the relationship between the smuggler and the smuggled person is thought to end upon entry into their destination country.[62] In reality, however, smuggled persons "may be forced into drug pushing, prostitution, begging, or theft" once in the country of destination in order to "repay smuggling debts".[63] They may also be exploited by persons other than smugglers in countries of transit and destination due to a lack of a right to work.[64] Indeed, both trafficked and smuggled persons may become victims of a range of crimes during migration, a reality that Rijken refers to as "victimmigration".[65] These similarities are not reflected in the trafficking and smuggling definitions and make it difficult to distinguish between both practices. Overall, when examining trafficked and smuggled persons' actual experiences, the distinction between the two, and the claim that the former need protection while the latter do not, appears extremely questionable.

Returning to the question of whether smuggled persons are victims of crime for the purpose of EU law, the foregoing discussion shows that they are, indeed, likely to meet the Victim Protection Directive's definition of "victim of crime". Smuggled persons are likely to have "suffered harm, including physical, mental or emotional harm . . . which was directly caused by a criminal offence".[66] It may, of course, be questioned how strictly the term "directly" should be interpreted in the context of smuggling, since it is states' migration management strategies that create the crime of smuggling and, therefore, the harm experienced in this context, a point I will return to below. In addition, since many irregular migrants die in the course of attempting to reach their destination countries, smuggled persons may also be "family members of a person whose death was directly caused by a criminal offence and who have suffered harm as a result of that person's death".[67] This, in turn, raises the question of why EU law does not recognise smuggled migrants as victims of crime who have protection needs similar to those of trafficked persons.

4.6 Who Is the "Vulnerable" Victim?

While smuggled persons are likely to fit the Victim Protection Directive's definition of "victim of crime", the Directive offers little in the way of concrete support, so that meeting the definition, in itself, is of limited use. The Directive focuses largely on providing information and referrals to support services,[68] rather than concrete assistance, while also providing for rights related to the participation in criminal proceedings[69]—guarantees which are less extensive than those provided by the Trafficking Directive and the Residence Permit Directive. The 2023 proposal for a recast Victim Protection Directive contains some more concrete assistance measures, notably free psychological assistance, and additional protection measures for child victims.[70]

Nevertheless, the Victim Protection Directive also contains information on the circumstances entitling victims of crime to special protection, which may also apply to smuggled persons. Recital 38 of the Directive states:

> Persons who are *particularly vulnerable* or who find themselves *in situations that expose them to a particularly high risk of harm*, such as persons subjected to repeat violence in close relationships, victims of gender-based violence, or persons who fall victim to other types of crime in a Member State of which they are not nationals or residents, *should be provided with specialist support and legal protection.*[71]

The Victim Protection Directive also states that Member States are obliged to

> ensure that victims receive a timely and individual assessment, in accordance with national procedures, to *identify specific protection needs* and to determine whether and to what extent they would benefit from special measures in the course of criminal proceedings . . . due to their *particular vulnerability to secondary and repeat victimisation, to intimidation and to retaliation.*[72]

The Directive then clarifies that it is the victims' "relationship to and dependence on the offender" that makes them "particularly vulnerable", going on to state that "[i]n this regard, victims of terrorism, organised crime, human trafficking, gender-based violence, violence in a close relationship, sexual violence, exploitation or hate crime, and victims with disabilities shall be duly considered".[73] The proposal for a recast Victim Protection Directive contains a similar list of "particularly vulnerable" groups, while expanding this to include different types of gender-based violence.[74] Notably, the EU has legislated to offer additional protections to some of these groups—victims of trafficking and terrorism, as well as child victims of sexual abuse.[75]

As mentioned already, smuggled persons, however, receive no special protection under EU law. While smuggled persons may be considered to be "particularly vulnerable" under the Victim Protection Directive—when the smugglers are part of an organised criminal group, and the smuggled persons in question are therefore victims of an organised crime, or when the smuggled persons have a disability—they are not named as a "vulnerable" group. Similarly, the proposal for a recast Facilitation Directive designates some smuggled persons as "particularly vulnerable, including unaccompanied minors", though for the purpose of establishing what constitutes an aggravated criminal offence, rather than for victim protection.[76] Again, smuggled persons generally are not seen as vulnerable. This is likely so because it is assumed that smuggled persons' relationship to and dependence on the offender end upon entry into the country of destination, so that there is no risk of secondary and repeat victimisation, intimidation, or retaliation. Yet, as mentioned above, it is well known that smuggled persons may face exploitation to repay smuggling debts.

This observation alone serves to question why smuggled persons receive no special protection under EU law, as the Victim Protection Directive explicitly mentions that "victims of exploitation" should be considered to be particularly vulnerable. In addition, smuggled persons may be said to experience secondary and repeat victimisation, not necessarily from smugglers, but from the state, a proposition I will explore below. In order to comment further on why smuggled persons, too, ought to be entitled to special protection and why they may be at risk of secondary and repeat victimisation, it is pertinent to explore in more detail the circumstances that render smuggled persons vulnerable. Thus, the next section examines the notion of vulnerability in some detail, while considering how vulnerability theory can be applied to smuggled persons as victims of crime.

4.7 Vulnerability as a Key to Understanding Protection Needs

The proposition that there is a connection between vulnerability and protection needs is widely accepted. Fineman developed vulnerability theory as an alternative to the anti-discrimination framework, proposing that it should be the responsibility of the state to address individual vulnerabilities to achieve equality.[77] She proposes that "[v]ulnerability initially should be understood as arising from [human] embodiment, which carries with it the ever-present possibility of harm, injury, and misfortune from mildly adverse to catastrophically devastating events, whether accidental, intentional, or otherwise".[78] At the same time, she explains that vulnerability is "experienced uniquely by each of us",[79] due to differences between individuals, for example, with respect to health or economic or social capital.[80] Thus, Fineman conceives of vulnerability as being both universal and particular. While personal characteristics and a lack of resources can exacerbate a person's vulnerability, such characteristics and resources can also "provide individuals with "resilience" in the face of vulnerability".[81]

Building on Fineman's vulnerability theory, Mackenzie et al. propose a "taxonomy of three different sources of vulnerability (i.e., *inherent*, *situational*, and *pathogenic*) and two different states of vulnerability (i.e., *dispositional* and *occurrent*)".[82] Inherent vulnerability broadly corresponds to Fineman's conceptualisation of vulnerability as universal, described by Mackenzie et al. as "intrinsic to the human condition" and related to the state of the physical body, including its age and health.[83] Situational vulnerability, on the other hand, is "context-specific" and is "caused or exacerbated by the personal, social, political, economic, or environmental situations of individuals or social groups".[84] Pathogenic vulnerability is "a subset of situational vulnerability" and arises through "morally dysfunctional or abusive interpersonal and social relationships and sociopolitical oppression or injustice".[85] Both forms of vulnerability—inherent and situational—Mackenzie et al. argue, can be either dispositional (where there is the potential to experience vulnerability) or occurrent (where, as the term suggests, vulnerability actually occurs).[86] What Fineman's and Mackenzie et al.'s approaches to conceptualising vulnerability have in common is an interest in understanding the reason(s) for exposure to harm by identifying the relevant sources of vulnerability.

Analysing the legislation governing trafficked and smuggled persons as victims of crime in light of Mackenzie et al.'s taxonomy thus serves to identify EU law's view of why victims of crime generally, and trafficked persons specifically, are at risk of harm and thus in need of protection. This analysis shows that the EU Directives take different views of the relevant sources of vulnerability. First, the Victim Protection Directive focuses mainly on situational vulnerability while adopting a group-based approach to defining such vulnerability. Thus, trafficked persons, as a group, are perceived as vulnerable[87] but smuggled persons are not, unless they are victims of organised crime or exploitation, or they have disabilities. Vulnerability for the purpose of the Victim Protection Directive largely stems from the victim's relationship to the offender and may, therefore, also be described as pathogenic. In addition, there is an inherent aspect to the Directive's conceptualisation of vulnerability, as evident from its mention of disability as a decisive factor.

Second, the Trafficking Directive mentions inherent and situational sources of vulnerability. Prior to its 2024 amendment, the Directive considered that where the offence of trafficking "is committed . . . against a particularly vulnerable victim, the penalty should be more severe", explaining that "particularly vulnerable persons should include at least all children", while "[o]ther factors that could be taken into account when assessing the vulnerability of a victim include, for example, gender, pregnancy, state of health and disability".[88] Thus, at the time, the Directive focused on the inherent vulnerabilities of a group—trafficked persons—that the Victim Protection Directive sees as situationally vulnerable. Notably, following the 2024 amendment, the Directive no longer mentions these factors in relation to offences committed against "particularly vulnerable" victims with the exception of age.[89] It does, however, refer to "victims with special needs", who are defined in a similar manner to the "particularly vulnerable persons" in the former version of the Directive, that is, in terms of inherent vulnerabilities like pregnancy, mental and physical health, and disability, as well as situational (or pathogenic) vulnerability brought about by having experienced violence.[90] In addition, the Directive offers an explanation of the situational factors that make individuals vulnerable to trafficking in the first place, mentioning "[p]overty, conflict, inequality, gender-based violence, the absence of viable employment opportunities or social support, humanitarian crisis, statelessness and discrimination".[91]

Finally, the Residence Permit Directive views all third-country nationals who fall within its scope—that is, both trafficked and smuggled persons—as vulnerable,[92] but it does not explain where this vulnerability stems from. Returning to the Victim Protection Directive assists in interpreting the Residence Permit Directive insofar as the former seems to suggest that third-country nationals, as a group, are situationally vulnerable, speaking of the vulnerability of "persons who fall victim to other types of crime in a Member State *of which they are not nationals or residents*".[93]

These different conceptualisations of vulnerability across related EU legal instruments illustrate some of the concept's shortcomings. Indeed, the vulnerability concept is both overused and undertheorised, which can result in its use "obscur[ing] the needs of specific groups and individuals".[94] Thus, designating an entire group as "vulnerable" can lead to essentialising and stigmatising members of that group and overlooking differences within the group.[95] At the same time, as demonstrated by the discussion above, it can exclude from protection those who are not part of the identified group.[96] In addition, vulnerability carries mainly negative connotations, and the use of the concept can result in a denial of agency, as well as attempts to impose assistance and to control the behaviour of "vulnerable" persons.[97] Nevertheless, as Mackenzie et al.'s taxonomy demonstrates, when theorised carefully, the vulnerability concept can illuminate the complexities surrounding the question of why an individual may be exposed to harm. Thus, the next section seeks to clarify where vulnerability stems from in the context of irregular migration and why both trafficked and smuggled persons are at risk of harm and are therefore in need of protection.

4.8 "Vulnerable" Irregular Migrants: Towards an Understanding of State-Sponsored and Consequential Vulnerability

The conceptualisation of vulnerability in the three Directives discussed above is extremely limited, as it only considers the victim's relationship to the offender, a range of "root causes" of trafficking,[98] and a number of inherent factors as sources of vulnerability, but without inquiring where the latter stem from. To fully understand why both trafficked and smuggled persons are vulnerable, it is important to acknowledge, first of all, that there is no singular experience of either trafficking or smuggling. Thus, rather than considering trafficked and smuggled persons' vulnerability on a group basis, it is necessary to consider each individual and their unique experiences.

Nevertheless, it is possible to make some general observations about the sources of vulnerability in the context of irregular migration. While irregular migrants may indeed have inherent vulnerabilities related to their age, gender, or disability, and while they may also experience pathogenic vulnerability as a result of abusive relationships with traffickers and smugglers, vulnerability in the irregular migration context is largely situational and produced not solely by "root causes" in countries of origin, but also by states of destination. As explained above, trafficking and smuggling, and therefore the abuse and harm experienced in this context, exist only because of destination states' migration policies. These policies may well be described as pathogenic—indicating sociopolitical injustice. Interestingly, the 2024 amendment of the Trafficking Directive introduces a Recital stating that "[s]tateless persons are at greater risk of becoming victims of trafficking in human beings", urging states to "pay particular attention to that vulnerable group".[99] The text does not, however, explain why this increased risk exists, that is, because stateless persons lack documents are therefore forced to travel irregularly.

Furthermore, once irregular migrants have arrived in their destination countries, they continue to experience the effects of restrictive migration policies. States force irregular migrants into punitive status determination processes, with restrictive rules on the right to work and on family reunification.[100] This, in turn, often leads to destitution and, as a result, to the risk of forced labour or exploitation.[101] As such, a continuing abusive relationship with traffickers or smugglers is not the only source of irregular migrants' situational vulnerability. On the contrary, migrants are exposed to harm, such as exploitation, as a result of the political choice to marginalise them in society. Yet, EU law does not take into account the state and its actions as a source of vulnerability.

Equally, EU law does not take into account the consequences of this state-sponsored vulnerability. It is important to understand that most of the inherent vulnerabilities mentioned in the legislation—especially pregnancy and state of health, but possibly also disability—are likely to be brought about by the experience of being trafficked (or smuggled).[102] Mackenzie et al.'s taxonomy lacks a term for vulnerability caused by a particular experience. Elsewhere, I have suggested "consequential vulnerability" to describe inherent or situational vulnerabilities brought about by the initial trafficking (or smuggling) experience.[103] Of course, trafficked and smuggled persons may already have a disability or health condition when embarking on an initial dangerous journey. However, it is likely that the harm experienced during such journeys—which, as mentioned above, includes, for example, incarceration, physical and sexual violence, and forced labour—can bring about additional disabilities or mental or physical health conditions, as well as pregnancy as a result of sexual exploitation and rape. As Mackenzie et al. note, there is no hard and fast distinction between inherent and situational vulnerabilities.[104] The same is true with regard to consequential vulnerability. Indeed, the irregular migration context shows that supposedly inherent vulnerabilities are, in fact, likely to be produced by the situation in which irregular migrants find themselves—having to undertake dangerous journeys and the consequences of harm experienced during such journeys.

By framing health-related vulnerabilities as inherent in the group of trafficked persons and by limiting the acknowledgement of the situational nature of irregular migrants' vulnerability to the situation in countries of origin or their relationship with traffickers and smugglers, rather than the host state, EU criminal law obscures the true sources of irregular migrants' vulnerability. The Residence Permit Directive and the Victim Protection Directive do allude to the state's role in creating irregular migrants' vulnerability, by suggesting that (trafficked and smuggled) third-country nationals are generally vulnerable, but do not name or interrogate the real reasons behind this vulnerability. Of course, this is not surprising, as EU criminal law is limited to protecting trafficked and smuggled persons as victims of crime and therefore operates within the confines of the relevant criminal law definitions, which, as discussed above, perpetuate assumptions about trafficked and smuggled persons and their protection needs. Nevertheless, the above analysis shows that it is unprincipled to confine the limited protections that EU criminal offers to trafficked persons without acknowledging that smuggled persons are often equally vulnerable.

4.9 Repeat and Secondary Victimisation of Irregular Migrants by the State

EU law is unlikely to acknowledge smuggled persons' vulnerability or to properly interrogate the sources of both trafficked and smuggled persons' vulnerability. Doing so would require engaging with the wider context of migration control policies and their harmful effects on the people at the receiving end of these measures. Since it is impossible to separate the "crimes" of trafficking and smuggling from the broader context of border control, a serious engagement with trafficked and smuggled persons' vulnerability and their protection needs would require interrogating how irregular migrants are re-victimised—not just by traffickers and smugglers but also by the state.

The Victim Protection Directive strongly emphasises the importance of preventing repeat and secondary victimisation. It calls on Member States to "ensure that measures are available to protect victims and their family members from secondary and repeat victimisation, from intimidation and from retaliation, including against the risk of emotional or psychological harm".[105] The Directive does not define either secondary or repeat victimisation; however, the former is generally understood to mean "victimization that occurs not as a direct result of the criminal act but through the response of institutions and individuals to the victim".[106] Repeat victimisation, meanwhile, as the term suggests, refers to repeatedly becoming a victim of crime, whether "the same or different crime types".[107]

4.9.1 Secondary Victimisation

Spena, in discussing secondary victimisation of smuggled persons in the context of the UN Smuggling Protocol, notes that since smuggled persons "have rights that states may infringe while fighting against smugglers", states may "victimize them through actions carried out against smugglers".[108] As Patanè argues, in the EU law context, this includes states criminalising migrants who facilitate their own (and others') journeys.[109] Furthermore, secondary victimisation includes the "refusal to recognize [an individual's] experience as criminal victimization".[110] Such a refusal is clearly present in cases of smuggled persons. As such, it is not only the response of the state and its institutions to smuggled persons but also the lack of a response towards them *as victims of crime* that leads to secondary victimisation through a resulting lack of protection and assistance. Trafficked persons, too, suffer secondary victimisation, for example, where they cannot benefit from further protection because they are unwilling or unable to cooperate in criminal proceedings (or because no criminal investigation is conducted) and therefore cannot obtain a residence permit.[111] Secondary victimisation may also occur where trafficked persons are not believed and therefore not correctly identified.[112]

This issue of failing to identify trafficked and other "vulnerable" persons is likely to be exacerbated by certain instruments of the EU's New Pact on Migration and Asylum. Even though the Screening Regulation foresees a "vulnerability check" for third-country nationals apprehended in connection with an unauthorised crossing of the external border of a Member State or disembarked after a search and rescue operation, it does not define vulnerability; the concept is conceived of as encompassing being a stateless person, a victim of torture, and other serious harm, or having a need for special reception or procedural guarantees.[113] Elsewhere in the Regulation, "individuals with vulnerabilities" are stated to include "pregnant women, elderly persons, single-parent families, persons with an immediately identifiable physical or mental disability, persons visibly having suffered psychological or physical trauma and unaccompanied minors".[114] Trafficked persons are not mentioned specifically in the Screening Regulation; however, "national authorities in charge of detecting and identifying victims of trafficking in human beings" shall be involved in vulnerability checks, "where appropriate".[115] Given the absence of a more specific provision on identifying trafficked persons in the Regulation and the lack of recognition in EU law generally that smuggled persons experience serious harm, neither group is likely to be considered in the assessment. The Pact instruments also provide for accelerated asylum procedures for a wide range of reasons,[116] and for border procedures,[117] both of which are designed to speed up the assessment of asylum claims and, ultimately, removal, leaving less time for considering applicants' vulnerability.

4.9.2 Repeat Victimisation

With regard to repeat victimisation, the Victim Protection Directive highlights the role of the original offender,[118] that is, in the context of the present discussion, the role of traffickers and smugglers. Yet, the migration management dynamics at play for victims of trafficking and smuggling mean that it is the state that plays the biggest role in the risk of repeat victimisation of trafficked and smuggled persons. As mentioned already, such repeat victimisation may occur where irregular migrants are marginalised and therefore fall victim to exploitation and forced labour in the host state. In addition, where irregular migrants are unable to regularise their status, for example, as refugees, they will be returned to their countries of origin and may be re-trafficked or re-migrate irregularly. Although trafficked and smuggled persons' vulnerabilities also serve as indicators for the risk of re-trafficking and irregular re-migration,[119] currently, only trafficked persons can claim refugee status based on their trafficking experience and the future risks related thereto, while smuggled persons cannot make a similar claim based on their smuggling experience. As such, smuggled persons are at particular risk of re-victimisation as, post return, they will once again be impacted by states' restrictive migration policies.

4.10 Conclusion

There is a definitive hierarchy between trafficked and smuggled persons as victims of crime under EU law. Even though both groups' experiences during migration are very similar, as victims of crime, their protection differs considerably. This differential treatment likely stems, at least in part, from assumptions introduced in the definitions of the offences of trafficking and smuggling, which paint trafficked persons as forced migrants in need of protection and smuggled persons as voluntary migrants who do not need protection.

In addition to limiting protection to a small group of irregular migrants, framing some victims as more worthy of protection than others helps the EU to justify its migration policies. Indeed, it is the framing of trafficked persons as victims of crime which suggests that irregular migrants experience harm only as a result of traffickers' intent to exploit them, rather than as a consequence of punitive migration policies. In refusing to recognise smuggled persons as victims and in presenting a limited view of trafficked persons' vulnerability, EU law obscures states' role in creating irregular migrants' vulnerabilities and protection needs.

Notes

1 For an overview of the rights of victims under EU law, see Valsamis Mitsilegas, *EU Criminal Law* (Bloomsbury Publishing 2022) chapter 6.
2 Directive 2012/29/EU of the European Parliament and of the Council of 25 October 2012 establishing minimum standards on the rights, support, and protection of victims of crime, and replacing Council Framework Decision 2001/220/JHA [2012] OJ L315 (hereinafter, in the chapter, Victim Protection Directive), article 2(1)(a).
3 Directive 2011/36/EU of the European Parliament and of the Council on preventing and combating trafficking in human beings and protecting its victims [2011] OJ L101 (hereinafter, in the Chapter, Trafficking Directive), as amended by Directive (EU) 2024/1712 of the European Parliament and of the Council of 13 June 2024 Amending Directive 2011/36/EU on Preventing and Combating Trafficking in Human Beings and Protecting its Victims [2024] OJ L2024/1712 (hereinafter, in the chapter, Trafficking Amendment Directive), consolidated version available at <https://eur-lex.europa.eu/legal-content/EN/TXT/HTML/?uri=CELEX:02011L0036-20240714> accessed 18 December 2024; Directive 2011/93/EU of the European Parliament and of the Council on combating the sexual abuse and sexual exploitation of children and child pornography [2011] OJ L335; Directive (EU) 2017/541 of the European Parliament and of the Council of 15 March 2017 on combating terrorism and replacing Council Framework Decision 2002/475/JHA and amending Council Decision 2005/671/JHA [2017] OJ L88.
4 Trafficking Directive (consolidated version) (n 3).
5 Council Directive 2004/81/EC of 29 April 2004 on the residence permit issued to third-country nationals who are victims of trafficking in human beings or who have been the subject of an action to facilitate illegal immigration, provided they cooperate with the competent authorities [2004] OJ L261 (hereinafter, in the chapter, Residence Permit Directive).
6 Valsamis Mitsilegas, 'Reforming EU Criminal Law on the Facilitation of Unauthorised Entry: The new Commission Proposal in the Light of the *Kinshasa* Litigation' (2024) 15(1) New Journal of European Criminal Law 3.
7 Rianne Letschert and Conny Rijken, 'Rights of Victims of Crime: Tensions Between an Integrated Approach and a Limited Legal Basis for Harmonisation' (2013) 4(3) New Journal of European Criminal Law 226, 229.
8 According to Eurostat, "in 2022, 37% of registered victims of trafficking in the EU were citizens of Member States". See Eurostat, 'Trafficking in Human Beings Statistics' (January 2024) <https://ec.europa.eu/eurostat/statistics-explained/index.php?title=Trafficking_in_human_beings_statistics&stable=1> accessed 8 March 2024.
9 Vicki Squire, 'The Contested Politics of Mobility: Politicising Mobility, Mobilising Politics' in Vicki Squire (ed), *The Contested Politics of Mobility: Borderzones and Irregularity* (Routledge 2011) 5 (emphasis in original).

10 Trafficking Directive (consolidated version) (n 3) article 2(1).
11 Trafficking Directive (consolidated version) (n 3) article 2(3).
12 Protocol to Prevent, Suppress and Punish Trafficking in Persons, Especially Women and Children, supplementing the United Nations Convention against Transnational Organized Crime (adopted 15 November 2000, entered into force 25 December 2003) 2237 UNTS 319 (hereinafter, in the Chapter, Trafficking Protocol) article 3(a).
13 Trafficking Directive (consolidated version) (n 3) article 2(1).
14 Trafficking Directive (consolidated version) (n 3) article 2(3).
15 Protocol against the Smuggling of Migrants by Land, Sea and Air, Supplementing the United Nations Convention against Transnational Crime (adopted 15 November 2000, entered into force 28 January 2004) 2241 UNTS 480 (hereinafter, in the chapter, Smuggling Protocol) article 3(a).
16 Council Directive 2002/90/EC of 28 November 2002 defining the facilitation of unauthorised entry, transit and residence [2002] OJ L328 (hereinafter, in the Chapter, Facilitation Directive) article 1(1)(a).
17 Proposal for a Directive of the European Parliament and of the Council laying down minimum rules to prevent and counter the facilitation of unauthorised entry, transit, and stay in the Union, and replacing Council Directive 2002/90/EC and Council Framework Decision 2002/946 JHA [2023] COM (2023) 755 final, article 3(1)(a).
18 Mitsilegas (n 6); Johannes Keiler, 'The EU's Facilitators' Package—in the Twilight of Fighting Organised Crime and the (Over)criminalisation of Solidarity: A Comparative Evaluation' in this volume; Flavia Patanè, 'Migrants' Agency in Smuggling Routes: Criminalising Practices and Socio-Legal Implications in the EU' in this volume.
19 See, e.g., Conny Rijken, 'Victimmigration: When Smuggling Becomes Trafficking' in Evangelia (Lilian) Tsourdi and Philippe De Bruycker (eds), *Research Handbook on EU Migration and Asylum Law* (Edward Elgar 2022) 474.
20 Anne T Gallagher, *The International Law of Human Trafficking* (CUP 2010) 29.
21 Benjamin S Buckland, 'Human Trafficking & Smuggling: Crossover & Overlap' in Cornelius Friesendorf (ed), *Strategies Against Human Trafficking: The Role of the Security Sector* (National Defence Academy and Austrian Ministry of Defence and Sports 2009) 155. See also Jayashri Srikantiah, 'Perfect Victims and Real Survivors: The Iconic Victim in Domestic Human Trafficking Law' (2007) 87 Boston University Law Review 157, 187. See further Anne T Gallagher, 'Human Rights and Human Trafficking: Quagmire or Firm Ground—a Response to James Hathaway' (2009) 49(4) Virginia Journal of International Law 789, 792.
22 Maria De Angelis, *Human Trafficking: Women's Stories of Agency* (Cambridge Scholars Publishing 2016) 45.
23 Nils Christie, 'The Ideal Victim' in Ezzat A Fattah (ed), *From Crime Policy to Victim Policy: Reorienting the Justice System* (Macmillan 1986).
24 Rita Haverkamp, 'Victims of Human Trafficking: Considerations from a Crime Prevention Perspective' in Rita Haverkamp, Ester Herlin-Karnell and Claes Lernstedt (eds), *What Is Wrong with Human Trafficking? Critical Perspectives on the Law* (Hart 2019) 55.
25 Haverkamp (n 24) 69.
26 Noemi Magugliani, 'Trafficked Adult Males as (Un)Gendered Protection Seekers: Between Presumption of Invulnerability and Exclusion from Membership of a Particular Social Group' (2022) 34 (3–4) International Journal of Refugee Law 353.
27 Alessandro Spena, 'Smuggled Migrants as Victims? Reflecting on the UN Protocol Against Migrant Smuggling and on Its Implementation' in Serena Forlati (ed), *The Palermo Convention at Twenty: The Challenge of Implementation* (Brill 2021) 52.

28 Anne T Gallagher and Fiona David, *The International Law of Migrant Smuggling* (CUP 2014) 44.
29 Proposal for a recast Facilitation Directive (n 17) article 3(1)(b).
30 cf Mitsilegas (n 6).
31 Rijken (n 19) 474. See also Elspeth Guild, 'Conclusions: The Variable Political and Legal Geography of People Smuggling and Trafficking in Europe' in Elspeth Guild and Paul Minderhoud (eds), *Immigration and Criminal Law in the European Union: The Legal Measures and Social Consequences of Criminal Law in Member States on Trafficking and Smuggling in Human Beings* (Martinus Nijhoff 2006) 411. See further Spena (n 27).
32 International Council on Human Rights Policy (ICHRP), 'Irregular Migration, Migrant Smuggling and Human Rights: Towards Coherence' (2010) 72 <https://documentation.lastradainternational.org/lsidocs/irregular%20migration%20smuggling%20hr_towards%20coherence.pdf> accessed 5 April 2023.
33 Vladislava Stoyanova, *Human Trafficking and Slavery Reconsidered: Conceptual Limits and States' Positive Obligations in European Law* (CUP 2017) 87.
34 Trafficking Directive (consolidated version) (n 3) articles 11(2) and 11(3).
35 Trafficking Directive (consolidated version) (n 3) article 11(5).
36 Trafficking Directive (consolidated version) (n 3) article 11(7).
37 Trafficking Directive (consolidated version) (n 3) 12(2).
38 Trafficking Directive (consolidated version) (n 3) article 11a(2).
39 Trafficking Directive (consolidated version) (n 3) article 14(1).
40 Residence Permit Directive (n 5) article 3(1); emphasis added.
41 Residence Permit Directive (n 5) article 6(1)–(2).
42 Residence Permit Directive (n 5) article 8(1).
43 Residence Permit Directive (n 5) article 9(2).
44 Residence Permit Directive (n 5) article 11.
45 Valsamis Mitsilegas and Niovi Vavoula, 'Criminal Law: Institutional Rebalancing and Judicialisation as Drivers of Policy Change' in Florian Trauner and Ariadna Ripoll Servent (eds), *Policy Change in the Area of Freedom, Security and Justice: How EU Institutions Matter* (Routledge 2015) 142.
46 Facilitation Directive (n 16); Council Framework Decision of 28 November 2002 on the strengthening of the penal framework to prevent the facilitation of unauthorised entry, transit and residence [2002] OJ L328.
47 Proposal for a recast Facilitation Directive (n 17).
48 Residence Permit Directive (n 5) article 3(2); emphasis added.
49 Residence Permit Directive (n 5) articles 6; 9(2); 11.
50 Residence Permit Directive (n 5) Recitals 1 and 2.
51 Residence Permit Directive (n 5) Recital 9.
52 Gallagher and David (n 28) 553.
53 Victim Protection Directive (n 2) article 2(1)(a).
54 Angeliki Dimitriadi, 'The Interrelationship Between Trafficking and Irregular Migration' in Sergio Carrera and Elspeth Guild (eds), *Irregular Migration, Trafficking and Smuggling of Human Beings: Policy Dilemmas in the EU* (CEPS 2016) 67 <www.ceps.eu/wp-content/uploads/2016/02/Irregular%20Migration,%20Trafficking%20and%20SmugglingwithCovers.pdf> accessed 4 April 2023.
55 See, e.g., Thomas Gammeltoft-Hansen, *Access to Asylum: International Refugee Law and the Globalisation of Migration Control* (CUP 2011); Maarten den Heijer, *Europe and Extraterritorial Asylum* (Hart Publishing 2012); Violeta Moreno-Lax, *Accessing Asylum in Europe: Extraterritorial Border Controls and Refugee Rights Under EU Law* (OUP 2017).
56 European Parliament, 'Resolution of 11 December 2018 with Recommendations to the Commission on Humanitarian Visas' (11 December 2018) 2018/2271(INL)

<www.europarl.europa.eu/doceo/document/TA-8-2018-0494_EN.html#title1> accessed 4 April 2023, Recital E.

57 Moreno-Lax (n 55) 119.

58 Khalid Koser, 'Asylum Policies, Trafficking and Vulnerability' (2000) 1 International Migration 91, 103; Luigi Achilli, '"The Good Smuggler": The Ethics and Morals of Human Smuggling Among Syrians' (2018) 676 The Annals of the American Academy of Political and Social Science 77; Tekalign Ayalew Mengiste, 'Refugee Protections from Below: Smuggling in the Eritrea-Ethiopia Context' (2018) 676 The Annals of the American Academy of Political and Social Science 57.

59 UNHCR, 'Guidelines on International Protection No 7: The Application of Article 1A(2) of the 1951 Convention and/or 1967 Protocol Relating to the Status of Refugees to Victims of Trafficking and Persons at Risk of Being Trafficked' (2006) HCR/GIP/06/07 (UNHCR Trafficking Guidelines) para 15.

60 UNHCR, 'Desperate Journeys: Refugees and Migrants Entering and Crossing Europe via the Mediterranean and Western Balkans Routes' (February 2017) <www.unhcr.org/uk/media/desperate-journeys-refugees-and-migrants-entering-and-crossing-europe-mediterranean-and> accessed 8 March 2024.

61 Vladislava Stoyanova, 'Victims of Human Trafficking: A Legal Analysis of the Guarantees for "Vulnerable Persons" Under the Second Phase of the EU Asylum Legislation' in Céline Bauloz and others (eds), *Seeking Asylum in the European Union: Selected Protection Issues Raised by the Second Phase of the Common European Asylum System* (Brill Nijhoff 2015) 77.

62 ICHRP (n 32) 80.

63 Claire Brolan, 'An Analysis of the Human Smuggling Trade and the Protocol Against the Smuggling of Migrants by Land, Air and Sea (2000) from a Refugee Protection Perspective' (2003) 14(4) International Journal of Refugee Law 561, 578–79.

64 Peter Dwyer and others, 'Socio-Legal Status and Experiences of Forced Labour Among Asylum Seekers and Refugees in the UK' (2016) 32(3) Journal of International and Comparative Social Policy 182. See also Rijken (n 19) 476.

65 Rijken (n 19).

66 Victim Protection Directive (n 2) article 2(1)(a)(i).

67 Victim Protection Directive (n 2) article 2(1)(a).

68 Victim Protection Directive (n 2) articles 3–9.

69 Victim Protection Directive (n 2) articles 10–17.

70 Proposal for a Directive of the European Parliament and of the Council amending Directive 2012/29/EU establishing minimum standards on the rights, support, and protection of victims of crime, and replacing Council Framework Decision 2001/220/JHA [2023] COM/2023/424 final.

71 Victim Protection Directive (n 2) Recital 38; emphasis added.

72 Victim Protection Directive (n 2) article 22(1); emphasis added.

73 Victim Protection Directive (n 2) article 22(3).

74 Proposal for a recast Victim Protection Directive (n 70) article 1(10).

75 See n 3 above.

76 Proposal for a recast Facilitation Directive (n 17) article 4(d).

77 Martha Albertson Fineman, 'The Vulnerable Subject: Anchoring Equality in the Human Condition' (2008) 20(1) Yale Journal of Law and Feminism 9.

78 Fineman (n 77) 9.

79 Fineman (n 77) 10.

80 Martha Albertson Fineman, 'Equality, Autonomy, and the Vulnerable Subject in Law and Politics' in Martha Albertson Fineman and Anna Grear (eds), *Vulnerability: Reflections on a New Ethical Foundation for Law and Politics* (Routledge 2016) 21–22.

81 Fineman (n 77) 13.

82 Catriona Mackenzie, Wendy Rogers and Susan Dodds (eds), *Vulnerability: New Essays in Ethics and Feminist Philosophy* (OUP 2014) 7 (italics in original).
83 Mackenzie and others (n 82) 7.
84 Mackenzie and others (n 82) 7.
85 Mackenzie and others (n 82) 9.
86 Mackenzie and others (n 82) 8.
87 It is worth noting that EU asylum law adopts a similar approach in Directive 2013/33/EU of the European Parliament and of the Council of 26 June 2013, which lays down standards for the reception of applicants for international protection (recast) [2013] OJ L180, article 21.
88 Trafficking Directive (2011 version) (n 3) Recital 12.
89 Trafficking Directive (consolidated version) (n 3) article 4(2)(a).
90 Trafficking Directive (consolidated version) (n 3) article 11(7).
91 Trafficking Amendment Directive (n 3) Recital 2.
92 Residence Permit Directive (n 5) Recital 12.
93 Victim Protection Directive (n 2) Recital 38; emphasis added.
94 Alyson Cole, 'All of Us Are Vulnerable, But Some Are More Vulnerable than Others: The Political Ambiguity of Vulnerability Studies, an Ambivalent Critique' (2016) 17(2) Critical Horizons 260, 267.
95 Lourdes Peroni and Alexandra Timmer, 'Vulnerable Groups: The Promise of an Emerging Concept in European Human Rights Convention Law' (2013) 11(4) International Journal of Constitutional Law 1056; Francesca Ippolito and Sara Iglesias Sánchez, 'Introduction' in Francesca Ippolito and Sara Iglesias Sánchez (eds), *Protecting Vulnerable Groups: The European Human Rights Framework* (Hart 2015).
96 Fineman (n 80); Ben Hudson, 'Migration in the Mediterranean: Exposing the Limits of Vulnerability at the European Court of Human Rights' (2018) 4 Maritime Safety and Security Law Journal 37.
97 Peroni and Timmer (n 95) 1056; Lewis Turner, 'The Politics of Labeling Refugee Men as "Vulnerable"' (2021) 28(1) Social Politics: International Studies in Gender, State & Society 1.
98 Trafficking Amendment Directive (n 3) Recital 2; cf Trafficking Protocol (n 12) article 9(4). On the flawed assumption that addressing 'root causes' reduces irregular migration, see Hein de Haas, 'Turning the Tide? Why Development Will Not Stop Migration' (2007) 38(5) Development and Change 819.
99 Trafficking Amendment Directive (n 3) Recital 22.
100 Dwyer and others (n 64) 182. See also Rijken (n 19) 476.
101 Dwyer and others (n 64).
102 Giussy and others note that gender-based violence migrants experience during migratory journeys "can have substantial and long-lasting negative effects on [their] mental, physical, reproductive, and sexual health", see Barbara Giussy and others, 'Sexual Violence and Unwanted Pregnancies in Migrant Women' (2017) 5(4) The Lancet 396, 396.
103 Maja Grundler, '"Route Causes" and Consequences of Irregular (Re-)Migration: Vulnerability as an Indicator of Future Risk in Refugee Law' (2024) 20 International Journal of Law in Context 35.
104 Mackenzie and others (n 82) 8.
105 Victim Protection Directive (n 2) article 18. See also Recitals 9, 17, 38, 46, 52, 53, 54, 55, 57, 58 and 65, as well as articles 9(1)(e), 9(3)(a), 12(1), 22(1), 22(4) and 26(2) of the Victim Protection Directive.
106 UNODC, 'Handbook on Justice for Victims' (1999) 9 <www.unodc.org/pdf/crime/publications/standards_9857854.pdf> accessed 30 March 2023.
107 Louise Nicholas and Graham Farrell, 'Repeat Victimization' in Bonnie S Fisher and Steven P Lab (eds), *Encyclopedia of Victimology and Crime Prevention* (Sage 2010).

108 Spena (n 27) 51.
109 Patanè (n 18).
110 UNODC (n 106) 9.
111 Rijken (n 19) 480–81.
112 Conny Rijken and others, '(Preventing) Secondary Victimisation of Trafficking Victims Through Law Enforcement Interventions' (2021) 2(1) Journal of Human Trafficking, Enslavement and Conflict-Related Sexual Violence 3.
113 Regulation (EU) 2024/1356 of the European Parliament and of the Council of 14 May 2024 introducing the screening of third-country nationals at the external borders and amending Regulations (EC) No 767/2008, (EU) 2017/2226, (EU) 2018/1240 and (EU) 2019/817 [2024] OJ L2024/1356 (hereinafter, in the Chapter, Screening Regulation), articles 1(b), 12(3) and Recital 27.
114 Screening Regulation (n 113) Recital 38.
115 Screening Regulation (n 113) article 8(9).
116 Regulation (EU) 2024/1348 of the European Parliament and of the Council of 14 May 2024 establishing a common procedure for international protection in the Union and repealing Directive 2013/32/EU [2024] OJ L2024/1348 (hereinafter, in the Chapter, Asylum Procedures Regulation) article 42.
117 Asylum Procedures Regulation (n 116) articles 43–45.
118 Victim Protection Directive (n 2) Recitals 53 and 55.
119 Grundler (n 103).

Bibliography

Achilli L, '"The Good Smuggler": The Ethics and Morals of Human Smuggling Among Syrians' (2018) 676 The Annals of the American Academy of Political and Social Science 77.

Albertson Fineman M, 'The Vulnerable Subject: Anchoring Equality in the Human Condition' (2008) 20 Yale Journal of Law and Feminism 9.

Albertson Fineman M, 'Equality, Autonomy, and the Vulnerable Subject in Law and Politics' in Albertson Fineman M and Grear A (eds), *Vulnerability: Reflections on a New Ethical Foundation for Law and Politics* (Routledge 2016).

Brolan C, 'An Analysis of the Human Smuggling Trade and the Protocol Against the Smuggling of Migrants by Land, Air and Sea (2000) from a Refugee Protection Perspective' (2003) 14 International Journal of Refugee Law 561.

Buckland BS, 'Human Trafficking & Smuggling: Crossover & Overlap' in Friesendorf C (ed), *Strategies Against Human Trafficking: The Role of the Security Sector* (National Defence Academy and Austrian Ministry of Defence and Sports 2009).

Christie N, 'The Ideal Victim' in Ezzat Fattah A (ed), *From Crime Policy to Victim Policy: Reorienting the Justice System* (MacMillan 1986).

Cole A, 'All of Us Are Vulnerable, But Some Are More Vulnerable than Others: The Political Ambiguity of Vulnerability Studies, an Ambivalent Critique' (2016) 17 Critical Horizons 260.

De Angelis M, *Human Trafficking: Women's Stories of Agency* (Cambridge Scholars Publishing 2016).

De Haas H, 'Turning the Tide? Why Development Will Not Stop Migration' (2007) 38 Development and Change 819.

Den Heijer M, *Europe and Extraterritorial Asylum* (Hart Publishing 2012).

Dimitriadi A, 'The Interrelationship Between Trafficking and Irregular Migration' in Sergio Carrera and Elspeth Guild (eds), *Irregular Migration, Trafficking and Smuggling of Human Beings: Policy Dilemmas in the EU* (CEPS 2016).

Dwyer P and others, 'Socio-Legal Status and Experiences of Forced Labour Among Asylum Seekers and Refugees in the UK' (2016) 32 Journal of International and Comparative Social Policy 182.
Gallagher AT, 'Human Rights and Human Trafficking: Quagmire or Firm Ground—a Response to James Hathaway' (2009) 49 Virginia Journal of International Law 789.
Gallagher AT, *The International Law of Human Trafficking* (CUP 2010).
Gallagher AT and David F, *The International Law of Migrant Smuggling* (CUP 2014).
Gammeltoft-Hansen T, *Access to Asylum: International Refugee Law and the Globalisation of Migration Control* (CUP 2011).
Giussy B and others, 'Sexual Violence and Unwanted Pregnancies in Migrant Women' (2017) 5 The Lancet 396.
Grundler M, '"Route Causes" and Consequences of Irregular (Re-)Migration: Vulnerability as an Indicator of Future Risk in Refugee Law' (2024) 20 International Journal of Law in Context 35.
Guild E, 'Conclusions: The Variable Political and Legal Geography of People Smuggling and Trafficking in Europe' in Guild E and Minderhoud P (eds), *Immigration and Criminal Law in the European Union: The Legal Measures and Social Consequences of Criminal Law in Member States on Trafficking and Smuggling in Human Beings* (Nijhoff 2006).
Haverkamp R, 'Victims of Human Trafficking: Considerations from a Crime Prevention Perspective' in Haverkamp R, Herlin-Karnell E and Lernstedt C (eds), *What Is Wrong with Human Trafficking? Critical Perspectives on the Law* (Hart 2019).
Hudson B, 'Migration in the Mediterranean: Exposing the Limits of Vulnerability at the European Court of Human Rights' (2018) 4 Maritime Safety and Security Law Journal 37.
Ippolito F and Iglesias Sánchez S, 'Introduction' in Ippolito F and Iglesias Sánchez S (eds), *Protecting Vulnerable Groups: The European Human Rights Framework* (Hart 2015).
Keiler J, 'The EU's Facilitators' Package—in the Twilight of Fighting Organised Crime and the (Over)criminalisation of Solidarity: A Comparative Evaluation' in this volume.
Koser K, 'Asylum Policies, Trafficking and Vulnerability' (2000) 1 International Migration 91.
Letschert R and Rijken C, 'Rights of Victims of Crime: Tensions Between an Integrated Approach and a Limited Legal basis for Harmonisation' (2013) 4 New Journal of European Criminal Law 226.
Mackenzie C and others (eds), *Vulnerability: New Essays in Ethics and Feminist Philosophy* (OUP 2014).
Magugliani N, 'Trafficked Adult Males as (Un)Gendered Protection Seekers: Between Presumption of Invulnerability and Exclusion from Membership of a Particular Social Group' (2022) 34 International Journal of Refugee Law 353.
Mengiste TA, 'Refugee Protections from Below: Smuggling in the Eritrea-Ethiopia Context' (2018) 676 The Annals of the American Academy of Political and Social Science 57.
Mitsilegas V, *EU Criminal Law* (Bloomsbury Publishing 2022).
Mitsilegas V, 'Reforming EU Criminal Law on the Facilitation of Unauthorised Entry: The New Commission Proposal in the Light of the *Kinshasa* Litigation' (2024) 15 New Journal of European Criminal Law 3.
Mitsilegas V and Vavoula N, 'Criminal Law: Institutional Rebalancing and Judicialisation as Drivers of Policy Change' in Trauner F and Servant AR (eds), *Policy Change in the Area of Freedom, Security and Justice: How EU Institutions Matter* (Routledge 2015).

Moreno-Lax V, *Accessing Asylum in Europe: Extraterritorial Border Controls and Refugee Rights Under EU Law* (OUP 2017).
Nicholas L and Farrell G, 'Repeat Victimization' in Fisher BS and Lab SP (eds), *Encyclopedia of Victimology and Crime Prevention* (Sage 2010).
Patanè F, 'Migrants' Agency in Smuggling Routes: Criminalising Practices and Socio-Legal Implications in the EU' in this volume.
Peroni L and Timmer A, 'Vulnerable Groups: The Promise of an Emerging Concept in European Human Rights Convention Law' (2013) 11 International Journal of Constitutional Law 1056.
Rijken C, 'Victimmigration: When Smuggling Becomes Trafficking' in Tsourdi E and De Bruycker P (eds), *Research Handbook on EU Migration and Asylum Law* (Edward Elgar 2022).
Rijken C and others, '(Preventing) Secondary Victimisation of Trafficking Victims Through Law Enforcement Interventions' (2021) 2 Journal of Human Trafficking, Enslavement and Conflict-Related Sexual Violence 3.
Spena A, 'Smuggled Migrants as Victims? Reflecting on the UN Protocol Against Migrant Smuggling and on its Implementation' in Forlati S (ed), *The Palermo Convention at Twenty: The Challenge of Implementation* (Brill | Nijhoff 2021).
Squire V, 'The Contested Politics of Mobility: Politicising Mobility, Mobilising Politics' in Squire V (ed), *The Contested Politics of Mobility: Borderzones and Irregularity* (Routledge 2011).
Srikantiah J, 'Perfect Victims and Real Survivors: The Iconic Victim in Domestic Human Trafficking Law' (2007) 87 Boston University Law Review 157.
Stoyanova V, 'Victims of Human Trafficking: A Legal Analysis of the Guarantees for "Vulnerable Persons" Under the Second Phase of the EU Asylum Legislation' in Bauloz C and others (eds), *Seeking Asylum in the European Union: Selected Protection Issues Raised by the Second Phase of the Common European Asylum System* (Brill | Nijhoff 2015).
Stoyanova V, *Human Trafficking and Slavery Reconsidered: Conceptual Limits and States' Positive Obligations in European Law* (CUP 2017).
Turner L, 'The Politics of Labeling Refugee Men as "Vulnerable"' (2021) 28 Social Politics: International Studies in Gender, State & Society 1.

5 Crimmigration as Hate Speech

Alessandro Spena

5.1 Introduction

Crimmigration is the merging of migration law and criminal law through which Western states today typically pursue the goal of tackling mass immigration with a view to the territorial and social exclusion of the unwanted foreigner.[1] The subject of this contribution is the complex relationship of crimmigration with hate speech. Crimmigration finds in hate speech against the mass-foreigner (in the discursive construction, on a widespread and media level, of the unwanted foreigner as a dangerous open crowd,[2] an enemy, and a parasite) a possible basis of legitimisation: An alternative basis to the democratic–republican-inspired one that the use of criminal law generally claims for itself, at least on a rhetorical level.[3] Racial, ethnic, xenophobic stereotypes and corresponding scaremongering and securitarian constructions of the migration theme then serve to shape the platform of problems and needs to which crimmigration purports to respond.[4] In this way, it ends up taking on political contents and goals which, at least in part, themselves trace the model of hate speech against the mass-foreigner: The verbalisation of crimmigration (the discursive illustration of its contents and aims) cannot but unmask its hate-speaking soul, that is, the fact that those contents and goals are typical of hate speech.

By aiming crimmigration against unwanted foreigners, states make them the targets of an institutional hate speech, of coercive norms and practices whose meaning is, precisely, hatred towards them:[5] A hate speech endowed with the authoritativeness, the illocutionary force inherent in institutional, official discourse. This, in turn, triggers a circular process whereby crimmigration—as authoritative hate speech—ends up reinforcing the sense of self-legitimisation that already underpins the widespread hate speech against the mass-foreigner. Crimmigration backs up this hate speech, providing institutional confirmation of the stereotypes and alarmism that the circulating hateful narratives of the mass-foreigner feed on, and thus sublimates them into official truths.

DOI: 10.4324/9781003378440-5

5.2 A Brief Account of Hate Speech

What is hate speech exactly? At the normative level, this concept has, by now, taken on a rather well-established definition at its core: An aggressive or derogatory manifestation of hostility towards a discriminated social group or an individual regarded as an exponent of such a group. In the Appendix to the Recommendation of the Committee of Ministers of the Council of Europe on combating hate speech, to give but one example,

> hate speech is understood as all types of expression that incite, promote, spread or justify violence, hatred or discrimination against a person or group of persons, or that denigrates them, by reason of their real or attributed personal characteristics or status such as 'race', colour, language, religion, nationality, national or ethnic origin, age, disability, sex, gender identity and sexual orientation.[6]

Hate speech is thus, first of all, a kind of intergroup behaviour, in which "individuals belonging to one group interact, collectively or individually, with another group or its members in terms of their group identification":[7] The hate speaker, claiming to be speaking as an exponent of a certain social group (*ingroup*), manifests hostility either towards a different social group (*outgroup*, or *target group*) or towards certain individuals only by virtue of their being (identified as) instances of the outgroup (*individual target*). Group identification (the identification of a target group, and the identification of an individual target with a target group) takes place through the use of highly depersonalised/collective rhetoric figures (the "nigger", the "faggot", the "southern redneck", the "Sicilian mafioso", the "Muslim") revolving around the possession of certain traits (skin colour, sexual orientation, geographical origin, religious beliefs) considered as indicators of the overall behaviour and way of being of the people who possess them, and therefore capable of defining their very quintessence. The members of the outgroup are thus reduced to "undifferentiated items in a unified social category":[8]

> The phenomena of depersonalisation, dehumanisation, and social stereotyping which tend to increase in scope as and when intergroup relations deteriorate are no more than special instances of this wider principle of the increased *un*differentiation of the outgroup.[9]

A specific hostility is at work in the construction of the target group as a "depersonalised, dehumanised, and socially stereotyped" category: A hostility funded on reasons and arguments that are not specific to the speaker as a private individual, but public in nature, since they relate to the availability of the social space, the possibility of accessing it, and finding a place in it. Those who utter hate speech locate themselves within the perspective of a given sociocultural order, characterised by an asymmetry of power between ingroup and outgroup,[10] an order in which the relevant (physical or virtual) social space is subdivided in such a way that the members of the outgroup are either radically excluded from it or participate in it in a subordinate position: An order in which, in any case, the members of the outgroup are denied full recognition.

The hate speaker speaks to defend, or to re-establish, this order against the claim by members of the outgroup to inhabit the same social space as the ingroup, and to do so on an equal footing with the ingroup's members: Hate speech implies imputing to the target group the wrong of aspiring to full social recognition, of "sneakily mixing"[11] with members of the ingroup. From the perspective of the hate speaker, this is a very serious wrong, since it calls into question "the very foundations of the cultural order, the family and hierarchical differences without which there would be no social order" (Girard calls it *evil of undifferentiation*).[12] Hate speech, in short, serves to claim the exclusion or marginalisation of the target group and its members, as well as the correlative position of privilege and power of the ingroup and its members.

In pronouncing hate speech, the hate speaker takes on certain tasks: (1) The *unmasking/exposition* of the target as a foreign subject, as an alien, as an ontological bearer/carrier of a danger of undifferentiation: By insulting a gay person, the hate speaker points to her as an ontologically different subject; the target is informed that they have been recognised as being different, and, if the insult is uttered in the presence of others, their diversity is also made recognisable as such by them; (2) the *interception* of the target while they are trying to cross the borders of the ingroup's social space or—even worse, from the hate speaker's perspective—while they are roaming undisturbed within those borders; (3) the target's *symbolic repulsion/expulsion* out of this space, the declaration that they must be excluded from there, not necessarily in the physical sense, but more generally in the sense that they must be excluded from enjoying an equal social position—in terms of rights, privileges, dignity—to that of the ingroup's members, bringing them back to their proper role as an excluded or marginalised subject; (4) the *symbolic re-establishment*, or *re-affirmation*, of the integrity/purity of the ingroup, and of the persisting force/validity of the related model of asymmetric power, so as to save the social order from the risk of breaking up.[13]

Understood in this way, not only does hate speech stand in direct contrast to the values of "tolerance and respect for the equal dignity of all human beings [that] constitute the foundations of a democratic, pluralistic society",[14] but it also has a clear political dimension, which is expressed in its presupposing and iterating asymmetries in social power;[15] uttering it is thus a—not necessarily successful—exercise of political power, of the power to define the borders of a certain social space and to establish the limits within which certain people are entitled to stay therein.

5.3 Hate Beach: The Gospel of Crimmigration According to Matthew

Having thus reconstructed the meaning of hate speech, it is not difficult to realise its affinity with crimmigration. First, crimmigration finds its cultural premises in a sociopolitical media narrative steeped in hostility towards the foreigner, conceived not as an individual, but as a mass-foreigner, as the personification of a mass pressing against the boundaries of the community, threatening to break them and overflow into it, to invade its social space and subvert its social and cultural coordinates (not just barbaric invasion, ethnic replacement, Islamisation of the West, but also the increase in crime rates, the burdening of the social welfare system, etc.): Crimmigration is the institutional epiphenomenon of this cultural process of construction of the migrant foreigner as an open mass, of migration as mass deviance, as a massive violation of the norms that define access to the community, and that therefore define the community itself and its social order. This narrative is interwoven with hate speech as it feeds on an endless network of acts of propaganda, verbal aggression, or discrimination against the foreigner, which take shape daily in one-to-one interactions, in traditional media, especially social media, and even in political and institutional discourse.

It is precisely from the political context that it may be useful to draw a concrete example of this type of discourse. One such episode, which has had some media resonance at least in Italy, featured Matteo Salvini, an Italian politician, who, in recent years, has distinguished himself as a swaggering defender of crimmigration policies, to which he actively contributed between 2018 and 2019 as Minister of the Interior, with two "security decrees" (largely focused on immigration issues) and an unprecedented campaign of criminalising NGOs engaged in rescuing migrants in the Mediterranean Sea.[16]

On 24 July 2020, Salvini, who was in the opposition at the time (after being forced to resign as minister in August 2019), commented, while live on Facebook from the beach of Lampedusa, on the arrival of an Italian coast guard ship carrying migrants:[17]

> [T]he government has difficulty in finding money for Lampedusa, but . . . [pointing with his finger to the ship behind him] but . . . now . . . live . . . example of tourists who do not pay, but who are paid to be tourists . . . boat, barge, yet other clandestines who will remain here scrounging at the expense of the Italians. Today we visited the centre which is supposed to host 190 and hosts 800, of which 700 are male, between 20 and 30 years old, robust, adults, strong, mobile phone, hat, sunglasses, nice shoes.[18]

The point of this speech is quite clear: It seeks to dismantle the idea that foreigners rescued at sea are vulnerable individuals in need of assistance and replace it with their portrayal as foreign parasites, well-off people ("mobile phone, hat, sunglasses, nice shoes")[19] light-heartedly choosing to come to Italy in order to exploit the generosity of Italians, who are all, by definition, honest people, forced to work and pay taxes in return for those public benefits and services, which these "other clandestines"[20] (first evocation of the theme of the mass) will enjoy "scrounging".[21] With extreme nonchalance, Salvini completely glosses over the fact that many of these foreigners, if they remain in Italy, will end up picking tomatoes in Sicilian or Apulian fields or otherwise exploited to work in the black economy. His comments are certainly not meant to point out the complexity of the issues raised by immigration but only to plead the need for more severity in the exclusion of unwanted foreigners, hence more crimmigration.

Building on the reputation he gained during his previous experience in government, Salvini is there, in Lampedusa, to show how those who succeeded him in the leadership of the country are unfit to carry out that task (a few seconds later, in the same video on Facebook, he even accused them of being "accomplices of criminals", i.e., migrant smugglers) and to instead credit himself, and his own political party, as the most suitable to pursue securitarian policies to control and limit unwanted immigration:

> [Y]ou see? This is the dock, this is the spectacle of Lampedusa in the evening, with people who are struggling, who have a business, who have a bar, who have a restaurant, who have a shop . . . and that's a warehouse of barges and barges. And you see? There are dozens and dozens in the last few days alone, with landings of hundreds of illegal immigrants, organised landings, with a government that is accomplice to the criminals. Let us say it: it is a government accomplice to criminals! Yesterday there was a record in recent years of landings in Lampedusa. It is not possible! So, I can't wait to go back to government, with serious people, to shut the ports and the criminals [and, at this point, Salvini, it is unclear how intentionally, turns his index finger behind his back, in the direction of the foreign nationals who had just arrived in port] and reopen them to decent people, fishermen, and tourists. All live [the index finger again pointing towards the boat]: this is a day at the end of July; however, I can tell you, if you have saved 2 euro, stay in Italy and have a holiday, come to Lampedusa, come to Sicily, stay in Italy, because the Sicilian and Italian seas are the most beautiful in the world, and [Salvini indicates the vessel once again] we don't need those people there anymore.[22]

5.3.1 "Me Dicen el Clandestino/Yo Soy el Quiebra Ley"

Speeches like this one, which, for several decades, have contributed to defining the political and media narrative about immigration, are, as we can see, explicitly xenophobic, and therefore offensive and discriminatory. Words and expressions used serve first to evoke the arrival of a mass ("*ennesimi clandestini*", "*il centro . . . dovrebbe ospitarne 190 e ne ospita 800*", "*un deposito di barchini e barconi*", "*decine e decine e decine solo negli ultimi giorni*", "*con sbarchi di centinaia di clandestini*", "*il record degli ultimi anni degli sbarchi a Lampedusa*"), and then to describe it in a deliberately frightening and offensive manner: "*clandestini*", "*delinquenti*", "*quella gente là*", or the repeated use of diminutives ("*telefonino, cappellino, occhiali da sole, scarpino*"; "*telefonino, scarpe, catenina, orologino*"), to derogatorily belittle the vulnerable condition in which these people generally find themselves at the moment of disembarkation.

It is worth dwelling, in particular, on the word "clandestine".[23] As the Italian Court of Cassation recently ruled in a case that bears broad similarities with this one,[24] this is a slur, which has now "concretely assumed, in current usage, a derogatory content and a strongly negative valence". This is especially the case if inserted into a more general discourse, in which foreigners referred to as "clandestines" are explicitly portrayed as parasites, usurpers of board and lodging, dedicated to unspecified vices to the detriment of Italian citizens, who suffer from their "invasion", causing such harmful consequences as increased taxation and reduced pensions.[25]

Literally, when used as a noun, "clandestine" is something or someone who is in hiding, who escapes the gaze of an authority that instead claims to see and control her. In this sense, foreigners who, relying on smugglers, undertake the journey across the Mediterranean Sea are, in reality, in most cases, anything but clandestine, since they generally end up turning to the Italian and European authorities in search of rescue and reception.[26] To call them "clandestine" essentially serves to criminalise them, to point to their existential condition as "illegal", "outlawed" subjects. It is no coincidence that Salvini also calls them "delinquents". In fact, the two terms are used as synonyms, or rather, the "clandestine" is depicted as a *species* of delinquent, to refer to the foreigner's criminal status of being an undocumented person, the author of the crime of irregular entry or stay. Theirs is an ontological delinquency, which, from them being a person in a condition of irregularity (an embodied violation of the immigration laws), radiates to their entire social action: The clandestine immigrant, who is a criminal *qua irregular*, is also seen as someone who will also violate other criminal norms (especially norms protecting property or *ordre dans la rue*), because delinquency is in their nature.

Even in this criminalising meaning, however, the use of the term is technically inappropriate. Not only is the implicit assumption of an alleged natural vocation of the irregular foreigner to commit non-migratory crimes obviously unfounded; it is even more radically inaccurate, or at least naïve, to say that all foreigners who arrive in Italy without passing through the established border crossings are in an irregular condition. Many of them are rescued at sea in situations of distress and then brought to an Italian safe port, which makes their entry legal, in accordance with domestic and international law on rescue at sea.[27] Many others apply or aspire to apply for asylum in Italy, and this too makes their presence perfectly regular under domestic and international law.[28]

The word "clandestine", however, also has another meaning, which renders very well the opinion those who use it hold of the people to whom they apply it. Namely, that the unwanted foreigner is a subject without individual identity, a mass-foreigner, a person whose singularity is completely indifferent, since she assumes relevance not as an individual, but as a grain of an indefinite mass, in which each of the people who make it up is dispersed and hidden.

In addition to being replete with slurs, however, Salvini's discourse also bears other features of xenophobic and discriminatory discourse: The people who are the subject of it—in addition to being collectively identified as Other and being gratuitously attributed characteristics, intentions, or aspirations, such as to generate contempt or fear ("*turisti che non pagano, ma che vengono pagati per fare i turisti*", "*ennesimi clandestini che rimarranno qua a scrocco e a spese degli italiani*", "*700 maschi, fra i 20 e 30 anni, robusti, adulti, belli forti*"—subtext: They are many and dangerous; "*telefonino, cappellino, occhiali da sole, scarpino*"—subtext: they are not at all poor victims)—are also explicitly compared with both the Italians (the fishermen, the shopkeepers, all assumed to be honest and hardworking) and the category of the good foreigner, the genuine tourist, the rich one, who is willing to pay for her stay: "Close the ports", "lock up the delinquents (i.e., the 'clandestines')", and open the doors "to good people, fishermen and tourists": A concentration of hostility and discrimination ("the good people" *v* '"hose people over there"), in which one glimpses the elementary enunciation of some of the cornerstones of crimmigration—closing of borders and selection of the foreigner on a national, ethnic. and economic basis; criminalisation of the foreigner who does not pass the border selection (mass-foreigner); use of imprisonment as an ordinary tool of migration management.

There is every reason to hold that acts of political propaganda of this kind, all the more so when they are carried out close to the persons targeted and in such a way that these people can grasp their meaning,[29] constitute forms of discriminatory harassment, as defined in Article 2(3) of Council Directive 2000/43: "an unwanted conduct related to racial or ethnic origin tak[ing] place with the purpose or effect of violating the dignity of a person and of creating an intimidating, hostile, degrading, humiliating or offensive environment".[30] These speeches, in any case, fit squarely into the various definitions of hate speech that exist at national, European, and international levels. They certainly fit, for example, into the definitions of hate speech provided by the Council of Europe in both the Appendix to Council of Europe Recommendation No. R (97) 20 and the Appendix to Recommendation CM/Rec(2022)16), as "forms of expression which spread . . . racial hatred [and] xenophobia . . ., including: intolerance expressed by aggressive nationalism and ethnocentrism, discrimination and hostility against minorities, migrants and people of immigrant origin".[31]

They also fit the notion of "offences concerning racism and xenophobia" in Article 1 of the Council Framework Decision of 28 November 2008 on combatting certain forms and expressions of racism and xenophobia by means of criminal law, as they clearly consist of "intentional conduct[s]" which "publicly incit[e . . .] to hatred directed against a group of persons . . . defined by reference to race, colour, religion, descent or national or ethnic origin".[32] Finally, they also meet the requirements of national legislation incriminating hate speech, such as, for instance, Article 604-bis, paragraph 1(a), of the Italian Criminal Code, which criminalises "whoever spreads ideas based . . . on racial or ethnic hatred, or . . . commits acts of discrimination on racial, ethnic, national or religious grounds".

In order to exclude the relevance of such conduct as a form of hate speech, it is not sufficient to appeal to the right to political criticism. This right, as the Court of Cassation judgement mentioned earlier has made clear,[33] is not a free pass to allow any kind of utterance, but must be balanced with other rights recognised by constitutions and by international and supranational law, including the right to non-discrimination, which is enshrined in Article 14 of the European Convention on Human Rights (ECHR), Article 21 of the Charter of Fundamental Rights of the European Union (EUCFR), Article 10 of the Treaty on the Functioning of the European Union (TFEU), and the Council Directive 2000/43/EC. It is not, in fact, political criticism that constitutes a limit to the moral and legal relevance of discriminatory propaganda (which would be absurd, because such propaganda—having, like any hate speech, an intrinsic political dimension[34]—is always a form of political criticism), but rather the opposite. It is political criticism that finds in discriminatory hate propaganda an external limitation that, if pursued in a proportionate manner, "may be considered necessary in certain democratic societies to sanction or even prevent all forms of expression which spread, incite, promote or justify hatred based on intolerance"[35] and thus to protect those rights that could be intolerably attacked by such extreme and derogatory forms of criticism.[36]

5.4 Crimmigration as Discriminatory Harassment

Speeches of this kind constitute the extreme version of a political and media narrative that has become widespread about immigration in the twenty-first century. And it is precisely in this narrative—in the idea that a person, just because she possesses certain extrinsic characteristics (race, ethnicity, nationality, etc.), is a potential danger to the social order and its orderly functioning, and that society is therefore legitimised to reject or marginalise her—that crimmigration finds its ultimate horizon of meaning, the background of shared beliefs and values on the basis of which it claims to legitimise itself in terms of social consensus, despite its purely expulsive-repulsive nature and the numerous deviations it entails from certain fundamental principles of the system.[37]

These speeches are not mere interpretations that look at crimmigration from the outside without affecting its nature. Instead, they define its purposes, so that crimmigration, seen in the light of these purposes, appears to be itself a hostile speech, a way of using law and bureaucracy that, beyond asepticism and technicalities and beyond the proclaimed deference for the rights of the persons concerned, *communicates* hatred—repulsion and discrimination—towards these persons. I do not mean to say that every single norm and act of crimmigration is hate speech; there are many such norms and acts that, taken individually, have nothing to do with the expression of hatred towards foreigners. What I mean is that the whole political, legal, and administrative strategy we call crimmigration is a complex set of speeches—norms, ministerial circulars, judicial and administrative decisions, police orders and executions of orders, and so on—which, taken as a whole, conveys content, performs functions, and produces effects that are largely the same as the collective hate speech that shapes its horizon of meaning.

Moreover, although I will devote some reflections below to the more specifically verbal dimension of crimmigration,[38] my argument refers, more generally, to a concept of "(hate, hostile) speech or discourse" understood in a broad sense, to include all expressions, verbal and non-verbal.[39] In this sense, crimmigration is the way in which contemporary states enact their hatred against mass-foreigners; hatred against mass-foreigners is the (meta-)meaning overall communicated through that complex set of speeches (statutes, regulations, decisions, and orders) and corresponding actions that we call crimmigration.

However, it could be objected that there is a significant conceptual difference between crimmigration and hate speech, which could make the idea of lumping them together as manifestations of a common logic problematic. In the perspective of crimmigration, indeed, it is necessary that the Other to be excluded is a foreigner, a non-citizen, whereas it is not required that she belongs, or is formally qualified as belonging, to socially discriminated groups. The target of crimmigration is the foreigner who enters or is on the territory of the state in violation of rules established by the latter. It remains formally irrelevant whether she possesses further characteristics, such as belonging to a particular ethnic group or race, professing a certain religion, or having a certain sexual orientation. In short, the irregular foreigner to be excluded is generally not explicitly identified on the basis of other discriminating factors.[40] The opposite is somewhat the case for hate speech: Its target is not necessarily a foreigner;[41] instead, it is a subject who belongs to groups that are socially discriminated against on account of hate factors such as race, ethnicity, religion, sexual orientation, etc.

This difference plays an essential role in the legitimisation of crimmigration. Indeed, the possibility for states to present crimmigration as an aseptic and non-discriminatory policy of enforcing the rules of entry and permanence of foreigners on their territory depends on it. Crimmigration allegedly does not discriminate; it does not treat non-citizens differently due to discriminating factors; it merely enforces the sovereign prerogative of states to close their borders and control migratory flows in order to protect their citizens.

But, it is not difficult to realise how discriminatory crimmigration actually is, despite its apparent aseptic nature, and how discriminatory it is even when judged by the legal standards that the EU and its Member States set themselves to counter discrimination as unlawful behaviour. Both in its abstract normative dimension and in its concrete implementation, crimmigration involves acts and practices that can be subsumed under the legal definition of discrimination, such as that in Article 2 para 2(a) of Council Directive 2000/43/EC, according to which "direct discrimination shall be taken to occur where one person is treated less favourably than another is, has been or would be treated in a comparable situation on grounds of racial or ethnic origin". Suffice it to consider that the European system (EU, but also of the individual Member States) of selection, management, and consequent criminalisation of irregular foreigners is not addressed to any foreigner but only to certain categories of people who are selected, already on an abstract regulatory level, not only on the basis of individual dangerousness indexes but also on the basis of other presumptive and categorising indexes, such as nationality and economic means.[42]

For example, the combined provisions of Article 3 para 1(7) of Council Regulation 2018/1240,[43] and Article 6 of Council Regulation 2016/399[44] identify as the bearer of an "illegal immigration risk" (and therefore as the main target of crimmigration), in addition to the foreigner "considered to be a threat to public policy, internal security, public health or the international relations of any of the Member States", also the indigent foreigner who cannot justify her entry, except with the search for better living conditions, and the one who—for most of the same reasons just mentioned—has not obtained a visa. However, an entry visa is not required of all foreigners, but only of those who come from specific countries, as listed in Council Regulation (EC) 2018/1806,[45] which are basically identified either because they are considered hostile or problematic from the point of view of international relations and public order, or—and this is the most relevant point here—because they are poor or developing countries (mostly African, Asian, or Eastern European). Statistics concerning some aspects of the functioning of crimmigration show data that are perfectly consonant with these premises: Most of the non-EU citizens found to be illegally present in the EU, between 2015 and 2022, come from countries such as Syria, Afghanistan, Morocco, Tunisia, Algeria, Moldova, etc.,[46] and most of the non-EU citizens ordered to leave the EU, in 2021 and 2022, come from Algeria, Morocco, Afghanistan, Pakistan, etc.[47]

In short, crimmigration presupposes and contributes to enforcing a selection of foreigners that is anything but neutral and aseptic from the point of view of factors such as nationality and economic capacity, which have a strong and well-known discriminatory force. The conditions of access to

European territories are decidedly more burdensome for foreigners of certain nationalities, especially if destitute, and this means that they are essentially the ones who flow into the capacious reservoir of irregularity, from which crimmigration then draws its targets.

Moreover, it is difficult not to notice that the combination of the national and economic factors ends up resulting, in practice, in a more creeping, but nevertheless evident and very significant, relevance of other discriminatory factors, such as race, ethnicity, or religion. First of all, those caught in the wheels of crimmigration are essentially foreigners belonging to groups that have historically been the object of social stigmatisation also for racial or ethnic reasons: In Europe, the sub-Saharan African, the North African/Maghreb, the Middle Eastern, the Eastern European. Moreover, scholars have pointed out that, in general, the treatment of irregular migrants is selective: "in practice not all the aliens deprived of legal status are persecuted with the same determination by public authorities".[48] It is often the case that the criteria used to select foreigners to be controlled, and thus persecuted, are the result of racial biases or the application of other discriminating factors.

Consequently, even though it is not explicitly based on those factors, it frequently happens that crimmigration in action makes them concretely relevant. For instance, the link between crimmigration and the war on terror and the substantial identification of terrorism and Islamic terrorism made by European criminal policies has determined, especially in the first three decades of the 2000s, a creeping emergence of the religious factor as a substantial criterion for the selection of the foreigner who is considered undesirable because dangerous and, as such, to be subjected to the hostile and scrutinising eye of crimmigrationist surveillance.[49]

5.5 The Linguistic Games of Crimmigration

How are these contents legally verbalised? Is the language of crimmigration (here, for reasons of space, I will only consider the language of abstract legal norms) an openly hateful language? Is, therefore, crimmigration also hate speech in a verbally explicit sense?

In order to answer these questions, one must consider that crimmigration must legitimise itself in an overall political, legal, and cultural context in which public coercion finds a limit in fundamental rights, including equality and non-discrimination,[50] and in the idea that criminal law must have a democratic foundation and an inclusive character.[51] More generally, the crimmigration practised by states that profess to be liberal-democratic must come to terms with the fact that

> liberal democracies define themselves as being opposed to hatred and the violent othering that hatred is thought to imply. They are founded in part on a fear of passions, hatred being the passion most feared of all because it is strongly associated with violence and with a devaluation of the other.[52]

Consequently, if it is to appear legitimate, crimmigration cannot be overtly hateful, xenophobic, and discriminatory; it must conceal this nature, or at least mitigate it, through a series of expedients that make it appear, rather, as a reasonable compromise between the respect due to those rights and other demands, also fundamental, such as public security and the fair distribution of available public resources, which would depend, among other things, on the closure of borders and the exclusion of undesirable foreigners.

In the setting of these legitimising devices, language plays a central role. It is understandable, then, that the formal language of crimmigration is generally not the same language that politicians, especially sovereigntist and populist politicians, pronounce in its support; it is, instead, the aseptic language of law and administrative practices, formally polite and deferential towards the dignity of persons and fundamental legal principles. In the "*whereas* clauses" or among the provisions of those very normative acts (laws, decrees, regulations, Directives, memoranda of understanding, etc.) that provide for criminalisation, administrative detention, and expulsion, one cannot count the solemn declarations that all these measures will be carried out with the strictest respect for the rights and dignity of the foreigners who will be subjected to them.

And yet, this formal—and, shall we say, hypocritical—surface fails to entirely conceal the hostile, stigmatising, and xenophobic substance of the overall strategy. If one reads it carefully, it is not difficult to see how even between the folds of the technocratic neutrality of that language there are glimpses of that substance. What emerges is a complex interplay of the said and unsaid, which serves to legitimise the hateful vocation of these policies, without, however, stating it explicitly or brutally. On the one hand, the scaremonger of the mass-foreigner is raised, but indirectly and surreptitiously evoked rather than explicitly pointed out; on the other hand, measures of social exclusion are reserved for this subject, but an attempt is made to wrap them in euphemisms and circumlocutions that soften their meaning and conceal their scope as far as possible.

5.5.1 Euphemisms: The Return of UFOs

In the perspective of this second linguistic strategy, it is significant that, for example, Council Directive 2008/115 never speaks of expulsion, let alone deportation, but of "returning illegally staying third-country nationals". "Return" is clearly a euphemism with respect to expulsion or deportation. The latter two expressions, in fact, indicate acts that the foreigner undergoes, of which she is evidently an object, not an active subject. The term "return", on the contrary, evokes an active role of the foreigner, equal and opposite to her action of entering or staying illegally: With her "return'" in short, the foreigner cancels, undoes her own original wrong, reproducing it backwards, as if she were literally retracing her steps.

Even the definition clearly alludes to an active role of the returning foreigner. According to Article 3(3),

> "return" means the process of a third-country national *going back* . . . to his or her country of origin, or a country of transit in accordance with Community or bilateral readmission agreements or other arrangements, or another third country, to which the third-country national concerned *voluntarily decides* to return and in which he or she will be accepted. (emphasis added)

Although this act may also be "enforced" (in which case it becomes more properly a "removal"), nevertheless, in its ontological status, it remains an act of the foreigner. It is she who, as she came, *goes back* (active verb) whence she came. And in fact, the ordinary form that this process must take is, again according to the Directive, that of "voluntary return" (in the Preamble) or "voluntary departure", envisaged in Article 7, which Article 3(8) defines as "compliance with the obligation to return within the time-limit fixed for that purpose in the return decision", and that clearly serves to euphemise the fact that, in any case, the returning foreigner is a subject who is coercively forced to leave the territory.

Another emblematic example of the euphemising use of language in the context of crimmigration can be found in the way in which the so-called administrative detention of the foreigner is sometimes referred to. Administrative detention of foreigners is, properly speaking, a mass detention, detention of collectivities rather than individuals, of foreigners treated as UFOs (*unidentified fleeing objects*). Under Article 14(1) *decreto legislativo* (d.lgs.) 286/1998, for example, it is applied to foreigners "[w]hen it is not possible to carry out expulsion by accompanying them to the border or rejection with immediacy, due to transitory situations that hinder the preparation of repatriation or the carrying out of removal". This happens, for the most part, when the foreigner does not have an ascertained identity (see, e.g., Article 14, in combination with Article 13 para 4 bis, d.lgs. 286/1998), that is, she is not, by law, an individual person, but a fragment of the irregular mass looming threateningly in the background. Migrant detention—a typically punitive device, but employed as an ordinary instrument of the administrative management of the foreigner to be expelled[53]—condenses in this ancipite nature (formally administrative, but substantially repressive) the vocation, peculiar to crimmigration, to interweave the criminal and the migratory, in a mutual reinforcement all aimed at the pursuit of the ultimate objective of the exclusion/expulsion—territorial and juridical, but also social[54]—of the unwanted foreigner.

It has been debated whether confinement in migrant centres entails a deprivation of liberty within the meaning of Article 5(1) of the ECHR and thus constitutes a true form of detention. Governments have sometimes argued that detained foreigners are not really detained, but "sheltered" or "accommodated" while awaiting their situation to be dealt with.[55] Italy is an interesting example thereof.[56] Since the mid-1990s, when these centres were first built, Italian legislation has never been formulated in terms of "detaining" foreigners for immigration management purposes. Instead, it has resorted to hypocritical circumlocutions, according to which the detention of immigrants is defined as "hosting" them (in so-called "migrant reception centres" or "reception centres for asylum seekers"), or "holding" them (in so-called "temporary residence centres", "identification and expulsion centres", "residence centres for returning foreigners", or even "welcome centres").

It is, however, beyond serious doubt that the situation of those held in at least some of these centres amounts, or is "equivalent in practice, in view of the restrictions suffered, to a deprivation of liberty".[57] This can be easily inferred if we move beyond labels and take account of "a whole range of factors such as the nature, duration, effects and manner of execution of the measure in question".[58] Among the centres existing within the Italian system, for instance, it is clear that at least those referred to in Article 14 d.lgs. 286/1998 have a liberty-limiting nature.[59] Not only are they closed centres surrounded by high fences with barbed wire all around them, but Article 21 para 1 d.p.r. 394/1999 places on foreigners an "absolute duty not to leave" them; moreover, though their leaving one of these centres does not amount to committing a crime of escape, the police are nonetheless expressly empowered to use force as a means to restore their detention.[60] And yet, in the recent Decreto-legge 124/2023,[61] reference continues to be made, euphemistically, to "reception, permanence and repatriation facilities", despite the decision to entrust the design and construction of a "suitable number" (Article 21 para 2) of these centres to the Ministry of Defence, declaring them "by right as works intended for defence and national security" (Article 21 para 3) and despite the announcement that these facilities will be located "in very low population density areas and will be fenced and guarded".[62]

The unwillingness of certain legislators to speak of immigration "detention" underlines a truth, though. As detention is commonly deemed to be a typical criminal law instrument, this linguistic strategy strikes one as an attempt to send the message that migrant confinement does not stem from punitive intentions. By avoiding the word "detention", the practice is thus presented as if it was more humane, or at least less intrusive than carceral punishment, hence less urgently in need of strong justification.

5.5.2 Surreptitious Stigmatisation: (1) Migrant Smuggling as Facilitation of Unauthorised Immigration

In the cases considered so far, language is used euphemistically, to conceal the real scope of certain crimmigration measures and make their impact on the rights of foreigners seem less problematic and pervasive, less hateful. In other cases, it happens instead that, through formally aseptic language, without resorting to overtly and aggressively hateful verbal forms, the linguistic effects of criminalisation and stigmatisation are pursued or, in any case, obtained in a concealed, surreptitious manner. They therefore evoke, without stating it explicitly, the image of the mass-foreigner as a sinister subject, deserving of the treatment—criminalisation, hostility, and exclusion—that is reserved for her.

An emblematic case of this kind of linguistic strategy can be found in the criminalisation of smuggling of migrants. This, in principle, is directed against smugglers, subjects who, in order to make a profit, exploit the difficult situation in which a foreigner who aspires to irregularly enter a state other than her own finds herself. This is, in fact, how the conduct is described in Article 6 of the UN Protocol against the Smuggling of Migrants.[63] However, if one looks at the EU rules on the subject, one realises that these follow a different approach, only apparently or incidentally hinging on smugglers, but essentially concerned with smuggled migrants themselves. The language used in the relevant provisions clearly shows this approach. It is already indicative that, in the EU Facilitators' Package, comprised of Council Directive 2002/90[64] and Council Framework Decision 2002/946,[65] which still defines the foundations of EU law on the matter, the phenomenon is not even identified as migrant smuggling, but as facilitation of irregular migration.

Speaking of "smuggling" is a way of attributing to the foreigner the essentially passive role of the object of the smuggler's conduct. EU law, however, does not refer to the crime as "smuggling", but as "facilitation of unauthorised entry, transit, and residence", and this makes it clear from the outset that the conduct by which European policies are really concerned is ultimately that of the foreigner who enters, transits or stays illegally; only indirectly does that of the smuggler come into the picture, as facilitating activity. Congruently with these premises, the Facilitators' Package describes the offence as the act of "assisting" a foreigner to enter the territory of a member state irregularly, or to transit through it (Article 1 para 1(a)), or else to stay there irregularly (Article para 1(b)); it thus delineates for the foreigner themselves an essentially active role: Not the object of another's conduct, but an acting subject, whom the facilitator merely helps. The facilitation's wrongness is thus constructed in terms of complicity in the wrongful act of illegal immigration committed by the migrant. A wrongness that is not autonomous, but accessory, a reflection of that of irregular immigration.[66] Preventing irregular immigration is the true purpose of criminalising facilitation, not protecting the smuggled foreigner or, in any case, targeting smugglers as profiteers of the foreigner's vulnerability. It is the smuggled foreigner who is implicitly criminalised as a subject who enters, transits, or resides "in breach of the laws of the state concerned". It is she, the would-be migrant, who, with her aspiration to enter or remain in a state that does not want her, ultimately breaches these laws, which makes her the ultimate law-breaker.

5.5.3 Surreptitious Stigmatisation: (2) Clandestine Immigration, Clandestine Migrants

In a manner entirely congruent with this approach—using the repression of smuggling/facilitation to indirectly criminalise the would-be migrant herself—Italian law labels the norms against these crimes (Article 12 d.lgs. 286/1998) as "provisions against clandestine immigration". This rubric gives the cue for a different kind of consideration: If the configuration of smuggling as facilitation of irregular immigration serves to conceal the indirect criminalisation of the migrant, the use of the expression "clandestine immigration" to refer to the migrant's situation adds to criminalisation a nuance of offensive and dehumanising stigmatisation. Surprisingly, notwithstanding the highly offensive and discriminatory meaning assumed by the usage of terms such as "clandestine" or "clandestinity" to capture the condition of the foreigner who enters or remains irregularly in the territory of the state,[67] this usage is still found in Italian legal language today. For example, the Memorandum of Understanding signed by Italy and Libya on 2 February 2017 speaks of "clandestine migrants".

At the legislative level, there is no provision directly affixing the qualification of "clandestinity" to the foreigner. This is generally identified, in a more aseptic way, as "a foreigner who enters or remains in the territory of the state in violation of its laws" (e.g., Article 10 bis d.lgs. 286/1998). In the law, in short, the term "clandestine" is not normally used as a synonym for "a foreigner who irregularly enters or remains in the territory of the state", but rather as an adjective referring to the phenomenon of irregular immigration, which is, in fact, indicated by and large (not only in the heading of Article 12 d.lgs. 286/1998) as "clandestine immigration". Nevertheless, even this is, on closer inspection, a use of the term that has become problematic today, although apparently fair and not directly offensive. Qualifying the position of the foreigner as "clandestine immigration" has, in fact, the obvious implication that the foreigner is a "clandestine". This brings back in through the back door the stigmatising value of the term directly referring to the foreigner irregularly present on the territory of the state. Not to mention the circular effect that is produced in this way: The current use of the term, directly referring to the person of the foreigner, can in fact claim legitimacy precisely in the coverage that the legislative language provides for it.

5.6 Conclusion: What Is the Use of Conceptualising Crimmigration in Terms of Hate Speech?

It thus seems possible to conceptualise crimmigration in terms of hatred and hate speech. But why do so? What conclusions can be drawn from this? From a specifically legal point of view, the fact of recognising in crimmigration a form of hate speech first highlights the existence of an axiological antinomy[68] between the inspiring principles and norms of crimmigration itself, and those in which counter-hate speech policies are articulated. This is true not only at the state level but also at the European Union level: At both levels, in different but complementary and synergic forms and with different instruments, the coexistence of crimmigration and the fight against hate speech creates an obvious inconsistency. This has repercussions on the credibility of the political message sent through both; the coexistence of one and the other empties both of them of meaning, or in any case undermines them from within, making them, in different ways and to different degrees, less credible.

The existence of norms and the implementation of practices that, without great straining, can be considered forms of institutional discriminatory harassment or in any case expressions—even violent ones (detentions, expulsions and rejections)—of hatred for racial, ethnic, religious or national reasons, can only make it less convincing for states to also commit themselves to combating discrimination and hate speech. And the fact that the instruments of crimmigration are envisaged in legal norms of legislative rank in no way detracts from their problematic nature as forms of hatred and hate speech. On the contrary, it has the effect of making this problematic nature more serious, giving it a structural, institutional dimension, which prevents it from being downplayed as a mere occasional, accidental deviation and instead highlights its overall character of systemic abuse.

But the qualification of crimmigration as hate speech highlights its problematic nature not only because of its legal content, but also because of its socio-conversational repercussions. As we have already seen,[69] between the two levels—of crimmigration and the hostile sociopolitical media narratives that shape its backdrop—there is a circular interaction, made possible by the fact that both are but dimensions of the same hate speech. In addition to presupposing those narratives, crimmigration also contributes to nourishing and iterating them, and indeed endows them with a further illocutionary force (greater than that of ordinary hate speech), since it seals them with the formal authority of the state and provides them with new arguments of a legal-bureaucratic nature. For instance, once the irregular entry and stay of foreigners in the territory of the state is made a crime, and these people are dubbed, directly or indirectly, as "clandestines", they become more than just undocumented foreigners: They are made criminal strangers, marked with a foreignness/extraneousness/Otherness that is no longer only national, but also criminal; this formalises their status as deviant subjects (and doubly so: For both the migratory and the criminal law), and their social stigmatisation finds in criminal law a reason, an argument, additional to those found in migration law.[70]

Moreover, the locking up of foreigners in detention centres for the purposes of their identification and expulsion confines them in differentiated physical and social spaces. This reaffirms, also symbolically, their Otherness (their being outside the community boundaries) and subordination. The social sense of their Otherness is only increased by the fact that they are known to be detained, or detainable, in such mysterious non-places, only by virtue of their being foreigners in an irregular position. In a circular manner, crimmigration, on the one hand, is rooted in the discursive and rhetorical construction of the foreigner as unwanted, dangerous, enemy, or parasite and, on the other hand, is part of it, actively contributing to it.

Crimmigration is thus problematic in two ways: Directly, because of the legal-bureaucratic treatment it reserves to the foreigner, and because of the contrast between this treatment and certain fundamental legal principles; and indirectly, because by setting itself as a seal and a legal foundation of the social subordination of the mass-foreigner, it ends up—intentionally or not—fuelling and legitimising widespread discriminatory behaviour towards its target. Thus, it contributes, like any successful hate speech in general does,[71] to polluting the conversational context involving and concerning the foreigner, in such a way that, the widespread, everyday social environment (not only the institutional one) becomes more hostile and inhospitable.

Notes

1 Scholarship on crimmigration, and more generally on the criminalisation of migration, is now countless. See, e.g.: Juliet Stumpf, 'The Crimmigration Crisis: Immigrants, Crime, and Sovereign Power' (2006) 56 American University Law Review 367; Juliet Stumpf, 'Crimmigration and the Legitimacy of Immigration Law' (2023) 65 Arizona Law Review 113; Stephen Legomsky, 'The New Path of Immigration Law: Asymmetric Incorporation of Criminal Justice Norms' (2007) 64 Washington and Lee Law Review 469; Jennifer Chacón, 'Managing Migration Through Crime' (2009) 109 Columbia Law Rev 138; Allegra McLeod 'The U.S. Criminal-Immigration Convergence and its Possible Undoing' (2012) 49 American Criminal Law Review 105; Yolanda Vázquez, 'Crimmigration: The Missing Piece of Criminal Justice Reform' (2017) 51 University of Richmond Law Review 1093; Cesar Cuauhtemoc García Hernández, *Crimmigration Law* (2nd edn, American Bar Association 2021); Idil Atak and James Simeon (eds), *The Criminalization of Migration: Context and Consequences* (McGill-Queen's UP 2018); Peter Billings (ed), *Crimmigration in Australia. Law, Politics, and Society* (Springer 2019); Valsamis Mitsilegas, *The Criminalisation of Migration in Europe. Challenges for Human Rights and the Rule of Law* (Springer 2015); Maria João Guia, Maartje van der Woude and Joanne van der Leun (eds), *Social control and Justice: Crimmigration in the Age of Fear* (Eleven International Publishing 2013); Luisa Marin and Alessandro Spena 'Introduction: The Criminalization of Migration and European (Dis)Integration' (2016) 18 European Journal of Migration and Law 147; Alessandro Spena, 'Iniuria Migrandi: Criminalization of Immigrants and the Basic Principles of the Criminal Law' (2014) 8 Criminal Law and Philisophy 635; Alessandro Spena 'The Double-Deviant Identity of the Mass-Foreigner and the Lack of Authority of the Crimmigrationist State' (2019) 22 New Criminal Law Review 301; Emmanuel Melissaris, 'Non-Citizens as Subjects of the Criminal Law' (2017) 2 LSE Law, Society and Economy Working Papers 1; Gian Luigi Gatta, Valsamis Mitsilegas and Stefano Zirulia (eds), *Controlling Immigration Through Criminal Law. European and Comparative Perspectives on "Crimmigration"* (Hart 2021); Christine Graebsch, 'Crimmigration and Pre-Crime in German Law Connecting the International Debate to the German National (Legal) Context' (2022) 15 Kriminologisches Journal 16; Rottem

Rosenberg-Rubins, *Crimmigration Under International Protection. Constructing Criminal Law as Governmentality* (Routledge 2023).

2 According to Elias Canetti, *Crowds and Power* (first published 1960, Continuum 1981) 16, "[t]he natural crowd is the *open* crowd; there are no limits whatever to its growth; it does not recognize houses, doors or locks and those who shut themselves in are suspect. 'Open' is to be understood here in the fullest sense of the word; it means open everywhere and in any direction. The open crowd exists so long as it grows; it disintegrates as soon as it stops growing" (emphasis added).

3 Antony Duff, *The Realm of Criminal Law* (OUP 2018); Richard Dagger, 'Republicanism and the Foundations of Criminal law' in Antony Duff and Stuart Green (eds), *Philosophical Foundations of Criminal law* (OUP 2011); Alessandro Spena, 'The Good, the Bad and the Ugly: Images of the Foreigner in Contemporary Criminal Law' (2018) 4 International Journal of Migration and Border Studies 287.

4 On the securitisation of migration, see, e.g., Ayse Ceyhan, '"Migrants as a Threat": A Comparative Analysis of Securitarian Rhetoric: The European Union (France) and the United States (California)' (Paper presented at the ECSA 5th Biennial International Conference, 29 May–1 June 1997) <http://aei.pitt.edu/2551/1/002850_1.PDF> accessed 20 December 2024; Ayse Ceyhan and Anastassia Tsoukala, 'The Securitization of Migration in Western Societies: Ambivalent Discourses and Policies' (2002) 27 Alternatives: Global, Local, Political 21; Didier Bigo, 'Security and Immigration: Toward a Critique of the Governmentality of Unease' (2002) 27 Alternatives: Global, Local, Political 63; Alessandro Dal Lago, *Non-persone. L'esclusione dei migranti in una società globale* (Feltrinelli 2004); Elspeth Guild, *Security and Migration in the 21st Century* (Polity Press 2009); Zygmunt Bauman, *Strangers at Our Door* (Polity Press 2016).

5 In a similar direction, see already Kathryn Abrams, 'When the State Hates' in Thomas Brudholm and Birgitte Schepelern Johansen (eds), *Hate, Politics, Law: Critical Perspectives on Combating Hate* (OUP 2018) 237, who applies this idea to the specific case of Arizona, which "[i]n the mid-to late-2000s . . . adopted a series of laws aimed explicitly at making life so difficult for the state's undocumented immigrants that they would return to their countries of origin" (237). More generally, on the possibility that even states, and democratic states in particular, can act in ways that can be connoted as expressions of hatred, see, e.g., Mikkel Thorup, 'Democratic Hatreds: The Making of "the Hating Enemy" in Liberal Democracy' in Brudholm and Johansen (eds), *Hate, Politics, Law: Critical Perspectives on Combating Hate* (n 5).

6 Recommendation of the Council of Europe CM/Rem(2022)16 of 20 May 2022 on combating hate speech [2022] para 2.

7 On the concept of "intergroup behaviour", Muzafer Sherif, *In Common Predicament. Social Psychology of Intergroup Conflict and Cooperation* (Houghton Mifflin 1966) 12; more recently, Sik Hung Ng 'Intergroup Behaviour and Ethnicity: A Social Psychological Perspective' (2005) 6 Asian Ethnicity 19; Richard Crisp, *Social Psychology. A Very Short Introduction* (OUP 2015).

8 Henri Tajfel, *Human Groups and Social Categories. Studies in Social Psychology* (CUP 1981) 243.

9 Henri Tajfel, 'Social Psychology of Intergroup Relations' (1982) 33 Annual Reviews of Psychology 1, 13 (original emphasis).

10 According to Marija Branković and others, 'Social Identity Complexity and Inclusiveness as Predictors of Intergroup Emotions' (2016) 8 Primenjena Psihologija 364, "[a]ccording to Social Dominance Theory, . . . biases toward out-groups [– of which hate speech is a manifestation –] are more likely to be expressed if a group one belongs to is dominant rather than subordinate".

11 Furio Jesi, *L'accusa del sangue* (Bollati Boringhieri 2007) 37.

12 René Girard, *The Scapegoat* (first published 1982, The Johns Hopkins UP 1986) 15, 21–23.

13 Antony Duff and Sandra Marshall advocate a conception of the politico-legal relevance of hatred and hate speech very close to this one. See their 'Criminalizing Hate?' in Thomas Brudholm and Birgitte Schepelern Johansen (eds), *Hate, Politics, Law. Critical Perspectives on Combating Hate* (OUP 2018): "Hatred", they write, "involves a radical kind of alienation or exclusion. To hate is to exclude from fellowship and recognition" (120), and to do so, in particular, by "assert[ing the] inferiority" of the excluded (125). More specifically: "Hate speech . . . denies that [members of another group] are participants, let alone equal participants, in the polity's public discourse, and it denies them that place on the basis not of judgements about their qualities as individuals, but of a reaction to a group characteristic—their ethnicity, or religion, or sexuality" (124–25).
I find this way of putting things agreeable provided that: (1) the concept of "polity" is understood in a very broad sense, including any space of social interaction, not only physical, but also virtual (online hate speech would be very difficult to interpret as exclusion from a polity in the classical political sense); (2) relevance is attributed not only to hatred against those who are already part of the polity thus understood, but also to that against outsiders who aspire to be part of it; (2) relevance is attributed not only to hatred aimed at excluding the victim from any presence or participation in the polity, but also to hatred aimed at excluding her from equal participation in it, i.e., marginalising her, keeping her in the polity, but in a subordinate role (on the possibility of extending Duff and Marshall's conception in these directions, see pp 126–29).

14 *Erbakan v Turkey* [2006] ECLI:CE:ECHR:2006:0706JUD005940500, para 56.

15 See Rae Langton, 'Speech Acts and Unspeakable Acts' (1993) 22 Philosophy and Public Affairs 293; Ishani Maitra, 'Subordinating Speech' in Ishani Maitra and Mary Kate McGowan (eds), *Speech and Harm. Controversies over Free Speech* (OUP 2012); Mihaela Popa-Wyatt and Jeremy Wyatt, 'Slurs, Roles and Power' (2018) 175 Philosophical Studies.

16 Salvini is certainly not the only one among prominent Italian politicians to have used, over the years, openly hostile arguments against mass-foreigners as justifications for advocating exclusionary and discriminatory policies of a crimmigrationist kind. Giorgia Meloni, the current Italian Prime Minister, also distinguished herself, e.g., before assuming her current position, by employing xenophobic rhetoric in particularly heated tones, sometimes even veiled in anti-Semitism. In 2018, e.g., in expressing her and her party's (Fratelli d'Italia) opposition to Italy's signing of the Global Compact, she proclaimed:

> The Global Compact is an apparently innocuous document, but at its core it contains a devastating principle for the existence of nation states: it says that immigration is a fundamental principle of every human being. Mind you, any kind of immigration: those fleeing war, those fleeing hunger, those fleeing the heat, those moving simply because they feel like moving. If Italy subscribes to this pact, any policy of controlling our borders that we make tomorrow will be recalled by the United Nations.
>
> (Fratelli d'Italia, Global Compact: Flash mob FdI sotto Palazzo Chigi)

Meloni: "*Se su Immigrazione Governo cambia politica torna a votare*" (29 November 2018) <https://www.fratelli-italia.it/global-compact-flash-mob-fdi-sotto-palazzo-chigi-meloni-se-su-immigrazione-governo-cambia-politica-tornare-a-votare/> accessed 20 December 2024. Later on, Meloni herself commented on the fact that George Soros had announced his support for Emma Bonino's +Europa party in the run-up to the 2019 European elections: "Soros is entering the field for the European elections by financing Emma Bonino's party with 200,000 Euros. He chose the left as an ally and us sovereignists as enemies. A great pride for Fratelli d'Italia: keep the money from usurers, our strength is the Italian people".

Ilaria Myr, "*Giorgia Meloni e 'Soros l'usuraio': quando l'antisemitismo non ha bisogno della parola 'ebreo'*" (*Bet Magazine Mosaico*, 26 March 2019) <https://www.mosaico-cem.it/attualita-e-news/italia/giorgia-meloni-e-soros-lusuraio-quando-lantisemitismo-non-ha-bisogno-della-parola-ebreo/> accessed 20 December 2024; the same article comments the anti-Semitic implications of using the term "usurer" to refer to a wealthy person of Jewish origin. Finally, as late as the summer of 2022, during the general elections after which she became Prime Minister, Giorgia Meloni and her party proposed "The naval blockade off the Libyan coast [as] the only useful concrete measure to stop the influx of irregular immigrants from North Africa: more than 600,000 people in five years, 90% adult men, only 8% political refugees. The 'naval blockade' that FDI proposes is a European military mission, carried out in agreement with the Libyan authorities, to prevent barges of immigrants from leaving in the direction of Italy. These are not pushbacks, because pushbacks properly said take place on the open sea". See Alessandro Della Guglia, 'La Meloni (ri)propone il blocco navale, ma è una voce troppo debole' (*Il Primato Nazionale*, 22 March 2023) <https://www.ilprimatonazionale.it/esteri/meloni-ripropone-il-blocco-navale-voce-deboli-258573/> accessed 20 December 2024.

17 Corriere della Sera, 'Lampedusa, Salvini mostra lo sbarco dei migranti in diretta Facebook' (24 July 2020) <https://www.youtube.com/watch?v=MkoNceQNfp0> accessed 20 December 2024.

18

> *I soldi il governo per Lampedusa fatica a trovarli, però . . . però . . . adesso . . . live . . . esempio di turisti che non pagano, ma che vengono pagati per fare i turisti . . . barchino, barcone, ennesimi clandestini che rimarranno qua a scrocco e a spese degli italiani. Oggi abbiamo visitato il centro che dovrebbe ospitarne 190 e ne ospita 800, di cui 700 maschi, fra i 20 e 30 anni, robusti, adulti, belli forti, telefonino, cappellino, occhiali da sole, scarpino.*

19 "*Telefonino, cappellino, occhiali da sole, scarpino*". This idea that foreigners who cross the Mediterranean Sea to come to Europe are generally well-off people is a workhorse for Salvini, who, on 24 September 2023, reiterated it in a TV programme, claiming that "many arrive (with): smartphone, shoes, necklace, watch" ["*Molti arrivano: telefonino, scarpe, catenina, orologino*"]. Paolo del Debbio and Matteo Salvini, 'Paolo del Debbio intervista Matteo Salvini' (*Dritto e rovescio*, 24 September 2023) <https://mediasetinfinity.mediaset.it/video/drittoerovescio/puntata-del-24-settembre_F312803901000501> accessed 20 December 2024.

20 "Ennesimi clandestini".

21 "A scrocco".

22 Corriere della Sera,'Lampedusa, Salvini mostra lo sbarco dei migranti in diretta Facebook' (n 17). The original text reads: "*Vedete? Questo è il porto, questo è lo spettacolo di Lampedusa di sera, con gente che fatica, che ha un'attività, che ha un bar, che ha un ristorante, che ha un negozio . . . e quello è un deposito di barchini e barconi. E vedete? Sono decine e decine e decine solo negli ultimi giorni, con sbarchi di centinaia di clandestini, sbarchi organizzati, con un governo complice dei criminali. Ce lo diciamo: è un governo complice dei criminali! Ieri c'è stato il record degli ultimi anni degli sbarchi a Lampedusa. Non è possibile! Quindi, non vedo l'ora di tornare al governo, con gen te seria, per richiudere i porti e i delinquenti e riaprirli alle persone per bene, ai pescatori e ai turisti. Tutto in diretta: questa è una giornata di fine luglio; comunque, vi posso dire, se avete risparmiato 2 euro, state in Italia a far vacanza, venite a Lampedusa, venite in Sicilia, state in Italia, ché il mare siciliano e il mare italiano è il più bello del mondo, e di quella gente là non ne abbiamo più bisogno*".

23 The use of this term in this context is mainly characteristic of the Italian language (as well as of the Spanish language, as shown, for example, by the verse used as

the title of this paragraph, which comes from a song by Manu Chao, entitled "Clandestino"). The English-language discussion has rather focused on the widespread and derogatory use of the concept of "illegality" and its variants ("illegal immigration", "illegal migrant", "illegals"), which, in many ways, raise similar concerns to those associated with the concept of "clandestine migrants". See Catherine Dauvergne, *Making People Illegal—What Globalization Means for Migration and Law* (CUP 2008); Cecilia Menjívar and Daniel Kanstroom, *Constructing Immigrant "Illegality"—Critiques, Experiences, and Responses* (CUP 2013).

24 Cass civ, sez III, 22 May 2023 (dep 16 August 2023) 24686/2023, para 14(3). The case was as follows: a cooperative company had agreed with the Prefecture of Varese to make available its own facility, in the municipality of Saronno, to accommodate 32 asylum seekers. In protest against this decision, the local section of the Lega Nord (the party of which, by the way, Salvini is the national secretary) organised a demonstration, during which about 70 posters were put up throughout the municipality, bearing not only the party symbol, but also phrases such as:

> Saronno does not want clandestines; Renzi [*then Italian PM*] and Alfano [*then Minister of the Interior*] want to send 32 clandestines to Saronno: board, lodging and pampering paid for by us. In the meantime, they are cutting pensions and increasing taxes for the Saronnesi; Renzi and Alfano are accomplices of the invasion.

Placards that had been posted for about a month; this message was later reinforced by further statements by the secretary of the Lega Nord of Saronno against the reception of "clandestines". At the end of a trial initiated at the behest of the Asgi and Naga associations, the Lega Nord was condemned to pay compensation for the non-pecuniary damage caused to the 32 asylum seekers concerned, precisely because of the discriminatory nature of the conduct on that occasion.

25 For comments on this decision, see Federico Faloppa, 'Perché è giusto vietare la parola clandestino' (*La Stampa*, 20 August 2023) <https://www.lastampa.it/editoriali/lettere-e-idee/2023/08/20/news/perche_e_giusto_vietare_la_parola_clandestino-13003146/> accessed 20 December 2024; Marco Brando, 'Clandestini, la pseudo-verità tra politica e giornalismo' (*Lingua Italiana—Treccani*, 29 August 2023) <https://www.treccani.it/magazine/lingua_italiana/articoli/scritto_e_parlato/clandestini2.html> accessed 20 December 2024.

26 Alessandro Spena, 'Smuggling umanitario e scriminanti' (2019) 62 Rivista italiana di diritto e procedura Penale.

27 See, e.g., Stefano Zirulia, *Il favoreggiamento dell'immigrazione irregolare—Tra overcriminalisation e tutela dei diritti fondamentali* (Giappichelli 2024).

28 For example, see Maurizio Ambrosini and Minke Hajer, *Irregular Migration—IMISCOE Short Reader* (Springer 2023).

29 As, for example, in Cass civ, sez III, 22 May 2023 (dep 16 August 2023) 24686/2023 (v 25).

30 Council Directive 2000/43/EC of 29 June 2000 implementing the principle of equal treatment between persons irrespective of racial or ethnic origin [2000] OJ L180/22.

31 Recommendation CM/Rec(1997)20 on "hate speech", 107. See (n 6).

32 Council Framework Decision 2008/913/JHA of 28 November 2008 on combatting certain forms and expressions of racism and xenophobia by means of criminal law [2008] OJ L328/55.

33 But see also, among many others, Cass civ, sez III, 31 January 2023 (dep 26 May 2023) 14836/2023.

34 Alessandro Spena, 'La dimensione pubblica del discorso d'odio' in Salvatore Di Piazza and Alessandro Spena (eds), *Parole cattive—La libertà di espressione tra linguaggio, diritto e filosofia* (Quodlibet 2022).

35 *Erbakan v Turkey* [2006] ECLI:CE:ECHR:2006:0706JUD005940500, para 56.
36 For example, see *Gündüz v Turkey* [2004] ECLI:CE:ECHR:2003:1204JUD003507197, para 40; *M'Bala M'Bala v France* [2015] ECLI:CE:ECHR:2015:1020DEC002523913; *Affaire Zemmour v France* [2022] ECLI:CE:ECHR:2022:1220JUD006353919.
37 The deviations to which I refer have long been highlighted and denounced by scholars: for example, the works already mentioned (n 1). I will limit myself here to a brief exemplification. At the *abstract normative level*: excessive use of, direct and indirect, criminalisation, with an exponential increase in the number of migratory offences; recourse to offences much closer to the logic of the *Täterstrafrecht* than to that of the *Tatstrafrecht*; *ad hoc* trial tracks for migratory offences, strongly lacking in procedural guarantees; detention as an instrument for managing the irregular foreigner during the identification and expulsion phase (so-called administrative detention); the multiplication of cases in which the commission of a non-migratory crime leads to the expulsion of the foreigner or to the deprivation of acquired citizenship; the denial, not only of the enjoyment of political rights, and therefore of the possibility of active participation in the political life of the community, but also of full access to social and economic rights concerning fundamental human needs, such as health, housing, and fair working conditions. On the *level of practical implementation*, things are even more problematic: overcrowding of migrant detention facilities and poor hygienic and sanitary conditions there; lack of adequate legal assistance (at best left to the goodwill of voluntary organisations) and thus absolute uncertainty in which irregular foreigners generally find themselves regarding their legal and social status; recourse to detention as the main criminal sanction applied (hence an overrepresentation of foreigners in prisons); insistent attention reserved for them by the forces of law and order, characterised by an arbitrary and racially sensitive application of the rules; the consequent substantial unpredictability of a legal and coercive reaction that is manifested in forms that leave much to be desired from the point of view of the rule of law; the risk of being discovered and apprehended as irregular foreigners as a further factual obstacle to the effective enjoyment of even those few rights that are formally recognised.
38 Section 5.5.
39 I will not, therefore, follow, as it seems to me unnecessary and all things considered formalistic, the choice of Eric Heinze, *Hate Speech and Democratic Citizenship* (OUP 2016) 18–19, to refer to this more general sense of "speech" using the word "expression".
40 Even the so-called Muslim Ban—Executive order 13769, 'Protecting the Nation from Foreign Terrorist Entry into the United States', 82 FR 8977—issued by Donald Trump on 27 January 2017 does not actually make any explicit mention to discriminatory factors, merely referring to "remaining inadequacies" that would allegedly characterise the approach of certain states (Chad, Iran, Libya, North Korea, Syria, Venezuela, Yemen, Somalia) in "address[ing] both terrorism-related and public-safety risks" <https://trumpwhitehouse.archives.gov/presidential-actions/presidential-proclamation-enhancing-vetting-capabilities-processes-detecting-attempted-entry-united-states-terrorists-public-safety-threats/> accessed 20 December 2024. An explicitly racist immigration law was, instead, the Chinese Exclusion Act of 1882, "a law infamous for using explicitly race-based criteria to identify people prohibited from entering the United States": García Hernández (n 1) 5.
41 Indeed, according to Duff and Marshall (n 13), the target of hate speech should necessarily be a fellow citizen, albeit in a broad sense.
42 Spena (n 1); Cathryn Costello, 'Victim or Perpetrator? The Criminalization of Migration and the Idea of "Harm" in the Labour Market Context' in Alan Bogg and others (eds), *Criminality at Work* (OUP 2020).

43 Council Regulation (EC) 2018/1240 of 12 September 2018 establishing a European Travel Information and Authorisation System (ETIAS) and amending Regulations (EU) No 1077/2011, (EU) No 515/2014, (EU) 2016/399, (EU) 2016/1624 and (EU) 2017/2226 [2018] OJ L236/1.

44 Council Regulation (EC) 2016/399 of 9 March 2016 on a Union Code on the rules governing the movement of persons across borders (Schengen Borders Code) [2016] OJ L77/1.

45 Regulation (EU) 2018/1806 of the European Parliament and of the Council of 14 November 2018 listing the third countries whose nationals must be in possession of visas when crossing the external borders and those whose nationals are exempt from that requirement (codification) OJ L303/39.

46 Eurostat, 'Top 20 Countries of Citizenship of Non-EU Found Illegally Present in the EU, 2015–2022' (2023) <https://ec.europa.eu/eurostat/statistics-explained/images/9/9b/EIL_2022_tab1_2.png> accessed 20 December 2024.

47 Eurostat, 'Top 20 Countries of Citizenship of Non-EU Citizens Ordered to Leave the EU, 2021 and 2022' (2023) <https://ec.europa.eu/eurostat/statistics-explained/index.php?title=File:Top_20_countries_of_citizenship_of_non-EU_citizens_ordered_to_leave_the_EU,_2021_and_2022_(number).png> accessed 20 December 2024.

48 Ambrosini and Hajer (n 28) 48.

49 For example, see Tufyal Choudhury, 'Suspicion, Discrimination and Surveillance: The Impact of Counter-Terrorism Law and Policy on Racialised Groups at Risk of Racism in Europe' (*European Network Against Racism*, 2021) <https://www.enar-eu.org/wp-content/uploads/suspicion_discrimination_surveillance_report_2021.pdf> accessed 20 December 2024.

50 For example, see Deborah Hellman and Sophia Moreau (eds), *Philosophical Foundations of Discrimination Law* (OUP 2013).

51 See, e.g., Duff (n 3).

52 Thorup (n 5) 215.

53 Galina Cornelisse, *Immigration Detention and Human Rights. Rethinking Territorial Sovereignty* (Brill | Nijhoff 2010); Daniel Wilsher, *Immigration Detention: Law, History, Politics* (CUP 2012); Giuseppe Campesi, *La detenzione amministrativa degli stranieri. Storia, diritto, politica* (Carocci 2013); Alessandro Spena, 'Resisting Immigration Detention' (2016) 18 European Journal of Migration and Law 201.

54 Spena (n 1).

55 For example, see the Turkish Government's submissions in *Abdolkhani and Karimnia v Turkey* [2009] ECLI:CE:ECHR:2009:0922JUD003047108, para 120, and *Z.N.S. v Turkey* [2020] ECLI:CE:ECHR:2020:0128JUD002758207, para 54. But this is a quite old approach, dating back at least to the 'prison with three walls' argument, first set out by the US Supreme Court in *Shaughnessy v Mezei* [1953] 345 US 206. See Wilsher (n 53) 60–61, 112–13, 146–48, 227.

56 Alberto di Martino, 'Centri, campi, Costituzione. Aspetti d'incostituzionalità dei CIE' (2014) 1 Diritto, immigrazione e cittadinanza; Asher Colombo, 'Foreigners and Immigrants in Italy's Penal and Administrative Detention Systems' (2013) 10 European Journal of Criminology 746; Giuseppe Campesi, 'Hindering the Deportation Machine: An Ethnography of Power and Resistance in Immigration Detention' (2015) 17 Punishment and Society; Campesi (n 53) 14–17; Andrea Pugiotto, 'La "galera amministrativa" degli stranieri e le sue incostituzionali metamorfosi' (2014) 3 Quaderni costituzionali. Rivista italiana di diritto costituzionale.

57 For example, see *Amuur v France* [1996] ECLI:CE:ECHR:1996:0625JUD001977692, para 49; *Abdolkhani and Karimnia v Turkey* (n 56) para 125; *Z.N.S. v Turkey* (n 56) paras 56–57.

58 *Engel v The Netherlands* [1976] ECLI:CE:ECHR:1976:0608JUD000510071, para 59: *Guzzardi v Italy* [1980] ECLI:CE:ECHR:1980:1106JUD000736776, para 92.

59 See, e.g., Alberto di Martino, 'La disciplina dei C.I.E. è incostituzionale. Un pamphlet' (*Diritto penale contemporaneo*, 11 May 2012) <https://archiviodpc.dirittopenaleuomo.org/d/1487-la-disciplina-dei-cie-e-incostituzionale> accessed 20 December 2024.

60 See Decreto legislativo "Testo unico delle disposizioni concernenti la disciplina dell'immigrazione e norme sulla condizione dello straniero" 25 July 1998, n 286, Article 14 para 7 and Decreto del Presidente della Repubblica "Regolamento recante norme di attuazione del testo unico delle disposizioni concernenti la disciplina dell'immigrazione e norme sulla condizione dello straniero, a norma dell'articolo 1, comma 6, del decreto legislativo 25 luglio 1998, n 286" 31 August 1999, n 394, Article 20 para 9.

61 Decreto-legge "Disposizioni urgenti in materia di politiche di coesione, per il rilancio dell'economia nelle aree del Mezzogiorno del Paese, nonche' in materia di immigrazione" 19 September 2023, n 124.

62 Marco Iasevoli, 'Migranti, nuovi Cpr e "trattenimento" di 18 mesi. Meloni: sinistra Ue rema contro' (*Avvenire*, 18 September 2023) <https://www.avvenire.it/attualita/pagine/norme-migranti-meloni-sinistra-ue-rema-contro> accessed 20 December 2024.

63 United Nations, Protocol Against the Smuggling of Migrants by Land, Sea and Air, Supplementing the United Nations Convention Against Transnational Organised Crime, adopted on 15 November 2000, Resolution A/RES/55/25. In addition, see, e.g., Tom Obokata, 'The Legal Framework Concerning the Smuggling of Migrants at Sea Under the UN Protocol on the Smuggling of Migrants by Land, Sea and Air' in Bernard Ryan and Valsamis Mitsilegas (eds), *Extraterritorial Immigration Control* (Brill | Nijhoff 2010); Anna Gallagher and Fiona David, *The International Law of Migrant Smuggling* (CUP 2014); Alessandro Spena, 'Smuggled Migrants as Victims? Reflecting on the UN Protocol Against Migrant Smuggling and on its Implementation' in Serena Forlati (ed), *The Palermo Convention at Twenty; The Challenge of Implementation* (Brill Nijhoff 2021).

64 Council Directive 2002/90/EC of 28 November 2002 defining the facilitation of unauthorised entry, transit and residence [2002] OJ L328/4.

65 Council Framework Decision 2002/946/JHA of 28 November 2002 on the strengthening of the penal framework to prevent the facilitation of unauthorised entry, transit and residence [2002] OJ L328/1.

66 Alessandro Spena, 'Human Smuggling and Irregular Immigration in the EU: From Complicity to Exploitation?' in Sergio Carrera and Elspeth Guild (eds), *Irregular Migration, Trafficking and Smuggling of Human Beings* (CEPS 2016) 37; Spena (n 64) 55; Valsamis Mitsilegas, 'The Normative Foundations of the Criminalization of Human Smuggling: Exploring the Fault Lines Between European and International Law' (2019) 10 New Journal of European Criminal Law 68.

67 See above, Section 5.3.1.

68 According to Karl Engisch, *Einführung in das juristische Denken* (Kohlhammer 1968), there is an axiological antinomy, or antinomy of evaluation, 'when the legislator, without actually falling into conflict of norms, does not stick to an evaluation made previously'.

69 Section 5.5.3.

70 Spena (n 1).

71 Mari Matsuda, 'Public Response to Racist Speech: Considering the Victim's Story' (1989) 87 Michigan Law Review 2320; Jeremy Waldron, *The Harm in Hate Speech* (Harvard UP 2014); Rae Langton, 'The Authority of Hate Speech' in John Gardner, Leslie Green and Brian Leiter (eds), *Oxford Studies in Philosophy of Law* (OUP 2018).

Bibliography

Abrams K, 'When the State Hates' in Brudholm T and Schepelern Johansen B (eds), *Hate, Politics, Law: Critical Perspectives on Combating Hate* (OUP 2018).

Ambrosini M and Hajer M, *Irregular Migration—IMISCOE Short Reader* (Springer 2023).

Atak I and Simeon J (eds), *The Criminalization of Migration: Context and Consequences* (McGill-Queen's UP 2018).

Bauman Z, *Strangers at Our Door* (Polity Press 2016).

Bigo D, 'Security and Immigration: Toward a Critique of the Governmentality of Unease' (2002) 27 Alternatives: Global, Local, Political 63.

Billings P (ed), *Crimmigration in Australia. Law, Politics, and Society* (Springer 2019).

Branković M and others, 'Social Identity Complexity and Inclusiveness as Predictors of Intergroup Emotions' (2016) 8 Primenjena Psihologija 364.

Campesi G, *La detenzione amministrativa degli stranieri. Storia, diritto, politica* (Carocci 2013).

Campesi G, 'Hindering the Deportation Machine: An Ethnography of Power and Resistance in Immigration Detention' (2015) 17 Punishment and Society.

Canetti E, *Crowds and Power* (first published 1960, Continuum 1981).

Ceyhan A and Tsoukala A, 'The Securitization of Migration in Western Societies: Ambivalent Discourses and Policies' (2002) 27 Alternatives: Global, Local, Political 21.

Chacón J, 'Managing Migration Through Crime' (2009) 109 Columbia Law Review 138.

Choudhury T, *Suspicion, Discrimination and Surveillance: The Impact of Counter-Terrorism Law and Policy on Racialised Groups at Risk of Racism in Europe* (European Network Against Racism 2021).

Colombo A, 'Foreigners and Immigrants in Italy's Penal and Administrative Detention Systems' (2013) 10 European Journal of Criminology 746.

Cornelisse G, *Immigration Detention and Human Rights. Rethinking Territorial Sovereignty* (Brill | Nijhoff 2010).

Costello C, 'Victim or Perpetrator? The Criminalization of Migration and the Idea of "Harm" in the Labour Market Context' in Bogg A and others (eds), *Criminality at Work* (OUP 2020).

Crisp R, *Social Psychology. A Very Short Introduction* (OUP 2015).

Cuauhtemoc García Hernández C, *Crimmigration Law* (2nd edn, American Bar Association 2021).

Dagger R, 'Republicanism and the Foundations of Criminal Law' in Duff A and Green S (eds), *Philosophical Foundations of Criminal Law* (OUP 2011).

Dal Lago A, *Non-persone. L'esclusione dei migranti in una società globale* (Feltrinelli 2004).

Dauvergne C, *Making People Illegal—What Globalization Means for Migration and Law* (CUP 2008).

di Martino A, 'Centri, campi, Costituzione. Aspetti d'incostituzionalità dei CIE' (2014) 1 Diritto, immigrazione e cittadinanza.

Duff A, *The Realm of Criminal Law* (OUP 2018).

Duff A and Marshall S, 'Criminalizing Hate' in Brudholm T and Schepelern Johansen B (eds), *Hate, Politics, Law. Critical Perspectives on Combating Hate* (OUP 2018).

Engisch K, *Einführung in das juristische Denken* (Kohlhammer 1968).

Gallagher A and David F, *The International Law of Migrant Smuggling* (CUP 2014).

Gatta GL, Mitsilegas V and Zirulia S (eds), *Controlling Immigration Through Criminal Law. European and Comparative Perspectives on "Crimmigration"* (Hart 2021).

Girard R, *The Scapegoat* (first published 1982, The Johns Hopkins UP 1986).

Graebsch C, 'Crimmigration and Pre-Crime in German Law Connecting the International Debate to the German National (Legal) Context' (2022) 15 Kriminologisches Journal 16.

Guild E, *Security and Migration in the 21st Century* (Polity Press 2009).
Heinze E, *Hate Speech and Democratic Citizenship* (OUP 2016).
Hellman D and Moreau S (eds), *Philosophical Foundations of Discrimination Law* (OUP 2013).
Hung Ng S, 'Intergroup Behaviour and Ethnicity: A Social Psychological Perspective' (2005) 6 Asian Ethnicity 19.
Jesi F, *L'accusa del sangue* (Bollati Boringhieri 2007).
João Guia M, Van der Woude M and Van der Leun M (eds), *Social Control and Justice: Crimmigration in the Age of Fear* (Eleven International Publishing 2013).
Langton R, 'Speech Acts and Unspeakable Acts' (1993) 22 Philosophy and Public Affairs 293.
Langton R, 'The Authority of Hate Speech' in Gardner J, Green L and Leiter B (eds), *Oxford Studies in Philosophy of Law* (OUP 2018).
Legomsky S, 'The New Path of Immigration Law: Asymmetric Incorporation of Criminal Justice Norms' (2007) 64 Washington and Lee Law Review 469.
Maitra I, 'Subordinating Speech' in Maitra I and McGowan MK (eds), *Speech and Harm. Controversies over Free Speech* (OUP 2012).
Marin L and Spena A, 'Introduction: The Criminalization of Migration and European (Dis)Integration' (2016) 18 European Journal of Migration and Law 147.
Matsuda M, 'Public Response to Racist Speech: Considering the Victim's Story' (1989) 87 Michigan Law Review 2320.
McLeod A, 'The U.S. Criminal-Immigration Convergence and its Possible Undoing' (2012) 49 American Criminal Law Review 105.
Melissaris E, 'Non-Citizens as Subjects of the Criminal Law' (2017) 2 London School Economy Law, Society and Economy Working Papers 1.
Menjívar C and Kanstroom D, *Constructing Immigrant "Illegality"—Critiques, Experiences, and Responses* (CUP 2013).
Mitsilegas V, *The Criminalisation of Migration in Europe. Challenges for Human Rights and the Rule of Law* (Springer 2015).
Mitsilegas V, 'The Normative Foundations of the Criminalization of Human Smuggling: Exploring the Fault Lines Between European and International Law' (2019) 10 New Journal of European Criminal Law 68.
Obokata T, 'The Legal Framework Concerning the Smuggling of Migrants at Sea Under the UN Protocol on the Smuggling of Migrants by Land, Sea and Air' in Ryan B and Mitsilegas V (eds), *Extraterritorial Immigration Control* (Brill | Nijhoff 2010).
Popa-Wyatt M and Wyatt J, 'Slurs, Roles and Power' (2018) 175 Philosophical Studies.
Pugiotto A, 'La "galera amministrativa" degli stranieri e le sue incostituzionali metamorfosi' (2014) 3 Quaderni costituzionali. Rivista italiana di diritto costituzionale.
Rosenberg-Rubins R, *Crimmigration Under International Protection. Constructing Criminal Law as Governmentality* (Routledge 2023).
Sherif M, *In Common Predicament. Social Psychology of Intergroup Conflict and Cooperation* (Houghton Mifflin 1966).
Spena A, 'Iniuria Migrandi: Criminalization of Immigrants and the Basic Principles of the Criminal Law' (2014) 8 Criminal Law and Philosophy 635.
Spena A, 'Human Smuggling and Irregular Immigration in the EU: From Complicity to Exploitation?' in Carrera S and Guild E (eds), *Irregular Migration, Trafficking and Smuggling of Human Beings* (CEPS 2016).
Spena A, 'Resisting Immigration Detention' (2016) 18 European Journal of Migration and Law 201.
Spena A, 'The Good, the Bad and the Ugly: Images of the Foreigner in Contemporary Criminal Law' (2018) 4 International Journal of Migration and Border Studies 287.
Spena A, 'Smuggling umanitario e scriminanti' (2019) 62 Rivista italiana di diritto e procedura Penale.

Spena A, 'The Double-Deviant Identity of the Mass-Foreigner and the Lack of Authority of the Crimmigrationist State' (2019) 22 New Criminal Law Review 301.

Spena A, 'Smuggled Migrants as Victims? Reflecting on the UN Protocol Against Migrant Smuggling and on its Implementation' in Forlati S (ed), *The Palermo Convention at Twenty; the Challenge of Implementation* (Brill Nijhoff 2021).

Spena A, 'La dimensione pubblica del discorso d'odio' in Salvatore Di Piazza and Alessandro Spena (eds), *Parole cattive—La libertà di espressione tra linguaggio, diritto e filosofia* (Quodlibet 2022).

Stumpf J, 'The Crimmigration Crisis: Immigrants, Crime, and Sovereign Power' (2006) 56 American University Law Review 367.

Stumpf J, 'Crimmigration and the Legitimacy of Immigration Law' (2023) 65 Arizona Law Review 113.

Tajfel H, *Human Groups and Social Categories. Studies in Social Psychology* (CUP 1981).

Tajfel H, 'Social Psychology of Intergroup Relations' (1982) 33 Annual Reviews of Psychology 1.

Thorup M, 'Democratic Hatreds: The Making of "the Hating Enemy" in Liberal Democracy' in Brudholm T and Schepelern Johansen B (eds), *Hate, Politics, Law. Critical Perspectives on Combating Hate* (OUP 2018).

Vázquez Y, 'Crimmigration: The Missing Piece of Criminal Justice Reform' (2017) 51 University of Richmond Law Review 1093.

Waldron J, *The Harm in Hate Speech* (Harvard UP 2014).

Wilsher D, *Immigration Detention: Law, History, Politics* (CUP 2012).

Zirulia S, *Il favoreggiamento dell'immigrazione irregolare—Tra overcriminalisation e tutela dei diritti fondamentali* (Giappichelli 2024).

6 Migrants' Agency in Smuggling Routes

Criminalising Practices and Socio-Legal Implications in the EU

Flavia Patanè

6.1 Introduction

The term "crimmigration" refers to the intertwining of crime control and migration control that has been taking place over the past two decades.[1] One of the main techniques used in the crimmigration process is the use of criminal penalties and proceedings for immigration law purposes.[2] In this regard, several studies show how the law on human smuggling has become a tool to curb migration and prevent the presence of undesirable individuals within the territory of the state.[3] In this debate, one main criticism revolves around the legitimacy of the European and domestic legal frameworks on human smuggling in light of the over-criminalisation of solidarity with migrants.[4] Another, less researched, area of concern regarding anti-smuggling policies in the EU lies in the impacts such policies have not on the humanitarian actors helping irregular migrants, but on the migrants themselves. While the agency of migrants within their own smuggling is at the centre of recent studies, including criminological studies, on human smuggling,[5] a less explored question is how justice systems react to this agency. The aim of this chapter is to address the latter question by looking into the increased use of anti-smuggling laws and policies against irregular migrants and asylum seekers who facilitate their own journey to Europe, and to discuss the socio-legal implications of this trend.

The chapter is organised into three sections. Section 6.2 explores previous literature on the role played by migrants in the smuggling process and provides the necessary background of the study. It shows how, in the prevailing literature on human smuggling, the active role played by migrants is either silenced or overemphasised, whereas a more meaningful approach is to reconcile such binary views. Section 6.3 focuses on the position of smuggled migrants within the international and EU legal frameworks on human smuggling. After analysing the limitations of supranational laws in respect to risks of criminalisation of migrants, the section provides evidence of such criminalisation taking place in different contexts of smuggling to and through the EU. Particularly, by analysing recent legal cases, the section shows how, as migrants increasingly participate in smuggling-related offenses as a way to secure their own entry or stay in

DOI: 10.4324/9781003378440-6

EU Member States, they are often criminalised under laws and policies targeting smugglers rather than irregular migrants. Section 6.4 reflects on the socio-legal implications of the criminalisation of migrants who play an active role in their own smuggling. It is therefore argued that a proper re-conceptualisation of human smuggling should be informed by the active role migrants play within smuggling processes in order to avoid over-criminalisation and their unfair exclusion from protection.

6.2 The Role of Migrants in Criminological Models on Human Smuggling

This section examines the role of migrants within criminological models of human smuggling, presenting a nuanced analysis of two predominant frameworks. First, it outlines the organised crime model, which emphasises smuggling as a global business run by institutionalised networks for profit, treating migrants as passive commodities. Next, it explores the human network model, which shifts focus to the agency of migrants and their active role in navigating migration processes. Finally, it reconciles these models, discussing how the interplay between the sophistication of smuggling networks and the agency of migrants shapes contemporary smuggling practices.

6.2.1 Organised Crime Model of Human Smuggling

Both practitioners and researchers conceptualise human smuggling as an aspect of international migration.[6] The classical model of human smuggling approaches migration solely in terms of its relation to organised crime. Salt and Stein elaborated a model that conceptualises international migration as a global business in which institutionalised networks operate in pursuit of a commercial gain.[7] In such a model, migrant smuggling and human trafficking function as an intermediary part of the global migration business, facilitating movements of people between origin and destination countries.[8] The legal status of the migrants transported is, generally speaking, irrelevant and does not determine the illegality of the migration-facilitating process (i.e., smuggling). The focus is therefore on the institutions invested in the facilitating business rather than on the migrants themselves. The model usually recognises that asylum seekers and irregular migrants alike rely on illegal means to reach their destination countries; however, they are themselves seen only as "commodities" at the disposal of rational profit makers.[9]

The business model has gained popularity in the European Union, with the European Union Agency for Law Enforcement Cooperation (Europol) and the European Union Agency for Criminal Justice Cooperation (Eurojust) endorsing it in their policies. In Eurojust's documents, migrant smuggling crimes are usually attributed to organised criminal groups working in smuggling routes, who often ruthlessly endanger the lives of migrants throughout their journey, whether by land, air, or sea.[10]

The main characteristics of the business model, as presented by EU agencies, are:

(1) Migrants are mostly considered "passive objects" who are "recruited" by smugglers.[11] Therefore, they do not retain much control over their own migration process.[12] Smuggling is a business that exploits the pain and hardship of people; however, states usually do not identify smuggled migrants as victims of a crime. This is due to the fact that smuggled migrants do not fully resemble the archetypical victim who has not caused or provoked her own predicament,[13] as they are generally presumed to consent to their own smuggling.
(2) Human smuggling is a flexible business that responds rapidly to controls put in place by states. Therefore, there is a focus on trying to grasp the sophistication of smuggling procedures, including the separation of tasks and different trafficker and organisational roles.
(3) The human smuggling business represents a major security threat.[14] Human smuggling is primarily an organised crime phenomenon run by networks that are usually involved in other organised crime areas, such as drug trafficking. The prevention of document fraud becomes a core part of the fight against human smuggling, as it is identified as a typical smugglers' *modus operandi.*
(4) As stipulated by the 2000 UN Smuggling Protocol (the Protocol),[15] there is a need for stronger cooperation between police forces and judiciaries. For instance, in 2016, Europol established the European Migrant Smuggling Centre (EMSC) with the aim to support "police and border authorities to coordinate highly complex cross-border anti-smuggling operations" in order to address the "multi-billion-euro trade" of human smuggling.[16]
(5) There is a very clear distinction between human smuggling and trafficking. While a smuggled migrant would have made an agreement with a smuggler with the aim to obtain entry into a country, a trafficked person is someone who, through force, fraud, or deception, is recruited, transported, transferred, harboured, or received for the purpose of being exploited.[17]

The organised crime model seems to generate a portrayal of migrants as mere objects, incapable of assuming control over their own destinies. At the same time, it puts great emphasis on consent as the distinguishing line between smuggling and trafficking that rules out extending the protection afforded to trafficked victims to smuggled migrants. During criminal investigations, migrants are granted an active role only as providers of information about the *modus operandi* and the dynamics of the organised criminal networks;[18] in order words, they are instrumental in building up cases for prosecution. The qualification of the migrant as a victim, witness, or suspect derives from their level of involvement in the smuggling case.

The global business model lacks a comprehensive view of migration, as it fails to acknowledge the responsibility of states and border controls for the exploitation of migrants.[19] Furthermore, by putting their emphasis on the smugglers, EU agencies and governments usually deny the agency of migrants in their own smuggling. Such accounts aim to label smuggling as the cause of irregular migration to the EU and do not recognise how, in the absence of safe channels to migrate to the EU, smuggling is often the only way people can fulfil their migratory journey.

6.2.2 *Human Network Model on Human Smuggling*

The assumption made by organised crime theories that migrants are merely objects of human smuggling procedures has been questioned by studies on the active role migrants take in their migration process.[20] This second model of human smuggling is based on a view that sees international migration mainly as a human network. In this model, the focus is on migrants as independent subjects, and their migration journey is seen as an expression of self-determination. The migrant's agency is a key concept for this understanding of international migration, which allows one to examine the "lived experience of the migrant and their strategies of navigating a dangerous and complex world of control and deterrence as well as of opportunity and hope".[21] There is an emphasis on migration processes as being, at least partly, the result of an individual choice by the migrant or by their community. For example, in the context of migration from Eritrea to Ethiopia and Europe, Mengiste reports of a proactive role on the part of migrants and their friends and family members and shows how the facilitation of irregular transit by migrants themselves reproduces a "collective system of migratory knowledge that aims to bring refugees to safety".[22]

Literature on migration systems also emphasises human agency in the different phases of the migration project. Bakewell et al., for instance, reflect on the agency of those engaged in pioneering migration systems and argue that migrants are not passive recipients of the opportunity structures presented to them by the origin and destination countries, but that in making their decision to migrate or assisting others to follow their footsteps they exercise a certain degree of choice.[23] Studying the Angolan migration process to the Netherlands, Van Wijk reports how asylum seekers arrange travel documents themselves through informal social networks and corrupt practices rather than using large-scale human smuggling organisations.[24]

At the same time, ethnographic studies have shed light on the strong bonds between the smugglers and the smuggled that challenge the conceptualisations of smugglers as "wicked villains" who exploit migrants.[25] Scholars like Sanchez have undertaken extensive empirical research that shows how ordinary people and migrants themselves operate independently and within personal networks to facilitate border crossing.[26] According to this literature, the role of transnational organised crime in the facilitation of movement has been overestimated in the policies of Western states. Empirical studies have also demonstrated that in some contexts those who facilitate migratory movements are committed to protecting people throughout their journey, rather than acting as unscrupulous criminals.[27] The human network model has the advantage of incorporating migrants' perspectives on their personal life journey, as well as of collocating them within the structural challenges faced by irregular migrants in the current securitarian environment of Western states. It effectively dismantles the state-centred view of facilitation of migration and sheds light on the instrumental depiction of smugglers as the sole root of the evils of human rights abuses suffered by migrants.

When analysing the shortcomings of this model, one main point arises. This model might be criticised for being simplistic in ruling out the possible involvement of criminal smugglers. While there is indeed evidence showing that in most cases irregular migrants are not "recruited" by the smugglers, it is demonstrated that in many contexts, throughout the journey, migrants enter into a relationship with the smuggler, that is, someone whose motivation for facilitating irregular migration is not primarily altruistic. Such relationships can have varying natures, ranging from mutual respect to severe exploitation. As noted by Staring in 2004, an enormous diversity of actors and motivations is characteristic of the immigration industry, from family or community members supporting their relatives' journeys, to violent criminal networks.[28] De Bondt et al. also conclude that there is "an enormous diversity in the landscape of organised criminal involvement" in both human smuggling and trafficking, "but also there is an enormous diversity as to the different types of actors active in these markets".[29] The relationship between smugglers and smuggled individuals is quite diverse and dynamic over time,[30] and migrants might have space for negotiations with smugglers while at the same time being in an extremely vulnerable position.[31] While organised criminal involvement is certainly not an essential part of smuggling, evidence from different sources suggests that smuggling may, depending on the route, simultaneously be both a criminal issue and a human network phenomenon.[32]

6.2.3 Reconciling the Two Models: Sophistication of Smuggling Networks and Agency of Migrants

According to the traditional view on migration management and smuggling, the imposition by states of new obstacles or the heightening of old ones leads to the sharp diminution of a long, continued flow of people to state borders.[33] Such a position does not take into account the evolving strategies of both smugglers and migrants. In 2000, the UNHCR noted that the control and deterrence measures implemented by Western states with the turn of the millennium would have little lasting impact because the need of people to move prevails.[34] If one route narrows or closes, the pressure is directed at another.[35] Similarly, in 2007, Broeders and Engbersen predicted that the strengthening of new policies of identification and exclusion by European states would lead to the ability of the state "to intervene in the crucial strategies of irregular migrants, particularly in the use of migration networks and the manipulation of their identity".[36] Consequently, according to these scholars, as states raise protective walls and develop control systems around a logic of exclusion, "traveling to and staying in Europe may very well become an affair of professional and criminal activity".[37]

The main point to realise here is that while the "fight against human smuggling" has brought about the sophistication of smuggling networks,[38] it has also impacted the roles played by smuggled migrants. In other words, the proliferation of criminal networks enabling mobility of people has not eliminated the self-determination of migrants, quite the opposite. Both smugglers and migrants have started developing strategies to decrease risk and overcome the challenges posed by the context of irregular migration and securitisation of borders.[39]

At the same time, a more active role for migrants and increasing solidarity among them do not necessarily exclude the involvement of organised crime. Members of smuggling networks easily adapt to changing circumstances and vary strategies according to the measures taken by governments in order to avoid their jurisdictional reach. In the EU, since states and institutions have included the fight against human smuggling in their migration management agendas, there has been growing evidence of the attempts by smugglers to remain "invisible".[40] For example, in Italy, when prosecutors started arresting professional smugglers operating on boats in international waters, criminal organisations responsible for the smuggling market in Libya started leaving vessels to be conducted by smuggled migrants themselves in order to secure impunity of their own members.[41]

This approach has also been registered in smuggling operations via land. For instance, in Bulgaria, in response to increased arrests of hired "inland" drivers, facilitators started to buy cars and buses and instead of driving migrants to Sofia, they would leave the car near the border refuelled and with the keys inside for the migrants to drive by themselves.[42] A dangerous pattern has also been reported at the Greek–Turkish border: Vehicles driving at high speed in an attempt to reach Greece, piloted by migrants who agree to drive in order to pay off a debt to smugglers.[43] Along the Balkan route, researchers are showing how direct violence used to control cross-border crime shapes migrants' aspirations to shift their role from clients to workers in smuggling organisations.[44]

The overview above suggests that criminal organisations may use migrants as a deliberate *modus operandi* aimed at securing their own impunity, but also that migrants increasingly participate in their own smuggling to the EU in response to state border measures. It is in the interaction between systems of exclusion by states and the advancement of organised criminal groups' strategies that the agency of migrants should be interpreted. As human smuggling is a reaction to the militarisation of border controls of the last two decades,[45] the self-organisation of smuggled migrants can be read as an agentic response to the closure of borders. Importantly, the strategies developed by migrants throughout migratory routes do not rule out their vulnerability and possible various degrees of exploitation.[46] As argued by de Rebetz, most cases of smuggling within the EU fall in an in-between grey area, where smuggled migrants can, at times, be in full control of their migration paths but at other times choose to relinquish their agency to the migrant smugglers.[47]

One main problem with agency played by migrants is that, as demonstrated, for example, by van Liempt, the individual strategies developed by migrants introduce a complexity into human smuggling cases that do not fit the typical categories in the law of human smuggling.[48] As smuggled migrants actively interpret immigration policies and base their actions on these interpretations, this situation progressively shows the shortcomings of the binary distinction between the "smuggler" and the "smuggled" on which human smuggling laws and policies rely.[49] One of the shortcomings of such categorisation is that it does not take into account the interaction between vulnerability and agency of migrants. As will be shown below, while supranational laws on human smuggling have introduced the obligation for states to criminalise facilitation of irregular migration, including in its organised forms, they have also left protection gaps in relation to smuggled migrants and their agentic strategies. Such gaps have contributed to smuggled migrants being directly exposed to criminalisation at the national level under human smuggling laws and policies.

Until now, I have explored the criminological conditions that lead to the criminalisation of migrants under human smuggling laws (namely, the sophistication of human smuggling networks and the increased agency of migrants). The chapter now moves to the analysis of the legal cause underlying the exposure of migrants to criminalisation with human smuggling laws and policies, that is, the protection gaps in the international and EU frameworks on human smuggling.

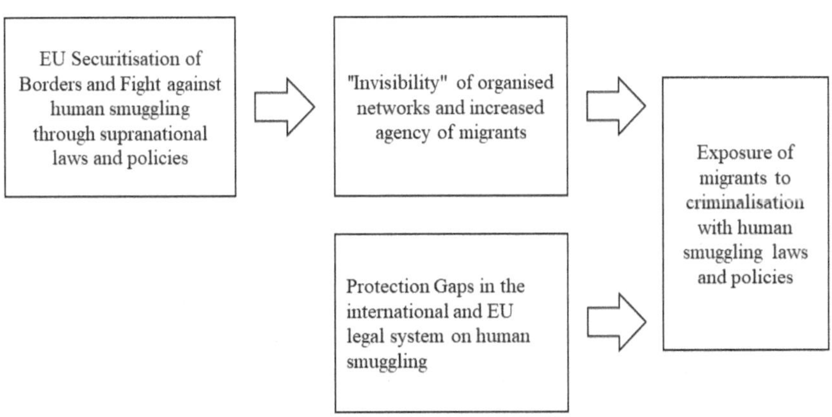

Figure 6.1 Causes leading to the criminalisation of migrants via human smuggling laws

6.3 Protection Gaps in International and EU Law and Criminalisation

This section explores the tension between the criminalisation of human smuggling and the protection of smuggled migrants under international, EU, and domestic law. It first examines the ambivalence of the Smuggling Protocol, treating migrants as both objects and agents (3.1). Next, it addresses the broad definition of smuggling in the EU's Facilitation Directive and its impact on migrants (3.2). The section concludes by examining domestic practices in the EU, exploring case studies of smuggling via land (3.3.1), sea (3.3.2), and air (3.3.3), to demonstrate the criminalisation of migrants as active participants in their smuggling journeys. These analyses highlight the complex relationship between migration management and criminal justice responses, illustrating the protection gaps and unintended consequences of current legal frameworks.

6.3.1 Smuggled Migrants in International Law

The Smuggling Protocol represents the primary international law framework for the criminalisation of human smuggling.[50] It introduces human smuggling as a transnational crime in order to protect states' interest to secure their own borders, while simultaneously protecting smuggled migrants.[51] States attempted to reconcile these two interests—states' borders and migrants' position—by attributing an active role to organised networks involved in smuggling,[52] whereas migrants were seen as having a quiet, passive role. More particularly, Article 5 of the Smuggling Protocol affirms that "[m]igrants shall not become liable to criminal prosecution under this Protocol for the fact of having been the object of conduct set forth in Article 6 of this Protocol". Smuggled migrants are, therefore, constructed as "objects" of the conduct of smuggling, acted upon rather than actors. As argued by Spena, framing smuggling as a transnational crime

> implicitly depicts smuggled migrants as mere instruments exploited by others for their own benefit, as subjects taken into consideration not so much for any action they may perform, but because of the mere fact that they represent sources of illicit enrichment of other persons.[53]

As long as they remain passive, migrants can be identified as "smuggled" and are entitled to exemption from prosecution.

The approach of the Protocol, however, changes with regard to migrants who are labelled as *agents* in the migratory journey. More particularly, Article 6(4) of the Protocol states: "nothing in the Protocol shall prevent a State from taking measures against a person whose conduct constitutes an offence under its domestic law".[54] Indeed, while the objective of the Smuggling Protocol is to criminalise and prosecute those who smuggle others for gain, and not the migrants themselves, the latter can still be prosecuted for having smuggled others or for the commission of any other smuggling-related offense defined in national laws. This is the position of both the United Nations Office on Drugs and Crime (UNODC)[55] and the recent UN Global Compact Migration from 2018.[56] As "active migrants" are not "smuggled migrants" for the purpose of the Protocol, it seems that they fall outside its protective scope. By introducing a clear-cut dichotomy between "migrant objects" and "migrant agents", the international framework on human smuggling has taken an ambivalent stance that has not adequately solved the tension between the logics of criminalisation and of protection in relation to categories of migrants who are active agents within their own migration journey.

6.3.2 EU Law

In the EU, states have adopted a definition of smuggling that is much broader than the one in the Smuggling Protocol. The EU Facilitators' Package, consisting of the Facilitation Directive and its accompanying Framework Decision,[57] do not require evidence that there has been any financial gain or profit for the facilitation of irregular entry to come into effect.[58] Because of the broad contours of the facilitation offence and the obligation on states to criminalise such conduct within their national systems, the EU legislation on smuggling is a doorway to the sweeping use of anti-smuggling policies. More particularly, critiques of the Facilitation Directive have focused on the uncritical use of the facilitation offence against categories of people and institutions that do not have any link with organised crime.[59] This seems to be in line with what a few scholars have identified as the real aim of the Directive, that is, the fight against irregular migration and not human smuggling.[60]

A related question concerns the portrayal of smuggled migrants within the Directive. In EU law, smuggling does not consist of "procuring" illegal entry of a person, but rather "assisting" a non-national to enter, transit, or stay in the EU.[61] Therefore, migrants are not portrayed as "objects", but more as beneficiaries of human smuggling. Spena goes even further, concluding that the definition of the offence is drafted "in complicity terms" as if "the migrants themselves are actively involved in the perpetration of the crime".[62] Does this also mean that smuggled migrants could be investigated and prosecuted for facilitation of irregular migration when they play an active role in smuggling, for example, when they transport other migrants or asylum seekers while securing their own entrance to the EU? A cursory look at the description of the identified target category of the Facilitation Directive, as "any person who intentionally assists a person who is not a national of a Member State to enter, or transit across, the territory of a Member State", suggests an affirmative answer.

This conclusion seems corroborated by the fact that Article 1 of the Facilitation Decision states that "when appropriate", criminal penalties for facilitation of irregular entry and stay "may be accompanied" by deportation,[63] thus suggesting that perpetrators may have an immigration status and introducing an immigration-related consequence for those involved in smuggling procedures. Furthermore, while a specific (non-mandatory) exception for those assisting irregular entry and transit out of humanitarian reasons has been included in the Directive,[64] no specific provision has been included in relation to migrants. Indeed, while the provision does not offer a definition of "humanitarian assistance", it was introduced after civic society organisations expressed concerns over their own possible prosecution for assisting third-country nationals and does not concern criminalisation of smuggled migrants as such.[65]

In November 2023, the European Commission adopted a proposal for a Directive which is supposed to replace the Facilitators' Package.[66] This proposal has potential for limiting the overbroad reach of criminal law in human smuggling cases; however, it presents some limitations in relation to the possible criminalisation of migrants within anti-smuggling policies.[67]

6.3.3 *Domestic Approaches in the EU: Evidence of Criminalisation of "Migrant-Agents"*

This section aims to provide evidence of a correlation between the migration strategies developed by migrants during the smuggling process (either by land, sea, or air) and the response of domestic criminal justice systems (in particular, the use of criminal law and the recognition of asylum-seeking situations). It offers an analysis of domestic legal cases and national practices in EU Member States as examples of prosecution, conviction, or penalisation of migrants for active participation in their own smuggling.

6.3.3.1 *Smuggling by Land*

Agency of migrants in smuggling via land has been reported on different occasions. For instance, in episodes of mass crossing, migrants often organise themselves to synchronise their crossing as a way to enhance their chances to successfully get past the border.[68] While formal policies attribute these episodes to mafia-like organisations or non-EU countries, there can be different legal consequences for the migrants involved in such acts.[69]

Less reported are cases in which migrants show active roles in smuggling others, such as in the "*Procès de la solidarité*" in Belgium. This trial concerns 11 people—seven migrants (with Eritrean, Egyptian, Syrian, Sudanese, and Tunisian nationalities) and four "hosts"—prosecuted by the public prosecutor's office of East Flanders in 2017 for facilitating irregular migration across Belgian borders. In 2018, the Tribunal of First Instance of Brussels acquitted the four Belgian hosts, while the migrants were sentenced to 12 to 40 months in prison for having acted as *passeaurs*. Acts for which they were convicted were: Guiding the "victims" of the smuggling from a train station to the parking lots; opening and closing truck doors; helping victims to board with their luggage; inquiring about the location of different motorway car parks; or collecting money from victims (Sudanese and Eritrean asylum seekers who wanted to cross into Britain).[70]

The seven migrants who acted as *passeaurs* in the case were convicted under Article 77 *bis* of the Belgian law of 15 December 1980. Article 77 *bis* applies the offence of human smuggling to anyone assisting the entry, transit, or residence of a third-country national in violation of state legislation and with a view towards obtaining, directly or indirectly, a financial benefit.[71] At the same time, the tribunal did not confirm the charge of participation in a (structured) criminal association under Article 324 *bis* of the Belgian Criminal Code, which had been charged by the prosecutor in relation to the migrants. It instead requalified the conduct as an aggravating circumstance under Article 77.7 *quarter* of Belgian law of 15 December 1980, namely "participation in the main or ancillary activity of an association". During the trial, it was not disputed that the defendants only participated in the smuggling in the hope of being able to cross the English Channel themselves, at a lower cost or for free, and not to participate in a criminal organisation.[72] The Court of Appeal of Brussels even acknowledged that the defendants were "victims" of the smuggling network.[73] However, the fact that they were participating in the smuggling process to facilitate themselves was only considered in order to assess the sentence to be imposed and not their criminal liability.[74] Both the Tribunal of First Instance and the Court of Appeal concluded that the fact that the defendants were participating in an arrangement with others whereby they were trying to secure their own passage to the UK was sufficient proof that they were pursuing an indirect financial gain, even if none of them had derived any particularly significant income from their activity in the association[75]

6.3.3.2 *Smuggling by Sea—Criminalisation of Boat Drivers*

Smuggling by sea offers the highest number of examples of prosecutions of migrants under anti-human smuggling laws. In the last decade, the criminalisation of those who steer or otherwise take an active role on boats transporting migrants has been widespread in some EU Member States. Different sources confirm that most of the arrested boat drivers in European waters are asylum seekers themselves. Already in 2015, a study commissioned by the European Commission noted that there was "a significant increase in the number of Syrians apprehended for smuggling (131% since 2013) due to the fact that smuggled migrants turn into smugglers themselves".[76] According to an article from 2022 in *The New Humanitarian*, the number of migrants accused of facilitating irregular migration between 2015 and 2021 amount to more than 2000 in Italy, to hundreds in the UK, and to around 7000 in Greece.[77] Different NGO reports and academia articles report that most boat crew members arrested in Greece and Italy for human smuggling from 2014 onwards are in fact migrants who agreed to take an active role in exchange for transportation to Europe.[78]

The motivations for migrants to play an active role on boats may differ. Sometimes, migrants accept an active role in the smuggling chain in exchange for their own transportation to Europe; at other times, they have been forced to do so by the smugglers;[79] or they have been pushed into driving the boat due to their socio-economic background. While the motivations for migrants to play an active role on boats might differ, these cases have one thing in common: They concern people who are themselves in need of migrating—in many times looking for protection—rather than members of criminal associations.

Nevertheless, the approach taken by some prosecution offices in relation to boat drivers in the Mediterranean is particularly severe and takes after the "anti-organised crime approach" introduced by the Smuggling Protocol. For instance, in Italy, cases of migrants prosecuted for human smuggling have often been considered by prosecutorial offices as "the last links of the smuggling chain" and therefore of interest to the anti-mafia prosecutorial offices.[80] A detailed report from Greece shows that out of 48 trials against migrants steering boats monitored between 2014 and 2019, the average sentence for facilitation of illegal entry and related crime was about 48 years, with a mandatory prison sentence of about 19 years.[81]

In cases where no charges of criminal association and no aggravating circumstances are applied, boat drivers are still often prosecuted and convicted for facilitation of irregular migration in basic forms (not requiring profit as an element of the crime), which may still impose a few years in detention.[82] The position of national courts in the EU has been that the specific status of the suspect (smuggled migrant, asylum seeker, etc.) does not relieve the person of their criminal responsibility for helping others to reach their destination. For instance, in 2014, the Supreme Court of Spain made the point that intending to reach the EU does not exclude or exculpate the criminal responsibility for the crime of migrant smuggling, as in these cases, the person is convicted for enabling irregular migration rather than for irregularly entering the state themselves.[83]

The conclusion seems to be similar even when the "use" of smuggled migrants is part of a deliberate *modus operandi* of smuggling networks. According to a judgement of the Italian Court of Cassation from 2021, when there is no proof of a criminal link between the driving migrant and members of a criminal organisation, but nevertheless the driving of the vessel by the migrants themselves is part of an organised plan of "full-fledged smugglers", the migrant still bears responsibility for occasional cooperation with the smuggler.[84] In Italy, only a proven state of necessity has worked as an exonerating circumstance in the cases of boat captains.[85]

Different sources have identified the criminalisation of boat drivers in the Mediterranean as a "collateral effect of the EU migration management",[86] an "orchestrated selection of a scapegoat to allay the security concerns".[87] The approach to these cases shows that there is a binary categorisation, smuggled/smuggler, in which migrants who actively participate in their own smuggling lose protection for not fitting the stereotypical idea of an "object" of the crime. Furthermore, not only do migrants prosecuted for human smuggling lose protection from penalisation; they may also encounter difficulties in accessing asylum procedures.[88] When convicted for facilitation of irregular migration, they might be might be denied international protection as "foreigners constituting a danger to public order",[89] or excluded from subsidiary protection.[90]

6.3.3.3 *Smuggling via Air*

A common strategy used by smuggled migrants to secure their entry into a state involves the use of false or stolen documents. Asylum seekers are often obliged to use the services of smugglers who provide them with false or forged documents in order to get around the vigilance of commercial carriers.[91] At the very least, such criminal law focus on document fraud exposes irregular migrants and asylum seekers using false documents to more penetrating examination by law enforcement actors. This should not be underestimated. A study by the European Migration Network, for instance, shows that the use of false documentation to reach the EU, depending on the specific national legislation, may have severe impacts on the asylum procedure of the person involved.[92] There is evidence that prosecution of migrants for document-related fraud in the EU actually starts before and independently of the determination of their status under international law. Costello, for instance, notes that "a general problem in States in Europe appears to be the failure to avoid or suspend criminal prosecution while the asylum claim is determined".[93]

The conduct of using a false document does not amount to the criminal offence of smuggling, which usually presupposes a difference between the facilitator and the facilitated. However, there is a strong correlation between the use of false documents and human smuggling, as the former is often seen as a component of smuggling. At the policy level, there is a recent emphasis on document fraud as the "new" *modus operandi* of smugglers.[94] In a recent report, Europol estimates that the increased controls and restrictions on travel and entry in some EU countries will likely fuel this strategy.[95]

The relationship between the use of false documents and prosecution under human smuggling laws remains underexplored. The conflation of the use of false documents with the "fight against smugglers" was evident in a recent Italian judicial case. In 2019, a woman from the Republic of Congo attempted to circumvent border controls at Bologna airport by showing false Senegalese passports for herself and two children traveling with her (later found to be her daughter and niece). What makes this case interesting, for the purpose of our analysis, is that the arrested woman was an asylum seeker herself who had showed false passport documents in order to enter Italy and ask for asylum. She was arrested and charged with both possession of false documents[96] and facilitation of irregular migration in the aggravated form because she had used international transportation and false IDs to facilitate the illegal entry of the two minors.[97]

This case gave the Italian Constitutional Court the opportunity to intervene in the definition of the domestic offence of human smuggling for the first time.[98] In the case, the state advocate argued that the aggravated form of smuggling was justified by the fact that the woman had relied on a smuggler for procuring for herself the false documents.[99] The Constitutional Court promptly rejected the argument and ruled that the aggravating circumstance of "using false documents" with a penalty from 5 to 15 years in detention constituted "a manifestly irrational legislative choice",[100] rendering it unconstitutional. To arrive at its conclusion, the court clearly distinguished between the facilitation of irregular migration for solidarity or mutual aid and human smuggling perpetrated by organised criminal groups. In other words, the court said it is irrational to prosecute a migrant facilitating her own and her family's entrance with penalties equal to those designed for smugglers.

The decision by the Italian Constitutional Court is to be welcomed, as it seems to open the door to a more nuanced conceptualisation of human smuggling that resembles the model of human smuggling as a social network grounded in solidarity. At the same time, it falls short of providing protection to those smuggled migrants who use false documents to secure their own entry or those of their family members, as migrants with an asylum-seeking status can still be prosecuted, not only for the use of false documents but also for the basic offence of facilitation of irregular migration.

6.4 Implications of the Study

This section explores the multifaceted implications of the study, particularly focusing on the intersection between criminal law, migration policy, and the treatment of smuggled migrants. The discussion highlights the need for a nuanced understanding of migrant smuggling, focusing on how current EU frameworks often fail to differentiate between the smuggling of persons for exploitation and humanitarian acts. The analysis culminates in examining how international law, particularly refugee law, might offer a more protective and human rights-oriented approach to smuggled migrants, ultimately providing a foundation for reforming EU policy in this area.

6.4.1 *Migrants as Complicit with Smugglers: A Crimmigration Strategy*

Crimmigration scholars have identified three main patterns of criminal policy strategies operating both in the US and in the EU, namely: The use of criminal law to punish immigration law breaches; the introduction of administrative consequences following criminal convictions; and the introduction of criminal-type tools, such as custodial measures, for immigration law violations.[101] More recently, a "fourth path" of crimmigration in the EU has extended to the over-criminalisation of human smuggling (indirect criminalisation of migration).[102] Indeed, since the 2015 EU "refugee crisis", the main strategy has consisted of the over-criminalisation of those assisting irregular migration rather than the direct criminalisation of migrants. What this chapter shows is an additional crimmigration technique adopted by some local criminal policy strategies: The criminalisation of migrants via laws and policies supposedly designed to protect them from the harms of risky journeys organised by smugglers.

More particularly, there seems to be a tendency to conflate smuggled migrants with smugglers every time the smuggled migrants' conduct moves beyond that ascribed to them as "objects" (e.g., consent to being transported, negotiation with the smuggler about routes and price of the journey). This is particularly relevant in those cases in which migrants are prosecuted and convicted for facilitation of irregular migration in its aggravated forms, by applying elements of smuggling, such as the profit requirement or the endangerment of lives, that were designed to fight serious forms of smuggling, not mutual solidarity among migrants. In this regard, the prosecution of migrants for serious forms of human smuggling underscores an instrumentalisation of the organised crime paradigm, which exposes the inconsistency between high-level goals and the reality of domestic cases. The conflation of the smuggled migrant and the smuggler gives credence to the argument by the Guild that the call of the Protocol to criminalise human smuggling has led states to shift their focus "from the plight of the people using smugglers' services to the evils of smugglers and traffickers", eventually compromising international human rights protection.[103]

Nevertheless, the Smuggling Protocol clearly states that migrants should not be penalised for relying on smugglers. Furthermore, the wording of Article 5, that "[m]igrants shall not become liable to criminal prosecution under this Protocol for the fact of having been the object of conduct set forth in Article 6 of this Protocol", conveys the clear message that the transnational fight against smugglers should not bring about more criminalisation of migrants. If states have enhanced their focus on human smuggling as a consequence of the call of the Protocol, they should also implement its protection objectives.[104] Furthermore, in order for this protection to retain any value, it should also be interpreted by keeping in mind the development of both smugglers' and migrants' strategies. As evidence is showing that migrants have stopped being only "objects" of human smuggling, the exercise of their agency should be better incorporated in the judicial responses implementing the fight against human smuggling, as to do otherwise amounts to endorsing the *modus operandi* of full-fledged smugglers.

6.4.2 Unsuitability of EU Human Smuggling Laws and Possible Reforms

The unsuitability of laws on human smuggling that criminalise the facilitation of irregular migration without imposing more stringent requirements on the definition of the crime has been extensively highlighted by various studies. Some scholars have argued that adding a profit requirement to the EU definition of human smuggling may help to limit the scope of criminalisation of human smuggling.[105] While this might prevent the criminalisation of humanitarian actors, it might have no effect on the growing framing of migrants as perpetrators or aiders within the smuggling process. Indeed, in the cases assessed in this study, the migrant's act of securing a journey to the EU may still be interpreted as a "profit" or benefit. A broad interpretation of the concept of profit could indeed include benefitting from the promise to travel free or at a reduced cost to an EU state, as, for instance, interpreted by the Brussels Criminal Court in the "*Procès de la solidarité*" case.[106]

As said above, in 2023, the European Commission proposed to redefine the offence of facilitating irregular migration as assisting a third-country national to enter, transit across, or stay within the territory of any Member State, where either the person requests, receives, or accepts, directly or indirectly, a financial or material benefit, or there is a high likelihood of causing serious harm to a person.[107] This definition addresses the breadth of the smuggling offence and is supposed to provide "clarity on which offences should be criminalized".[108]

The proposal by the Commission seems to introduce a more migrant-centred definition of human smuggling, and in this regard, it could be seen as a step towards a definition of the crime that focuses more on fundamental rights than on protecting borders.[109] However, it falls short of sufficiently circumscribing the reach of criminal law in relation to migrants playing an active role in their own smuggling in several ways. First, the element of direct or indirect benefit in the proposed definition remains broad and, as noted above, might continue to be interpreted in an instrumental way by national authorities in cases of migrants participating in smuggling. Second, the alternative element of "high likelihood of serious harm to a person" might maintain the systematic prosecution and conviction of those who act in contexts of smuggling that are inherently dangerous for life, such as third-country nationals who help others to escape in a collective flight by sea. Finally, not only does the proposal reproduce the portrayal of migrants as passive objects in their smuggling, it also specifically provides that

> considering the possible risk to public policy and public security that they may pose, third-country nationals who committed the offences defined in this Directive should be subject to return . . . either after having served the prison sentence in a Member State or in view of serving the prison sentence.[110]

These third-country nationals should then be subject to entry bans.[111]

The assumption that facilitators of irregular migration may pose risks to public policy or security and therefore should be returned may sanction the national practices of prosecuting and returning third-country nationals who participate in smuggling without looking at their status as asylum seekers or refugees. This could conflict with international law. Indeed, engagement in people smuggling for the purpose of seeking protection does not constitute a legitimate ground for expulsion under Article 32 of the Refugee Convention.[112]

A situation in which asylum seekers and smuggled migrants, who (according to official EU policies) are the protected group of anti-smuggling policies, might bear the severe consequences of such policies, calls into question the legitimacy and effectiveness of the current EU anti-smuggling system. The adoption of anti-smuggling legislation might be an opportunity to address this situation. In this regard, the status of smuggled migrants within human smuggling cases might be discussed, and a specific provision could be introduced in EU law that provides a basis for non-criminalisation of smuggled migrants and clarifies their status within criminal proceedings. This would also make the status of smuggled migrants more uniform across the EU.[113]

While such a provision could be inspired by the non-criminalisation clause in Article 5 of the Smuggling Protocol, it should take into account the evolved nature of human smuggling and the dynamic role that migrants play within it instead of reproducing the binary of smugglers/objects of the crime. Therefore, it should exempt from prosecution those migrants who have facilitated their own and others' flight to the EU and who do not belong to a criminal organisation. Otherwise, the use of criminal law in this area may remain a form of secondary victimisation that clashes with the idea of the criminalisation of human smuggling in order to advance migrants' protection in line with the purposes of international protection.

6.4.3 *International Refugee Law as a Basis for Non-Criminalisation in the Framework of Smuggling*

As explained above, the criminalisation and securitisation of migration shape the behaviour of migrants. As EU Member States fortify their borders and enhance the fight against smugglers, migrants will continue to rely on human smuggling and undertake actions to secure their journey. This is especially the case for those who are refugees or asylum seekers. In the criminal cases analysed above, while it is recognised that the defendants are often asylum seekers themselves, the created collusion with smugglers annihilates any legal consideration of the possible asylum-seeker status of the person, including their right to asylum. It is striking that in the many cases of prosecution of migrants within anti-smuggling approaches, the protection afforded by Article 31 of the Refugee Convention (hereinafter "Article 31") is not analysed.

Article 31 stipulates that refugees should not be penalised for their illegal entry.[114] Although EU law prevents Member States from holding a person in detention for the sole reason that they have applied for asylum,[115] it does not explicitly establish a duty to refrain from penalising refugees for unlawful entry or presence, as mandated by Article 31 of the Refugee Convention.[116] In 2014, the Court of Justice of the EU (CJEU) was called to clarify the application of this provision within the EU in the *Qurbani* case. The question was whether Article 31 must be interpreted as precluding a person from being punished under criminal law in the Member State in which he or she seeks asylum, for offences connected with her/his unauthorised entry into that Member State's territory (in particular, unauthorised entry with the assistance of people smugglers and use of a forged identity document).[117] However, the CJEU concluded it did not have the jurisdiction to directly interpret Article 31, or any other article, of the Refugee Convention, as "it is undisputed that the Member States have retained certain powers falling within that field, in particular relating to the subject-matter covered by Article 31 of that convention".[118]

The decision of the court not to intervene in the interpretation of the non-penalisation clause makes it compelling to look at states' practice of the implementation of Article 31 of the Refugee Convention in the context of the EU.[119] In addition to the challenges surrounding the application of Article 31, it is necessary to discuss the possible scope of the non-penalisation clause and its potential for the non-criminalisation of migrants in the framework of smuggling laws and policies. Article 6 of the Facilitators Framework Decision, titled "International law on refugees", states that the decision applies without prejudice to the protection of refugees and asylum seekers in accordance with international refugee law and specifically Article 31 of the Refugee Convention. This imposes an application of human smuggling norms that is respectful of human rights.

According to Gallagher and David, migrant smugglers who are themselves claiming asylum from persecution could benefit from the Refugee Convention's non-penalisation clause in Article 31 with respect to their own entry and stay.[120] At the same time, they also concur that Article 31 does not prevent "migrant smugglers" from being penalised for criminal conduct related to the smuggling of other persons, therefore concluding that international refugee law does not offer protection for smuggling-related offenses.[121] However, a teleological interpretation of international refugee law could suggest otherwise. Instead of immunising refugees from a particular kind of penalty, the purpose of Article 31 is actually to prohibit all penalties when imposed in a particular context, namely as the result of unlawful entry or presence.[122] Importantly, Noll notes that in order for Article 31 to maintain any value, it has to be interpreted in the contemporary context of Northern states' migration policies, and in particular by keeping in mind the current practice of extraterritorial border control.[123] He therefore argues that "an international lawyer respectful of the will of the drafters and original signatories will have to remember this stark shift when interpreting Article 31 in the contemporary context of migration control".[124]

In other words, in order to respect the humanitarian purpose of the treaty, one needs to take into account the specific conditions of the contemporary migration scenario. In the current crimmigration scene—in which states have enhanced the use of criminal law for immigration purposes—Article 31 of the Refugee Convention deserves renewed attention.[125] If a migrant exercises their agency to resist state border controls and ask for protection, does this open a derogation from the rights of *non-refoulement* and to seek asylum that, according to both international and EU law, need to be respected in the implementation of human smuggling policies? The answer should be negative.

When discussing the scope of application of Article 31, Gallagher and David also conclude that

> international law is clear on the point that asylum claims are to be considered on their substantive merits: the right to protection is located within the reasons for flight, not the mode of arrival. In other words, an individual cannot be denied refugee status—or, most important, the opportunity to make a claim for such status through fair assessment procedures, solely because of the way in which that person sought or secured entry into the country of destination.[126]

For example, Hathaway argues that in a situation of "self-smuggling"[127] in which a refugee is seeking to ensure their own access to protection and in doing so leads "a collective flight to safety", the entry of others provoked by that refugee's actions should be viewed only as incidental to the primary and legally protected goal of accessing protection.[128] Prosecution in such a case would amount to an indirect means of unlawfully penalising a refugee for their illegal entry or presence.[129] As concluded by the Supreme Court of Canada in a relevant case of prosecution of "self-smuggling":

> Art. 31(1) of the Refugee Convention seeks to provide immunity for genuine refugees who enter illegally in order to seek refuge. For that protection to be effective, the law must recognize that persons often seek refuge in groups and work together to enter a country illegally. To comply with art. 31(1), a state cannot impose a criminal sanction on refugees solely because they have aided others to enter illegally in their collective flight to safety.[130]

To be sure, there should be a limit to the application of the non-penalisation clause in smuggling cases. In some contexts, participation in smuggling operations results in violence among migrants. Case law has shed light on cases of asylum seekers collaborating with smugglers and traffickers to earn their own trip to Europe in which they participated in kidnapping,[131] abuse, rape, torture, and murder.[132] These cases certainly should be prosecuted as serious violations of human rights.

Furthermore, migrants who have acted as violent smugglers of other migrants and later apply for asylum might be excluded from refugee status under Article 1F of the Refugee Convention, if the conduct amounts to an international crime or a serious non-political crime.[133] However, even in cases where migrants fulfil facilitating roles in organised smuggling networks, their exclusion from protection should be assessed with extreme caution, also keeping in mind that in some smuggling contexts migrants are under great pressure to collaborate with smugglers.[134]

Conclusion

The objective of this study was to shed light on the way in which domestic justice systems are responding to the increased use of agency by migrants along smuggling routes within the current EU migration management context, and to reflect on the socio-legal implications of such a response. It first focused on the criminological causes of the exposure of migrants to human smuggling laws and policies, namely the growing agency of migrants and the sophistication of smuggling networks. Second, the chapter moved to the analysis of the international and EU legal frameworks on human smuggling and exposed the protection gaps they leave in relation to migrants who are actively involved in their own migration experience. It further explored how some EU national systems have been responding to the increased agency played by smuggled migrants by providing evidence of trends of prosecution of smuggled migrants via anti-smuggling laws and policies.

The analysis confirmed that when applying human smuggling laws, national authorities may rely on a formalistic approach in which agency of migrants annihilates their status as asylum seekers and exposes them to different levels of criminalisation. In some cases, there is a clear instrumentalisation of Smuggling Protocol provisions, for instance, when migrants are prosecuted for aggravated forms of human smuggling. Thus, the implementation of human smuggling laws and policies in some EU Member States fails to grasp the nuanced status of smuggled migrants, who may be both "objects" and "agents" in their own journey. This renders the legislative and policy frameworks ill-suited to respond to current developments in smuggling and introduces doubts about the effectiveness of anti-smuggling policies designed at a supranational level.

Finally, the chapter contextualised the prosecution and penalisation of smuggled migrants under human smuggling laws within the crimmigration context. It therefore reflected on the need to come up with a conceptualisation of human smuggling that gives proper consideration to the agency played by migrants without disregarding their vulnerability and possible levels of exploitation. A migrant-centred definition of human smuggling may serve this purpose. Such a re-conceptualisation should be accompanied by a proper discussion at the EU level on a non-criminalisation clause for smuggled migrants and a non-penalisation clause for asylum seekers.

Notes

1 Maartje A. H. van der Woude, Joanne P. van der Leun and Jo-Anne A. Nijland, 'Crimmigration in the Netherlands' (2014) 39 Law & Social Inquiry 560. In the US, the term "crimmigration" has been used in a narrower sense, to indicate the convergence of criminal and immigration law, see Juliet Stumpf, 'The Crimmigration Crisis: Immigrants, Crime, and Sovereign Power' (2006) 56 American University Law Review 367.

2 On the different strategies used in crimmigration, see Gian Luigi Gatta, 'The Connections Between Migration, Crime and Punishment: Historical and Sociological Questions' in Gian Luigi Gatta and others (eds), *Controlling Immigration*

Through Criminal Law: European and Comparative Perspectives on "Crimmigration" (Hart 2021).

3 Valsamis Mitsilegas, 'The Normative Foundations of the Criminalisation of Human Smuggling: Exploring the Fault Lines Between European and International Law' (2019) 10(1) New Journal of European Criminal Law 68.

4 Sergio Carrera and others, *Policing Humanitarianism: EU Policies Against Human Smuggling and Their Impact on Civil Society* (Hart 2019); Stefano Zirulia, 'Is that a Smuggler? The Blurring Line Between Facilitating Illegal Immigration and Providing Humanitarian Assistance at the European Borders' in Gian Luigi Gatta and others (n 2).

5 Ilse van Liempt and Jeroen Doomernik, 'Migrant's Agency in the Smuggling Process: The Perspectives of Smuggled Migrants in the Netherlands' (2006) 44(4) International Migration 165.

6 See Theodore Baird 'Theoretical Approaches to Human Smuggling' (2013) DIIS Working Paper 10/2013 <https://pure.diis.dk/ws/files/56032/WP2013_10ted_baird_human_smuggling_web.pdf> accessed 13 April 2023.

7 John Salt and Jeremy Stein, 'Migration as a Business: The Case of Trafficking' (1997) 35(4) International Migration 467.

8 Salt and Stein (n 7) 476.

9 Salt and Stein (n 7) 471.

10 See, e.g., Eurojust, 'Eurojust's Work in the Fight Against Migrant Smuggling' (2022) <https://www.eurojust.europa.eu/sites/default/files/assets/2022-04-26-migrant-smuggling-leaflet.pdf> accessed 6 September 2022.

11 Salt and Stein (n 7) 479.

12 Salt and Stein (n 7) 479.

13 Gudrun Dahl, 'Sociology and Beyond: Agency, Victimisation and the Ethics of Writing' (2009) 37 Asian Journal of Social Science 391, 393.

14 UNODC, *Smuggling of Migrants a Global Review and Annotated Bibliography of Recent Publications* (UNODC 2010).

15 Protocol against the Smuggling of Migrants by Land, Sea and Air, Supplementing the United Nations Convention against Transnational Crime (adopted 15 November 2000, entered into force 28 January 2004) 2241 UNTS 480 (hereinafter, in the Chapter, Smuggling Protocol) in particular article 2 and article 7.

16 European Migrant Smuggling Centre, <https://www.europol.europa.eu/about-europol/european-serious-and-organised-crime-centre-esocc/european-migrant-smuggling-centre-emsc> accessed 6 September 2022.

17 See Protocol to Prevent, Suppress and Punish Trafficking in Persons, Especially Women and Children, supplementing the United Nations Convention against Transnational Organized Crime (adopted 15 November 2000, entered into force 25 December 2003) 2237 UNTS 319 (hereinafter, in the Chapter, Trafficking Protocol).

18 See, e.g., Eurojust, 'Tactical Meeting on Judicial Challenges in Illegal Immigrant Smuggling—Outcome Report' (2016) 9.

19 See Hein De Haas, 'Don't Blame the Smugglers: the Real Migration Industry' (2015) <http://heindehaas.blogspot.com/2015/09/dont-blame-smugglers-real-migration.html> accessed 13 April 2023.

20 van Liempt and Doomernik (n 5).

21 Anna Triandafyllidou, 'Beyond Irregular Migration Governance: Zooming in on Migrants' Agency' (2017) 19 European Journal of Migration and Law 1, 3.

22 Ayalew T. Mengiste, 'Refugee Protections from Below: Smuggling in the Eritrea-Ethiopia Context' (2018) 676(1) Annals of the American Academy of Political and Social Science 57.

23 Oliver Bakewell and others, 'Migration Systems, Pioneer Migrants and the Role of Agency' (2012) 11(4) Journal of Critical Realism 413, 422. See also Ċetta Mainwaring, 'Migrant Agency: Negotiating Borders and Migration Controls' (2016) 4(3) *Migration Studies* 269.

24 Joris van Wijk, 'Luanda—Holanda: Irregular Migration from Angola to the Netherlands' (2010) 48(2) International Migration 1.
25 See, e.g., Luigi Achilli 'The "Good" Smuggler: The Ethics and Morals of Human Smuggling Among Syrians' (2018) 676 Annals of the American Academy of Political and Social Science 77.
26 See Gabriella Sanchez, '"Circuit Children": The Experiences and Perspectives of Children Engaged in Migrant Smuggling Facilitation on the US-Mexico Border' (2018) 11 Anti-Trafficking Review 103.
27 Stephanie Maher, 'Out of West Africa: Human Smuggling as a Social Enterprise' (2018) 676 The Annals of the American Academy 36.
28 Richard Staring, 'Facilitating the Arrival of Illegal Immigrants in the Netherlands: Irregular Chain Migration Versus Smuggling Chains' (2004) 5 Journal of International Migration and Integration 273.
29 Gert Vermeulen and others, 'Perceived Involvement of "Organised Crime" in Human Trafficking and Smuggling' (2010) 81(1–2) Revue Internationale De Droit Pénal 247.
30 van Liempt and Doomernik (n 5) 166.
31 van Liempt and Doomernik (n 5) 186.
32 Paolo Campana and Loraine Gelsthorpe, 'Choosing a Smuggler: Decision-Making Amongst Migrants Smuggled to Europe' (2020) 27 European Journal on Criminal Policy and Research 5, 9; see also, Federico Alagna, 'Understanding the Complexity of Migrant Smuggling: The "Smuggling Spectrum" as a Comprehensive Analytical Framework' (2020) 6 International Journal of Migration and Border Studies 298, 308.
33 Everett S Lee, 'A Theory of Migration' (1966) 3(1) Demography 49, 53.
34 UNHCR, 'Reconciling Migration Control and Refugee Protection in Refugee Protection in the European Union: A UNHCR Perspective' (2000) 2.
35 UNHCR, 'Reconciling Migration Control and Refugee Protection in Refugee Protection in the European Union: A UNHCR Perspective' (2000) 2.
36 Dennis Broeders and Godfried Engbersen, 'The Fight Against Illegal Migration: Identification Policies and Immigrants' Counterstrategies' (2007) 50(12) American Behavioral Scientist 1592, 1606. See also Khalid Koser, 'The Smuggling of Asylum Seekers into Western Europe: Contradictions, Conundrums, and Dilemmas' in David Kyle and Rey Koslowski (eds), *Global Human Smuggling: Comparative Perspectives* (John Hopkins UP 2001). Koser explains that the implementation of restrictive policies on asylum since the late 1980s and early 1990s in Western Europe gradually led different migrants' categories to converge on a single migration channel monopolised by smugglers and traffickers.
37 Broeders and Engbersen (n 36) 1606.
38 Anna Triandafyllidou, 'Migrant Smuggling: Novel Insights and Implications for Migration Control Policies' (2018) 676(1) The Annals of the American Academy of Political and Social Science 212.
39 Campana and Gelsthorpe (n 32).
40 Yewa Holiday, 'Legal Perspectives on Migration Crime' in Valsamis Mitsilegas and others (eds), *Research Handbook on Transnational Crime* (Edward Elgar Publishing 2019).
41 See Flavia Patanè and others, 'Asylum-Seekers Prosecuted for Human Smuggling: A Case Study of Scafisti in Italy' (2020) 39 Refugee Survey Quarterly 123, 130.
42 European Commission, Directorate General for Migration and Home Affairs, 'A Study on Smuggling of Migrants: Characteristics, Responses and Cooperation with Third Countries' Final Report (September 2015) 39.
43 Nikolaos Chatzinikolaou, 'Crimmigration in Greece: A Story of Exceptional Derogations from the Rule of Law Within a Permanent Situation of Emergency' in Gatta and others (n 2).

44 Karolina Augustova and others, 'Becoming a Smuggler: Migration and Violence at EU External Borders' (2023) 28 Geopolitics 619.
45 De Haas (n 19).
46 Campana and Gelsthorpe (n 32) 6; van Liempt and Doomernik (n 5) 186.
47 Roxane de Massol de Rebetz, 'How Useful Is the Concept of Transit Migration in an Intra-Schengen Mobility Context? Diving into the Migrant Smuggling and Human Trafficking Nexus in Search for Answers' (2021) 27 European Journal on Criminal Policy and Research 41, 49.
48 Ilse van Liempt, *Navigating Borders: Inside Perspectives on the Process of Human Smuggling into the Netherlands* (Amsterdam UP 2007) 41.
49 van Liempt (n 48) 160. On the oversimplification of the human smuggling categories, see also Scott Watson, 'The Criminalisation of Human and Humanitarian Smuggling' (2015) 1 Migration, Mobility, & Displacement 39.
50 See Smuggling Protocol (n 15).
51 See Preamble of Smuggling Protocol (n 15). On the double objective of the Smuggling protocol, see Mitsilegas (n 3).
52 Smuggling Protocol (n 15) article 6. Article 6 of the Smuggling Protocol requires State Parties to criminalize the intentional facilitation of illegal entry or stay for financial or material benefit, including smuggling migrants, producing or using fraudulent documents for smuggling purposes, enabling illegal residence, as well as attempting, assisting, organizing, or directing such offenses.
53 Alessandro Spena, 'Smuggled Migrants as Victims? Reflecting on the UN Protocol Against Migrant Smuggling and on its Implementation' (2019) 3(4) Transnational Crime 43, 47.
54 In accordance with such a conclusion, an analysis of the preparatory works of the Protocol shows that several delegations were "apprehensive about the possibility of the Protocol granting immunity to illegal migrants, especially if they had committed a crime, including the smuggling of other illegal migrants". See Revised draft Protocol against the Smuggling of Migrants by Land, Air and Sea, supplementing the United Nations Convention against Transnational Organized Crime A/AC.254/4/Add.1/Rev.4, note 60.
55 UNODC, 'Global Study on Smuggling of Migrants' (2018) E.18.IV.9 United Nations Publication, 17; UNODC, 'Model Law Against the Smuggling of Migrants' (2010) 56.
56 UN Global Compact for Safe, Orderly and Regular Migration, 19 December 2018, Objective 9.
57 Council Directive 2002/90/EC of 28 November 2002 defining the facilitation of unauthorised entry, transit, and residence [2002] OJ L328 (hereinafter, in the chapter, Facilitation Directive); Council framework Decision 2002/946/JHA of 28 November 2002 on the strengthening of the penal framework to prevent the facilitation of unauthorised entry, transit, and residence [2002] OJ L328.
58 For an overview of the domestic legislation of EU States on the facilitation of irregular entry and stay, see FRA, 'Criminalisation of Migrants in an Irregular Situation and of Persons Engaging with Them, Annex: EU Member States' Legislation on Irregular Entry and Stay, as Well as Facilitation of Irregular Entry and Stay' (2014), <https://fra.europa.eu/en/publication/2014/criminalisation-migrants-irregular-situation-and-persons-engaging-them>.
59 See, e.g., Sergio Carrera and others, *Fit for Purpose? The Facilitation Directive and the Criminalisation of Humanitarian Assistance to Irregular Migrants* (Study commissioned by LIBE Committee, European Parliament 2016).
60 Valsamis Mitsilegas, 'The Criminalisation of Migration in the Law of the European Union: Challenging the Preventive Paradigm' (2021) in Gatta and others (n 2).
61 Council Directive 2002/90/EC, article 1.
62 Spena (n 53) 55–56.

63 See Framework Decision 2002/946/JHA, article 1.

64 Facilitation Directive, Article 1 para 2: Any Member State may decide not to impose sanctions with regard to the behaviour defined in paragraph 1(a) by applying its national law and practice for cases where the aim of the behaviour is to provide humanitarian assistance to the person concerned.

65 Carrera and others (n 59) 26. States' practice seems to confirm that the humanitarian exception in Article 1 para 2 of the Framework Directive aims to protect the acts of solidarity with migrants, rather than migrants themselves. For example, even though Greece has introduced an exemption from penalties in cases where people at sea are rescued and in cases where people in need of international protection are brought to safety, migrants have been prosecuted systematically for facilitating irregular migration: George Maniatis, 'Country Report Greece' in Sara Bellezza and Tiziana Calandrino (eds), *Criminalisation of Flight and Escape Aid* (KideM 2017) 224.

66 Proposal for a Directive of the European Parliament and of the Council laying down minimum rules to prevent and counter the facilitation of unauthorised entry, transit, and stay in the Union, and replacing Council Directive 2002/90/EC and Council Framework Decision 2002/946 JHA [2023] COM (2023) 755 final.

67 See Section 4.2.

68 Paul Adams and Joshua Nevett, 'Poland-Belarus: How Social Media Posts Fuelled the Migrant Crisis' *BBC* (11 November 2021) < https://www.bbc.com/news/world-europe-59253377>. The continuous cross-border attempts in Spain's African enclaves also show a conscious choice of migrants to put their life in peril as a way to enhance their migration chances. See Ashifa Kassam, 'A Bloodbath': Refugees Reel from Deadly Melilla Mass Crossing' *The Guardian* (Madrid, 30 June 2022) <https://www.theguardian.com/world/2022/jun/30/a-bloodbath-refugees-reel-from-deadly-melilla-mass-crossing>.

69 See, e.g., *N.D. and N.T. v Spain* Applications nos. 8675/15 and 8697/15 (ECtHR, 13 February 2020). In this case Grand Chamber of the ECtHR considered whether the lack of individual removal decisions and the denial of the possibility to claim asylum by Spain for two nationals of Mali and Côte d'Ivoire *refouled* to Morocco after climbing the fences in Melilla constituted a breach of the prohibition of collective expulsions. The answer of the court was in the negative, as the non-recognition of such rights was in fact a result of the applicants' own conduct. They had taken advantage of the mass group in order to cross borders and had not made use of the official entry procedures available for asserting their rights.

70 Tribunal De Première Instance Francophone De Bruxelles 47e Chambre Correctionnelle, 12 December 2018, 2018/6764.

71 As opposed to Article 77, which punishes the mere "facilitation of irregular migration".

72 Corr. Bruxelles, 12 décembre 2018, 2018/6764; Cour D'Appel de Bruxelles (2021) [49].

73 Cour D'Appel de Bruxelles 14ème Chambre Affaires Correctionnelles, 26 May 2021, [49].

74 In 2021, the Court of Appeal of Bruxelles confirmed the conviction but suspended the penalties for most of the accused migrants.

75 Cour D'Appel de Bruxelles [49].

76 European Commission, 'A Study on Smuggling of Migrants: Characteristics, Responses and Cooperation with Third Countries: Final Report' (2015) 51. See last Frontex Risk Analysis (2020).

77 For an overview of prosecutions of asylum seekers as human smugglers in these three countries, see Ottavia Spaggiari, Isobel Thompson and Iliana Papangeli,

'How European Courts are Wrongfully Prosecuting Asylum Seekers as Smugglers' *The New Humanitarian* (2022) <https://www.thenewhumanitarian.org/investigation/2022/09/01/European-courts-prosecution-asylum-seekers>.

78 For a comprehensive view on Italy, see ARCI Porco Rosso and Alarm Phone, 'From Sea to Prison: The Criminalisation of Boat Drivers in Italy' (2021) <https://fromseatoprison.info/introduction/> accessed 13 April 2023. For the prosecution of boat drivers in the Greek Aegean islands, see Valeria Hänsel and others, 'Incarcerating the Marginalized: The Fight Against Alleged "Smugglers" on the Greek Hotspot Islands' (2020).

79 For a spectrum of "captains" arrested in Italy, see ARCI Porco Rosso and Alarm Phone, 'From Sea to Prison: The Criminalisation of Boat Drivers in Italy' (n 78).

80 ARCI Porco Rosso and Alarm Phone (n 78) 20.

81 Hänsel and others (n 78) 70.

82 In the case of Italy, the basic form of facilitation of irregular migration can earn a punishment of between one to five years in prison and a fine of €15,000 for every person, while in Greece the sentence can be up to ten years of imprisonment and a fine of €20,000 as a minimum.

83 Supreme Court of Spain, sentencia 673/2014.

84 Cass pen (1) 3 February 2023, 4768.

85 Although not without many (legal) obstacles. See ARCI Porco Rosso and Alarm Phone (n 78) 64.

86 Alexandra Ricard-Guay, 'Criminalizing Migrants Who Steer the Dinghies in the Mediterranean: A Collateral Effect of Migration Management?' (2018) EUI Working Paper RSCAS 2018/32.

87 Lucia Borghi and Alberto Biondo 'Country Report: Italy' in Sara Bellezza and Tiziana Calandrino (n 65).

88 For the case of Italy, see Patanè and others (n 41).

89 Patanè and others (n 41).

90 For Greece, see Hänsel and others (n 78) 34; for Italy, see Legislative Decree 251/2007, article 16.

91 For an overview of the criminalisation of asylum seekers for using false documents and related offences, see Cathryn Costello, 'Article 31 of the 1951 Convention Relating to the Status of Refugees' (2017) UNHCR Legal and Protection Policy Research Series.

92 EMN, 'Ad-Hoc Query on Impact of False/Forged Documents in the Immigration and Asylum Procedures' (2018) <http://www.emnitalyncp.it/wp-content/uploads/2018/02/062_lu_impact_of_falseforged_documents.pdf> accessed 2 December 2021.

93 Costello (n 91) 54.

94 See, e.g., European Commission, 'A Renewed EU Action Plan Against Migrant Smuggling (2021–2025)' COM (2021) 591 final, 25–26; Europol (2021); Joint Interpol-Europol Report (2016).

95 Europol (2016) 10.

96 Tribunale Bologna, Sez. I, Ord. di rimessione, 01/12/2020, n. 92., article 497 *bis*.

97 Law on immigration, article 12, section 1 and 3.

98 Stefano Zirulia, 'La Corte costituzionale sul favoreggiamento dell'immigrazione irregolare: illegittima l'aggravante che parifica il trattamento sanzionatorio dei trafficanti a quello di coloro che prestano un aiuto per finalità solidaristiche' (*Sistema Penale*, 2022) <https://www.sistemapenale.it/it/scheda/corte-costituzionale-2022-63-favoreggiamento-immigrazione-irregolare-aggravato-nota-zirulia> accessed 13 April 2023.

99 Corte Costituzionale 63/2022, para 4.5.

100 Corte Costituzionale 63/2022, para 4.5.

101 See Gatta and others (n 2).
102 Giulia Mentasti, 'La "Crimmigration" nel Sistema Italiano: tra Scelte di Incriminazione e Ricorso al Trattenimento Amministrativo' (PhD thesis, University of Milan 2020).
103 Elspeth Guild, 'The Criminalisation of Migration in the Law of the European Union: Challenging the Preventive Paradigm' in Gatta and others (n 2) 15.
104 See Smuggling Protocol (n 15) article 4: the Protocol applies to the prevention, investigation and prosecution of the offences of migrant smuggling "as well as to the protection of the rights of persons who have been the object of such offences".
105 Mitsilegas (n 3); Stefano Zirulia, 'Non c'è smuggling senza ingiusto profitto' [2020] Diritto Penale Contemporaneo Riv Trim 3.
106 Tribunal de première instance francophone de Bruxelles, No 2018/6764, 12 December 2018.
107 Proposal for a recast Facilitation Directive (n 64) article 3 para 1(a).
108 Proposal for a recast Facilitation Directive (n 64) article 3.
109 For a possible re-conceptualisation of human smuggling as a crime aginst the dignity of migrants, see the contribution by Keiler in this volume.
110 Proposal for a recast Facilitation Directive (n 64), Recital 11.
111 Proposal for a recast Facilitation Directive (n 64), Recital 11. In its general approach on the proposal for a recast Facilitation Directive, the Council of the European Union removed the reference in the recital to the commission of the offence by third-country nationals. See Council of Europe, 2023/0439(COD) 13 December 2024.
112 For arguments supporting this conclusion, see James C. Hathaway, 'Prosecuting a Refugee for "Smuggling" Himself' (2014) Public Law and Legal Theory Research Paper Series 429/2014.
113 According to a booklet on human smuggling and the judicial use of information following debriefing of migrants at external borders by Eurojust from 2021, a smuggled migrant's legal status in criminal proceedings may vary from suspect to witness or victim. Many States declared that migrants' status depends on the specific circumstances of the case. See Eurojust, 'Migrant Smuggling in Focus' Issue 1 (October 2021).
114 "The Contracting States shall not impose penalties, on account of their illegal entry or presence, on refugees who, coming directly from a territory where their life or freedom was threatened." Since the conduct protected by Article 31 occurs before refugee status can be formally determined—and because refugee status is declaratory—the provision also applies to asylum seekers, treating them as refugees until it is determined that they are not.
115 Directive 2013/33/EU of the European Parliament and of the Council of 26 June 2013 laying down standards for the reception of applicants for international protection (recast) (Reception Conditions Directive) [2013] OJ L180 article 8.
116 The application of Article 31 in criminal cases initiated against migrants has been understudied in the EU. For a relevant exception, see Yewa Holiday, 'The Prosecution of Asylum Seekers' in Satvinder S Juss (ed), *Research Handbook on International Refugee Law* (Elgar 2019).
117 See Judgement of 17 July 2014, Qurbani, C-481/13, EU:C:2014:2101.
118 Judgement of 17 July 2014, Qurbani, C 481/13, EU:C:2014:2101, para 24. The decision has attracted great criticism for neglecting the relevance of Article 31 within EU law; see Yewa Holiday, 'Penalising Refugees: When Should the CJEU Have Jurisdiction to Interpret Article 31 of the Refugee Convention?' (*EU Law Analysis*, 2014) <http://eulawanalysis.blogspot.com/2014/07/penalising-refugees-when-should-cjeu.html> accessed 13 April 2023.
119 The application of Article 31 in criminal cases initiated against migrants has been understudied in the EU. For a relevant exception, see Yewa Holiday, 'The

Prosecution of Asylum Seekers' in Satvinder S Juss (ed), *Research Handbook on International Refugee Law* (Elgar 2019).
120 Anne T Gallagher and Fiona David, *The International Law of Migrant Smuggling* (CUP 2014) 167.
121 Gallagher and David (n 120).
122 James C Hathaway, *The Rights of Refugees Under International Law* (2nd edn, CUP 2021) 514–15. See also *R v Uxbridge Magistrates Court and Another, Ex parte Adimi*, [1999] EWHC Admin 765 [15] arguing that the objective of article 31 was to provide immunity anytime the breach of the law can be attributed to a bona fide desire to seek asylum.
123 Gregor Noll, 'Article 31 (Refugees Unlawfully in the Country of Refuge)' in Andreas Zimmermann (ed), *The 1951 Convention Relating to the Status of the Refugees and its 1967 Protocol: A Commentary* (OUP 2011) 1247.
124 Noll (n 123).
125 Hathaway (n 122) 487.
126 Gallagher and David (n 120) 165.
127 Hathaway (n 112).
128 Hathaway (n 122) 508.
129 Hathaway (n 112).
130 *R. v Appulonapa* [2015] SCC 59 (27 November 2015) [43].
131 See, for instance, District Court of The Hague, 19 December 2019, ECLI:NL:RBDHA:2019:13721.
132 This was the case, for instance, of a 24-year-old Somali citizen, Osman Matammud, who was arrested in 2017 after being recognised by fellow Somalis in a migrant reception centre in Milan. He was accused of committing heinous crimes against migrants at the detention camp of Bani Walid, in the Lybian desert. While recognising that Matammud was himself an asylum seeker working for the smugglers to get a free pass to Europe, the Court of Assizes of Milan (upheld by the Court of Appeal in 2019) sentenced him to life imprisonment on the basis of his personal involvement in the highest level of violence against migrants. See Corte ass. app. Milano, sez. I, 20 March 2019, n. 9/2019.
133 See Refugee Convention, article 1F(a) and (b) and Directive 2011/95/EU article 12(2).
134 Anne Aagten, 'Migrant Smuggling in the Mediterranean, An Excludable Act Under Article 1F(b) Refugee Convention?' (2018) 2 Crimmigratie & Recht 2.

Bibliography

Aagten A, 'Migrant Smuggling in the Mediterranean, An Excludable Act Under Article 1F(b) Refugee Convention?' (2018) 2 Crimmigratie & Recht 2.
Achilli L, 'The "Good" Smuggler: The Ethics and Morals of Human Smuggling Among Syrians' (2018) 676 Annals of the American Academy of Political and Social Science 77.
Alagna F, 'Understanding the Complexity of Migrant Smuggling: The "Smuggling Spectrum" as a Comprehensive Analytical Framework' (2020) 6 International Journal Migration and Border Studies 298.
ARCI Porco Rosso and Alarm Phone, *From Sea to Prison: The Criminalisation of Boat Drivers in Italy* (Self-Published 2021).
Augustova K, Carrapico H and Obradović-Wochnik J, 'Becoming a Smuggler: Migration and Violence at EU External Borders' (2023) 28 Geopolitics 619.
Baird T, 'Theoretical Approaches to Human Smuggling' (2013) DIIS Working Paper.
Bakewell O, De Haas H and Kubal A, 'Migration Systems, Pioneer Migrants and the Role of Agency' (2012) 11 Journal of Critical Realism 413.

Borghi L and Biondo A, 'Country Report: Italy' in Bellezza S and Calandrino T (eds), *Criminalisation of Flight and Escape Aid* (KideM 2017).

Broeders D and Engbersen G, 'The Fight Against Illegal Migration: Identification Policies and Immigrants' Counterstrategies' (2007) 50 American Behavioral Scientist 1592.

Campana P and Gelsthorpe L, 'Choosing a Smuggler: Decision-Making Amongst Migrants Smuggled to Europe' (2020) 27 European Journal on Criminal Policy and Research 5.

Carrera S and others, *Fit for Purpose? The Facilitation Directive and the Criminalisation of Humanitarian Assistance to Irregular Migrants* (Study commissioned by LIBE Committee, European Parliament 2016).

Carrera S and others, *Policing Humanitarianism: EU Policies Against Human Smuggling and Their Impact on Civil Society* (Hart 2019).

Chatzinikolaou N, 'Crimmigration in Greece: A Story of Exceptional Derogations from the Rule of Law Within a Permanent Situation of Emergency' in Gatta GL, Mitsilegas V and Zirulia S (eds), *Controlling Immigration Through Criminal Law: European and Comparative Perspectives on "Crimmigration"* (Hart 2021).

Costello C, 'Article 31 of the 1951 Convention Relating to the Status of Refugees' (2017) UNHCR Legal and Protection Policy Research Series.

Dahl G, 'Sociology and Beyond: Agency, Victimisation and the Ethics of Writing' (2009) 37 Asian Journal of Social Science 391.

De Massol de Rebetz R, 'How Useful Is the Concept of Transit Migration in an Intra-Schengen Mobility Context? Diving into the Migrant Smuggling and Human Trafficking Nexus in Search for Answers' (2021) 27 European Journal on Criminal Policy and Research 41.

European Migration Network, 'Ad-Hoc Query on Impact of False/Forged Documents in the Immigration and Asylum Procedures' (Self-Published 2018).

European Union Agency for Fundamental Rights, 'Criminalisation of Migrants in an Irregular Situation and of Persons Engaging with them, Annex: EU Member States' Legislation on Irregular Entry and Stay, as Well as Facilitation of Irregular Entry and Stay' (Self-Published 2014).

Gallagher AT and David F, *The International Law of Migrant Smuggling* (CUP 2014).

Gatta GL, 'The Connections Between Migration, Crime and Punishment: Historical and Sociological Questions' in Gatta GL, Mitsilegas V and Zirulia S (eds), *Controlling Immigration Through Criminal Law: European and Comparative Perspectives on "Crimmigration"* (Hart 2021).

Guild E, 'The Criminalisation of Migration in the Law of the European Union: Challenging the Preventive Paradigm' in Gatta GL, Mitsilegas V and Zirulia S (eds), *Controlling Immigration Through Criminal Law: European and Comparative Perspectives on "Crimmigration"* (Hart 2021).

Hänsel V and others, *Incarcerating the Marginalized: The Fight Against Alleged "Smugglers" on the Greek Hotspot Islands* (Self-Published 2020).

Hathaway JC, 'Prosecuting a Refugee for "Smuggling" Himself' (2014) Public Law and Legal Theory Research Paper Series.

Hathaway JC, *The Rights of Refugees Under International Law* (2nd edn, CUP 2021).

Holiday Y, 'Legal Perspectives on Migration Crime' in Mitsilegas V, Hufnagel S and Moiseienko A (eds), *Research Handbook on Transnational Crime* (Edward Elgar Publishing 2019).

Holiday Y, 'The Prosecution of Asylum Seekers' in Satvinder SJ (ed), *Research Handbook on International Refugee Law* (Edward Elgar 2019).

Koser K, 'The Smuggling of Asylum Seekers into Western Europe: Contradictions, Conundrums, and Dilemmas' in Kyle D and Koslowski R (eds), *Global Human Smuggling: Comparative Perspectives* (John Hopkins UP 2001).

Lee EL, 'A Theory of Migration' (1966) 3 Demography 49.
Maher S, 'Out of West Africa: Human Smuggling as a Social Enterprise' (2018) 676 The Annals of the American Academy 36.
Mainwaring C, 'Migrant Agency: Negotiating Borders and Migration Controls' (2016) 4 Migration Studies 269.
Maniatis G, 'Country Report Greece' in Bellezza S and Calandrino T (eds), *Criminalisation of Flight and Escape Aid* (KideM 2017).
Mengiste AT, 'Refugee Protections from Below: Smuggling in the Eritrea-Ethiopia Context' (2018) 676 Annals of the American Academy of Political and Social Science 57.
Mentasti G, *La "Crimmigration" nel Sistema Italiano: tra Scelte di Incriminazione e Ricorso al Trattenimento Amministrativo* (University of Milan 2020).
Mitsilegas V, 'The Normative Foundations of the Criminalisation of Human Smuggling: Exploring the Fault Lines Between European and International Law' (2019) 10 New Journal of European Criminal Law 68.
Mitsilegas V, 'The Criminalisation of Migration in the Law of the European Union: Challenging the Preventive Paradigm' in Gatta GL, Mitsilegas V and Zirulia S (eds), *Controlling Immigration Through Criminal Law: European and Comparative Perspectives on "Crimmigration"* (Hart 2021).
Noll G, 'Article 31 (Refugees Unlawfully in the Country of Refuge)' in Zimmermann A, Einarsen T and Herrmann FM (eds), *The 1951 Convention Relating to the Status of the Refugees and its 1967 Protocol* (Oxford Commentaries on International Law 2024).
Patanè F and others, 'Asylum-Seekers Prosecuted for Human Smuggling: A Case Study of Scafisti in Italy' (2020) 39 Refugee Survey Quarterly 123.
Ricard-Guay A, 'Criminalizing Migrants Who Steer the Dinghies in the Mediterranean: A Collateral Effect of Migration Management?' (2018) European University Institute Working Paper.
Salt J and Stein J, 'Migration as a Business: The Case of Trafficking' (1997) 35 International Migration 467.
Sanchez G, '"Circuit Children": The Experiences and Perspectives of Children Engaged in Migrant Smuggling Facilitation on the US-Mexico Border' (2018) 11 Anti-Trafficking Review 103.
Spena A, 'Smuggled Migrants as Victims? Reflecting on the UN Protocol Against Migrant Smuggling and on its Implementation' (2019) 3 Transnational Crime 43.
Staring R, 'Facilitating the Arrival of Illegal Immigrants in the Netherlands: Irregular Chain Migration Versus Smuggling Chains' (2004) 5 Journal of International Migration and Integration 273.
Stumpf J, 'The Crimmigration Crisis: Immigrants, Crime, and Sovereign Power' (2006) 56 American University Law Review 367.
Triandafyllidou A, 'Beyond Irregular Migration Governance: Zooming in on Migrants' Agency' (2017) 19 European Journal of Migration and Law 1.
Triandafyllidou A, 'Migrant Smuggling: Novel Insights and Implications for Migration Control Policies' (2018) 676 The Annals of the American Academy of Political and Social Science 212.
Van der Woude MAH, Van der Leun JP, Nijland JA, 'Crimmigration in the Netherlands' (2014) 39 Law & Social Inquiry 560.
Van Liempt I, *Navigating Borders: Inside Perspectives on the Process of Human Smuggling into the Netherlands* (Amsterdam UP 2007).
Van Liempt I and Doomernik J, 'Migrant's Agency in the Smuggling Process: The Perspectives of Smuggled Migrants in the Netherlands' (2006) 44 International Migration 165.
Van Wijk J, 'Luanda—Holanda: Irregular Migration from Angola to the Netherlands' (2010) 48 International Migration 1.

Vermeulen G, Van Damme Y and De Bondt W, 'Perceived Involvement of "Organised Crime" In Human Trafficking and Smuggling' (2010) 81 Revue Internationale De Droit Pénal 247.

Watson S, 'The Criminalisation of Human and Humanitarian Smuggling' (2015) 1 Migration, Mobility, & Displacement 39.

Zirulia S, 'Non c'è smuggling senza ingiusto profitto' (2020) 3 Diritto Penale Contemporaneo Rivista Trimestrale 143.

Zirulia S, 'Is that a Smuggler?: The Blurring Line Between Facilitating Illegal Immigration and Providing Humanitarian Assistance at the European Borders' in Gatta GL, Mitsilegas V and Zirulia S (eds), *Controlling Immigration Through Criminal Law: European and Comparative Perspectives on "Crimmigration"* (Hart 2021).

7 Crimmigration through Administrative Surveillance of Civil Society at the EU's External Borders

*Niovi Vavoula and Evangelia (Lilian) Tsourdi**

7.1 Introduction

At the EU level (over)criminalising migration has spilled over to the criminalisation and prosecution of human smuggling in a rather sweeping manner, including where no financial gain is pursued and individuals or civil society actors provide humanitarian assistance.[1] Beyond this development that rests squarely in the realm of criminal justice, national policies have targeted civil society actors through a variety of further means, such as defamatory statements or disproportionate administrative requirements with a distinct criminal undertone. In our chapter, we critique this trend through the illustrative case of criminalising migration and asylum civil society organisations (CSOs) through administrative surveillance in Greece. Specifically, we scrutinise a wave of registration requirements targeting migration CSOs against national constitutional law, as well as EU law, with an emphasis on fundamental rights and the rule of law.

The civic space for migration-related CSOs has been shrinking in Greece. Actors such as the Greek National Commission for Human Rights,[2] the Conference of International Non-Governmental Organisations of the Council of Europe,[3] the Commissioner for Human Rights of the Council of Europe,[4] and the European Commission[5] have repeatedly criticised national legal and policy developments that have led to an obstructed civic space in Greece in what concerns CSOs active in the fields of migration and asylum. Crucial among these developments has been the practice around registration requirements for migration CSOs and their members, including staff and volunteers.

Against this backdrop, the next section traces and analyses the emergence of administrative registration requirements that amount to indirect criminalisation of CSOs in Greece (Section 7.2). Section 7.3 scrutinises the legal design of the most recent national legislation, followed by a sustained critique of national law and practice through three lenses: National constitutional law,

* This research was supported by a European Research Council Starting Grant (EU Grant Agreement 101165167, PI Lilian Tsourdi).

DOI: 10.4324/9781003378440-7

EU fundamental rights law, and EU rule of law (Section 7.4). This fine-grained analysis demonstrates violations of these different frameworks, and appraises efforts to enforce relevant legal standards. We conclude with overarching considerations on criminalisation of CSOs through surveillance and the suitability of existing enforcement mechanisms to address this newer phenomenon of crimmigration practice.

7.2 The Emergence of a Convoluted Administrative Legal Framework Restricting the Operational Space of Civil Society

Criminalisation of CSOs assisting refugees and migrants in Greece[6] has been coupled with administrative requirements that have a distinct criminal undertone. This section traces these developments in three waves: The first wave concerning efforts to map the activity of CSOs as a form of increasing transparency; the second wave characterised by the emergence of a hostile environment against CSOs, marked by repeated legislative interventions, tight deadlines, and increasing bureaucracy; and, finally, the third wave of direct criminalisation of CSOs operating without fulfilling the registration requirements and beyond the control of the Greek authorities.

7.2.1 The First Wave: Registration Requirements to Improve Transparency

The first steps took place in early 2016, following the peak of arrivals of asylum seekers in summer 2015 due to the escalation of armed conflict in Syria. At that point, Joint Ministerial Decision 4151.4183/166 envisaged the creation of a Coordinating Committee within the "General Secretariat of Aegean and Island Policy" for the registration, coordination, and evaluation of CSOs operating on the island of Lesvos, a location where numerous CSOs had been assisting arriving refugees for more than a year.[7] In February 2016, CSOs and volunteers assisting refugees and migrants were initially requested to fill out forms providing personal details of all their members to the government.[8]

The Coordinating Committee produced two forms, the "organisation profile" form and the "personal profile" form that all migration-related CSOs operating on the Greek islands had to complete and register with the police in order to remain operational. The "organisation profile" form required CSOs to provide personal details of all volunteers working with them; source(s) of income; affiliation with other groups active in Greece; proposed place of action and type of voluntary work; proposed analytical programme; and action description.[9] The "personal profile" form required the submission of personal data, such as name, address, date of birth, and passport number, as well as information on "professional capacity"; "previous actions"; "date of arrival and departure"; "affiliation/cooperation with organisation(s)"; "proposed voluntary action in Greece"; and "proposed place of action and type of voluntary work".[10]

This development was by no means a Greek novelty. In Slovakia, CSOs must register with the Interior Ministry, while foundations face a double registration requirement, as they must also register with the central body in their field of work.[11] Similarly, in Hungary, following the introduction of a new Civil Code, registered CSOs were required to go through a lengthy and resource-intensive process of amending their founding documents, which included deleting references to legal acts that had lost force.[12]

In the Greek case, later in 2016, Ministerial Decision 39487/2016[13] created a "National Transparency Registry" for CSOs, whether Greek or foreign, which were active in the field of international protection, immigration, and social inclusion. The Ministerial Decision placed all CSOs directly under state control, refusing to recognise the operations of independent and unregistered CSOs, a process which, according to the EU Agency for Fundamental Rights (FRA), amounted to "effectively criminalising them".[14] Criminalisation, in this context, involves controlling the activities of the CSOs through increasing administrative surveillance of them and their members/employees in the form of collecting and further processing information. The registry was designed to contain information on the geographical scope of activity of the CSO, including legal documents regarding its creation; tax information; financial information (such as its budget); its legal representative in Greece; the services offered (sector, target groups); its premises; details on all volunteers and employees, including their periods of employment or volunteer work, and detailed information on their activities in the past two years.

The same Ministerial Decision required an update of the information following any changes at regular intervals, and the CSOs were obliged to inform the government of any changes, particularly regarding the discontinuation of work of specific volunteers or employees (in this field or in general), or their departure from the Greek territory. However, the provisions were also contradictory. For example, Article 4 was addressed to CSOs that "wished to apply for registration"; however, that registration was a necessary prerequisite not only for their activity, but also for their certification and broader collaboration with the services of the Ministry of Interior and Administrative Reconstruction, which was responsible for migration affairs at the time. The creation of the national registry was also aligned with the EU approach towards the implementation of hotspots in Greece. The European Commission Progress Report of December 2015 referred to a "structured system for disembarkation at official disembarkation points" and the adoption of "[T]erms of Reference to coordinate all relevant governmental and non-governmental players involved in the hotspot locations".[15]

The Ministerial Decision was adopted even though several ministries already had lists of CSOs. Different registries had been operational for a number of years to facilitate financial audits as part of anti-money laundering efforts.[16] Therefore, the vilification of CSOs took place in a manifold manner: The increased attention to auditing their financial transactions suggested that they are prone to commit financial irregularities.[17] Overall, between 2016 and 2018, local authorities were registering both CSOs (legal persons) and physical persons, including volunteers seeking to access refugees and asylum seekers who are *de facto* detained in hotspots. The European Border and Coast Agency (Frontex) had also constituted lists of CSOs operating in Lesvos.[18] In addition, the United Nations High Commissioner for Refugees (UNHCR) regularly organised coordination meetings to avoid overlap.[19] Therefore, local and EU authorities, as well as UN agencies, closely monitored who was doing what in the field.[20] Nevertheless, different registration requirements were far from coordinated. The end result was that different CSOs managed or tried to register in different registries (local, national, and EU), with some of these organisations submitting an application to register many times, often unsuccessfully and awaiting a decision for prolonged periods of time.[21]

7.2.2 The Second Wave: An Emerging Hostile Environment

In 2018, Ministerial Decision 7586/18 was adopted without significantly modifying the previous Ministerial Decision 39487/2016.[22] The change of government at the end of 2019, however, led to increased restrictions and the creation of a hostile environment for CSOs working with migrants and refugees. This was partly in response to the rise of tensions between the local population, particularly in Lesvos, and the Greek Government over newly established pre-removal detention facilities and an increase in migrant flows.[23] In fact, in a little over a year after the first reform at the end of 2019, the national legislation on registration requirements was reformed and expanded four times.

At the centre of the reforms was compulsory registration, with strict deadlines for the submission of evidence or the lodging of an application from scratch for CSOs that had already requested registration. Article 66 of Law 4636/2019 adopted on 1 November 2019[24] required that only CSOs certified with the national Ministry of Citizens' Protection (then responsible for migration affairs) could access border crossing points, including transit zones, reception, and detention centres.[25] Furthermore, on 26 November 2019, the same Greek Ministry issued an announcement instructing all CSOs to lodge their application within ten working days along with all supporting documents.[26] However, the ministry did not specify the consequences if the ten-working-day deadline was not complied with, and upon expiration of that deadline, the ministry failed to proceed to further announcements.[27]

In 2020, the responsibility for the registry moved from the national Ministry of Citizens' Protection to the newly established Ministry of Migration and Asylum. Then, Law 4662/2020 of 7 February 2020,[28] along with the Joint Ministerial Decision 3063/2020 of 14 April 2020,[29] created a new online platform for mandatory registration and certification of CSOs. According to Decision 3062/2020, CSOs that had already registered were required to submit anew their registration within two months. Furthermore, Article 191 of

Law 4662/2020 explicitly set out that the registry must also contain information on the members, employees, and other partners of the CSOs active in Greece in the field. In addition, registration and certification of the CSOs and the connected persons was a *sine qua non* not only for their operational presence in Greece, but also for their collaboration with national authorities.

The government alleged that the rationale behind the necessity of the registry was the operation of "deep and dark networks" of CSO interests that sought to take advantage of refugees.[30] In a briefing note of February 2020, the Ministry of Migration and Asylum stated that the rationale behind the introduction of the registry relates to the operation of

> a large number of official and unofficial "organizations" and/or ordinary groups of people, self-proclaimed as CSOs which acted without control, taking advantage of the situation for other reasons, inciting residents of the accommodation facilities and triggering havoc, to the detriment of both refugees and migrants, as well Greek citizens and residents of these areas, resulting in preventing the Greek State from doing what needed to be done.[31]

According to the ministry, whereas CSOs were generally considered "helpful and invaluable allies", some CSOs questioned "Greek sovereignty over areas of the Greek islands where accommodation facilities are located".[32] In addition, the ministry argued that the uncontrolled entry of CSOs into accommodation facilities resulted in concerns regarding the safety of migrants and refugees and, in particular, of vulnerable groups, namely women and children, including unaccompanied ones.[33] The undertone of the note is remarkable; without providing concrete examples of CSOs or "self-proclaimed CSOs" that generated these risks, efforts to control and monitor the work of civil society were intensified.

Before the expiration of the two-month deadline for CSOs to register, the law changed again, superseding the previous regime. Law 4686/2020 of May 2020 provided anew for the minimum necessary terms and conditions of registration.[34] Its Article 58 stated that non-registered CSOs could not participate in activities related to asylum, migration, and social inclusion within the Greek territory, and in particular could not offer legal, psychosocial, or health services, nor provide information and advice. The law also granted power to the executive to lay down *additional* requirements for the registration, in violation of constitutional standards.[35] The relevant Joint Ministerial Decision 10616/2020, further specifying these requirements, was released only four months later and remains the current legal framework in December 2024.[36] In June 2020, the minister announced that out of the 40 organisations active on the ground, only 18 were at an advanced stage in the registration process, enabling them to continue accessing the centres.[37] Joint Ministerial Decision 10616/2020 therefore significantly altered registration requirements, resulting in CSOs that had requested registration pursuant to the previous Law 4662/2020, just a few months before, having to submit additional documentation within 40 days. That documentation concerned the financial audits of the CSOs.

The analysis above demonstrates that the multiple legislative reforms and adoption of ministerial decisions created a highly convoluted legal framework, which in view of the multiple reforms, challenged legal certainty. CSOs struggled to identify the applicable rules, submit the necessary evidence, and comply with strict deadlines that were not sufficient for the production of the required information. The confusion over the applicable rules led many CSOs to refer questions to the Ministry of Migration and Asylum, but almost half received no clarifications.[38] Among those that received an answer by phone or email correspondence, only around 10% found the answer useful, as the answers were vague, did not provide clarification, or directly contradicted the law.[39]

7.2.3 The Third Wave: Registration and Direct Criminalisation

The analysisabove illustrates that registration constitutes an essential requirement for operation of CSOs in Greece, and thus surveillance is the primary form in which indirect criminalisation takes place. Nevertheless, the legal framework has taken criminalisation up a notch, linking non-registration to direct criminalisation. A newer legislative framework, Law 4825/2021, imposes limitations and conditions on private persons and CSOs volunteering to work on SAR operations.[40] The new terms of cooperation delimit the involvement of civilian SAR operations to areas under the jurisdiction of the Hellenic Coast Guard.

In particular, Article 40 of Law No. 4825/2021 mandates that, in order to be active in such areas, national and international CSOs should be on the registry and under the orders and instructions of the Coast Guard authorities. Furthermore, CSOs may operate only under the conditions that they have already been included in local emergency plans for SAR operations; have not previously gone to sea with the aim of providing support without prior approval, and in circumstances that make it impossible for the Hellenic Coast Guard to take action; and have previously received written approval from the Coast Guard authorities. Non-compliance with these conditions may lead to deprivation of liberty (up to one year, rising up to three years in case of an accident) and a fine (€3000 to €6000 for entities and €500 to €1000 for individuals), which may be increased by 100% in case of a second infringement.

7.3 The Greek Registry Law in Scrutiny: Civil Society Criminalisation through Administrative Surveillance

This section examines more closely the contents and modalities of the principal legislative framework supporting the registration requirements, Joint Ministerial Decision 10616/2020, in order to then be able to scrutinise it against national, European, and EU standards (Section 7.4). The objective of Joint Ministerial Decision 10616/2020 is the regulation of the Registry of Greek and Foreign CSOs established and operating at the Ministry of Immigration and Asylum, ostensibly

> for reasons of public interest . . . in order to enable transparency in their mode of operation and, through it, the optimisation of the services provided by them; as well as to make it possible to guarantee the human rights of refugees, asylum seekers and all those who seek international protection and immigrants who are in the territory of Greece.[41]

Joint Ministerial Decision 101616/2020 mandates the registration of all CSOs, Greek and foreign alike, wishing to (1) work in state-sponsored facilities; (2) receive funding from national, EU, or other resources to provide material reception conditions; or (3) receive national funding for the implementation of social and humanitarian activities or activities of social integration, migration, and international protection.[42] Individual members of CSOs are also required to register separately in a dedicated registry.

For the registration in the CSO Registry, a rather broad list of documents regarding the legal personality and purpose of the CSOs are required, including their balance sheet, appointment of members of their board, appointment of a data protection officer, and registration of any estates.[43] Joint Ministerial Decision 10616/2020 doubles the time period within which the ministry can respond to requests for registration (from 30 to 60 days) and simultaneously reduces the period within which CSOs and individual applicants can respond to requests from the ministry for supplementary information (from 15 to 10 days).[44] If that deadline is missed, then the application will be rejected.[45]

Apart from registration, the Decision "construes certification as an automatic effect of registration on the CSO Registry".[46] Prior to this reform, certification was a separate and non-mandatory procedure for CSOs who wished to obtain access to state-sponsored facilities, or to access EU or national funding. Nonetheless, it has become a mandatory requirement and part of the registration process,[47] regardless of whether the CSOs operated in such facilities or wished such access to funding. Certification denotes that the CSO possesses the necessary characteristics and experience, as well as the requirements for quality assurance.[48] Certification is subject to compliance with the substantive criteria of efficiency, administrative/organisational ability, and accountability, in addition to the formal registration criteria.[49]

The Ministry of Migration and Asylum must carry out this assessment based on an indicative list of criteria. For example, to measure efficiency, the Joint Ministerial Decision refers to the implementation of the CSO's activities in the past two years, financial efficiency and stability as evidenced by the balance sheet, including the sources of funding and its stability, and the existence of quality assurance systems. Administrative/organisational ability is measured by the number and type of staff members and volunteers, the logistical infrastructure, or the "reasonable distribution of human resources" and organigram. Accountability can be provided by the "operation of a website" that publishes information on the CSO, including its mission statement, financial statement, and annual reports.

The examination of the application is undertaken by a three-member committee composed of a representative of a "Special Secretariat of Coordination of Involved Entities" or an officer of the Ministry of Migration and Asylum; a representative of the Greek Asylum Service; and a representative of the General Secretariat of Reception of Asylum Seekers.[50] The General Secretary of Reception of Asylum Seekers remains free to verify the submitted materials with the relevant national authorities and, notwithstanding a positive proposal from the aforementioned committee, retains the discretion to reject the registration application following an examination of the file and of elements that pertain to the CSO activities.[51]

Certified CSOs must then register their members, staff, and volunteers in the separate "Registry of CSO Members".[52] The registry will remain active for as long as the CSOs are active in Greece,[53] which means that if a CSO is active for another ten years, personal data on their employees and volunteers will be stored for that period. Prior to the introduction of Ministerial Decision 10616/2020, registration of individual employees or other individuals associated with CSOs was only required for a relatively limited group of persons carrying out activities at reception facilities and regional asylum offices.[54] However, under the revised rules, all CSO members, staff, and volunteers, irrespective of the work they carry out or of their contact with refugees and migrants, must be individually registered with the CSO Member Registry so that they can be authorised to carry out any activity pertaining to asylum, migration, and social inclusion.[55]

Article 10(2) of the Joint Ministerial Decision states that the CSO Member Registry is in the public interest. Furthermore, there is reference to the necessity to record all individuals who are in contact with asylum seekers or beneficiaries of refugee status, particularly women, children, and unaccompanied minors, and in particular those individuals who have access to reception and identification facilities, as well as to detention centres. Registration can ensure that persons who have been convicted of particularly heinous criminal offences, such as sexual abuse, child sexual abuse, human trafficking, drug trafficking, bodily harm, etc., are excluded from accessing facilities or having direct contact with migrants. Consequently, the stated purpose of the registry is protection of the fundamental rights of asylum seekers and refugees, especially their rights to life, security, physical safety, and mental health, as well as the prevention of crimes against refugees and migrants (e.g., physical abuse, etc.).

Individuals are registered provided that they have not been finally convicted of any criminal offences, with the exception of offences related to road traffic, disorderly conduct, begging, and any other crime that does not indicate criminal demeanour of particular gravity.[56] The offences that could lead to exclusion from registration (and consequent inability to be employed or volunteer with a CSO active in the field) are in particular (but not exhaustively): Participation in a criminal organisation, fraud, corruption, terrorism-related offences, money laundering and terrorism financing, human trafficking, drug trafficking, child abuse, endangerment of an individual, offences against the person, offences against personal freedom (such as kidnapping), sexual offences, and property offences. At first sight, it is already evident that this list does not correspond to Article 10(2) of the Joint Ministerial Decision and is far broader. For instance, property offences are rarely classified as "particularly heinous" and do not necessarily jeopardise the rights to life, security, physical safety, and mental health of refugees and migrants.

Those wishing to register must also provide their tax registration and health registration number, as well as information on professional activity, travel document information, address and contact details, that is, phone number and email. This information must be corroborated by supporting documents, notably a copy of a travel document, a copy of the criminal record accompanied by self-declaration of non-commission of the offences mentioned above, a CV, and the contract of employment or agreement for volunteer work. In case those individuals are themselves refugees, there is no need to provide the supporting documents; only the documents provided by the Greek Government are required.[57] The CSOs are responsible for updating the registry, and any changes in personal details must be declared within 24 hours of the occurrence of the event entailing change in these personal details (e.g., resignation of an employee, or end of a term of volunteer work). Especially in case of a person leaving a CSO, or activity in the field, failure to notify within 24 hours to request the deactivation of the registration of that person will lead to the automatic revocation of the certification of the entire CSO.

In line with Law 4686/2020, unregistered CSOs are excluded from carrying out any activity related to asylum or migration, including providing legal or psychosocial assistance. Therefore, registration is a necessary precondition for their activity, certification, and cooperation with the state authorities. Lawyers whose organisations have not been registered are only able to access migrants' facilities using their bar association identification cards and only after submitting a prior request. Natural persons whose registration is revoked from the CSO Member Registry can no longer be active as members, employees, or associates of CSOs, whether paid or not, or active in matters of asylum, immigration, and social inclusion within the territory of Greece.[58]

Such revocation can take place if, *inter alia*, they are involved in "illegal acts", as evidenced by a final conviction or demonstrated by a "document of the competent public authority", or if it is found that the implementation of their projects is "poor", as evidenced by a "relevant document" of the competent administrative authority.[59] Additionally, Law 4686/2020 repeats that a CSO and its members can be removed from the registry for failing to declare any change concerning the member's personal details within 24 hours from the occurrence of the event, especially if the individual leaves the country or finishes their employment and are inactive in the registry.[60] Once the registration of a CSO member is revoked, this person can no longer work for or be a member of any CSO active in the fields of international protection, migration, and social inclusion in Greece.[61]

7.4 Challenging Criminalisation through Administrative Surveillance: Constitutional Law, Fundamental Rights, and the Rule of Law

The modalities and operationalisation of the two national Greek registries, for CSOs and for their members, raise concerns as to their compliance with national constitutional principles, a number of fundamental rights, and the principle of the rule of law. The next subsections discuss these challenges.

7.4.1 *Dubious Legality? A National Constitutional Law Analysis*

From a Greek law perspective, the elaboration of the detailed requirements of the two registries via implementing acts—the various Joint Ministerial Decisions—poses significant constitutional law challenges. An implementing act is not capable of providing additional criteria for registration that should instead be established by law. It should rather only provide explanations and clarifications to an existing law (e.g., detailed information on an existing criterion). As a result, the latest Ministerial Decision, which provides concrete requirements on the members of CSOs, goes beyond its legislative delegation. This was recognised by the First Instance Court of Athens, which held that the Joint Ministerial Decision 10616/2020 exceeded the powers conferred upon the executive by the legislature and did not confine itself to specifying the procedure for registration, but also laid down conditions for registration of CSOs and their members, staff, and volunteers in the registries.[62] According to the court, this is a violation of Article 43(2) of the Greek Constitution, which permits delegation in cases concerning the regulation of, *inter alia*, more specific matters or matters of a detailed and technical nature.

7.4.2 *Fundamental Rights as an Effective Bulwark to Criminalisation through Surveillance?*

Joint Ministerial Decision 10616/2020 raises significant challenges regarding its compatibility with the fundamental right to freedom of association, as enshrined in Article 12 of the EU Charter of Fundamental Rights (Charter) and Article 11 of the European Convention on Human Rights (ECHR). Furthermore, as the Joint Ministerial Decision entails the processing of personal data of CSO members in a registry, it necessarily brings to the fore the rights to respect for private life and the protection of personal data, as laid down in Articles 7 and 8 of the Charter, respectively, as well as the application of Regulation 2016/679 (General Data Protection Regulation—GDPR).[63]

The applicability of the EU Charter is based on various considerations. First, access and provision of services by CSOs to asylum seekers is envisaged in the Reception Conditions Directive[64] and the Asylum Procedures Directive.[65] Second, registration of CSOs and their members is a precondition for accessing EU funding to ensure reception conditions.[66] The funding specifically is drawn from the Asylum, Migration, and Integration Fund (AMIF), governed by two relevant regulations, the AMIF Regulation and the Horizontal Regulation, outlining the operationalisation of a number of funds, including AMIF.[67] Therefore, the Charter is applicable when the Greek Government decides which CSOs will benefit from the allocation of AMIF grants. The Joint Ministerial Decision may also entail a restriction on the right to free movement of workers within the Union, as enshrined in Article 45 of the Treaty on the Functioning of the EU (TFEU). This is because the refusal of registration or removal from the Greek Registry of a CSO, or a CSO employee, will almost inevitably lead to the dismissal of this employee and, as seen above, prohibition from future employment in a Greek migration-related CSO.

7.4.2.1 *Freedom of Association: A Shrinking Space for CSOs Due to Burdensome Registration Requirements*

As regards the freedom of association, the Joint Ministerial Decision was not adopted through a participatory process and consultation with the CSOs concerned. As highlighted by HIAS,[68] this is not in line with the Joint Guidelines of the Organization for Security and Co-operation in Europe (OSCE)/ Office for Democratic Institutions and Human Rights (ODIHR) and the Venice Commission on Freedom of Association[69] or Council of Europe (CoE) Recommendation CM/Rec (2007)14 on the legal status of non-governmental organisations in Europe.[70] The registration requirements are arguably particularly cumbersome, as they include, for example, annual and detailed project reports of activities of the last two years, which, as a minimum, must include the operation of facilities (type, title, number of beneficiaries, cost of operation), services provided within accommodation facilities, actions undertaken by the entity in the previous two years, the number and titles of activities implemented per category, beneficiaries, cooperation with other agencies, and current interventions.[71] As CSOs must provide activity reports, balance sheets, and tax declarations of the two years preceding the application to register, newly established organisations are *per se* precluded from becoming active in the field of asylum, migration, and social inclusion in Greece, as they cannot provide the required documentation and thus they cannot register.[72] In addition, the Joint Ministerial Decision provides for the conduct of annual audits, including of CSOs that are not subject to a similar obligation under the Greek tax legislation.[73]

Another key challenge concerns the wide margin of discretion afforded to the administration to verify submitted applications and to reject them. The vague wording of the Ministerial Decision's provisions, particularly regarding measuring the efficiency and accountability of a CSO, allows a broad interpretation, thus granting excessive discretion to reject or remove CSOs and their members from the registries. As argued by various CSOs, this procedure violates the principle of foreseeability within the legality test under the jurisprudence of the European Court of Human Rights (ECtHR). In *Hasan and Chausch v Bulgaria*, the ECtHR opined that

> (i)n matters affecting fundamental rights it would be contrary to the rule of law, one of the basic principles of a democratic society enshrined in the Convention, for a legal discretion granted to the executive to be expressed in terms of an unfettered power. Consequently, the law must indicate with sufficient clarity the scope of any such discretion conferred on the competent authorities and the manner of its exercise.[74]

This unfettered discretionary power could be abused to ban or silence CSOs vocal in their criticism of state migration policies, or those that engage in litigation against the state, in breach of the right to freedom of expression. This is not a hypothetical argument; this discretion has led to arbitrary refusals to register key organisations operational on the ground, the most notable examples being Mare Liberum, which eventually decided to discontinue its activities in Greece and leave altogether,[75] and Refugee Support Aegean (RSA). The application for registration of the latter was rejected on the grounds that the CSO was active in favour of third-country nationals subject to removal, which, according to the ministry, was contrary to national law, a decision that even the Greek Ombudsman criticised as contrary to international, EU, and domestic law.[76] The application was rejected a year and a half after its lodging, which also raises concerns regarding the right to good administration, as enshrined in Article 41 of the Charter. RSA submitted an application for annulment before Greek administrative courts, and in the meantime, successfully registered in 2022.[77] However, the significant delay in securing registration to continue its operations created significant legal limbo.

Overall, the administrative burden of registration put a significant strain on CSOs. The registration requirements are costly and time-consuming. The reasons for rejecting an application are vague and rather broad, while revocation of an application can take place for reasons as trivial as non-adherence to very strict deadlines. The complexity is worsened by factors such as the constant and continuous reforms, the need for translation to Greek of all supporting documents, unjustified delays, the need for CSOs to abide anew with different registration requirements, and the fragility of the registration, which is dependent upon meeting very strict deadlines. The size of an organisation also plays a role. Individual human rights defenders are not able to obtain registration. The registration requirements therefore constitute a disproportionate interference with freedom of association.

Finally, the registration requirements only concern organisations involved in international protection, migration, and social inclusion. Other CSOs are not subject to such strict conditions, but the objective justification as to the need to place organisations working in a particular field of policy at a disadvantage has been, at best, flimsy. Such differentiated treatment not only constitutes a violation of freedom of association but also amounts to arbitrary discrimination on grounds of political opinion, contrary to Article 14 of the ECHR and Article 21 of the Charter.[78]

7.4.2.2 *Personal Data Protection: The Unlikely Hero?*

Additional challenges to the rights to respect for private life and personal data protection can be raised in two respects. The obligation of CSOs to publish information regarding their board members, managers, subscribers, and sponsors on their website as part of the substantive accountability assessment for certification is arguably disproportionate in light of the right to private life, as this information is excessive to the aim pursued.[79] It appears that it mostly constitutes an effort to make the registration process cumbersome for CSOs as a disincentive to operate in Greece or an excuse to reject the application. On the other hand, privacy and data protection concerns are chiefly raised by the separate registry for members of CSOs, as the Joint Ministerial Decision entails the collection and centralised storage of various categories of personal data of all staff and volunteers in these CSOs. On various occasions, both the Court of Justice of the EU (CJEU) and the ECtHR have highlighted that centralised storage of personal data constitutes an interference with the rights to private life and protection of personal data. These courts have laid down a series of safeguards to ensure that the processing of personal data for administrative purposes is necessary and proportionate in terms of, among other elements, the personal data processed, the bodies that have access to it, and the prescribed retention period.[80]

Furthermore, a close look at the applicable rules reveals that various principles enshrined in the GDPR have been violated. With regard to the principles of lawfulness, fairness, and transparency, laid down in Article 5(1)(a) of the GDPR, Joint Ministerial Decision 10615/2020 does not stipulate how the collected data will be processed, or which bodies and entities may have access to that data, including whether data can be transferred to other authorities outside the Greek territory. Furthermore, there is no specification of the retention period of the personal data collected, nor are there details regarding their erasure or periodic review by national authorities. Instead, the Joint Ministerial Decision links data storage to the activities of a CSO within Greece and to the work/volunteering period of an individual associated with a CSO. This signifies that the storage of personal data could effectively be from days to decades. This breach of the principle of storage limitation is coupled with the breach of the principles of integrity and confidentiality, enshrined in Article 5(1)(f) of the GDPR, as the Joint Ministerial Decision does not stipulate the specific technical and organisational measures implemented to ensure data security.[81]

Another disproportionate element concerns the amount and type of personal data collected from the CSO members (e.g., passport and ID number, Tax and Social Security ID number, CVs),[82] which do not meet the requirements of the principle of minimisation.[83] In particular, there is no exhaustive list of the categories of personal data to be collected and stored. There are certain types of personal data, such as passport number, which are concrete and specific. However, the requirement for all individuals to provide their CVs is problematic. CVs are not provided in a standardised format, which means that, depending on the individuals' preferences, they can be detailed or concise and can reveal very significant aspects of their personal life, such as their full educational and professional experiences, their skills, or extracurricular activities. As this requirement is imprecise and flexible, it is unclear why such a wealth of information is of relevance to the ministry, and how is it proportionate in light of the purpose of the registry. It is also unclear whether a CV with very basic and incomplete information, without providing an extensive resume of past and present activities, would be acceptable to the ministry. The ministry ought to have provided a very specific list of what elements the CVs of the members should cover in view of the aims pursued by the registry. Furthermore, the Joint Ministerial Decision also requires that CSOs submit the criminal records of their members,[84] although Greece has not adopted the necessary secondary legislation establishing appropriate safeguards for the processing of such information, as required by Article 10 of the GDPR.

A close look at the provisions of the Joint Ministerial Decision reveals a distinct lack of data protection culture, evidenced also by its adoption without being accompanied by an *ex ante* impact assessment. An impact assessment was essential, considering that the CSO Member Registry entails the processing of personal data relating to criminal convictions and offences, which, according Article 35(3) of the GDPR, requires the conducting of an impact assessment. Furthermore, impact assessments are also required when—in light of the nature, scope, context, and purposes of the processing—it is likely to result in a high risk to the rights and freedoms of natural persons. As the number of CSOs that have already successfully registered is about 100,[85] and the number of their members are in the thousands, an impact assessment ought to have been conducted. In addition, no data protection officer is foreseen.[86] There is also no reference to the competent supervisory authority, or to the right to information and access to personal data in accordance with the GDPR.[87] Finally, the Joint Ministerial Decision does not prescribe the maintenance of data logs for all data processing activities, in line with Article 30 of the GDPR,[88] which must also be made available to the supervisory authority on request, and it does not appoint a data controller for the CSO Member Registry.

Arguably, EU data protection law has been particularly instrumental in showcasing the challenges of the Joint Ministerial Decision. The fact that personal data protection constitutes a fundamental right enshrined in the Charter, and is fleshed out through various secondary legal instruments, makes it more tangible and thus more feasible to enforce and operationalise. Several organisations brought a case before the Greek Council of State claiming, among other arguments, that the Joint Ministerial Decision constitutes a violation of EU data protection law. The Council of State, sitting in plenary on 2 December 2022 heard the case, with the Greek Government focusing on downplaying the consequences of non-registration and steering the discussion away from the compatibility of the registries with fundamental rights.[89] At the time of writing in December 2024, the judgement was still pending, with the court presumably awaiting a revised Joint Ministerial Decision as a means to avoid striking down the current Joint Ministerial Decision. Notwithstanding efforts by the CoE Commissioner for Human Rights, and three UN Special Rapporteurs calling on Greece to review the Joint Ministerial Decision due its incompatibility with human rights,[90] the latest Joint Ministerial Decision 148104/2024 only made limited changes that did not address these crucial points.

7.4.2.3 *Knock-on Effect on Asylum Seeker and Migrant Rights*

The aforementioned fundamental rights challenges have a knock-on effect on the rights of asylum seekers and migrants. Without registration, CSOs are unable to operate and provide services and advice on Greek territory. Reception conditions and services in Greece are limited, with numerous academic commentators, CSOs, courts, and human rights bodies having found conditions to violate human dignity and to constitute inhuman and degrading treatment.[91] With even more limited access to service and assistance by CSOs, asylum seekers and refugees face even greater difficulties in accessing the asylum procedure, health services, legal aid, shelter, and food. As a result, the Joint Ministerial Decision does not serve its purported objective of safeguarding the rights of refugees and migrants, but rather creates a suffocating environment disregarding or sidelining the key role played by CSOs to realise migrants' rights.

Moreover, following the adoption of Law 4825/2021, SAR operations can only be carried out by CSOs that are registered on, and are included in, the local operational plan of the Hellenic Coast Guard, which creates an even more restrictive operational space for assisting refugees and migrants at sea. Even while meeting both of these criteria, organisations need to be specifically called to participate in a SAR operation. These measures amount to a *de facto* prohibition of civilian SAR.

Overall, the shrinking operational space for CSOs should be viewed within the broader hostile environment created in Greece and amidst accusations for violations of migrants' fundamental rights and pushbacks.[92] Reducing the number of CSOs and criminalising them for failing to comply with the convoluted legal framework not only creates a "chilling effect", as mentioned by the FRA,[93] but also reduces the likelihood of "eyes" witnessing those violations first hand. This links with the impact of these measures on the rule of law, as the next subsection explores.

7.4.3 *Criminalisation through Administrative Surveillance as a Rule of Law Violation?*

EU law accords to the rule of law the status of a foundational EU value.[94] The rule of law is an EU objective,[95] helps guide the Union's external action and foreign policy objectives,[96] and constitutes a condition for accession for candidate countries.[97] Fundamental rights and the rule of law are deeply intertwined in the EU's legal order.[98] Some commentators understand democracy, fundamental rights, and the rule of law to be co-constitutive.[99] Others have argued that by distinguishing the rule of law from the respect for human dignity, freedom, democracy, and equality, the Treaty on the European Union (TEU) seems to opt instead for a "thin" understanding.[100] It has also been argued that as the EU system of judicial review includes both procedural and substantive elements, it is probably best described as reflecting a version of the "thick" understanding of the rule of law.[101]

The European Commission understands the rule of law as containing the principles of legality, legal certainty, effective judicial protection, effective judicial review, separation of powers, and equality before the law.[102] Certain fundamental rights are contained within its scope; for example, effective judicial protection is intrinsically linked with the right to an effective remedy and a fair trial.[103] Finally, as CJEU case law made clear, the rule of law encompasses at least certain fundamental rights, such as the right to an effective remedy.[104]

Whichever understanding one adopts, criminalisation through administrative surveillance, as practiced in Greece, constitutes the violation of rule of law. As the previous subsections outlined, the Greek law and practice are problematic through the constitutional lenses of legality and legal certainty, as well as that of adherence to fundamental rights. In terms of legality concerns, additional requirements have been introduced through a ministerial decision, a legal instrument which is meant to only specify obligations rather than establish them.[105] In terms of legal certainty, the law and the Joint Ministerial Decision have been subject to consecutive reforms, creating significant confusion as to the applicable legal framework. In terms of fundamental rights violations, the ministerial decision directly challenges the rights to freedom of association, to privacy, and to personal life.[106] Indirectly, by weakening the operational capacity of civil society in a situation of underprovision, it further jeopardises absolute rights of migrants, such as the right to human dignity and the prohibition of inhuman or degrading treatment or punishment.[107]

Adopting a rule of law analysis, in addition to the constitutional and fundamental rights dimensions, can illustrate potential signs of broader constitutional capture, also known as rule of law backsliding. This can be understood in two ways. Building on Jan-Werner Müller's analysis of constitutional capture,[108] Laurent Pech and Kim-Lane Scheppele have defined rule of law backsliding as

> the process through which elected public authorities deliberately implement governmental blueprints which aim to systematically weaken, annihilate, or capture internal checks on power with the view of dismantling the liberal democratic state and entrenching the long-term rule of the dominant party.[109]

In situations that do not reach this level of gravity, rule of law backsliding could manifest in systemic breaches relating to judicial independence, harassment of CSOs or of educational institutions, and violations of the freedoms of expression and association. The Greek practice is taking this latter trajectory. Where connected with rule of law backsliding, these violations should not be viewed as "merely" policy-specific, that is migration-specific issues. They call for different responses, most notably streamlining the examination of these violations via the existing rule of law enforcement machinery.

Rule of law adherence is difficult to enforce. Institutional enforcement is essentially political in nature, as it is reserved to the procedures of Article 7 of the TEU and has thus been ineffective.[110] Individual enforcement of EU law cannot remedy this weakness. Article 2 of the TEU arguably cannot be considered directly effective and thus cannot be relied upon before domestic courts, which, in any event, are often targeted by backsliding governments.[111] Alternative mechanisms have emerged. A strand of mechanisms embed respect for rule of law in the operationalisation and discharge of EU funding.[112] A parallel approach developed by the Commission is an advisory and exchange framework, the Annual Rule of Law cycle. In operation since 2020, it consists of annual reporting at EU and national levels on rule of law adherence and challenges, including concrete recommendations to Member States, whose follow-up the Commission tracks.

The Commission scrutinised Greece's registration practices as a challenge to the rule of law since the inception of its Annual Rule of Law framework. Its first report, released in 2020, already alerted to restrictive space for action for migration CSOs in Greece,[113] with the national Greek chapter stating that several actors criticised the registry as including "too stringent and disproportionate requirements for registration and certification".[114] In its 2021 report, the Commission noted that the registration process "continues to raise questions".[115] The 2021 Greek national chapter elaborated that registration, as practiced by Greece, was challenging the capacity of CSOs to operate there and to receive financial support, while recommending to Greece that "registration requirements should not go beyond what is strictly necessary and proportionate and in particular should not be excessively burdensome".[116]

This scrutiny has continued in more recent reports. In 2022, the Commission noted in its report that "some registration requirements continue to be considered disproportionate".[117] In its recommendations, it asked Greece to "ensure that registration requirements for civil society organisations (CSOs) are proportionate in view of maintaining an open framework for them to operate".[118] This was one of five recommendations of the Commission to Greece in relation to the rule of law in the country, revealing the gravity of the issue. The 2023 Annual Report highlights that in Greece "the situation of the civil society raises concerns, in particular in relation to organisations working in specific areas".[119] In the national chapter, the Commission highlighted that some progress had been made, for example, through reducing delays in the processing of registration applications from 120 to 60 days.[120] However, in another recommendation on the rule of law, it also held that Greece should "take further steps to evaluate the current registration system for CSOs, including by initiating a structured dialogue with CSOs, and assess whether there is a need to amend it".[121]

The most recent report (2024) continues this scrutiny. The Commission highlights that "the registration framework still needs to be evaluated and concerns remain about the space for civil society".[122] The national chapter notes some positive developments, such as efforts to make different registries interoperable so that CSOs do not need to resubmit the same documentation, as well as the abolishment of the requirement for CSOs to renew their registration with the ministry every three years.[123] The ministry also announced its intention to review the legal framework in the fall of 2023 by submitting a proposal for legislation, and on this basis, CSOs provided feedback.[124] However, this proposal has not yet materialised. Therefore, the Commission noted that the civic space in Greece remains obstructed, specifically in relation to CSOs operating in the field of migration and asylum.[125] Thus, as one of four recommendations to Greece in relation to the rule of law, the Commission advised it to "strengthen efforts to evaluate the current legal framework for the registration system for CSOs and assess whether there is a need to amend it, while moving forward with a structured dialogue with CSOs".[126]

Overall, the Commission's sustained scrutiny of the Greek migration CSO registration practice, and its inclusion as one of the few recommendations to the country, attests to the seriousness of the matter in relation to Greece's adherence to the rule of law. The Commission has also indicated that it considers some of the registration requirements disproportionate. However, it has not clearly stated that it considers this practice to violate Greece's legal obligations. More broadly, this soft dialogical framework has yielded only limited advancements in practice. Four years after the Commission commenced its scrutiny, the national legal framework remains largely unaltered. In the meantime, as the Commission's latest national report reveals, CSOs' difficulties to register continue to result in the temporary suspension of their activities or, in some cases, in their complete inability to operate due to the freezing of their assets by banks.[127]

7.5 Conclusion

This chapter provided a detailed analysis of how criminalisation of CSOs in Greece has been realised through increased administrative surveillance in the form of registration requirements for migration-related CSOs and their members. Our analysis demonstrated that through continuous legal reforms since 2016, and particularly between 2019 and 2021, national law has imposed increased administrative burdens. The cumbersome and constantly shifting registration requirements have created a suffocating, untenable civic space for the operation of migration CSOs. These requirements have resulted in a major disincentive for CSOs to continue their activities in Greece, as they are unable to meet the disproportionate legal exigencies around registration. Even CSOs that have managed to surmount the administrative obstacles and gather the necessary documentation face the wide discretionary power of national authorities in evaluating the supporting documentation, which constitutes a disproportionate limitation of their freedom of association. Perhaps the most visible challenge of the Greek registration framework concerns the members of CSOs, who have to provide a wide range of personal data, without corresponding data protection safeguards laid down in law. Finally, the registration framework has indirectly affected the rights of migrants who, in an existing environment of underprovision, face additional limitations to accessing procedural rights and reception conditions.

Overall, the Greek registration framework, marked by legal uncertainty, raises broader concerns regarding the adherence to the rule of law. Although these concerns are acknowledged at the EU level through the European Commission's Annual Rule of Law Framework, they have not led to meaningful reform at the national level. With the decision of the Greek Council of State on the fate of the two registries still pending over two years after the relevant hearing took place, EU data protection law seems to be the only applicable field of law "with teeth". It remains to be seen whether the operational space of migration-related CSOs at the periphery of the EU, and ultimately the EU's rule of law, can be effectively secured.

Notes

1 See among others, Chapter 2 in this volume, as well as the previous volume of Sergio Carrera, Valsamis Mitsilegas, Jennifer Allsopp and Lina Vosyliūtė, *Policing Humanitarianism—EU Policies Against Human Smuggling and Their Impact on Civil Society* (Hart 2019).

2 National Commission for Human Rights, 'Statement of 22 April 2024 on Human Rights Defenders Working with Migrants and Asylum Seekers' (2024).

3 Conference of International Non-Governmental Organisations of the Council of Europe, Expert Council on NGO Law, 'Study on Stigmatisation of Non-Governmental Organisations in Europe' (2024).
4 Council of Europe: Commissioner for Human Rights, 'Letter to Prime Minister of Greece' (2023).
5 European Commission, '2024 Rule of Law Report: Country Chapter on the Rule of Law Situation in Greece' SWD (2024) 808.
6 In Greece, the Facilitators' Package was first implemented by Law 3386/2005 concerning the entry, stay, and social integration of third-country nationals (GG A 212/23.8.2005) and has been subject to multiple reforms in 2007 (Law 3536/2007, GG A 42/23.2.2007) and 2009 (Law 3772/2009, GG A 112/10.7.2009). The relevant provisions were replaced by the Immigration and Social Integration Code of 2014 (Law 4251/2014, GG A 80/1.4.2014). In comparison with other EU Member States, Greek law criminalises the facilitation of irregular entry, transit, and residence of third-country nationals with sanctions that place Greece at the higher end of the "criminalisation spectrum", and no material benefit is required for the commission of the offence. See Sergio Carrera and others, *Fit for Purpose? The Facilitation Directive and the Criminalisation of Humanitarian Assistance to Irregular Migrants* (Study commissioned by LIBE Committee, European Parliament 2016).
7 Joint Ministerial Decision 4151.4183/166, 'Setting up of a Coordination Committee within the General Secretariat of Aegean and Island Policy for the registration, coordination and evaluation of NGOs in the island of Lesvos' (2016) (Κοινή Υπουργική Απόφαση 4151.4183/166 'Σύσταση στη Γενική Γραμματεία Αιγαίου και Νησιωτικής Πολιτικής Συντονιστικής Επιτροπής καταγραφής, συντονισμού και αξιολόγησης Μ.Κ.Ο. στη νήσο Λέσβο') GG 114/28.1.2016.
8 Statewatch, 'NGOs and Volunteers Helping Refugees in Greece to Be Placed Under State Control' (22 February 2016) <https://www.statewatch.org/media/documents/news/2016/feb/greece-state-control-ngos.pdf> last accessed 18 January 2025, as all the hyperlinks included in this Chapter.
9 Statewatch (n 8).
10 Statewatch (n 8).
11 See the CIVICUS Monitor webpage on Slovakia <https://monitor.civicus.org/country/slovakia/>.
12 Act CLXXV (2011) on the right of association, the legal status of public benefit, and the operation and support of civil organizations, article 75, para 5.
13 Ministerial Decision 39487/16 'Joint Establishment of a National Registry of Greek and Foreign NonGovernmental Organizations (NGOs) active in the field of international Joint Ministerial Decision' (2016) (Υπουργική Απόφαση 39487/16 'Σύσταση Εθνικού Μητρώου ελληνικών και ξένων Μη Κυβερνητικών Οργανώσεων (ΜΚΟ) που δραστηριοποιούνται σε θέματα διεθνούς προστασίας, μετανάστευσης και κοινωνικής ένταξης') GG B 2930/14.9.2016.
14 FRA, 'Challenges Facing Civil Society Organisations Working on Human Rights in the EU' (2018) 22.
15 European Commission, 'Communication from the Commission to the European Parliament and the Council—Progress Report on the Implementation of the Hotspots in Greece' COM (2015) 678 final.
16 UN Special Rapporteur on the Situation of Human Rights Defenders, 'Situation of Human Rights Defenders—Visit to Greece' (2 March 2023) 8.
17 The National Herald, 'Greece's Refugee, Migrant NGO's Face Ban Unless Registered' (27 November 2019) <https://www.thenationalherald.com/greeces-refugee-migrant-ngos-face-ban-unless-registered/>.
18 Carrera and others (n 1).
19 Carrera and others (n 1).

20 Lina Vosyliute and Ngo Chun Luk, *Protecting Civil Society Space: Strengthening Freedom of Association, Assembly and Expression and the Right to Defend Rights in the EU* (Study requested by LIBE Committee, European Parliament 2020) 55.
21 Choose Love, 'Υπό Πίεση—Πώς η Ελλάδα περιορίζει τις οργανώσεις της κοινωνίας των πολιτών που δουλεύουν με πρόσφυγες' (2021) 15.
22 Ministerial Decision 7586/2018 'Operation of the Registry of Greek and Foreign Non-Governmental Organizations (NGOs) active in matters of international protection, migration and social integration' (2018) (Υπουργική Απόφαση 7586/18 'Λειτουργία Μητρώου Ελληνικών και Ξένων Μη Κυβερνητικών Οργανώσεων (ΜΚΟ) που δραστηριοποιούνται σε θέματα διεθνούς προστασίας, μετανάστευσης και κοινωνικής ένταξης' GG B 4794/26.10.2018.
23 UN Special Rapporteur on the Situation of Human Rights Defenders (n 16).
24 Law 4636/19 'On International Protection and Other Provisions' (2019) GG A 169/1.11.2019.
25 For reasons of national security, public security or reasons owing to the administrative management of a particular border crossing point.
26 Ministry of Citizen's Protection, '26-11-2019: Announcement Regarding the Finalisation of the Registration Process for NGOs in the Field of Migration/Refugee in the Relevant Register' (2019) ('26-11-2019: Ανακοίνωση σχετικά με προθεσμία για την ολοκλήρωση της διαδικασίας ένταξης Μη Κυβερνητικών Οργανώσεων, με πεδίο δράσης το μεταναστευτικό/προσφυγικό στο σχετικό μητρώο') <https://www.minocp.gov.gr/2019/11/26/26-11-2019-anakoinosi-schetika-me-prothesmia-gia-tin-oloklirosi-tis-diadikasias-entaxis-mi-kyvernitikon-organoseon-me-pedio-drasis-to-metanasteftiko-prosfygiko-sto-schetiko-mitroo/>.
27 Choose Love (n 21) 17.
28 Law 4662/2020, 'National Mechanism for Crisis Management and Risk Management, Restructuring of the General Secretariat of Civil Protection, Upgrading of the Voluntary Civil Protection System, Reorganization of the Fire Brigade and Other Provisions' (2020) (Εθνικός Μηχανισμός Διαχείρισης Κρίσεων και Αντιμετώπισης Κινδύνων, αναδιάρθρωση της Γενικής Γραμματείας Πολιτικής Προστασίας, αναβάθμιση συστήματος εθελοντισμού πολιτικής προστασίας, αναδιοργάνωση του Πυροσβεστικού και άλλες διατάξεις') GG A 27/7.2.2020, article 191, para 2.
29 Joint Ministerial Decision 3063/2020 'Regulation of the "Registry of Greek and Foreign Non-Governmental Organizations (NGOs)" and the "Registry of Members of Non-Governmental Organizations (NGOs)", which are active in matters of international protection, migration and social integration within the Greek Territory' (2020) (Καθορισμός λειτουργίας του "Μητρώου Ελληνικών και Ξένων Μη Κυβερνητικών Οργανώσεων (ΜΚΟ)" και του "Μητρώου Μελών Μη Κυβερνητικών Οργανώσεων (ΜΚΟ)", που δραστηριοποιούνται σε θέματα διεθνούς προστασίας, μετανάστευσης και κοινωνικής ένταξης εντός της Ελληνικής Επικράτειας') GG B 1382/14.4.2020.
30 TA NEA, 'Heavy Accusations by Koumoutsakos: Deep and Dark Networks of NGO Interests' (5 February 2020) ('Βαριές κατηγορίες Κουμουτσάκου: Βαθιά και σκοτεινά δίκτυα συμφερόντων με ΜΚΟ') <https://www.tanea.gr/2020/02/05/politics/varies-katigories-koumoutsakou-vathia-kai-skoteina-diktya-symferonton-me-mko/>.
31 Ministry of Migration and Asylum, 'National Legislation Regarding NGOs Participating in the Implementation of Actions in the Field of International Protection, Migration and Social Integration—Briefing Note' (2021) <https://commission.europa.eu/document/download/222d7e7c-4037-494d-af8b-50d4a700bc77_en?filename=el-additional_input.pdf>.
32 Ministry of Migration and Asylum (n 31).
33 Ministry of Migration and Asylum (n 31).

34 Law 4686/2020, 'Improvement of Immigration Legislation, Amendment of Provisions of Laws 4636/2019 (A΄ 169), 4375/2016 (A΄ 51), 4251/2014 (A΄ 80) and other provisions' (2020) ('Βελτίωση της μεταναστευτικής νομοθεσίας, τροποποίηση διατάξεων των νόμων 4636/2019 (A΄ 169), 4375/2016 (A΄ 51), 4251/2014 (A΄ 80) και άλλες διατάξεις' GG A 96/12.5.2020, article 58.

35 As explained by the Greek Parliament Scientific Service, the law empowers the government to set out additional substantive conditions beyond those set out in legislation. For an analysis of the constitutional challenges, see Section 4.1. Greek Parliament,'Έκθεση επί του νομοσχεδίου "Βελτίωση της μεταναστευτικής νομοθεσίας"' (2020) 9–10 <https://www.hellenicparliament.gr/UserFiles/7b24652e-78eb-4807-9d68-e9a5d4576eff/metanast-nomothesia-epist.pdf>.

36 Joint Ministerial Decision 10616/2020, 'Regulation of the functioning of the "Registry of Greek and Foreign Non-Governmental Organisations (NGOs)" and the "Registry of Members of Non-Governmental Organisations (NGOs)"' (2020) (Καθορισμός λειτουργίας του "Μητρώου Ελληνικών και Ξένων Μη Κυβερνητικών Οργανώσεων (ΜΚΟ)" και του "Μητρώου Μελών Μη Κυβερνητικών Οργανώσεων (ΜΚΟ)") GG B 3820/9.9.2020. Notably the Decision was finalised in August 2020, but was only released on 10 September 2020.

37 ERT, '18 NGOs Retain the Right to Enter the Reception Centres and Accommodation Facilities' (17 June 2020) ('18 Μη Κυβερνητικές Οργανώσεις διατηρούν το δικαίωμα εισόδου σε ΚΥΤ και δομές φιλοξενίας') <https://www.ertnews.gr/eidiseis/ellada/kinonia/mko18-diatiroyn-dikaioma-prosvasis-se-k-y-t-kai-domes/>; Ethnos, 'Migration: "Eviction" to 22 NGOs from the Reception Centres and Accommodation Facilities' (17 June 2020) ('Μεταναστευτικό: "Έξωση" σε 22 ΜΚΟ από τα ΚΥΤ και τις δομές φιλοξενίας') <https://www.ethnos.gr/greece/article/110956/metanasteytikoexoshse22mkoapotakytkaitisdomesfiloxenias>.

38 Choose Love (n 21) 15–16.

39 Chosse Love (n 21).

40 Law 4825/2021, 'Reform of Deportation and Return Procedures for Citizens of Third Countries, Attracting Investors and Digital Nomads, Issues of Residence Permits and Procedures for Granting International Protection, Provisions of the Competence of the Ministry of Immigration and Asylum and the Ministry of Citizen Protection and Other Urgent Provisions' (2021) (Αναμόρφωση διαδικασιών απελάσεων και επιστροφών πολιτών τρίτων χωρών, προσέλκυση επενδυτών και ψηφιακών νομάδων, ζητήματα αδειών διαμονής και διαδικασιών χορήγησης διεθνούς προστασίας, διατάξεις αρμοδιότητας Υπουργείου Μετανάστευσης και Ασύλου και Υπουργείου Προστασίας του Πολίτη και άλλες επείγουσες διατάξεις') GG A 157/4.9.2021.

41 Joint Ministerial Decision 10616/2020 (n 36), article 1, para 3.

42 Joint Ministerial Decision 10616/2020 (n 36), article 1.

43 Joint Ministerial Decision 10616/2020 (n 36), article 2.

44 Joint Ministerial Decision 10616/2020 (n 36), article 3, para 2 and article 14. para 2.

45 Joint Ministerial Decision 10616/2020 (n 36), article 3, para 2.

46 RSA, 'Repression Continued Greece Further Restricts Civil Society Supporting Refugees and Migrants' (2020) <https://rsaegean.org/wp-content/uploads/2020/09/RSA_Comments_New_NGO_Registry-1.pdf>.

47 Joint Ministerial Decision 10616/2020 (n 36), article 5.

48 Joint Ministerial Decision 10616/2020 (n 36), article 6, para 1.

49 Joint Ministerial Decision 10616/2020 (n 36), article 5.

50 Joint Ministerial Decision 10616/2020 (n 36), Article 6, para 3. The provision was amended by Article 1 of Ministerial Decision 148104/2024 'Amendment of Joint Ministerial Decision of the Ministers of Finance and Migration

and Asylum Regulation of the functioning of the "Registry of Greek and Foreign Non-Governmental Organisations (NGOs)" and the "Registry of Members of Non-Governmental Organisations (NGOs)", which are active in matters of international protection, migration, and social integration within the Greek Territory' (2024) ['Τροποποίηση της υπ' αρ. οικ.10616/24-8-2020 κοινής απόφασης των Υπουργών Οικονομικών και Μετανάστευσης και Ασύλου Καθορισμός λειτουργίας του "Μητρώου Ελληνικών και Ξένων Μη Κυβερνητικών Οργανώσεων (ΜΚΟ)" και του "Μητρώου Μελών Μη Κυβερνητικών Οργανώσεων (ΜΚΟ)", που δραστηριοποιούνται σε θέματα διεθνούς προστασίας, μετανάστευσης και κοινωνικής ένταξης εντός της Ελληνικής Επικράτειας'] GG B 2829/20.05.2024.

51 Joint Ministerial Decision 10616/2020 (n 36), article 6, para 4.

52 Joint Ministerial Decision 10616/2020 (n 36), article 10.

53 Joint Ministerial Decision 10616/2020 (n 36), article 10, para 2.

54 See Expert Council on NGO Law, 'Addendum to the Opinion of the Compatibility with European Standards of Recent and Planned Amendments to Greek Legislation on NGO Registration' (2020) <https://rm.coe.int/expert-council-conf-exp-2020-5-addendum-to-the-opinion-on-the-compatib/1680a076f2>.

55 Joint Ministerial Decision 10616/2020 (n 36), article 10, para 1 and article 13, para 2.

56 Joint Ministerial Decision 10616/2020 (n 36), article 11 para 1(a).

57 However, the individuals can only have access to the premises for two months renewable by the Director of the facility.

58 Joint Ministerial Decision 10616/2020 (n 36), article 14, para 2.

59 Joint Ministerial Decision 10616/2020 (n 36), article 8, para 1(d) and article 14, para 1(c).

60 Joint Ministerial Decision 10616/2020 (n 36), article 11, para 4 and 5.

61 Joint Ministerial Decision 10616/2020 (n 36), article 14, para 2.

62 First Instance Court of Athens, Decision 427/2022 [2022]. Also see Refugee Support Aegean (RSA), 'Risk of Repression: New Rules on Civil Society Supporting Refugees and Migrants in Greece' (2020) 1 <https://rsaegean.org/wp-content/uploads/2020/05/RSA_Comments_NGO_Registry.pdf>.

63 Regulation (EU) 2016/679 of 27 April 2016 on the protection of natural persons with regard to the processing of personal data and on the free movement of such data, and repealing Directive 95/46/EC (General Data Protection Regulation, GDPR) [2016] OJ L119/1.

64 Directive 2013/33/EU of 26 June 2013 laying down standards for the reception of applicants for international protection (recast) [2013] OJ L180/96, Article 10, para 4 and Article 18, para 2(b) and (c).

65 Directive 2013/32/EU of 26 June 2013 on common procedures for granting and withdrawing international protection (recast) [2013] OJ L180/60, Article 8, para 2 and Article 22, para 2.

66 Elli Kriona Saranti, 'Challenging the Crackdown on Migration NGOs in Greece: Contesting the Discriminatory Framework for the Registration of Migration NGOs and Their Members Before the Council of State' [forthcoming 2025] German Law Journal.

67 Regulation (EU) 514/2014 of 16 April 2014 laying down general provisions on the Asylum, Migration and Integration Fund and on the instrument for financial support for police cooperation, preventing and combating crime, and crisis management [2014] OJ *L150/112*; Regulation (EU) 2021/1147 of 7 July 2021 establishing the Asylum, Migration and Integration Fund [2021] OJ L251/1.

68 HIAS, 'Some Thoughts on the New Joint Ministerial Decision, Regulating the Registration of Migration-Related NGOs in Greece' (8 May 2020) <https://hias.org/wp-content/uploads/jmd_3063.2020_ngo_registry-version_4.

pdf?_gl=1*f3go9c*_gcl_au*MTIzMzE0OTYwNy4xNzM0ODY4NzUz*_ga*NzM2MzYyMjUxLjE3MzQ4Njg3ODk.*_ga_6Q0BQPF21C*MTczNDg2ODc4OC4xLjEuMTczNDg2ODkwMC41NS4wLjA>.

69 European Commission for Democracy through Law—Venice Commission and OSCE ODIHR, 'Joint Guidelines on Freedom of Association', adopted on 12–13 December 2014 <https://www.venice.coe.int/webforms/documents/default.aspx?pdffile=CDL-AD(2014)046-e>.

70 Council of Europe—Committee of Ministers, 'Recommendation CM/Rec (2007)14 of the Committee of Ministers to Member States on the Legal Status of Non-Governmental Organisations in Europe' (2007).

71 HIAS (n 68).

72 Kriona Saranti (n 66).

73 Kriona Saranti (n 66).

74 ECtHR, *Hasan and Chaush v Bulgaria* [2000] 30985/96, para 84.

75 Efysin, 'Departure-Slap of the NGO Mare Liberum' (5 May 2023) (Αποχώρηση—ράπισμα της ΜΚΟ Mare Liberum) <https://www.efsyn.gr/ellada/koinonia/388450_apohorisi-rapisma-tis-mko-mare-liberum>.

76 RSA, 'The Ombudsman Calls for Re-Examining the Refusal to Register RSA in the Registry of NGOs' (2021) (13 December 2021) (Ο Συνήγορος του Πολίτη καλεί για την επανεξέταση της απόρριψης εγγραφής της RSA στο Μητρώο ΜΚΟ) <https://rsaegean.org/el/o-synigoros-tou-politi-kalei-gia-tin-epanexetasi-tis-aporripsis-engrafis-tis-rsa-sto-mitroo-mko/>; RSA, 'Refusal to Register in the Registry of NGOs of the Ministry of Migration and Asylum Despite the Fulfillement of all the Conditions' (2021) [Απόρριψη εγγραφής στο Μητρώο ΜΚΟ του Υπουργείου Μετανάστευσης και Ασύλου παρά την ύπαρξη όλων των προβλεπόμενων προϋποθέσεων] <https://rsaegean.org/el/aporripsi-engrafis-sto-mitroo-mko/>.

77 RSA, 'Refugee Support in the Aegean—Report 2022' (2022) (Υποστήριξη Προσφύγων στο Αιγαίο (RSA) Έκθεση Πεπραγμένων 2022) <https://rsaegean.org/wp-content/uploads/2023/03/RSA_2022_-%CE%A0%CE%B5%CF%80%CF%81%CE%B1%CE%B3%CE%BC%CE%B5%CC%81%CE%BD%CF%89%CE%BD.pdf>.

78 See also HIAS (n 68); RSA (n 62) 5.

79 Joint Ministerial Decision 10616/2020 (n 36), article 6.

80 See in particular, CJEU, Joined cases C-293/12 and C-594/12 *Digital Rights Ireland Ltd v Minister for Communications, Marine and Natural Resources and Others and Kärntner Landesregierung and Others* [2014] ECLI:EU:C:2014:238; Joined Cases C-203/15 and C-689/15 *Tele2 Sverige AB v Post—ochtelestyrelsen and Secretary of State for the Home Department v Tom Watson and Others* [2016] ECLI:EU:C:2016:970; Opinion 1/15 ECLI:EU:C:2017:592; ECtHR, *Amann v Switzerland* [2000] 30 EHRR 843; *Rotaru v Romania* [2000] 8 BHRC 43.

81 Kriona Saranti (n 66).

82 Joint Ministerial Decision 10616/2020 (n 36), article 11.

83 GDPR (n 63), article 5, para 1(c).

84 Joint Ministerial Decision 10616/2020 (n 36), article 11, para 2(b).

85 The Registry can be found here: <https://ngo.migration.gov.gr/registered.php>.

86 GDPR (n 63), article 37.

87 GDPR (n 63), articles 13–15.

88 GDPR (n 63), article 30.

89 Kriona Saranti (n 66).

90 Expert Council on NGO Law (n 54); Council of Europe Commissioner for Human Rights, 'Letter to Greek Authorities' (2 May 2021) <https://rm.coe.int/letter-to-mr-michalis-chrysochoidis-minister-for-citizens-protection-o/1680a256ad>; 'Joint Communication of the Mandates of the Special Rapporteur on the Rights to Freedom of Peaceful Assembly and of Association, the Special Rapporteur on the

Situation of Human Rights Defenders, and the Special Rapporteur on the Human Rights of Migrants to Greece' (2021) GRC 1/2021 <https://spcommreports.ohchr.org/TMResultsBase/DownLoadPublicCommunicationFile?gId=26314>.

91 See Evangelia (Lilian) Tsourdi and Niovi Vavoula, 'Killing Me Softly? Scrutinising the Role of Soft Law in Greece's Response to COVID-19' (2021) 12 European Journal of Risk Regulation, 59; Refugee Service Aegean, 'Systemic Breaches of the Rule of Law and of the EU Asylum Acquis at Greece's Land and Sea Borders' (*RSA*, 2022) <https://rsaegean.org/en/greece_cso_briefing_libe/>; See Asylum Information Database/ECRE, 'Country Report: Greece' <https://asylumineurope.org/reports/country/greece/>; Council of Europe Commissioner for Fundamental Rights, 'Greek Authorities Should Investigate Allegations of Pushbacks and Ill-Treatment of Migrants, Ensure an Enabling Environment for NGOs and Improve Reception Conditions' (2021) CommHR/DM/sf 019-2021, and for a recent condemnation by the European Court of Human Rights, see ECtHR, *AR and others v Greece* [2024] 59841/19. See also, Special Rapporteur on the Human Rights of Migrants, 'A/HRC/44/42: Right to Freedom of Association of Migrants and Their Defenders—Report of the Special Rapporteur on the Human Rights of Migrants' (2020) <https://www.ohchr.org/en/press-releases/2020/03/greece-rights-violations-against-asylum-seekers-turkey-greece-border-must>.

92 Evangelia (Lilian) Tsourdi and Cathryn Costello, '"Systemic Violations" in EU Asylum Law: Cover or Catalyst?' (2023) 24 German Law Journal 982, 986–93, and ECtHR, *Alkhatib and others v Greece* [2024] 3566/16.

93 European Union Agency for Fundamental Rights, 'Legal Environment and Space of Civil Society Organisations in Supporting Fundamental Rights–Greece' (2021) 4–6 <https://fra.europa.eu/sites/default/files/fra_uploads/franet_greece_civic_space_2021.pdf>.

94 Treaty on the European Union (TEU) [2007], article 2 states that

> [t]he Union is founded on the values of respect for human dignity, freedom, democracy, equality, the rule of law and respect for human rights, including the rights of persons belonging to minorities. These values are common to the Member States in a society in which pluralism, non-discrimination, tolerance, justice, solidarity and equality between women and men prevail.

95 TEU, article 3, para 1.

96 TEU, article 21, para 1 and para 3; and for an analysis Joris Larik, *Foreign Policy Objectives in European Constitutional Law* (OUP 2016).

97 TEU, article 49.

98 Evangelia (Lilian) Tsourdi, 'Asylum in the EU: One of the Many Faces of Rule of Law Backsliding?' (2021) 17 European Constitutional Law Review 471, 477–80.

99 Sergio Carrera, Elspeth Guild and Nicholas Hernanz, *The Triangular Relationship Between Fundamental Rights, Democracy, and the Rule of Law in the EU: Towards an EU Copenhagen Mechanism* (CEPS 2013) <https://www.ceps.eu/ceps-publications/triangular-relationship-between-fundamental-rights-democracy-and-rule-law-eu-towards-eu/>.

100 Armin von Bogdandy and Michael Ioannidis, 'Systemic Deficiency in the Rule of Law: What it Is, What Has Been Done, What Can Be Done' (2014) 51 Common Market Law Review 59, 62–63, referring also to the writings of Christian Calliess, in Christian Calliess and Matthias Ruffert (eds), *EUV/AEUV: Kommentar* (4th edn, Beck 2011), article 2, marg. number 26.

101 Theodore Konstantinides, *The Rule of Law in the European Union: The Internal Dimension* (Hart Publishing 2017) 58.

102 See European Commission, *A New EU Framework to Strengthen the Rule of Law*, COM (2014) 158, 4; European Commission, *Further Strengthening the Rule of Law Within the Union*, COM (2019) 163, 1.

103 See Charter, Article 47. For an illustration in asylum, see Evangelia (Lilian) Tsourdi, 'Of Legislative Waves and Case Law: Effective Judicial Protection, Right to an Effective Remedy, and Proceduralisation in the EU Asylum Policy' (2019) 12 Review of European Administrative Law 143.

104 ECJ Case C-64/16 *Associação Sindical dos Juízes Portugueses v Tribunal de Contas* [2018] ECLI:EU:C:2018:117; and commentary in Matteo Bonelli and Monica Claes, 'Judicial Serendipity: How Portuguese Judges Came to the Rescue of the Polish Judiciary: ECJ 27 February 2018, Case C-64/16, Associação Sindical dos Juízes Portugueses' (2018) 14 EuConst 622; and Peter Van Elsuwege and Femke Gremmelperez, 'Protecting the Rule of Law in the EU Legal Order: A Constitutional Role for the Court of Justice' (2018) 16 EuConst 8, 23–25.

105 See analysis in section 3.1.

106 See analysis in section 3.2.

107 See analysis in section 3.2.

108 Jan-Werner Müller, 'Should the EU Protect Democracy and the Rule of Law Inside Member States' (2015) 21 European Law Journal 141.

109 Laurent Pech and Kim Scheppele, 'Illiberalism Within: Rule of Law Backsliding in the EU' (2017) 19 Cambridge Yearbook of European Legal Studies 3, 10.

110 See, Matteo Bonelli, 'From Sanctions to Prevention, and Now Back to Sanctions? Article 7 TEU and the Protection of the EU Founding Values' in Stefano Montaldo, Francesco Costamagna and Alberto Miglio (eds), *EU Law Enforcement the Evolution of Sanctioning Powers* (Routledge 2022) 47–70.

111 Antonia Baraggia and Matteo Bonelli, 'Filling the Enforcement Gap? Protecting the Rule of Law Through Funding Conditionality' in Evangelia (Lilian) Tsourdi and Marijn Van der Sluis (eds), *Governing Through Funding in the EU* (CUP, forthcoming 2026).

112 See, Baraggia and Bonelli (n 111), and Antonia Baraggia and Matteo Bonelli, 'Linking Money to Values: The New Rule of Law Conditionality Regulation and its Constitutional Challenges' (2022) 23 German Law Journal 131–56.

113 European Commission, '2020 Rule of Law Report: The Rule of Law Situation in the European Union', COM (2020) 580.

114 European Commission, '2020 Rule of Law Report: Country Chapter on the Rule of Law Situation in Greece', SWD (2020) 307, 12.

115 European Commission, '2021 Rule of Law Report: The Rule of Law Situation in the European Union', COM (2021) 700, 23.

116 European Commission, '2021 Rule of Law Report: Country Chapter on the Rule of Law Situation in Greece', SWD (2021) 709, 13.

117 European Commission, '2022 Rule of Law Report: The Rule of Law Situation in the European Union', COM (2022) 500; see also European Commission, '2022 Rule of Law Report: Country Chapter on the Rule of Law Situation in Greece', SWD (2022) 508, 21–22.

118 Annex to the European Commission, '2022 Rule of Law Report: The Rule of Law Situation in the European Union', COM (2022) 500.

119 European Commission, '2023 Rule of Law Report: The Rule of Law Situation in the European Union', COM (2023) 800.

120 European Commission, '2023 Rule of Law Report: Country Chapter on the Rule of Law Situation in Greece', SWD (2023) 508, 27–28.

121 European Commission (n 120) 2.

122 European Commission, '2024 Rule of Law Report: The Rule of Law Situation in the European Union', COM (2024) 800, 33–34.

123 European Commission, '2024 Rule of Law Report: Country Chapter on the Rule of Law Situation in Greece', SWD (2024) 808, 31–32.

124 European Commission (n 123).
125 European Commission (n 123).
126 European Commission (n 123) 2.
127 European Commission (n 123) 32.

Bibliography

Baraggia A and Bonelli M, 'Linking Money to Values: The New Rule of Law Conditionality Regulation and its Constitutional Challenges' (2022) 23 German Law Journal.

Baraggia A and Bonelli M, 'Filling the Enforcement Gap? Protecting the Rule of Law Through Funding Conditionality' in Tsourdi E and Van der Sluis M (eds), *Governing Through Funding in the EU* (forthcoming, CUP 2026).

Bonelli M, 'From Sanctions to Prevention, and Now Back to Sanctions? Article 7 TEU and the Protection of the EU Founding Values' in Montaldo S, Costamagna F and Miglio A (eds), *EU Law Enforcement The Evolution of Sanctioning Powers* (Routledge 2022).

Bonelli M and Claes M, 'Judicial Serendipity: How Portuguese Judges Came to the Rescue of the Polish Judiciary: ECJ 27 February 2018, Case C-64/16, Associação Sindical dos Juízes Portugueses' (2018) 14 EuConst 622.

Calliess C and Ruffert M (eds), *EUV/AEUV: Kommentar* (4th edn, Beck 2011).

Carrera S and others, *Fit for Purpose? The Facilitation Directive and the Criminalisation of Humanitarian Assistance to Irregular Migrants* (Study commissioned by LIBE Committee, European Parliament 2016).

Carrera S and others, *Policing Humanitarianism—EU Policies Against Human Smuggling and Their Impact on Civil Society* (Hart 2019).

Carrera S, Guild E and Hernanz N, *The Triangular Relationship Between Fundamental Rights, Democracy and the Rule of Law in the EU: Towards an EU Copenhagen Mechanism* (CEPS 2013).

Choose Love, *Υπό Πίεση—Πώς η Ελλάδα περιορίζει τις οργανώσεις της κοινωνίας των πολιτών που δουλεύουν με πρόσφυγες* (Self-Published 2021).

European Union Agency for Fundamental Rights, *Legal Environment and Space of Civil Society Organisations in Supporting Fundamental Rights–Greece* (Self-Published 2021).

HIAS, *Some Thoughts on the New Joint Ministerial Decision, Regulating the Registration of Migration-Related NGOs in Greece* (Self-Published 2020).

Konstantinides T, *The Rule of Law in the European Union: The Internal Dimension* (Hart Publishing 2017).

Müller J, 'Should the EU Protect Democracy and the Rule of Law Inside Member States' (2015) 21 European Law Journal 141.

Pech L and Scheppele K, 'Illiberalism Within: Rule of Law Backsliding in the EU' (2017) 19 Cambridge Yearbook of European Legal Studies 3.

Saranti EK, 'Challenging the Crackdown on Migration NGOs in Greece: Contesting the Discriminatory Framework for the Registration of Migration NGOs and Their Members Before the Council of State' [forthcoming 2025] German Law Journal.

Tsourdi E, 'Of Legislative Waves and Case Law: Effective Judicial Protection, Right to an Effective Remedy, and Proceduralisation in the EU Asylum Policy' (2019) 12 Review of European Administrative Law 143.

Tsourdi E, 'Asylum in the EU: One of the Many Faces of Rule of Law Backsliding?' (2021) 17 European Constitutional Law Review 471.

Tsourdi E and Costello C, '"Systemic Violations" in EU Asylum Law: Cover or Catalyst?' (2023) 24 German Law Journal 982.

Tsourdi E and Vavoula N, 'Killing Me Softly? Scrutinising the Role of Soft Law in Greece's Response to COVID-19' (2021) 12 European Journal of Risk Regulation.
Van Elsuwege P and Gremmelperez F, 'Protecting the Rule of Law in the EU Legal Order: A Constitutional Role for the Court of Justice' (2018) 16 EuConst 8.
Von Bogdandy A and Ioannidis M, 'Systemic Deficiency in the Rule of Law: What it Is, What Has Been Done, What Can Be Done' (2014) 51 Common Market Law Review 59.
Vosyliūtė L and Luk NC, *Protecting Civil Society Space: Strengthening Freedom of Association, Assembly and Expression and the Right to Defend Rights in the EU* (Study requested by LIBE Committee, European Parliament 2020).

8 Punitive Immigration Control for Difficult, Troublesome, or "Low-Recognition" Asylum Seekers

On Waterbed Theory and Globalised Vagrancy Law

Galina Cornelisse

8.1 Introduction

On 20 March 2024, the Dutch newspaper NRC reported that a number of public prosecutors in the Netherlands are raising objections against a work instruction issued by the Office of the Public Prosecutor.[1] According to the work instruction, prosecutors are to impose a punitive sanction in the form of an administrative fine if asylum seekers are apprehended for minor offences, such as shoplifting. Asylum seekers are to "pay" for this fine by detention: They are detained on remand, and for each day that they spend in a police cell, 50 euros is deducted from the fine. Hence, after three days, the asylum seeker has paid a fine of 150 euros. In addition, the asylum seeker will have obtained a criminal record, which can subsequently be used to reject the asylum application more swiftly in an expedited procedure.

Essentially, the Public Prosecutor's office is instructing its officials to act in violation of the right to personal liberty. Persons being detained on remand should be brought before a judge promptly,[2] but the authorities do not intend to bring these asylum seekers before a judge at all. Moreover, the detention of a person suspected of a criminal offence should be proportionate and necessary, for example, because it is necessary in the interest of the investigation.[3] In the work instruction, prosecutors are advised to come up with spurious investigative interests, such as the need to request and wait for judicial documentation abroad. This violates domestic constitutional law as well as European and international human rights law. In this contribution, I argue that such instances of openly unlawful state acts show the inevitable stresses that arise at the fault lines of the global system of mobility regulation.

The intertwining of criminal justice and immigration control in Europe has received ample scholarly attention over the last few years. Research has highlighted how non-citizens who have been convicted of criminal offences may become subject to immigration enforcement measures, such as the expulsion of long-term residents.[4] Other scholars have addressed the penalisation

DOI: 10.4324/9781003378440-8

of infractions of migration law with criminal law sanctions, as can be seen in Member States that have made irregular entry or stay a criminal offence or enacted migration-related offences, such as the facilitation of irregular entry or stay.[5] A large body of criminological research has focused on the intermingling of the two areas of law, with particular attention for the use of administrative immigration measures that are not formally designated as criminal law but which are distinctly shaped by the criminal justice system, immigration detention being the ultimate example of such a measure.[6]

In this chapter, I will focus on yet another instance of the linkage between the criminal law paradigm and the regulation of international mobility. My focus here is on *explicit* punitive sanctions to discipline migrants that the state portrays as difficult, troublesome, or less deserving. Notwithstanding their openly punitive character, these sanctions do not follow ordinary criminal law procedures, either because they violate the fundamental principles inherent in those procedures (as in the aforementioned example) or because they remain administrative in nature, if only formally. An example of such punitive sanctions are the strict and sober regimes in specialised reception centres for asylum seekers who display undesirable behaviour in the normal reception system.[7] Other instances concern special measures taken with regard to asylum seekers coming from countries with a low recognition rate.[8] A similar dynamic is at play in immigration detention centres in which "foreign nationals [are] often and routinely subjected to solitary confinement",[9] for example, because they do not want to be accommodated in a shared room.[10]

These instances, in which liberal democratic states look for the limits of the law, at times deliberately overstepping these limits, show that the "management" of unwanted migration cannot be exercised in full conformity with constitutional principles, when the deep structure of our world order is characterised by profound legal and political inconsistencies where transborder human mobility is concerned. These inconsistencies mean that repairing one constitutional problem, be it through regulation or judgement, will inevitably cause another one to appear elsewhere. In this sense, the current global system of mobility regulation can be understood with reference to the waterbed theory: Attempting to "push down" the complexity of such a system in one place will invariably cause complexity to "pop up" somewhere else.

The complexity of the global system of mobility regulation is caused by the fact that its underlying premises are not aligned with the fundamental legal principles of equality and dignity, which modern human rights discourse accords to *everyone*. Simply put, the premise of the global system of mobility regulation is that the only lawful crossers of borders are either the rich, or those persons falling within the narrow confines of the refugee definition from the 1951 Refugee Convention. States who are confronted with unwanted migration classify, sort, and exclude people on the basis of this premise. Distinctions on the basis of (global) economic inequality and nationality are therefore inherent in the current system of mobility regulation. As a result, "constitutional inconsistencies" are inevitable, and the question is not *whether* they will emerge, but *where*. This chapter argues that in the Netherlands, the way in which the government deals with "nuisance" asylum seekers shows these constitutional inconsistencies with a particular acuteness.

In order to make my argument, I proceed as follows. In Section 8.2, I set out a number of Dutch policies designed to deal with difficult, troublesome, or "low-recognition" asylum seekers. Next (in Section 8.3), I turn to constitutional challenges to these policies, arguing that these are not adequate to address the particular forms of social control that are applied to difficult, troublesome, or "low-recognition" asylum seekers. Thus, insisting on legality and fundamental rights of refugees will simply not be sufficient for formulating answers to the questions of global redistributive justice that underlie immigration from the so-called low-recognition countries to welfare states in the global North (Section 8.5). In some instances, such narrow critiques also run a risk of downplaying, or even denoting as irrelevant or xenophobic, the concerns of the poor populations of rich states, a group that has shifted down the global inequality index quite dramatically over the last few years. If we care about justice in the migration debate, we need an approach that sees the interests of immigrants from sending states as co-constitutive with those of precarious populations living in receiving countries. In my conclusions (Section 8.6), I revisit the waterbed theory analogy, by addressing the question, "who should bear the costs of the system's complexity?"

8.2 Discipline and Deter: Dutch Policies to Deal with Difficult, Troublesome, or Low-Recognition Asylum Seekers

Since 2020, the Netherlands has a tailored approach to deal with criminal or troublesome asylum seekers: The so-called Top-X list. The list's purpose is to gain insight into the size and nature of the most substantial group of nuisance-causing or criminal asylum seekers. Once persons are placed on the list by (most often local) authorities, it is made clear to them that "their criminal or nuisance behaviour will not be tolerated in the Netherlands".[11] Where appropriate, use is made of the palette of measures available when dealing with criminal and "nuisance" asylum seekers:

> [T]his includes the strict enforcement of the house rules and the imposition of measures at the reception centres, immigration law measures and other administrative law measures, the maintenance of public order outside the reception locations (especially in public transport and in residential and shopping areas), scaling up where necessary and criminal prosecution when appropriate.[12]

Hence, for conduct by an asylum seeker to be seen as problematic and to be targeted by these measures, it does not necessarily have to be criminal in nature. On the contrary, they may also be subject to these measures when they display acts of nuisance. However, nuisance is a concept that remains largely undetermined, in both law and policy. Instead of a clear definition, the Dutch Aliens Circular merely provides some examples of nuisance, which not only include criminal acts but also denote behaviour such as arguing with or harassing other asylum seekers, staff, or other persons in the vicinity of the centre, or an unmanageable addiction problem or psychiatric problems.[13] Other policy documents addressing nuisance by asylum seekers employ equally ambiguous language, for example, mentioning subjective feelings of insecurity of other individuals. Thus, an information sheet of the Dutch Government on the national approach to "nuisance" asylum seekers sets off along the following lines:

> [S]ome asylum seekers create nuisance. This includes shoplifting, violence, threats and vandalism. In 2022, 83,000 asylum seekers spent some time in a reception facility. Of these, 7% were involved in an incident and 3% were suspected of a criminal offense. People living or working at a reception location, residents and business owners in the neighbourhood may feel unsafe due to incidents.[14]

The concept of nuisance in the first sentence is thus brought to life with a number of examples in the second sentence, but all these examples simply consist of criminal offences. For policy makers, however, the fuzzier concept of nuisance is much more useful than the concept of crime, precisely *because* it is blurry and operates outside the well-defined parameters of criminal law. The main effect of its use in policies is that it opens up space for the taking of disciplinary measures *outside* formal procedural criminal law, not only for those who have committed a (minor) criminal offence, but also for those who have not overstepped the line of clearly defined substantive criminal law. That dynamic becomes evident when we have a closer look at some of the measures that have been taken in the Dutch reception system.

8.2.1 "Low-Recognition" Asylum Seekers: The Procedure Availability Location

On 29 June 2022, the Dutch Minister of Justice presented a new kind of reception centre: The "Procedure Availability Location" (in Dutch: *Procesbeschikbaarheidslocatie*, hereafter PBL): A special reception centre for asylum seekers who have filed an asylum claim with little chances of success, such as by persons coming from safe countries or Dublin claimants.[15] For the rationale of this centre, he referred to research from which it had transpired that asylum seekers who come from countries with a low recognition rate were more often involved in "incidents" or crimes.[16] The PBL, launched as a pilot, consists of a number of rooms and communal areas. There are fences around the PBL, closing it off from the rest of the site. A very strict and sober regime applies: Asylum seekers receive (limited) benefits in kind, have a compulsory day and evening programme, and are only allowed to leave the PBL for an hour, twice per day. As a result, their stay in the centre resembles a deprivation of liberty. If asylum seekers refuse to live by the rules, they lose the right to reception conditions. The minister used stern language to get his message of toughness clearly across:

> I am committed to take measures to prevent nuisance and a tough, integrated approach to nuisance and criminal behaviour in cooperation with organizations in the migration chain, municipalities, police and the Office of the Public Prosecutor. These nuisance-makers are a burden on, among others, employees in the migration chain, fellow residents of reception centres, local residents, shopkeepers and public transport operators. The current level of nuisance and criminal behaviour is unacceptable and dealing with this group of asylum seekers is my absolute priority.[17]

Initially, asylum seekers who filed an asylum claim with low chances of success could only be placed in this facility if they had caused nuisance in the regular reception system. Later, the pilot was expanded to cover all asylum seekers coming from low-recognition countries. Early policy documents on the PBL kept the definition of nuisance deliberately vague so that a large number of low-recognition asylum seekers could be placed in the PBL.[18] As such, the PBL is a prime example of a mechanism that governs by "recasting potential acts of nuisance to that of criminal status".[19] The recasting is not done formally through criminal law, but it certainly occurs in terms of substance, considering that once in the PBL, asylum seekers undergo a very sober regime, and they have so many compulsory appointments to attend, from early morning to late at night, that they cannot leave the centre at all.[20]

The Minister acknowledges that all this occurs at the outer limits of the law, by explaining that these "asylum seekers are required to be available at all times", but that "(semi)closed reception is out of the question, as this would meet with legal objections".[21] Restricting rights in practice while a formal legal basis for interferences with individual liberty is lacking is reminiscent of the example with which this chapter opened: The prosecution of asylum seekers for minor offences, such as shoplifting, for which they are then punished with an administrative fine, which they can "pay" for by detention. This is opposed to the ordinary course of events when persons are arrested for shoplifting: Since 2022, Dutch policy determines that people arrested will get a mere warning. A criminal prosecution is resorted to only in cases of repeat offenders. The "coordinator nuisance" of the Immigration Service suggested a different approach for asylum seekers, and as a result, the Public Prosecutor's Office confirmed that "crimes committed by nuisance asylum seekers, including shoplifting, must in principle receive a criminal law response".[22]

The PBL as well as the work instruction of the Public Prosecutor's Office has encountered protest from *within* the state. Public Prosecutors protested against the unequal treatment between citizens and asylum seekers and the political interference in their work. Moreover, the aliens police refused to cooperate with the PBL pilot in the absence of crimes, protesting the vagueness of the notion of nuisance and drawing attention to the risk of ethnic profiling:

> Nuisance is a broad term. . . . . For example, asylum seekers may be frustrated because they have to wait for their procedure, this may cause riots or they may violate COA's house rules. But these are by no means always criminal offenses on the basis of which the police can detain someone. . . . The police in the Netherlands is there for everyone, and that does not fit with a way of working that could in practice lead to profiling of a target group on the basis of nationality.[23]

Meanwhile, however, in December 2023, the minister informed the parliament that 480 cases of "nuisance" asylum seekers had been processed in an accelerated procedure, using the PBL approach, concluding that his nuisance approach "runs like a charm".[24] Also, the scope of the PBL pilot was extended to cover all asylum seekers who have filed a claim with low chances of success, and need no longer involve "nuisance" asylum seekers.[25] This incremental extension of the categories eligible for disciplinary measures, now being merely based upon the nationality of individuals, shows the normalisation of unconstitutional measures through the use of a concept such as nuisance, when managing unwanted mobility.

8.2.2 "Nuisance" Asylum Seekers in the Reception System: The Enforcement and Supervision Location

While the PBL is a pilot launched in 2022, targeting specifically asylum seekers who file a claim with a low chance of success, other measures had been established for troublesome asylum seekers in the reception system before. Thus, the Enforcement and Supervision Location (in Dutch: *Handhavings en toezichtslocatie*, hereafter HTL) is a separate reception centre for asylum seekers who cause nuisance within the normal reception system. Nuisance, in this context, "includes (repeated) aggressive verbal and non-verbal behaviour towards fellow residents or staff at the (reception) location or outside, causing havoc, or discrimination or intimidation of residents in the reception system".[26] The measure lasts 12 weeks and can be continued if the conduct by the asylum seeker gives rise to this, and if there are no grounds for detention. The measure may also be imposed on unaccompanied minors aged 16 and above.

The HTL is located on a (limited) portion of a former prison site, and the complex itself is enclosed by fences and walls. The asylum seekers may leave the facility to go outside between 2 p.m. and 4 p.m., but only to access a green space that is fenced off. In the communal areas of the complex, asylum seekers are subject to 24-hour camera surveillance. They must participate in a daily programme every day. If they do not do this, there is the possibility of placing them in a time-out room. Twice a day, the asylum seekers are required to check in, during which time their fingerprints are taken. There is a room check every day at a set time, which also involves looking in the closets. Security searches take place upon entry into the HTL and thereafter on an occasional basis.

Benefits at the HTL are provided in kind. Asylum seekers are not allowed to leave the complex, except in exceptional cases, such as church visits, medical appointments, or meetings with a lawyer. In these cases, they are accompanied by a staff member of the HTL. Hence, asylum seekers are never present outside the fenced complex unaccompanied. Moreover, residents are not allowed to receive visitors freely; this requires explicit permission from a staff member. Each asylum seeker gets a mentor and a counselling plan to help them improve their behaviour. With "good behaviour", an asylum seeker can return to a normal reception centre. If a resident leaves the HTL, he loses his right to reception conditions.[27]

According to the minister, placement in the HTL does not constitute detention but a restriction on freedom of movement. As we will see below, Dutch courts agreed with his point of view. Nonetheless, the Inspectorate of Justice and Security, the independent body that monitors the implementation of decisions under the jurisdiction of the Ministry of Justice—such as prison sentences, placement in juvenile facilities, and immigration detention—issued a number of reports that called attention to unlawful practices in the HTL. It had received reports of abuses in the HTL, upon which it decided to act, by requesting information, interviewing staff and asylum seekers that had resided in the HTL. Moreover, it visited the HTL twice unannounced and analysed camera footage, among other things. It concluded that living conditions and safety were compromised at the HTL. More specifically, the rights of asylum seekers were not sufficiently safeguarded, because of the disproportionate use of violence, insufficient daily activities, limited access to legal assistance, and opaque house rules, for example, relating to visits:

> [T]he Inspectorate heard numerous examples of incidents where asylum seekers were punched or kicked, even in cases where an asylum seeker was not aggressive or already running away. Some staff say they consider such instances of the use of force normal, whereas it is only permissible as a last resort. It is unclear to what extent the staff is allowed to use coercion, the Inspectorate is having that investigated. Furthermore, the Inspectorate has observed that some employees laugh or swear at asylum seekers, a practice that actually encourages escalation.[28]

In a follow-up report based on further investigations, the Inspectorate found that there was actually no legal basis for the use of force and searches by residential supervisory staff.[29] Apart from updating the code of conduct for staff at the HTL and developing a complaint procedure, the minister has not acknowledged the gravity of these findings by his own monitoring body, as became apparent from his reaction:

> [W]ith regard to assessing whether unlawful and disproportionate use of force was applied in an incident, it is important that in doing so all circumstances are considered. The residential supervisors of the HTL have no authority to use force or coercion. Such use of force only occurs in exceptional cases, such as when the asylum seeker shows such aggressive behaviour towards staff or other asylum seekers that no other way out is possible. The target group in question consists of asylum seekers for whom lighter measures have not have proven to be sufficient and restricting negative behaviour is required to guarantee the safety of everyone. Application of disproportionate coercion and violence, however, is never justified. The conclusion [by the Inspectorate] that there would be a pattern in this regard is not recognised.[30]

Responding to ensuing questions by two Members of Parliament, the minister answered that coercion had indeed been applied by staff, which, at times, had been "harsh". He noted that the staff of the HTL can escort an asylum seeker out of a room with light touch, which would only be done in exceptional cases, such as when there is a risk of a situation escalating. He added that the staff may also physically defend themselves, in a proportionate manner, when an asylum seeker displays aggressive behaviour.[31]

8.2.3 Solitary Confinement: A Public Order Measure and a Disciplinary Sanction in Immigration Detention

The lack of clear rules limiting the use of coercion as a disciplinary measure for immigrants is also apparent from the frequent use of solitary confinement in immigration detention, an issue that has been flagged by Dutch lawyers and NGOs,[32] and was corroborated by the findings of the Committee for the Prevention of Torture and Inhuman or Degrading Treatment or Punishment (CPT) in its 2022 visit to the Netherlands. In its report, the CPT noted that immigrants detained at Rotterdam Detention Centre were "routinely subjected to solitary confinement, both as a [public order] measure and as a disciplinary sanction", and it considered the use of this measure "excessive". The CPT gave an example of a migrant who had spent 19 days in solitary confinement, after which, five days later, he spent an additional 14 days in solitary confinement.[33] It advised the Netherlands to cease applying solitary confinement as a disciplinary measure in the immigration detention context. The response by the Netherlands on this particular point was dismissive: Instead of pledging a reflection on the reasons for the excessive (and increasing) use of this measure, it responded by saying that "current practice follows these recommendations, in so far as it aims to avoid as much as possible the need to resort to measures or disciplinary punishments within detention centres".[34]

8.3 Challenging Disciplinary Measures: On Legality and Human Rights Conformity

Legal challenges to the disciplinary measures discussed in the section above have been abundant.[35] The aim of this section is to zoom in on the most pertinent and serious constitutional failings of the measures discussed above. Therefore, I will discuss issues pertaining to the legal basis of these measures and their qualification as detention or restriction on freedom of movement, and related questions on available remedies to contest the interferences with fundamental rights that these measures entail. Legality and judicial review of interferences with individual rights are core values of the constitutional state.

8.3.1 No Judicial Review of the Treatment of Immigration Detainees

In the first place, Dutch courts tasked with reviewing the legality of immigration detention have been dismissive of complaints relating to the treatment of persons formally kept in immigration detention, arguing that they are not competent to review such complaints. This is particularly relevant with regard to the frequent and widespread use of isolation in immigration detention. According to the Council of State, the highest administrative court in the Netherlands, courts reviewing the lawfulness of immigration detention are not allowed to take into account particular complaints relating to the disproportionate use of force or other disciplinary measures taken in the detention centres.[36] This, however, seems in direct contradiction with the constitutional role of a *habeas corpus* judge. It is also difficult to reconcile with EU law, in particular the Return Directive, which requires that measures taken against immigration detainees be proportionate.[37]

Thus, the CJEU has held that the national court that reviews the legality of detention must pay particular attention to the arrangement of the premises dedicated to the detention of third-country nationals, the rules which specify their conditions of detention, and the classification and duties of the staff responsible for the establishment in which the detention takes place. On the basis of all these factors, the court can determine whether the constraint imposed on the third-country nationals concerned is limited to what is strictly necessary in order to ensure an efficient removal procedure and avoids resembling detention in a prison environment suitable for punitive purposes.[38] The possibility of imposing disciplinary measures and their implementation are relevant factors to be taken into account against this context. This is affirmed by the Recital of the Return Directive, which holds that third-country nationals in detention should be treated in a humane and dignified manner, with respect for their fundamental rights and in compliance with international and national law. These factors are also taken into account by the European Court of Human Rights (ECtHR) when deciding whether detention is arbitrary, and thus in violation of the right to personal liberty protected by Article 5 of the European Convention on Human Rights (ECHR).[39]

8.3.2 Is It Actually Detention?

When it comes to the centres discussed above (both HTL and PBL), the most pertinent legal issue is the question of whether the situation of an asylum seeker who has been placed there should be qualified as deprivation of liberty. Dutch courts have ruled that the situation of asylum seekers in the HTL entails a severe restriction on the right to freedom of movement but that it cannot be qualified as detention, because the asylum seeker may at any time leave the facility voluntarily. A voluntary departure means that the asylum seekers lose their right to reception conditions, but that does not turn the restriction on the freedom of movement into a deprivation of liberty.[40] All appeals against rulings by the district courts on this matter have fallen on deaf ears at the Council of State, which has dismissed them without reasoning. That is striking, if only because the district courts have used differing, sometimes even conflicting, reasoning.[41]

But it is even more surprising in light of the more fundamental question their approach raises: What should be understood by personal liberty in the migration context? According to the ECtHR, the difference between deprivation and restriction of liberty is one of degree or intensity, not of nature or substance.[42] In order to determine whether someone has been "deprived of his or her liberty", the starting point must be their individual situation, and account must be taken of a range of factors, such as the type, duration, effects, and manner of implementation of the measure in question.[43] In the *FMS* judgement, the CJEU ruled that detention should be understood as "a coercive measure that deprives [the] applicant of his or her freedom of movement and isolates him or her from the rest of the population, by requiring him or her to remain permanently within a restricted and closed perimeter".[44] The CJEU dismissed the argument raised by the Hungarian Government, that the applicants in the main proceedings were free to leave the Röszke transit zone to travel to Serbia, stating it could not "call into question the assessment that the placing of those applicants in that transit zone cannot be distinguished from a regime of detention".[45] It is unclear how the possibility of leaving the PBL voluntarily relates to this judgement, precisely because leaving means that *all* reception conditions would be lost, which is in clear violation of EU law. Thus, the CJEU has ruled that a failure to provide for the basic needs of applicants for asylum amounts to a breach of their right to human dignity.[46]

In a more recent decision, a Dutch district court addressed a further disciplinary measure, taken *within* one of the centres, namely the placement of an asylum seeker in a timeout room (an "Regeling onthouding verstrekkingen" room). Such a measure

> physically restricted the claimant's freedom by requiring him to stay in a very confined space and preventing him from entering the regular sections of the HTL [. . . he] was also further restricted in his opportunities for social contact. Because he was not allowed to enter the normal part of the HTL, he could not, for example, use the computers there. Nor was he offered any daytime activities. Furthermore, the court considers the duration of the placement in the ROV room. The court does not see how the purpose of imposing the measure, namely to restore peace and order at the HTL, justifies a standard period of two weeks in an ROV room.[47]

The court concluded that the additional measure (placement in ROV room) turned the restriction of freedom of movement at the HTL into detention, for which there was no legal basis. The circumstance that the asylum seeker could leave the HTL at any time, including the ROV room, did not alter its conclusion. It is worth emphasising, as the court did in its judgement, that providing reception to "nuisance" asylum seekers—"a complex group with erratic behaviour"—is a complicated matter. The Dutch authorities have indicated that they will appeal the decision.[48]

Meanwhile, Dutch parliamentarians have raised questions, as they see this judgement as "undermining an effective approach to nuisance asylum seekers".[49] A similar dynamic between courts and politics is played out with regard to the PBL. Thus, a district court ruled very recently that an applicant for asylum has the right to reception conditions and that the particular form of reception in the PBL entails a restriction on the right to free movement, which finds no basis in either EU law or national law.[50] As a result, the PBL is no longer in use, but an overwhelming majority of the parliament has called for a "legal or practical solution to reopen the PBL as soon as possible, and its reopening is foreseen in the very near future".[51]

8.3.3 The Constitutional Gaps of Globalised Vagrancy Law

In the litigation analysed here, we see a number of issues coming together. In the first place, and in line with European and international human rights law, courts apply a case-by-case approach to determine whether the measures that have been applied to "nuisance" or "low-recognition" asylum seekers can be qualified as detention. But such a case-by-case approach obscures the fact that these measures entail a novel form of social control, one that can be qualified most fittingly as globalised vagrancy law. A case-by-case approach obscures the blurring of the lines between detention and restrictions on freedom of movement when dealing with "nuisance" or "low-recognition" asylum seekers.

It is precisely this tendency that is typical for contemporary migration governance. The EU legislature has perfected this mode of governance in the new border procedures that have been introduced in the newly adopted Asylum Procedures Regulation.[52] These procedures have become mandatory for certain categories of asylum seekers, such as "low-recognition" asylum seekers (in EU law, this concerns applicants from a country for which the average EU-wide recognition rate for asylum claims is less than 20%).[53] These persons *must* be kept at the border while their claims are being processed, but the legislator has not made clear how such a situation of containment should be legally qualified. In any case, it holds the opinion that border procedures do not necessarily entail detention.[54]

The most pertinent question raised by such practices of containment, be they at the border or within the state, is to what extent our current fundamental rights framework is capable of addressing the resulting challenges.[55] As we have seen above, in human rights law, the distinction between deprivation of liberty (detention) and restriction on freedom of movement is one of degree or intensity and not one of nature or substance. However, once a situation is qualified as detention, a number of safeguards kick in. Most notable is the *habeas corpus* guarantee, giving the detainee the right to have the lawfulness of the detention speedily reviewed by a court and to have the detention lifted if it is unlawful. But the implications of blurriness in this field extend far beyond the *habeas corpus* safeguard.

These further implications become apparent from the way in which the findings by the Inspectorate (that there is no legal basis for the use of force by the residential supervisors in the HTL) have featured in Dutch case law. We saw above that in a case in which an asylum seeker argued that he had been pushed by a residential supervisor in the HTL, the court dismissed the claim, referring to the reply by the minister that he did not recognise a pattern of disproportionate coercion and violence in the HTL. However, if these HTL measures had been qualified as detention, the ruling of the court would have been irreconcilable with ECtHR case law regarding persons who are under the control of the state, for example, when they are held in police custody.[56] In respect of a person deprived of his liberty, recourse to physical force, which has not been made strictly necessary by his own conduct, diminishes human dignity and is in principle an infringement of the right set forth in Article 3 of the ECHR.[57] It goes without saying that there needs to be a legal basis for such coercive power and that its exercise can only be assessed on an individual basis.

Similar constitutional problems arise with regard to the applicability of Article 6 of the ECHR on the right to a fair trial, in particular as regards its criminal charge limb, to the disciplinary measure of placement in the HTL. This is a particularly relevant question with regard to the presumption of innocence and the right not to be tried twice for the same offence (*ne bis in idem*), protected by Article 4 of Protocol No. 7 of the ECHR. Thus, the HTL measure is often applied after a criminal conviction and the application of a sanction, potentially raising issues with regard to the principle of *ne bis in idem*. The ECtHR has held that for establishing whether a measure constitutes a "criminal charge", reference must be made to the "three alternative criteria laid down in its case-law, namely the legal classification of the offence under domestic law, the nature of the offence and the nature and degree of severity of the penalty".[58] According to the ECtHR, "deprivations of liberty liable to be imposed as a punishment" generally "belong to the 'criminal' sphere".[59]

In a case in which the asylum seeker held that placement in the HTL constituted a violation of the principle of *ne bis in idem*, because he had already been punished by criminal law for the conduct that gave rise to his placement there, the district court considered that placement in the HTL cannot be viewed as a criminal charge:

> [T]he measure qualifies as administrative in domestic law and its purpose is to act against unacceptable behaviour. In addition, the measure aims to promote the safety and well-being of residents and staff at regular reception facilities. The severity of the measure, in this case defined by its duration, is in principle maximised at three months. The duration does not depend on the severity of the incident that led to the measure, but depends on the extent to which the third[-]country national shows that he can behave properly. What is important here is that the alien can voluntarily renounce staying in the HTL. The fact that the measure was imposed for the duration of three months is related to the fact that the claimant did not complete previously imposed measures, but chose to leave the HTL voluntarily and he has not yet shown any improvement in behaviour.[60]

In conclusion, the fact that disciplinary measures are not qualified as detention has repercussions for effective remedies that extend beyond the right to personal liberty, also impacting remedies against the use of force and fair trial rights. When it comes to disciplinary measures for difficult, troublesome or "nuisance" asylum seekers, some of the more troubling constitutional shortcomings have thus remained immune to judicial correction. In only a few cases, legal challenges have resulted in judicial outcomes that required a policy change, or at least better regulation of rights' restricting measures. At the same time, these disciplinary measures constitute somewhat of a moving target. Thus, when constitutional challenges are effective in one area, another measure is put forward to negate the constraining effects on the executive. In this context, it is relevant that the newly adopted European Pact on Migration and Asylum legitimises some aspects of the Dutch practices described above, for example, by introducing a new ground for the detention of applicants for asylum, namely if they have not complied with a public order obligation to reside only in a specific place.[61]

Moreover, the Dutch parliament, the core function of which is to provide a check on executive power, has often remained silent in the face of constitutional shortcomings, for example, when it concerns solitary confinement in detention, a practice that has gone unchecked for years and continues to do so, notwithstanding the grave consequences for the mental and physical health of detainees subjected to the measure. At other times, such as when the judiciary ruled that the restrictions on fundamental rights of asylum seekers lacked a legal basis, it has called for immediate practical or legal solutions, so that the "tough approach" for "nuisance" asylum seekers can continue and even be scaled up. In that respect, the way in which the Netherlands deals with difficult, troublesome, or low-recognition asylum seekers displays worrying elements of democratic and rule of law backsliding.[62] It also shows that our current legal and political framework may not be fit to deal with new forms of social control that have emerged as a response to unwanted migration. Disciplinary sanctions that are tied to the system of mobility regulation call for novel forms of legal and political correction, which explicitly take into account the injustices that underlie the current system of regulating global mobility. It is to these injustices that I turn to in the following section.

8.4 Regulating the Mobility of "Nuisance" Asylum Seekers: Operating at the Fault Lines of Global Inequality

Research shows that "nuisance" asylum seekers in the Netherlands are often asylum seekers from low-recognition countries, such as Morocco, Algeria, and Tunisia.[63] An abundance of research indicates the particular complexity of the problems that this group suffers from.[64] Indeed, research based upon interviews shows that this group consists predominantly of children and young adults from North Africa, who often come from poor family backgrounds, including poor housing conditions and little to no access to education.[65] These young people have little prospect of a better life in their country of origin (even less so after economies suffered on account of the war in Ukraine and COVID) and venture across to Europe, applying for asylum. These asylum seekers relatively often have psychiatric problems and are frequently addicted to alcohol, drugs, or medication. Staff working at reception centres report that they regularly request medication immediately upon arrival at the centre, sometimes even under the threat of suicide.[66] Instead of "nuisance" asylum seekers, this group may more fittingly be described as transnational street children.

As the Inspectorate of Justice and Security has emphasised, it is the immigration system itself which makes it difficult to address the multitude of problems that these young people suffer from, with nuisance as a result, and sometimes with more serious consequences. In a case where the Inspectorate investigated the killing of a therapist by an asylum seeker with psychiatric problems, the Inspectorate concluded that it is "the legal status of an asylum seeker" that is an obstacle to realising appropriate care, because institutions cannot work on "resocialisation with this target group". It recommended that the government put care first with regard to a group of foreign nationals with no prospect of both (permanent) residence in the Netherlands and return. According to the Inspectorate, this in the interest of society as a whole, employees in the reception system, co-residents, and the foreign national himself. It concluded that legislation should be adapted for this purpose if necessary.[67]

The predominant emphasis in legal and political discourse on the refugee legal framework obscures the fact that the current regulation of forms of mobility that fall outside its scope is deeply flawed. The focus on the rights of refugees, both in official policies (where "real refugees" are contrasted with abusers of the reception system) and in critiques of governmental policies, solidifies a particular conception of the world, in which transnational injustices that occur outside the context of war or persecution remain unaddressed. The emphasis on refugees as the only legitimate "crossers of sovereign borders" in international law makes distinctions and classifications that can be traced back to national origin inescapable.

Legal critiques of these distinctions mostly revolve around the question of whether some of these classifications, when used in qualification procedures, constitute discrimination within the framework of refugee law.[68] Such critiques, however, do not contest the core assumptions of an outdated legal framework that does not perceive poverty as a legitimate reason to cross borders. This outdated legal framework needs disciplinary measures to suppress, not so much the "nuisance" asylum seekers themselves, but the accompanying complexity of a flawed system. This paradox becomes apparent when we take a closer look at the way in which the Dutch Minister of Justice has defended the new mandatory border procedures in the EU to detain low-recognition asylum seekers at the borders of Europe:

> That is precisely what we need this mandatory border control. . . . For there is also the element in it that you can then also keep this group inside. Now you can't keep them in [the PBL]. The moment a Moroccan or an Algerian applies for asylum in the Netherlands, we have to treat him the same as we treat Syrians, Afghans and Yemenis. Then we cannot keep him in, other than through criminal law if someone has committed a criminal offense. And that still has to be of such a nature that it simply includes detention. That is something that, unfortunately . . . is very often not the case. That would not only not apply to Algerians and Moroccans, but also not to [you] and me if we were to exhibit the same behaviour. So, then that is not possible. So that is why there is the PBL. Then we just say: we give you so many appointments in one day, you do have to stay inside. That's one. And second, there is the HTL. These are means, or rather palliatives, but what's really going to help is the ability to just keep this group inside. Because we know that this group doesn't come here to seek asylum at all. They just come here to stay for a while, be facilitated by us and then move on again.[69]

The minister hence affirms that all asylum seekers have the right to file an application. He then admits that it is *unfortunate* that most of the crimes committed by "nuisance" and "low-recognition" asylum seekers are not of such a seriousness that these individuals can be detained in the criminal justice system. And he concedes that the right to liberty in the criminal law context is protected for asylum seekers and citizens ("you and me") alike. But instead of attempting to come to terms with the complexity of a phenomenon that could best be described as transnational homelessness or globalised street children,[70] he instead supports a solution that merely suppresses such complexity. However, as the solution consists of measures that fall squarely outside the parameters of constitutional law, which requires that interferences with fundamental rights should be kept to the minimum and subject to stringent judicial review, the system's complexity is merely shifted to a different place.

Current critical scholarship that addresses policies of criminalisation has rightly pointed out that these policies are the result of racialised and postcolonial perceptions of who is entitled to mobility and who is not.[71] At the same time, by its emphasis on the rights of refugees, much of this scholarship has failed to provide credible and sustainable solutions that take account of the context of stark global inequality that drives some of these migratory movements. We need more engagement with the fact that it is not either/or: Migration is often driven by both security concerns *and* economic concerns. Our legal framework addressing mobility needs to incorporate this complexity. Also, for countries in North Africa and sub-Saharan Africa, migration represents an important source of economic revenue.[72]

In a globalised world, sustainable migration policies need to take account of the link between global redistribution and migration. Research has shown that "global inequalities seem to be about as great today as they were at the peak of Western imperialism in the early 20th century".[73] Moreover, inequality *within* countries has increased over the last 40 years, particularly affecting the very poor. Especially over the last decade, in-country inequality in all European states has grown starkly. For example, in the Netherlands, the poorest 10% of the population have seen their income decrease by more than a third. At the same time, the richest 30% of the population had a growth of household income of around 60%.[74] In the Netherlands, one million people currently live in poverty. A large group of the very poor (25%) consists of children, and 70% of that group are children with parents with a migration background.[75] As such, the interests of the global and local poor are aligned.

"Nuisance" asylum seekers from low-recognition countries provide the ideal "problem" for governments that do not want to address issues of redistribution, globally or locally. These governments can be seen to take a firm stance and to act decisively in response to concerns that the local populations experience with regard to immigration. It is a deeply cynical move on their part, however, because the worries expressed by these resident populations, often those with a weaker socioeconomic position (i.e., the poorest residents in immigrant-receiving countries) have, for a long time, been dismissed as irrelevant or even xenophobic by the centre-left. At the same time, neoliberal policies introduced by the centre-right have made sure that precisely these domestically precarious groups have been disproportionately confronted with the burdens of inadequate social policies, such as in the area of housing or labour. Some of these negative impacts have in turn been reinforced by asylum immigration, family migration, or immigration by low-skilled workers, as these forms of immigration put additional pressure on the availability of social housing and on social protection in an ever more flexible labour market.

The social burdens caused by particular policies aimed at restricting or deterring asylum immigration have also landed on the shoulders of precarious resident populations. Thus, in the Netherlands, municipalities where people with a low income reside have housed three times as many asylum seekers over the last ten years as those inhabited by rich people.[76] At least some of the nuisance experienced in these areas is a direct result of intentional policies: asylum seekers are not housed in small-scale reception centres scattered over diverse locations but are instead "warehoused" in large reception centres. Overrepresentation of asylum seekers in property crime statistics will put the burden of this overrepresentation disproportionately on these few municipalities.[77] Moreover, the overall number of available places for asylum seekers has decreased over the last few years, so asylum seekers have had to sleep outside, in waiting rooms, and in tents. That such a setup carries a risk of causing "incidents" or nuisance can hardly be surprising. Finally, research has shown that in the Netherlands, asylum seekers who filed an asylum claim with good chances of success were *deprioritised*, which in turn resulted in very long waiting times spent idly in reception centres, with few opportunities for integration, by persons who would eventually receive a positive decision.[78]

8.5 Conclusions: A Global Mobility Tax for the Wealthy

Stressing the rights of refugees alone when criticising the policies described in this chapter may be a self-defeating strategy, in that it will not help to formulate adequate answers to address the issues of global redistributive justice that underlie immigration from low-recognition countries to welfare states in the global North. Indeed, the emphasis on the rights of refugees obscures the fact that a world in which the only legitimate crossers of borders are those with enough money or those who fit the narrow definition of the 1951 Refugee Convention will inevitably require the sorting of persons, the enforcement of which will be in direct violation of equality and dignity. Critical analysis of the criminalisation of migration must therefore also engage with questions of global redistributive justice in order to provide alternative ways of imagining our global political and legal order, in which socioeconomic rights are recognised as being of the same value as civil and political rights.

Concrete policy proposals, such as a global minimum income, would provide the much-needed impetus to the discussion on transnational mobility.[79] Similarly, realistic solutions to deal with non-returnable migrants, such as periodic regularisations, are long overdue. New forms of transnational constitutional identity building could emerge from the legal and political contestation of the globalised vagrancy law at work in immigrant-receiving countries. Political mobilisation on the left needs to make explicit that the interests of local precarious populations and transnational migrants are aligned and threatened by the same neoliberal policies, instead of opposed to each other in a zero-sum game.[80] More work needs to be done on the implementation of international proposals, such as a global tax for the very wealthy, as such measures are key to battling global inequality.[81]

Most importantly, when it comes to complexity in computer code, it is normal to engage with the question of who should bear the costs of such complexity: The user or the designer of the software.[82] Likewise, when we talk about the regulation of migration, we should explicitly engage with questions regarding the fair distribution of the costs of our imperfect, complex, and inconsistent system of regulating of global mobility. Our current globalised economic order has made global mobility for the wealthy incredibly smooth and uncomplicated. At the same time, thousands of unwanted migrants are exposed to social and economic hardship, severe human rights and dignity violations and even lose their lives when they attempt to cross seas or closely guarded borders in search of safety or a better life. In the face of such obscene inequality, a global mobility tax for the wealthy could be an important step towards a more even distribution of the costs of the complexity of the system. Such a tax could be calculated on the basis of criteria such as distances travelled; numbers of borders crossed; means of transport (a private jet should be taxed higher than a trip by train); individual wealth; and the ranking of the traveller's passport on the global passport index. The proceeds of such a tax could be used to cater for the reception needs of displaced persons and persons on the move all over the world, as well as for public goods for precarious (both migrant and local) populations in both sending and receiving countries.

Notes

1 Andreas Kouwenhoven, 'Onrust binnen het OM over aanpak van overlastgevende asielzoekers, die een boete betalen middels een celstraf' (*NRC*, 12 March 2024).
2 European Convention on Human Rights (hereafter ECHR), article 5 para 3.
3 ECHR, Article 5 para 1 under c. See European Court of Human Rights (ECtHR) 18 March 2008; *Ladent v Poland* App No 11036/03 (ECHR, 18/06/2008), paras 55–56.
4 Ana Aliverti, *Crimes of Mobility* (Routledge 2013); Eleonora Di Molfetta and Jelmer Brouwer, 'Unravelling the "Crimmigration Knot": Penal Subjectivities, Punishment and the Censure Machine' (2020) 20(3) Criminology & Criminal Justice.

5 Marq Wijngaarden and Frederieke Dölle, 'Is hulp aan asielzoekers strafbaar?' (2020) 6 (1) Crimmigratie & Recht 78–82.
6 Katja Aas and Mary Bosworth (eds), *The Borders of Punishment: Citizenship, Crime Control, and Social Exclusion* (OUP 2013); Mary Bosworth, 'Immigration Detention, Punishment and the Transformation of Justice' (2019) 28(1) Social & Legal Studies 81–99; Isabella Leroy, 'Migrant Reception Centres and Coercive Social Control: Rule by Legal Uncertainty?' [2024] Social & Legal Studies 1.
7 See AIDA, 'Country Report, The Netherlands, Types of Accomodation', <https://asylumineurope.org/reports/country/netherlands/reception-conditions/housing/types-accommodation/>
8 AIDA (n 7).
9 Report to the Government of the Netherlands on the periodic visit to the Kingdom of the Netherlands carried out by the European Committee for the Prevention of Torture and Inhuman or Degrading Treatment or Punishment (CPT) from 10 to 25 May 2022, CPT/Inf (2023) 12. Solitary confinement consists in keeping an inmate alone in a cell for over 22 hours a day, has harmful effects on detainees, and is a punitive measure.
10 Response of the Kingdom of the Netherlands to the 2022 CPT report, Kamerstukken II 2022–2023, 24587 (*Justitiële Inrichtingen*), n 899.
11 Kamerstukken II 2021–2022, 19 637 (Vreemdelingenbeleid), Nr. 2908 (Brief van de Staatsscretaris van Justitie en Veiligheid).
12 Kamerstukken II 2021–2022, 19 637 (Vreemdelingenbeleid), Nr. 2908 (Brief van de Staatsscretaris van Justitie en Veiligheid).
13 Besluit van de Staatssecretaris van Justitie en Veiligheid, 21 May 2021, number WBV 2021/7, houdende wijziging van de Vreemdelingencirculaire 2000, *Staatscourant* 2021, 28438.
14 Dutch Government, 'Nationale aanpak overlast asielzoekers' <https://www.rijksoverheid.nl/onderwerpen/asielbeleid/aanpak-overlastgevende-asielzoekers> accessed 5 August 2024.
15 Kamerstukken II 2021–2022, 19 637 (Vreemdelingenbeleid), Nr. 2908, Brief van de Staatsscretaris van Justitie en Veiligheid.
16 Wetenschappelijk Onderzoek en Datacentrum, *Incidenten en misdrijven door COA-bewoners 2017–2021*, WODC Cahier 2022–6.
17 Kamerstukken II 2021–2022, 19 637 (Vreemdelingenbeleid), nr. 2908, Brief van de Staatsscretaris van Justitie en Veiligheid.
18 Stichting Marechaussee Contact, 'Artikel in Het NRC over Het Opzoeken van de Rand van de Wet' (*Marechaussee Contact*, 11 February 2024) <https://www.marechausseecontact.nl/12133-artikel-in-het-nrc-over-overlast-en-overlastgevers> last accessed 11 April 2024.
19 Paul Hodge, 'A Grievable Life? The Criminalisation and Securing of Asylum Seeker Bodies in the 'Violent Frames' of Australia's Operation Sovereign Borders' (2015) 58 Geoforum 122–31.
20 Kamerstukken II 2022–2023, 19637 (Vreemdelingenbeleid), nr. 3157 (Verslag van een Commissiedebat).
21 Kamerstukken II 2021–2022, Aanhangsel van de Handelingen, nr. 3675.
22 Stichting Marechaussee Contact (n 18).
23 Stichting Marechaussee Contact (n 18).
24 Kamerstukken II 2023–2024, 19 637 (Vreemdelingenbeleid), nr. 3199 (Verslag van een Commissiedebat).
25 See District Court The Hague, 1 March 2024, ECLI:NL:RBDHA:2024:2653, para 5.10.
26 Besluit van de Staatssecretaris van Justitie en Veiligheid, 27 January 2020, number WBV 2020/2, houdende wijziging van de Vreemdelingencirculaire 2000, *Staatscourant* (2020) 5922.

27 See District Court The Hague, 10 July 2022, ECLI:NL:RBDHA:2020:6252; District Court The Hague 3 February 2023, ECLI:NL:RBDHA:2023:1079.
28 Ministry of Justice, Inspectie Justitie en Veiligheid, 'Onderzoek naar de leefomstandigheden en de veiligheid op de handhavings- en toezichtlocatie Hoogeveen' (The Hague, 12 October 2022). Lawyers representing asylum seekers at the HTL have documented evidence of physical harm done to asylum seekers in the HTL (personal email correspondence on record with the author).
29 Ministry of Justice, Inspectie Justitie en Veiligheid, 'Vervolgonderzoek naar onder andere de wettelijke basis geweldgebruik boa's HTL (The Hague, 27 March 2023).
30 Kamerstukken 2022–2023, 19 637 (Vreemdelingenbeleid), nr. 2995 (Brief van de Staatssecretaris vanJustitite en Veiligheid aan de Voorzitter van de Tweede Kamer der Staten-Generaal).
31 Kamerstukken 2022–2023, Aanhangsel van de Handelingen, nr. 1865. In a later letter to Parliament, the Minister merely stated that the issues that had been brought to attention by the Inspectorate were adequately monitored by now. TK 2023–2024, 19 637 (Vreemdelingenbeleid), nr. 3175.
32 Amnesty International, 'Isolatie in Vreemdelingenbewaring' (September 2020) <https://www.amnesty.nl/content/uploads/2020/09/AMN_20_26_rapport-isolatie_digitaal.pdf?x52822>.
33 Committee for the Prevention of Torture and Inhuman or Degrading Treatment or Punishment, 'Report to the Government of the Netherlands on the Periodic Visit to the Kingdom of the Netherlands Carried Out by the European Committee for the Prevention of Torture and Inhuman or Degrading Treatment or Punishment (CPT) from 10 to 25 May 2022', 23 June 2023, CPT/Inf (2023) 12.
34 TK 2022–2023, 24587 (Justitiële Inrichtingen) 899 (Response of the Kingdom of the Netherlands to the 2022 CPT report).
35 See for an overview Lieneke Slingenberg, 'Over de rechtsstaat en het 'aso-azc' (2021) 14 Nederlands Juristenblad 1062–70.
36 Raad van State, 21 August 2023, ECLI:NL:RVS:2023:3184; 15 June 2022, ECLI:NL:RVS:2022:171025; 25 November 2020: ECLI:NL:RVS:2020:2795; and 10 December 2010: ECLI:NL:RVS:2010:BO8075.
37 Directive 2008/115/EC of the European Parliament and of the Council of 16 December 2008 on common standards and procedures in Member States for returning illegally staying third-country nationals [2008] OJ L348, 98–107.
38 Case 519/20 *Landkreis Gifhorn* [2022] ECLI:EU:C:2022:178.
39 See for example *Saadi v the United Kingdom* [GC] App No 13229/03 (ECHR, 29 January 2008) 73.
40 District Court The Hague, 3 Februari 2023, ECLI:NL:RBDHA:2023:1079.
41 Slingenberg (n 35).
42 *Guzzardi v Italy* App No 7367/76 (ECHR, 6 November 1980) 93.
43 *Ilias and Ahmed v Hungary* [GC] App No 47287/15 (ECHR, 21 November 2019) 212.
44 Joined Cases C-924/19 PPU and C-925/19 PPU, *FMS*, ECLI:EU:C:2020:367, para 223.
45 Joined Cases C-924/19 PPU and C-925/19 PPU, *FMS*, ECLI:EU:C:2020:367, para 228.
46 Case C-233/18 *Haqbin* [2019] ECLI:EU:C:2019:956; Case 79/13 *Saciri* [2014] ECLI:EU:C:2014:103.
47 District Court The Hague, 16 February 2024, ECLI:NL:RBDHA:2024:1889.
48 In light of the aforementioned unresolved issues, it seems that the Council of State, as the highest court, will have to refer the case for a preliminary ruling to the CJEU on the basis of Article 267 of the TFEU.

49 Kamerstukken II 2023–2024, Aanhangsel van de Handelingen, nr. 1450.
50 District Court The Hague, 1 March 2023, ECLI:NL:RBDHA:2024:2653; ECLI:NL:RBDHA:2024:2669.
51 A motion requesting such solutions was supported by 142 of the 150 votes. See Kamerstukken II 2023–2024, 19 637 (Vreemdelingenbeleid), nr. 3221. See also Kamerstukken II 2023–2024, 19637 (Vreemdelingenbeleid), nr. 3250 (Brief van de Staatssecretaris).
52 Regulation of the European Parliament and of the Council establishing a common procedure for international protection in the Union and repealing Directive 2013/32/EU [2024] OJ L2024/1348 (hereinafter, in the chapter, Asylum Procedures Regulation).
53 Directive 2013/32/EU (n 52), Article 44 para 2 and Article 46 jo Article 43.
54 The use of border procedures is mandatory until adequate capacity is reached, see articles 47–51. See Galina Cornelisse and Marcelle Reneman, 'Border Procedures in the Commission's New Pact on Migration and Asylum: A Case of Politics Outplaying Rationality?' (2021) 26(3–4) European Law Journal 181–98; Maarten den Heijer, 'The Pitfalls of Border Procedures' (2022) 59(3) Common Market Law Review 641–72.
55 Galina Cornelisse, 'Border Control and the Right to Liberty in the Pact: A False Promise of "Certainty, Clarity and Decent Conditions"?' in Daniel Thym (ed), *Reforming the Common European Asylum System: Opportunities, Pitfalls, and Downsides of the Commission Proposals for a New 'Pact' on Migration and Asylum* (Nomos 2022) 61–80.
56 *Ribitsch v Austria* App No 18896/91 (ECHR, 4 December 1995) 38.
57 *Ribitsch v Austria* App No 18896/91 (ECHR, 4 December 1995) 38.
58 *Campbell and Fell v the UK* App No 7819/77 and 7878/77 (ECHR, 28 June 1984) 67.
59 *Engel and Others* App No 5100/71 (ECHR 8 June 1976) 82, para 82.
60 District Court The Hague 10 July 2020, ECLI:NL:RBDHA:2020:6252.
61 Directive (EU) 2024/1346 of the European Parliament and of the Council of 14 May 2024 laying down standards for the reception of applicants for international protection (recast) [2024] (hereinafter, in the chapter, Reception Conditions Directive), Articles 9 and 10. See Lieneke Slingenberg, 'Political Agreement on a Recast Asylum Reception Conditions Directive: Continuation of Tents, Containment and Discipline?' in Thym (ed), *Reforming the Common European Asylum System: Opportunities, Pitfalls, and Downsides of the Commission Proposals for a New 'Pact' on Migration and Asylum* (Nomos 2022) 257–76.
62 Evangelia (Lilian) Tsourdi, 'Asylum in the EU: One of the Many Faces of Rule of Law Backsliding?' (2021) (17)3 European Constitutional Law Review 471–97.
63 Ministry of Justice, Inspectie Justitie en Veiligheid, *Vervolgonderzoek naar de aanpak van overlastgevende asielzoeker, Een onderzoek naar aanleiding van het overlijden van een asielzoeker uit de EBTL Hoogeveen* (2019).
64 Vervolgonderzoek naar de aanpak van overlastgevende asielzoekers. <https://www.inspectie-jenv.nl/Publicaties/rapporten/2019/01/22/de-opvang-van-overlastgevende-asielzoekers>.
65 Işık Kulu-Glasgow and other, 'I have Nothing to Lose, Nomadic Unaccompanied Minors in Europe' (Cahier 2023-9, Research and Documentation Centre, 2023).
66 Kulu-Glasgow and others (n 65).
67 Ministry of Justice, Inspectie Justitie en Veiligheid, *Rapport Onderzoek naar aanleiding van het steekincident in CTP Veldzicht* (2023).
68 Julia Kienast and Jens Vedsted-Hansen, 'Differential Treatment and Temporary Protection Arrangements: Discrimination or Legitimate Distinctions?' (2024) 26(1) European Journal of Migration and Law 1–25; Cathryn Costello and

Michelle Foster, '(Some) Refugees Welcome: When Is Differentiating Between Refugees Unlawful Discrimination?' (2022) 22(3) International Journal of Discrimination and the Law 244–80.

69 Kamerstukken II 2022–2023, 19 637 (Vreemdelingenbeleid), nr. 3157 (Verslag van een Commissiedebat), at 38.

70 Or, in the words of Zygmunt Bauman, "the superfluous populations of migrants and refugees". See Zygmunt Bauman, *Wasted Lives: Modernity and its Outcasts* (Polity 2003).

71 Nicholas De Genova, 'The European Question: Migration, Race, and Postcoloniality in Europe' (2016) 34(3) Social Text 75–102.

72 Teresa Nogueira Pinto, 'Between a Rock and a Hard Place: The EU's Transactional Approach to Migration' (*Mixed Migration Review*, 2023) <https://mixed-migration.org/mmr2023/>; Matteo Villa and Alissa Pavia, 'Irregular Migration from North Africa: Shifting Local and Regional Dynamics' (*Atlantic Council*, 3 August 2023) <https://www.atlanticcouncil.org/in-depth-research-reports/report/irregular-migration-from-north-africa-shifting-local-and-regional-dynamics/>.

73 Lucas Chancel and others, 'World Inequality Report 2022' (*World Inequality Lab*, 2022) 12 <https://wir2022.wid.world/www-site/uploads/2021/12/WorldInequalityReport2022_Full_Report.pdf>.

74 Heike Vethaak and Egbert Jongen, 'Stille wateren hebben diepe gronden: Een analyse van de inkomensverdeling en haar determinanten over de afgelopen veertig jaar' (*Universiteit Leiden*, 2024) <https://www.universiteitleiden.nl/binaries/content/assets/rechtsgeleerdheid/fiscaal-en-economische-vakken/economie/rm_2024_01_13022024.pdf>.

75 Vethaak and Jongen (n 74).

76 Ben Meindertsma, 'Arme gemeenten vangen meer asielzoekers op dan rijke' (*NOS*, 21 September 2015).

77 As regards crime and incidents, research shows that asylum seekers in reception centres are mostly suspected of property crimes; by 2023, 74% of registered suspects were involved in this type of crime. This percentage is higher than for the general Dutch population in 2022 (32%) while the proportion of registered suspects of violent crimes among applicants for asylum in reception centres is relatively low (12% compared to 18% for the Dutch population). See Wetenschappelijk Onderzoek- en Datacentrum, 'Incidenten en misdrijven door bewoners van COA- en crisisnoodopvanglocaties 2017–2023' (Cahier 2024–12, Wetenschappelijk Onderzoek en Datacentrum 2024) <https://repository.wodc.nl/handle/20.500.12832/3374>.

78 Marcelle Reneman and Martijn Stronks, 'What Are They Waiting for? The Use of Acceleration and Deceleration in Asylum Procedures by the Dutch Government' (2021) 30(3) Time & Society 302–31.

79 Galina Cornelisse, 'Links moet weer het lef hebben om simpele oplossingen voor te stellen voor het migratievraagstuk' (*Volkskrant*, 5 December 2024) <https://www.volkskrant.nl/columns-opinie/opinie-links-moet-weer-het-lef-hebben-om-simpele-oplossingen-voor-te-stellen-voor-het-migratievraagstuk~b87ba7c1/>.

80 See also Lorenzo Gabrielli, Blanca Garcés-MascareÑas and Olatz Ribera-Almandoz, 'Between Discipline and Neglect: The Regulation of Asylum Accommodation in Spain' (2022) 35(1) Journal of Refugee Studies 262–81 <https://doi.org/10.1093/jrs/feab049>.

81 Adrien Fabre, Thomas Piketty and Rick van der Ploeg, 'Belast het vermogen van de superrijken en geef de opbrengst aan arme landen' (*Volkskrant*, 9 juni 2024) <https://www.volkskrant.nl/columns-opinie/opinie-belast-het-vermogen-van-de-superrijken-en-geef-de-opbrengst-aan-arme-landen~b0b97108/>.

82 Dan Saffer, *Designing for Interaction* (New Riders 2010).

Bibliography

Aliverti A, *Crimes of Mobility* (Routledge 2013).

Amnesty International, *Isolatie in Vreemdelingenbewaring* (Self-Published 2020).

Bauman Z, *Wasted Lives: Modernity and its Outcasts* (Polity 2003).

Bosworth M, 'Immigration Detention, Punishment and the Transformation of Justice' (2019) 28 Social & Legal Studies 81.

Cornelisse G, 'Border Control and the Right to Liberty in the Pact: A False Promise of "Certainty, Clarity and Decent Conditions"?' in Thym D (ed), *Reforming the Common European Asylum System: Opportunities, Pitfalls, and Downsides of the Commission Proposals for a New 'Pact' on Migration and Asylum* (Nomos 2022).

Cornelisse G and Reneman M, 'Border Procedures in the Commission's New Pact on Migration and Asylum: A Case of Politics Outplaying Rationality?' (2021) 26 European Law Journal 181.

Costello C and Foster M, '(Some) Refugees Welcome: When Is Differentiating Between Refugees Unlawful Discrimination?' (2022) 22 International Journal of Discrimination and the Law 244.

De Genova N, 'The European Question: Migration, Race, and Postcoloniality in Europe' (2016) 34 Social Text 75.

Den Heijer M, 'The Pitfalls of Border Procedures' (2022) 59 Common Market Law Review 641.

Di Molfetta E and Brouwer J, 'Unravelling the "Crimmigration Knot": Penal Subjectivities, Punishment and the Censure Machine' (2020) 20 Criminology & Criminal Justice.

Franko KA and Bosworth M (eds), *The Borders of Punishment: Citizenship, Crime Control, and Social Exclusion* (OUP 2013).

Gabrielli L, Garcés-Mascareñas B and Ribera-Almandoz O, 'Between Discipline and Neglect: The Regulation of Asylum Accommodation in Spain' (2022) 35 Journal of Refugee Studies 262.

Hodge P, 'A Grievable Life? The Criminalisation and Securing of Asylum Seeker Bodies in the 'Violent Frames' of Australia's Operation Sovereign Borders' (2015) 58 Geoforum 122.

Kienast J and Vedsted-Hansen J, 'Differential Treatment and Temporary Protection Arrangements: Discrimination or Legitimate Distinctions?' (2024) 26 European Journal of Migration and Law 1.

Kulu-Glasgow I and others, *I Have Nothing to Lose, Nomadic Unaccompanied Minors in Europe* (Cahier 2023–9, Research and Documentation Centre, 2023).

Leroy I, 'Migrant Reception Centres and Coercive Social Control: Rule by Legal Uncertainty?' [2024] Social & Legal Studies 1.

Nogueira Pinto T, 'Between a Rock and a Hard Place: The EU's Transactional Approach to Migration' (*Mixed Migration Review*, 2023).

Reneman M and Stronks M, 'What Are They Waiting For? The Use of Acceleration and Deceleration in Asylum Procedures by the Dutch Government' (2021) 30 Time & Society 302.

Saffer D, *Designing for Interaction* (New Riders 2010).

Slingenberg L, 'Over de rechtsstaat en het 'aso-azc' (2021) 14 Nederlands Juristenblad 1062–1070.

Slingenberg L, 'Political Agreement on a Recast Asylum Reception Conditions Directive: Continuation of Tents, Containment and Discipline?' in Thym D (ed), *Reforming the Common European Asylum System: Opportunities, Pitfalls, and Downsides of the Commission Proposals for a New 'Pact' on Migration and Asylum* (Nomos 2022).

Tsourdi L, 'Asylum in the EU: One of the Many Faces of Rule of Law Backsliding?' (2021) 17 European Constitutional Law Review 471.

Vethaak H and Jongen E, 'Stille wateren hebben diepe gronden: Een analyse van de inkomensverdeling en haar determinanten over de afgelopen veertig jaar' (*Universiteit Leiden*, 2024).

Wijngaarden M and Dölle F, 'Is hulp aan asielzoekers strafbaar?' (2020) 6 Crimmigratie & Recht 78.

9 From Prevention to Repression

Penal Populism and the Changing Paradigm of Criminal Law to Counter Irregular Migration and Humanitarian Assistance

Marta Minetti

9.1 Introduction

In October 2013, an overcrowded boat carrying migrants from Eritrea, Somalia, and Ghana capsized within sights of the Lampedusa Island, in the Italian region of Sicily.[1] The boat, which departed from the Libyan port of Misurata on 1 October 2013, had a capacity of 35 passengers, but was carrying over 500 people, 339 of whom died in the Mediterranean after the boat capsized. Ten years later, in 2023, two shipwrecks took place only months apart and made international headlines: One in Cutro, close to the southern Italian shores, in February 2023, where 100 people lost their lives; and one in the international waters off the coast of Pylos, Greece, where over 500 people drowned. In the ten years that separate the two events, an estimated 17,000 people lost their lives in the central Mediterranean,[2] making of it one of the deadliest—if not the deadliest—migration routes in the world, while over 56,000 forced migrants have disappeared in the perilous journeys across the same central Mediterranean waters.

Despite these disturbing figures, European and Italian authorities have not made any genuine efforts to provide safe and legal routes for asylum seekers and migrants to Europe. On the contrary, the responses, both at national and EU levels, have shown an attitude which has been described as "normalisation of migrant deaths",[3] consistently reiterating the need to further strengthen border controls allegedly aimed at tackling human trafficking and smuggling activities. This approach has *de facto* resulted in three inter-related developments: (1) Further restrictions to accessing the asylum system—and in many cases, the dismantling of the system altogether[4]—and sharper penalties for those migrants excluded from the asylum seeker category; (2) the creation of a criminal and administrative law action targeting the humanitarian actors carrying out SAR operations in the Mediterranean area; and (3) extraterritorial migration control aimed at curbing new departure through multiple bilateral agreements signed by the EU and its several Member States on the one side and Northern and sub-Saharan African governments on the other.[5]

DOI: 10.4324/9781003378440-9

In parallel, the previous decade has been characterised by the rise of populist movements across the western world and particularly in the EU. The political legitimation of such movements relies on electoral consent,[6] achieved largely through the rhetoric counterposing nationals and foreigners, the latter described by political leaders as security threats.[7] Consequently, EU Member States have gradually moved towards models of migration management and control based on the usage of punitive measures against non-citizens and those assisting them outside and within their borders.

In this sense, the EU strategy to combat the facilitation of illegal entry has differentiated itself because of its focus on the prevention of irregular arrivals and of the crime of facilitation of illegal entry. To achieve these goals, the Facilitators' Package[8] was ratified in 2002: A set of provisions that, since its ratification, has been subject to harsh critiques due to its lack of normative foundations, its over-extensive scope and, more recently, its alleged incompatibility with the European Charter of Fundamental Rights.[9] In fact, although the package is part of the EU criminal law domain, the ultimate function of which is—or should be—rehabilitative,[10] the legal instrument dealing with the establishment and strengthening of the penal framework surrounding the facilitation of illegal entry is explicitly aimed at the prevention of that crime.[11] For this reason, although its effectiveness in achieving the stated goals was confirmed in the REFIT assessment by the EU Commission released in 2017, legal scholarship has taken a completely different direction, citing the package as an example of the preventive role taken by EU criminal law.[12]

The criminal law-based countering action to the facilitation of irregular migration has nevertheless encountered the resistance of the judiciary, which, on more than one occasion, has declared SAR activities carried out by humanitarian actors as legitimate.[13] For this reason, the authorities drifted towards the application of administrative law tools, having similar coercive effects to the criminal ones, but escaping the judicial checks.[14] Nevertheless, the application of punitive instances against both irregular migrants and those assisting them has highlighted a disparity between criminal and immigration law in terms of protections available to persons caught between the two systems.[15] The interpretation of immigration control solely through the lens of criminalisation would be insufficiently precise, because, while immigrants and those assisting them face restrictions and measures drawn from criminal law, they are not afforded the same fundamental protections as are available to criminal defendants.[16]

Jacobs refers to the disparity between the "common" criminal law applicable to the citizens and an *ad hoc* criminal law applicable to the "enemies" of the citizens as "Criminal Law of the Citizen" and "Criminal Law of the Enemy" ["*Buergerstrafrecht und Feindstrafrecht*"].[17] The theory consists of the argument that societies tend to suspend certain laws and their related protections in order to protect themselves from certain (real or perceived) dangers. In this sense, the "over-criminalisation" of migration control advances along the process of "under-criminalisation",[18] where the protections usually provided by criminal law measures are not available to those identified as enemies of the society.

The legal and policy provisions (of which the Facilitators' Package is one example) adopted at the EU level and transposed into the Member States' domestic frameworks have enabled the instrumentalisation of law—both criminal and administrative—against the rescue activities carried out by humanitarian actors in the context of irregular migration, connecting the EU and national legal frameworks regulating the issue to the discourses regarding the increasing reach of the populistic misuse of law.

Against this backdrop, this chapter will unpack the relationship between immigration control, the rise of right-wing populism in Europe, and the distortion of the preventive justice paradigm for the repression of irregular migration and its facilitation. It will argue that the rise of right-wing populist parties across Europe (on the political side) and the increased reliance on a securitised approach and the preventive justice paradigm (on the legal side) resulted in abuses of the criminal and administrative legal frameworks (on the legal side) against the depersonalised phenomenon of irregular migration and its facilitation, depicted by these parties as a common enemy. In turn, the influence of populism in the legal field has led to the distortion of the preventive and rehabilitative aim of criminal law, to a much blurrier application of criminal and administrative legal measures aimed at the repression of irregular migration and its facilitation. The misuse of the framework to achieve essentially political goals, in turn, ultimately results in the contraventions of the Rule of Law Principle of Legality, codified in Article 49 of the Charter of Fundamental Rights of the European Union as well as in Article 7 of the European Convention on Human Rights.[19]

A paradigmatic example of the misuse of the criminal law framework to counter irregular migration and the related humanitarian activities has been offered by the Italian authorities, which, since 2017, have been at the centre of public and academic scrutiny for the criminalisation of NGOs saving migrants at sea.[20] Additionally, Italy has been defined as a "laboratory" for the study of populism and its implications in the repression of the irregular migration phenomenon.[21] For these reasons, the chapter will examine the Italian case to study the interplay between the preventive function of criminal law, its repressive distortion, and the influence of populism.

The interplay between populism, penal populism, and the rule of law for the purposes of immigration control has been the object of two more articles published by the author, in 2020 and 2022, respectively, in the New Journal of European Criminal Law and International Community Law Review.[22] The first article offers an analysis of the European and Italian criminalisation of humanitarian assistance offered to migrants in distress at sea by civil society groups. The study ultimately argues that the transposition of the EU

Facilitators' Package in the Member State's internal legislation opens the gate to abuses of criminal law for the purpose of serving the anti-immigration political agenda of the government fed by and feeding populistic movements.[23] The analysis in the second article focuses on the incompatibilities of the criminalisation of humanitarian assistance in the irregular migration context with the international law dimension.

More specifically, the chapter argues that the criminalising approach adopted by the EU and its Member States towards irregular migration and solidarity in this context, which is rooted in the nationalistic elements characterising populist movements, results in (1) non-compliance with state duties and obligations deriving from international law and (2) misuse of the transnational criminal law framework to justify non-compliance with principles of human rights and refugee law, ultimately eroding the international legal space.[24] While these previous studies take into account the effects of the intertwinement of the criminal law framework, populism, and immigration control, this chapter will take a step back in the analysis and unpack the relationship between these three elements in order to shed some light on the ways in which the preventive function of criminal law can be distorted to serve anti-immigration political agendas.

9.2 Penal Populism and Immigration Control

The modern anti-immigration rhetoric, on which right-wing populist governing parties have based their claims, sets its roots in the deep discontent that spread among the lower-middle layers of society, in turn originating from the economic recession followed by the economic crisis of 2007–2008.[25] As Funke, Schularick, and Trebesch confirm:

> [p]olitics takes a hard right turn following financial crises. . . . This pattern is visible in data both before and after WWII . . . the gains of extreme right-wing parties were particularly pronounced after the global crises of the 1920s–1930s and after 2008.[26]

In this context of widespread anger, the former dichotomy between regular and irregular migration, depicting as a potential threat only the latter, is replaced by a much more aggressive narrative targeting economic migrants, described as potential invaders, job thieves, false refugees, and criminals.[27] It is in this climate of mistrust in the democratic process that the field of criminal law becomes a fertile ground for the populistic discourses to find immediate application, a phenomenon that triggered the introduction of the concept of penal populism by Pratt.[28] Penal populism refers to the use for political purposes of diffused punitive instances and as an expressive political orientation guided by consensus obtained through the promise of quick, exemplary, and definite intervention for the reassuring of the citizens against a perceived common enemy.[29]

The origins of the concept of penal populism parallel those of political populism. Both concepts set their roots in the social and cultural changes, which began in the 1970s and now extend across much of modern society. As Pratt notes,

> [t]he rise of penal populism is a reflection of a fundamental shift in the axis of contemporary penal power brought about by these changes, even if the extent of the shift differs from society to society, depending on their local impact.[30]

Where public opinion previously operated simply as a boundary constraint on policy, it now is the preferred source of policy. Expert opinions and empirical research are downgraded, while "popular experience" is preferred as a decision- and policymaking basis.[31]

Additionally, penal populism involves a change in the emotional aspect of the penal process: From striving for objectivity and cool detachment of professional decision-makers, to an emotional appeal by the populist politicians to pass legislation designed to soothe the emotional needs of the electorate, whose anger or fear is stimulated by the populist rhetoric. In this sense, and in the interplay between cool and detached decision-making with the emotional political need, the boundary between the executive and legislative powers often gets blurred. Penal populist policies and laws are rarely evidence-led and aim at gathering an immediate political and electoral consensus, rather than tackling an actual issue in the pursuit of long-term penological results.[32]

9.3 Populism and Immigration Control in Italy

In Italy, in the past few years, the characteristic aspects of penal populism have been instrumental for the feeding of political populism that, in 2018, resulted in a coalition government between the right-wing party Lega Nord and the leftist Five Stars Movement. The electoral consent, which at the time enabled their appointment, was built on the promotion of security-oriented policies, based on two types of juxtaposition: The first one, typical of populist movements, opposing the people and the elite;[33] and the second one, counterposing Italian citizens and foreigners,[34] the latter described by political leaders as security threats. The Italian misuse of legislative measures to counter irregular migration, deriving from the expansion of right-wing populist political trends in the legal field, has been studied by comparative lawyers, to the point that Italy has been defined as a "laboratory" for the study of populism and its implications in tackling irregular migration.[35]

Italy, in this sense, constitutes a paradigmatic example of how populism and penal populism have worked towards the creation of a hostile environment for NGOs and migrants. In the Italian imagination, a fear of invasion from Syrian and sub-Saharan migrants and refugees was constructed by right-wing populist politicians on the massive increase in arrivals via sea, which followed the Arab Spring of 2011 and the "refugee crisis". More specifically, in the Italian case, the restrictions of the rights of the migrants and the creation of a hostile environment for all actors involved in the process of irregular migration, resulting from the expansion of populism in the legal field, represent a form of democratic decay that has become increasingly evident since 2015—year of origin of the so-called migration crises—but whose roots should be found even earlier.[36] For these reasons, the southern Italian border represents an ideal field of investigation to assess both the impact of populist policies on immigration law and the "resilience" of the legal system with respect to their spreading.[37]

In the past decade, the characteristic aspects of *penal* populism have been instrumental for the feeding of *political* populism, which has, more recently, resulted in the election of the first far-right prime minister since before the Second World War, Giorgia Meloni, the leader of *Fratelli d'Italia*.[38] The electoral consensus that enabled Meloni's election was built on the promotion of security-oriented policies, based on Eurosceptic and anti-immigration views.[39] The parties that came to government after 2017 expended their resources in the creation of a hostile environment through the consistent application of criminal and administrative laws against humanitarian and civil society actors providing assistance to irregular migrants in distress.[40] These parties position themselves within a migration control strategy that started long before the governments openly declared themselves as populist.[41]

The rhetoric that brought about the election of a populist radical right party in Italy, and unprecedented success of similar political factions in many other Member States,[42] has rested precisely on the depiction of the phenomenon of irregular migration and of the humanitarian actors carrying out SAR operations at sea as a security threat. Among the best-known examples of far-right populist governing parties is Viktor Orban's Fidesz, which has ruled Hungary since 2010 and whose hostile views and policies on immigration have played a vital role in the longevity of its government.[43] A more recent example is given by the dramatic win in the Netherlands' 2023 election of Geert Wilders' populist Party for Freedom, whose campaign was opposing migration and Islam.[44]

In particular, Meloni's rhetoric referred to the facilitation of illegal entry for humanitarian assistance as threatening to make Italy the "refugee camp of Europe" and advocated for naval blockades, defined in international law as an act of war, and for the use of European funds for the strengthening of the border instead of using them for the management of irregular migration.[45]

The electoral programme that brought Meloni to government included, among its first aims, the "defence and promotion of the Classical and Judaeo-Christian cultural and historical roots of Europe".[46] Additionally, point six of the electoral programme is entirely dedicated to "security and the countering actions to irregular migration" and lists among its aims a further production or *mise a jour* of the security decrees as well as the fight against irregular migration and the correct and ordinary management of migration flows, the creation of hotspots outside of the EU territory to process asylum applications, and the fight against "Islamist integralism".[47] The migration-related promises are listed among other security threats, such as the fight against mafia, terrorism, and youth violence and micro-criminality, as well as cyber-threats. The phrasing of the electoral programme and the reference to the need for defence suggest that there is a threat, supposedly posed by external and foreign influences, menacing the existence of a European identity.

It is on these ideological premises that the "closed ports" policies—indicating the prohibition of entry into Italian ports by the local authorities, imposed on NGO vessels conducting SAR operations in the Mediterranean to prevent the disembarkation of the rescued migrants—and the legal and policy responses to the facilitation of illegal entry for the purposes of providing humanitarian assistance have been based.[48] The new types of narratives and arguments supporting the anti-immigration policies and the firm political choice of closing borders display the characteristics that helped to establish this new political approach to the rescue work of the NGOs.[49]

9.4 From Regulation to Prevention to Repression: The Laws Tackling Irregular Migration

Security has always been a core function of the modern state.[50] Therefore, the reasons for the increase in production of new norms and laws focused on security lie in the perceived necessity to minimise risk and forestall harm in order to fulfil that function.[51] In this sense, the preventive element has followed the development of criminal law, which has led to the creation of inchoate offences, declaring criminal liability of people before they have actually committed the crime or caused the prohibited harm. In order for liability to arise, the law on these pre-emptive offences typically requires the proof of the person's intent to cause the prohibited harm and of the fact that a substantial step towards that goal has been taken. Most criminal law systems include inchoate offences as an element of the general part of criminal law. In the British Criminal Law framework, for example, these include attempts, conspiracy, and encouraging or assisting a crime.[52] Similarly, Article 56 of the Italian criminal code criminalises attempts (*delitto tentato*), while Article 110 criminalises conspiracies (*concorso di persone*).

On this basis, the preventive justice paradigm in its original form was aimed at minimising the risk of a clearly defined harm to an equally clearly identified legal interest against a clearly defined threat. However, due to the increasing influence of mostly right-wing populist parties across different EU Member States, the preventive justice paradigm (applicable in the fields of both criminal law and administrative law) has been over-stretched to minimise risk of a non-specified harm to a very blurrily defined protected legal interest from the similarly blurrily defined criminalised and depersonalised phenomenon of irregular migration and its facilitation. In this sense, the creation of "pre-inchoate offences"—intended as inchoate offences which do not meet the requirement of proof of the person's intent and the taking of substantial steps for their commission—has proliferated across Europe and the UK.[53] A prominent example is Section 5 of the UK Terrorism Act, which established criminal liability for actions taken at very early preparatory stages and allows for a sentence of life imprisonment.[54] This preventive expansion of criminalisation has not been confined to anti-terrorist law.

The term "preventive justice" has been used in connection with domestic criminal law and has been defined as a phenomenon extending the scope of criminal law to gradually remove the link between criminalisation and prosecution on the one hand and the commission of concrete acts on the other.[55] In the aftermath of the 9/11 attacks, the state's focus on prevention of harm intensified, marking a shift toward a precrime society that challenged the foundational principles of criminology.[56] Risk and security, already objects of enquiry in the 1990s, became more central objects of research after 11 September 2001, when the potential for further terrorist events significantly increased existing pressure on states to act pre-emptively to forestall the gravest harms. In this sense, the definition of preventive justice as a criminological construct acting as guarantor for the safety of the citizens and as defender of the security of the nation goes hand-in-hand with the conception of border control as essential to the preservation of national security, as well as with the right to exclude non-citizens as the ultimate prerogative of national sovereignty.[57] This exclusionary definition of national sovereignty works in combination with the "desire to reduce, monitor and police" those who seek to evade these exclusions.[58]

These developments, combined with the expansions of the right-wing populist parties, resulted—both at EU and national levels—in the proliferation of laws of various nature, ultimately aimed at preventing irregular arrivals to the European shores, through the deterrence and repression of the phenomenon of irregular migration and its facilitation. In this sense, the expansion of "preventive control", described as a criminological construct, which acts as a guarantor of safety of its citizens and defender of the nation's security,[59] represents the drive behind the creation and increase of powers of the European border control agency (Frontex, now European Border and Coast Guard Agency), the transnational surveillance system *Eurosur*, and the establishment of a European database collecting information on and fingerprints of asylum seekers (Eurodac).[60] Further examples of this preventive justice paradigm are given by the externalisation of European border control: "a range of processes whereby European actors and Member States complement policies to control migration across their territorial boundaries with initiatives that realise such control extra-territorially and through other countries and organs rather than their own".[61]

In this spirit, the legislative development implemented in the past two decades by European states included an intensification of the production of new measures aimed at preventing irregular migrants from accessing the physical external borders of EU Member States, and, consequently, the rule of law protections available within them.[62]

9.5 Preventive Laws: The Risks of Over- and Under-Criminalisation

The term "preventive state" also connotes a more recent tendency for states to pass preventive laws and measures designed to enhance their capacity to forestall risk and reduce or avert harms. The graver the risk and the more serious the prospective harms, the greater the powers the state accords itself to combat them. This paradigm is valid regardless of whether the risk of harm is real or artificially created. The analysis of the Italian case shows that the application of criminal law-derived tools used to perpetuate the populist anti-immigration agenda results in a distortion of the function of criminal law as a tool for repression and deterrence. The preventive justice paradigm has developed along two main paths: One of over-criminalisation[63] and the other of under-criminalisation.[64]

The term "over-criminalisation", studied by Husak in the context of the American criminal justice system,[65] is used to refer to the creation of criminal offences lacking a real justification or normative foundation. The over-extensive creation of criminal offences whose normative foundations and justifying factors are, at best, shaky, is undesirable insofar as it expands the reach of state power to deprive citizens of freedoms and liberties with no real reason. In fact, the function of criminal law, as defined by Beccaria, is not to punish, but to administer the least possible punishment.[66] Beccaria advocated for the application of the law to reduce the arbitrary power of the state through the introduction of the principles of legal certainty, legality, and certainty of the law: Principles constituting the pillars of the modern conception of the rule of law.[67] Therefore, the over-extensive production and application of criminal law-deriving tools, regardless of the purpose, is problematic both in terms of deprivation of liberty of the citizens and in terms of its consequences for the rule of law and its constitutive principles.

The under-criminalisation strategy presents similar issues. In fact, it includes the creation of and reliance on civil preventive orders/measures, such as prolonged and unjustified seizure of rescue vessels and burdensome pecuniary fines, which lack the safeguards foreseen in the criminal law framework. Where the criminalisation criteria are not met and the civil preventive orders are appropriate, the coercive elements should be reduced to ensure that the use of coercion is an exceptional measure of last resort, and stigmatising effects are minimised. Nevertheless, in practice, in the field of irregular migration and humanitarian assistance, it happens exactly the opposite. The use of administrative law to counter the activities of SAR NGOs in Italy contributes to the creation of stigma and of a hostile environment for humanitarian actors and irregular entrants alike. The perils of under-criminalisation may be less immediately apparent than those of over-criminalisation, but they are no less grave where the result is that disproportionate, ill-defined, and often burdensome intrusion upon individual liberty is imposed in the name of prevention without appropriate procedural safeguards.[68]

9.6 From Traditional Criminal Law to Criminal Law of the Enemy: Prevention through Repression

The preventive function of coercive measures, particularly in the field of inchoate offences and the limits of criminalisation, has been extensively debated among criminal law scholars and practitioners.[69] It logically follows that when the legal framework with the greatest coercive and stigmatising power lacks clearly defined boundaries, the risk of misuse and distortion increases significantly. In fact, "systematic [and less simple] explanations cannot compete with the simplicity and emotive power of invoking the spectre of the foreigner as an intrinsic menace to national security".[70] Furthermore, if the emotional rhetoric is adopted by right-wing populist groups and aimed at the depersonalised phenomenon of irregular migration, the limits of the law and the boundaries between legal fields get muddled and lead to the almost uncontrolled production of hybrid measures, whose nature and normative foundations are unclear.

In other words, this apparatus of prevention and security, through the influence of penal populism, results in real disregard for the leading principles of the rule of law in which traditional criminal and administrative law are rooted.[71] In this sense, penal populism in the field of migration control creates a veritable distortion of the functions of criminal law, which surpasses prevention and reaches repression.

The peculiarity of this distortion of criminal law, in particular, is the absence of constitutional or human rights protections for those subjected to these types of criminalisation.[72] Because those protections tend to be focused on criminal trials and punishment, it seems that coercive preventive and deterrent measures fall into a jurisprudential black hole. Similarly, the production and application of administrative law measures having similar repressive aims and similar coercive and stigmatising effects has the same shortcomings in terms of compliance with a rule of law-compatible reading of the examined measures. In fact, the misuse of the criminal law framework to counter irregular migration and its facilitation result in a disproportion between the infraction committed and the sanction imposed, raising questions about its compliance with the principle of proportionality.[73] Furthermore, the incompatibility of the criminalisation of irregular migration with the leading principles of international human rights law, international refugee law, international humanitarian law, and transnational criminal law challenges the principle of *pacta sunt servanda* and results in shortcomings with regard to the principle of legality.[74] The principle of legality is further endangered by the lack of normative foundations and the vagueness of the criminalising scope of the Facilitators' Package.[75]

The interplay between the risk posed by a—real or imagined—security threat and the consequent (artificially created) need for more restrictive approaches, particularly in the field of irregular migration, has thus led to the proliferation of law enforcement, criminalisation, and externalisation measures aimed at prevention, but which border on repression. Together, they significantly expand the state's exercise of coercive power over its citizens and thereby threaten core liberal values of individual liberty and autonomy.

9.7 Prevention through the Symbolic Use of Criminal Law of the Enemy in Immigration Control

According to Durkheim, in every society, there must exist a set of beliefs and sentiments that are shared by the average citizen and which constitute the *conscience collective,* on which the constitution of social solidarity is based.[76] According to this view, criminal law and the related sanctions for its violations are the manifestation of this *conscience collective*. In fact, violations of criminal law are often associated with strong sentiments or emotions deeply rooted in the values of the society.[77] Durkheim's theory could account for the symbolic dimension of criminal law policies, where criminal justice seems nowadays to be oriented towards crime control and grounded in instrumental rationality.[78] Traditional theories of punishment emphasise the need for deterrence, incapacitation, or rehabilitation of offenders. Durkheim takes the view that criminal law is also a means to express common moral values and social solidarity. Criminal law can be used to foster moral cohesion and to create some sense of collective identity. It can also be used to reinforce the legitimacy of the legal authority which expresses popular punitive passions, sometimes at the expense of marginalised segments of society.

In many European jurisdictions, including Italy, the rhetoric depicting the phenomenon of irregular migration as the scapegoat for rampant social discontent has resulted in the rise of mostly right-wing populist movement. This rise has contributed to a tidal wave of production of legislation (either of criminal nature, or having the same effect) lacking normative foundations, which are rarely applied, and which contribute to the creation of the climate of insecurity that populist governments feed.[79]

In Italy, the recurrent use of symbolic penal legislation creates a reaffirmation of some sort of ideological unity in a society that has never been very prone to dynamic adaptation, especially to the relatively abrupt changes and challenges that the globalisation processes have entailed. In this sense, the stigmatising and unifying power of criminal law is easily instrumentalised to reassure the public of the presence and stability of a *conscience collective* through the stigmatisation of irregular migration and the association of its facilitation with organised crime. It is on this climate of constant insecurity that the production of criminal law measures having only symbolic power to counter irregular migration and its facilitation has flourished and has resulted in the ratification by the Italian legislators of numerous legislative decrees increasing the administrative and criminal sanctions for breaches of immigration law.[80] The Italian criminalisation of facilitation of illegal entry, applied by the national authorities since 2017 against humanitarian actors providing assistance to migrants in distress at sea, is particularly exemplary of this trend. In fact, of the numerous investigations started against the NGOs rescuing migrants at sea, only the one against the crew of the Iuventa has reached the trial stage.[81]

In this sense, in the context of irregular migration and its facilitation, criminal legislation targeting irregular migration and its facilitation has been designed at the European and national levels as a sign of ministerial virility—a display of force that is characteristic of populist leaders. This display of force against a threat that is artificially created by the populist rhetoric itself, is presented as necessary to respond to and soothe the emotional needs of the electorate. However, the over-extensive application of criminal law measures remains *de facto* almost completely ineffective in achieving convictions.[82]

9.8 Prevention through Deterrence

The extensive production of criminal law measures having symbolic significance in the field of immigration control has the further aim to deter irregular migrants from departing and humanitarian actors from conducting SAR operations. In fact, across the globe for the past decades, the deterrence of crime has been a component of criminal law reform for the construction of the prevention-through-securitisation paradigm. Lawmakers in both the USA and the EU have sought greater control over the various security threats—posed, in particular, by transnational mobility crimes—through the creation of a penalty-setting system that provides for criminal punishments of sufficient magnitude to deter from the commission of the crime.[83]

Besides the issues of compatibility with the proportionality principle that this approach to criminal law might entail, it also regularly proves ineffective as well as having hidden criminogenic costs.[84] More specifically, the criminalisation of migration and humanitarian assistance relies on a distortion of the preventive function of criminal law into a deterrent and repressive one in order to obtain electoral consensus and achieve political goals.

Nevertheless, there is growing evidence that suggests scepticism about the effectiveness in deterring crime through the manipulation of criminal law rules and penalties, since potential offenders do not know the law nor make rational choices, nor perceive an expected cost for a violation that outweighs the expected gain.[85] Consequently, the ineffectiveness in achieving these deterrence goals has threefold consequences: It undermines the credibility of the law, has criminogenic effects, and causes increased vulnerability and death in the migration process. The infrequency of being able to achieve a meaningful deterrent effect through doctrinal manipulation reveals that the deterrence strategy is seriously out of touch with the reality of its limitations.

9.9 The Harms of the Expansion of Populism in the Penal Field

The problem with the penal declination of the right-wing populist parties in the field of immigration control is that they create moral panic around a perfectly normal process that has been going on since human history began, which has led human evolution and whose beneficial impacts on society, economy, and culture have been proved by countless studies in various academic fields, for the mere purpose of remaining in power.[86] To achieve this goal, the right-wing populist parties have deflected the anger and fear of the electorate, exacerbated by socio-economic changes, to initially target the character of the irregular migrant, the general phenomenon of irregular migration, and more recently—in Italy since 2017—its facilitation, even if carried out for humanitarian purposes.

By depicting the macro-area of irregular migration and its facilitation as an enemy, the right-wing populist political parties rely on rhetoric and appeal to the emotions of the electorate to create more demand for the production of new laws and norms that lack normative foundations, but are allegedly aimed at the prevention and deterrence of the irregular entry of the migrants on the national territory, while proving completely ineffective. This over-extensive creation of immigration-related offences attempts *ad hoc* to communicate to the citizens "a semblance of security" in fulfilment of those artificially created emotional needs. The resulting laws are rarely enforced in a proportionate manner and have, on multiple occasions, proven ineffective at deterring both irregular departures and SAR operations from every perspective.[87]

9.9.1 *Increased Deaths*

However, the failure of these laws to prevent or deter irregular departures does not imply that the widespread anti-immigration rhetoric—through which electoral support for such measures is gained—is harmless. The systematic introduction of new policies and norms targeting humanitarian actors and their activities—both through the use of criminal law and administrative seizures and fines—results in the creation of a hostile environment for both irregular migrants and the NGOs assisting them. Furthermore, the anti-smuggling criminal law framework and the organised crime framework have been instrumentalised by many Member States, of which Italy is only one very prominent example.[88] Similarly, Greece criminalised acts related to the receipt of donations of money and objects from private sources, using organised crime legislation pertaining to money laundering, fraud, and espionage, for which a defendant faces 25 years in prison.[89] In the UK, activists involved in peaceful protests to prevent a deportation flight at Stansted airport were charged and prosecuted for terror-related offences.[90]

The creation of such hostile environments by European states, particularly Italy, driven by the need to assert national sovereignty, results in the disregard of the fundamental rights of the migrants and of the rule of law obligation, in order to uphold the preventive paradigm, in turn ultimately aimed at the repression of the phenomenon of irregular migration.[91] The combination of criminal investigations and policy restrictions has severely hindered SAR operations, which has consequently increased the number of disappearances and deaths at sea.[92]

9.9.2 *Criminogenic Effects*

These repressive and deterrent legal and policy responses, virtually aimed at preventing irregular migrants from accessing the rule of law protections in the EU jurisdiction,[93] have resulted in the creation of a hostile environment for asylum seekers, migrants, and NGOs. Additionally, the recent dismantling of the Italian reception system, which began in 2018 with the Salvini Decrees,[94] started with the revocation of humanitarian residence permits,[95] and has resulted in the "warehousing" of asylum seekers.[96] This complete lack of systematic management of irregular migration, combined with the reduction (or elimination) of integration measures and of other channels for the obtainment of international protection and the recognition of the trafficking victim status, fosters the processes of dehumanisation and victimisation—of which the recent images from the hotspot of Lampedusa are only one testimony.[97] The migrant therefore has no other choice but to resort to solutions outside the law to support themselves, consequently feeding the narrative associating immigration and criminality upon which the populist rhetoric thrives and which provided the justification for the dismantling of the reception system in the first place.[98]

The new measures included in the most recent NGO-targeting decrees, making the ability of the vessels to rescue people at sea contingent to a variety of senseless requirements, constitute a new qualitative leap in the evolution of penal populism. Penal populism relies on "soliciting hatred and on the criminalisation of not just lawful, but indeed heroic conduct . . . in order to obtain consent for policies that are themselves unlawful, criminal and criminogenic".[99]

9.9.3 *Threatening Democracy and Undercutting the Credibility of the Law*

Political scientists have highlighted how populism and its penal declination have showed a tendency to instrumentalise and exploit the law to manipulate policymaking institutions and to subvert their capacity to disrupt the political will.[100] By reducing and discrediting the views and opinions of experts in the legal field, the resulting policymaking is increasingly concentrated in the hands of the executive in order to avoid interference by the legislative power, *de facto* resulting in harming the system of checks and balances: One of the pillars of modern democracy. In fact, the differences in the sources of legitimation between the executive (electoral consensus) and the judicial powers (constitutional principles) are at the root of the issue of the expansion of populism in the penal field.[101]

Moreover, as Garland states,

> [t]he problem with penal populism is that it embodies a kind of politics in which reductive representations of public opinion are allowed to dominate public debate . . . it facilitates a kind of know-nothing politicised policy making that ignores pertinent information and fails to address relevant values.[102]

In this sense, the know-nothing politicised policymaking—put in place by the right-wing populist parties advocating for harsher measures to curb irregular migration in all its forms—has resulted in the ratification of an "electorally driven" form of legislation (on both the European and national levels), whose normative foundations are extremely fragile and which endangers the separation of powers.

In Italy, the former Interior Minister Salvini has, on more than one occasion, attacked the judiciary by publicly challenging the qualification of the judges because they have not been elected by the people. Additionally, he declared indifference towards the legal proceedings against him, further disparaging the relevance of the judiciary in the eyes of the public. Nevertheless, the consensus of the electorate does not justify the arbitrary abuse of the law to achieve the goals of the executive, as the judicial power cannot allow an "electorally driven" form of legislation. In fact, if this trend were permitted to continue, democracy would be distorted into some sort of "elective autocracy", in which the legislative power is the only source of legitimacy, and no protection from abuse is envisaged.[103] The separation of powers is, in fact, a principle that is closely intertwined with the guarantee of rights: There is no constitution without separation of powers and guarantee of rights.[104]

Ultimately, the infrequency of being able to achieve a meaningful deterrent effect through doctrinal manipulation of the law reveals that the right-wing populist approach to irregular migration—relying on the distortion of the rehabilitative function of criminal law and the misapplication of the administrative legal measure—is seriously out of touch with the reality of its limitations.[105] Additionally, by deviating from (part of) the community's sense of justice, these rules undercut the criminal law's moral credibility and thereby reduce the law's long-term crime control effectiveness.[106]

Therefore, through the continuous attacks on the pillars of democratic principles—such as party pluralism, the separation of powers, and constitutionalism—this new form of penal populism is slowly but steadily damaging the democratic character of European society.[107]

9.10 Conclusion

This chapter has unpacked the relationship between immigration control, the rise of right-wing populism in Europe, and the distortion of the preventive justice paradigm for the repression of irregular migration and its facilitation.

It has argued that the rise of right-wing populist parties across Europe (on the political side) and the increased reliance on a securitised approach and on the preventive justice paradigm (on the legal side) is consequential to the rule of law crisis. This has ultimately resulted in abuses of the criminal and administrative legal frameworks (on the legal side) against the depersonalised phenomenon of irregular migration and its facilitation, depicted by these parties as a common enemy. The influence of populism in the legal field has consequently led to the distortion of the preventive and rehabilitative aim of criminal law, to the much blurrier application of criminal and administrative legal measures aimed at the repression of this depersonalised phenomenon and its facilitation.

Notes

1 Matthew Chance, 'Lampedusa Boat Sinking: Survivors Recall Awful Ordeal' *CNN* (9 October 2013) <https://edition.cnn.com/2013/10/08/world/europe/italy-lampedusa-boat-sinking/index.html> accessed 10 September 2024, as all the hyperlinks included in this Chapter.

2 For a more complete estimate of the number of deaths in the Mediterranean, 2000 more have been recorded in the western route and 1700 in the eastern route since 2014. The actual death toll is supposed to be much higher. For more information on the available data, see International Organization for Migration, 'Missing Migrant Project' (*Global Data Institute*, 2023) <https://missingmigrants.iom.int/region/mediterranean>.

3 Hyab Teklehaimanot Yohannes, 'The Normalisation of Migrant Deaths and its Implications for Humanity' (*Border Criminologies*, 16 June 2023) <https://blogs.law.ox.ac.uk/border-criminologies-blog/blog-post/2023/06/normalisation-migrant-deaths-and-its-implications>; Heidi Mogstad, 'Why Doesn't Europe Grieve Deaths in the Mediterranean?' *AlJazeera* (25 May 2023) <https://www.aljazeera.com/opinions/2023/5/25/why-doesnt-europe-grieve-deaths-in-the-mediterranean>.

4 Lorenzo Vianelli, 'Warehousing Asylum Seekers: Salvini's Attempt to Dismantle the Italian Reception System' (*Border Criminologies*, 25 April 2019) <https://blogs.law.ox.ac.uk/research-subject-groups/centre-criminology/centreborder-criminologies/blog/2019/04/warehousing#:~:text=These%20minimum%20provisions%2C%20it%20is,processes%20of%20dehumanisation%20and%20victimisation.&text=Javier%20Marcelo%20Cabrera)-,Law%20no.,and%20beneficiaries%20of%20international%20protection>.

5 Martino Reviglio, 'Externalizing Migration Management Through Soft Law: The Case of the Memorandum of Understanding Between Libya and Italy' (2019) 20 Global Jurist 1; Violeta Moreno-Lax and others, 'The EU Approach on Migration in the Mediterranean' (Study Requested by the LIBE Committee, European Parliament 2021) <https://www.europarl.europa.eu/thinktank/en/document/IPOL_STU(2021)694413>.

6 Jan-Werner Muller, *What Is Populism* (University of Pennsylvania Press 2017).

7 Roberto Cornelli, 'Contro Il Panpopulismo: Una Proposta Di Definizione Del Populismo Penale' (2019) 4 Diritto Penale Contemporaneo—Rivista Trimestrale 128.

8 Council Framework Decision 2002/946/JHA of 28 November 2002 on the strengthening of the penal framework to prevent the facilitation of unauthorised entry, transit and residence [2002] OJ L328/1; Council Directive 2002/90/EC of 28 November 2002 defining the facilitation of unauthorised entry, transit and residence [2002] OJ L328/17.

9 Marta Minetti, 'The Facilitators Package, Penal Populism and the Rule of Law: Lessons from Italy' (2020) 11 New Journal of European Criminal Law 335; Stefano Zirulia, 'Non c'é Smuggling Senza Ingiusto Profitto: Profili Di Illegittimitá Nella Normativa Italiana Ed Europea in Materia Di Favoreggiamento Irregolare' (2020) 3 Diritto Penale Contemporaneo—Rivista Trimestrale 143; Valsamis Mitsilegas, 'The Normative Foundations of the Criminalization of Human Smuggling: Exploring the Fault Lines between European and International Law' (2019) 10 New Journal of European Criminal Law 68; Valsamis Mitsilegas, 'Reforming the EU "Facilitators Package": The New Commission Proposal in the Light of the Kinshasa Litigation' (*University of Liverpool School of Law and Social Justice Blog*, 12 February 2024) <https://www.liverpool.ac.uk/law/blog/reforming-the-eu-facilitators-package/>; Case C 460/23 *Kinsa* [2023] ECLI:EU:C:2023:784. The case was formerly named as 'Kinshasa'.

10 Valsamis Mitsilegas, *EU Criminal Law After Lisbon* (Hart Publishing 2018); Adriano Martufi, 'The Paths of Offender Rehabilitation and the European Dimension of Punishment: New Challenges for an Old Ideal?' (2018) 25 Maastricht Journal of European and Comparative Law 672.

11 The complete title of the Council Framework Decision 2002/946/JHA (n 8) is 'Council Framework Decision of 28 November 2002 on the strengthening of the penal framework to *prevent* the facilitation of unauthorised entry, transit and residence' (emphasis added).

12 Valsamis Mitsilegas, 'The Changing Landscape of the Criminalisation of Migration in Europe: The Protective Function of European Union Law' in Maria Joao Guia, Maartje Van der Woude and Joanne Van der Leun (eds), *Social Control and Justice: Crimmigration in an Age of Fear* (Eleven International Publishing 2013); Maria Chiara Ricci, 'Criminalising Solidarity? Smugglers, Migrants and Rescuers in the Reform of the "Facilitators' Package"' in Valsamis Mitsilegas, Violeta Moreno-Lax and Niovi Vavoula (eds), *Securitising Asylum Flows* (Brill | Nijhoff 2020); Sergio Carrera and others, *Policing Humanitarianism—EU Policies Against Human Smuggling and their Impact on Civil Society* (Hart Publishing 2019).

13 The most prominent example in Italian jurisprudence is given by the "Rackete Judgement": Cass pen, sez III, 16 January 2020 (dep 20 February 2020) 6626/2020. For a critical account on the judgement see Luca Masera, 'Soccorsi in Mare e Diritto Penale Nella Stagione Dei Porti Chiusi. Alcune Riflessioni a Partire Dal Caso Di Carola Rackete' (*La Legislazione Penale*, 22 April 2022) <https://www.lalegislazionepenale.eu/soccorsi-in-mare-e-diritto-penale-nella-stagione-dei-porti-chiusi-alcune-riflessioni-a-partire-dal-caso-di-carola-rackete-luca-masera/>.

14 Luca Masera, 'Il Contrasto Amministrativo Delle ONG Che Operano Soccorsi in Mare, Dal Codice Di Condotta Di Minniti, al Decreto Salvini Bis e Alla Riforma Lamorgese: Le Forme Mutevoli Di Una Politica Costante' (*Questione Giustizia*, 15 June 2021) <https://www.questionegiustizia.it/articolo/nm60c4b77c1d7670-26683604>; Lucia Gennari, 'Navi in Porto, Naufragi Nel Mediterraneo: La Dimensione Amministrativa Del Contrasto Alle Operazioni Di Soccorso' (2021) 21 Diritto e Questioni Pubbliche 83.

15 Amanda Spalding, 'The Treatment of Immigrants in European Court of Human Rights: Moving Beyond Criminalisation' (2024) 26 European Journal of Migration and Law 137.

16 Spalding (n 15); Juliet Stumpf, 'The Crimmigration Crisis: Immigrants, Crime, and Sovereign Power' (2006) 56 American University Law Review 367; Federico Alagna, 'The Continuation of Criminalization by Other Means: The Role of Judicial Agency in the Italian Policing of Humanitarian Assistance at Sea' (2022) 29 Mediterranean Politics 235; Vicky Taylor, 'Evidence from Courtwatching: Documenting the Criminalisation of People Seeking Asylum in the UK' (*Border Criminologies*, 19 June

2023) <https://blogs.law.ox.ac.uk/border-criminologies-blog/blog-post/2023/06/evidence-courtwatching-documenting-criminalisation>.

17 Jakobs Guenther, 'Buergerstrafrecht Und Feindstrafrecht' (*Onlinezeitschrift fuer Hoechstrichterliche Rechtsprechung zum Strafrecht*, 5 March 2004) <https://www.hrr-strafrecht.de/hrr/archiv/04-03/index.php3?sz=6>.

18 Andrew Ashworth and Lucia Zedner, *Preventive Justice* (OUP 2014); Spalding (n 15).

19 Charter of Fundamental Rights of the European Union [2000] OJ C364/1, Article 49: "No one shall be held guilty of any criminal offence on account of any act or omission which did not constitute a criminal offence under national law or international law at the time when it was committed"; Article 7 of the European Convention on Human Rights [1950] mimics the contents of Article 49 of the Charter of Fundamental Rights of the European Union. For a commentary, see Valsamis Mitsilegas and Emmanouil Billis, 'Article 49—Principles of Legality and Proportionality of Criminal Offences and Penalties' in Steve Peers and others (eds), *The EU Charter of Fundamental Rights—a Commentary* (2nd edn, Hart Publishing 2022).

20 Roberta Barberini, 'Il Sequestro Della Iuventa: ONG e Soccorso in Mare' (*Questione Giustizia*, 18 September 2017) <https://www.questionegiustizia.it/articolo/il-sequestro-della-iuventa_ong-e-soccorso-in-mare_18-09-2017.php>.

21 Stefano Zirulia and Giuseppe Martinico, 'Criminalising Migrants and Securitising Borders—the Italian "No Way" Model in the Age of Populism' in Vladislava Stoyanova and Stijn Smet (eds), *Migrants' Rights, Populism and Legal Resilience in Europe* (CUP 2022).

22 Marta Minetti, 'International Legal Principles, Penal Populism and Criminalisation of 'Unwanted Migration'. An Italian Cautionary Tale (2022) 24 International Community Law Review 358; Minetti (n 9).

23 Minetti (n 9).

24 Minetti (n 22).

25 Bojan Bugaric, 'The Two Faces of Populism: Between Authoritarian and Democratic Populism' (2019) 20 German Law Journal 390.

26 Manuel Funke, Moritz Schularick and Cristoph Trebesch, 'Going to Extremes: Politics After Financial Crises, 1870–2014' (2016) 88 European Economic Review 227, 232.

27 Zirulia and Martinico (n 21).

28 Cornelli (n 7).

29 John Pratt, *Penal Populism* (Routledge 2007).

30 Pratt (n 29) 3.

31 David Garland, *The Culture of Control: Crime and Social Order in Contemporary Society* (OUP 2002).

32 David Garland, 'What's Wrong with Penal Populism? Politics, the Public, and Criminological Expertise' (2021) 16 Asian Journal of Criminology 257.

33 The Five Stars Movement defines itself as a "free association of citizens" and refuses the political party definition. Such defiance derives from the rejection to be associated with the Italian political dimension and ruling class, perceived and depicted as corrupted. See Filippo Tronconi, *Beppe Grillo's Five Star Movement* (Routledge 2015).

34 Among Salvini's electoral slogans, one of the most well-known was "Italians first'"["*prima gli Italiani*"].

35 Zirulia and Martinico (n 21).

36 Zirulia and Martinico (n 21).

37 Zirulia and Martinico (n 21) 260.

38 Mark Lowen, 'Giorgia Meloni: Far-Right Leader Poised to Run Italy' *BBC* (26 September 2022) <https://www.bbc.com/news/world-europe-62659183>.

39 Marina Cino Pagliarello and Davide Tedesco, 'What Giorgia Meloni's Policy Agenda Could Mean for Italy and Europe' (*LSE Blog*, 29 September 2022) <https://blogs.lse.ac.uk/europpblog/2022/09/29/what-giorgia-melonis-policy-agenda-could-mean-for-italy-and-europe/>.

40 The creation of a hostile environment goes beyond the mere criminal law-based approaches, but rests on the application of a wider set of legal and policy responses as well as practices employed by the EU and its Member States, which impact negatively—directly or indirectly—the civil society actors' activities.

41 Giuseppe Conte notoriously and repeatedly referred to himself as populist, see Agenzia Vista, 'Conte: "Rivendico Natura Populista Del Governo"' *Il Giornale* (28 December 2018) <https://www.ilgiornale.it/video/politica/conte-rivendico-natura-populista-governo-1622063.html>; Voltaire Network, 'Remarks by Giuseppe Conte to the 73rd Session of the United Nations General Assembly' (*Voltaire Network*, 26 September 2018) <https://www.voltairenet.org/article 203153.html>

42 Paul Taggart and Andrea Pirro, 'European Populism Before the Pandemic: Ideology, Euroscepticism, Electoral Performance, and Government Participation of 63 Parties in 30 Countries' (2021) 51 Italian Political Science Review 281.

43 Christian Lamour and Renáta Varga, 'The Border as a Resource in Right-Wing Populist Discourse: Viktor Orbán and the Diasporas in a Multi-Scalar Europe' (2017) 35 Journal of Borderlands Studies 335.

44 Pola Cebulak and Florian Lippert, 'Shocks to the System. Lessons from Geert Wilders' Victory in the Dutch Elections' (Research Centre for the Study of Democratic Cultures and Politics, KEW Publishing February 2024) <https://research.rug.nl/en/publications/shocks-to-the-system-lessons-from-geert-wilders-victory-in-the-du>.

45 For more information on Meloni's appeals for a naval blockade, see Gisella Ruccia, '"Blocco Navale Subito" "Impedire La Partenza Dei Barconi". "Affondare Le Barche Delle Ong". Così Parlava Giorgia Meloni—Il Videoblob' *Il Fatto Quotidiano* (15 August 2023) <https://www.ilfattoquotidiano.it/2023/08/15/blocco-navale-subito-impedire-la-partenza-dei-barconi-affondare-le-barche-delle-ong-cosi-parlava-giorgia-meloni-il-videoblob/7260612/>. The video at the link below (in Italian) shows Giorgia Meloni addressing the Parliament and receiving praise for refusing the EU proposal of funds destined to Italy to manage irregular migrants. She labels the proposal as aimed at making Italy the "refugee camp of the EU" and refuses the offer, suggesting that those funds be invested in further securing the border to more effectively contrast the phenomenon. See Askanews, 'Ue, Meloni: Mai Soldi per Un'Italia Trasformata in Campo Profughi' *Il Sole 24 Ore* (28 June 2023) <https://stream24.ilsole24ore.com/video/italia/ue-meloni-mai-soldi-un-italia-trasformata-campo-profughi/AEy2jRsD?refresh_ce=1>.

46 Giorgia Meloni and the political party 'Fratelli d'Italia con Giorgia Meloni', 'Programma Elettorale Del Movimento Politico' (Elezioni della Camera dei Deputati e del Senato della Repubblica del 2022, August 2022) 3 <https://dait.interno.gov.it/documenti/trasparenza/POLITICHE_20220925/Documenti/68/(68_progr_2_)-programma.pdf>.

47 Meloni and the political party 'Fratelli d'Italia con Giorgia Meloni' (n 46) 8.

48 Masera (n 14).

49 Zirulia and Martinico (n 21).

50 For two of the founding documents on the role of criminal law and the state, see Cesare Beccaria, *On Crimes and Punishment* (1764 Livorno); Jean-Jacques Rousseau, *The Social Contract* (1762 Amsterdam). For an analysis of the role of the state in the guarantee of security and the role of criminal law, see Lucia Zedner

and Andrew Ashworth, 'The Rise and Restraint of the Preventive State' (2019) 2 Annual Review of Criminology 429.

51 Ashworth and Zedner (n 18).

52 Serious Crime Act 2007.

53 Zedner and Ashworth (n 50); Andrew Ashworth and Lucia Zedner, 'Preventive Orders: A Problem of Undercriminalization?' in Antony Duff and others (eds), *The Boundaries of Criminal Law* (OUP 2010).

54 Terrorism Act 2006.

55 Ashworth and Zedner (n 18).

56 Zedner and Ashworth (n 50).

57 Audrey Macklin, 'Borderline Security' in Audrey Macklin (ed), *The Security of Freedom: Essays on Canada's Anti-Terrorism Bill* (University of Toronto Press 2001).

58 Mary Bosworth, 'Border Control and the Limits of the Sovereign State' (2008) 17 Social and Legal Studies 199, 201.

59 Zedner and Ashworth (n 50).

60 For a comprehensive examination and analysis of the privacy and Rule of Law challenges raised by some of these systems see Niovi Vavoula, *Immigration and Privacy in the Law of the European Union* (Brill | Nijhoff 2022).

61 Violeta Moreno-Lax and Martin Lemberg-Pedersen, 'Border-Induced Displacement: The Ethical and Legal Implications of Distance-Creation Through Externalization' (2019) 56 Questions of International Law 5; Violeta Moreno-Lax, 'The Architecture of Functional Jurisdiction: Unpacking Contactless Control—on Public Powers, S.S. and Others v Italy, and the "Operational Model"' (2020) 21 German Law Journal 385; Masera (n 14).

62 Valsamis Mitsilegas, 'The EU External Border as a Site of Preventive (in)Justice' (2022) 28 European Law Journal 263.

63 Douglas Husak, *Overcriminalization: The Limits of the Criminal Law* (OUP 2007).

64 Ashworth and Zedner (n 53); Spalding (n 15).

65 Husak (n 63).

66 Beccaria (n 50). For a beautiful reading of Beccaria's work see Philippe Audegean, 'Dei Delitti e Delle Pene Di Cesare Beccaria' (16 September 2022) <https://www.youtube.com/watch?v=Q0W6PPBIynU>; and Bernard Harcourt, 'Beccaria's "On Crimes and Punishments": A Mirror on the History of the Foundations of Modern Criminal Law' in Markus Dubber (ed), *Foundational Texts in Modern Criminal Law* (OUP 2014).

67 Harcourt (n 66); European Commission for Democracy Through Law, *Rule of Law Checklist* (Study 711/2013, 106th Plenary Session of the Venice Commission 18 March 2016) <https://www.venice.coe.int/webforms/documents/default.aspx?pdffile=CDL-AD(2016)007-e>.

68 Ashworth and Zedner (n 53); Spalding (n 15).

69 David Ormerod and John Child, 'General Inchoare Offences' in David Ormerod and John Child (eds), *Smith, Hogan and Ormerod's Essentials of Criminal Law* (5th edn, OUP 2023); Jeremy Horder, 'Criminal Attempt, the Rule of Law, and Accountability in Criminal Law' in Lucia Zedner and Julian Roberts (eds), *Principles and Values in Criminal Law and Criminal Justice: Essays in Honour of Andrew Ashworth* (OUP 2012); Jonathan Herring, 'Inchoate Offences', *Criminal Law: Text, Cases, and Materials* (10th edn, OUP 2022).

70 Macklin (n 57) 384.

71 Tom Bingham, *The Rule of Law* (Penguin 2011); Jeremy Waldron, 'The Concept and the Rule of Law' (2008) 43 Georgia Law Review 1.

72 Garland (n 31).

73 Francesca Cancellaro and From the Sea to Prison Project, 'Summary of the Request of Admission to the Italian Constitutional Court in Relation to the Case against the Crew of the *Iuventa*' (European Centre for Constitutional and Human Rights May 2023) <https://www.ecchr.eu/fileadmin/user_upload/IUVENTA_Summary_of_Constitutional_Complaint.pdf>.
74 Minetti (n 22); European Commission for Democracy Through Law (n 67).
75 Minetti (n 9); Mitsilegas (n 9).
76 Émile Durkheim, 'The Division of Labour in Society' in Steven Lukes (ed), *Durkheim: The Division of Labour in Society* (2nd edn, Bloomsbury Academic 2013).
77 Durkheim (n 76).
78 Thomas Elholm and Renaud Colson, 'The Symbolic Purpose of EU Criminal Law' in Renaud Colson and Stewart Field (eds), *EU Criminal Justice and the Challenges of Diversity: Legal Cultures in the Area of Freedom, Security and Justice* (CUP 2016).
79 Minetti (n 9).
80 See among others, the now repealed so-called "Security Decree bis" or Decreto-Legge "Disposizioni Urgenti in Materia di Ordine e Sicurezza Pubblica" 14 June 2019, No 53.
81 Examples of dismissal of legal procedures against the NGOs are numerous. Among the most prominent examples is that of the case of Open Arms, whose vessel was seized and subsequently released thrice, and the allegation of facilitation of illegal entry was dismissed in November 2020. Similarly, in the Sea Watch 3 case, the vessel was seized and released thrice; the criminal investigations were discontinued and the charges dismissed. For more information, see European Union Agency for Fundamental Rights, 'June 2023 Update—Search and Rescue Operations in the Mediterranean and Fundamental Rights' (October 2023) <https://fra.europa.eu/en/publication/2023/2023-update-ngo-ships-sar-activities>.
82 Elholm and Colson (n 78); Pratt (n 29).
83 Paul Robinson and John Darley, 'The Role of Deterrence in the Formulation of Criminal Law Rules: At its Worst When Doing its Best' (2003) 91 The Georgetown Law Journal 949.
84 Robinson and Darley (n 83).
85 Robinson and Darley (n 83).
86 George Borjas, 'The Economic Benefits from Immigration' (1995) 9 Journal of Economic Perspectives 3; Munz Rainer and others, 'The Costs and Benefits of European Immigration' HWWI Policy Report 3 (Hamburg Institute of International Economics 2006) <https://hdl.handle.net/10419/46220>.
87 Ana Aliverti, 'Making People Criminal: The Role of the Criminal Law in Immigration Enforcement' (2012) 16 Theoretical Criminology 417; Minetti (n 9).
88 Minetti (n 9); Alagna (n 16); Eugenio Cusumano and Matteo Villa, 'From "Angels" to "Vice Smugglers": The Criminalization of Sea Rescue NGOs in Italy' (2021) 27 European Journal on Criminal Policy and Research 23.
89 Carla Ferstman, 'Using Criminal Law to Restrict the Work of NGOs Supporting Refugees and Other Migrants in Council of Europe Member States' (Thematic Study prepared on behalf of the Expert Council on NGO Law, Conference of INGOs of the Council of Europe December 2019) <https://rm.coe.int/expert-council-conf-exp-2019-1-criminal-law-ngo-restrictions-migration/1680996969>.
90 Sue Clayton, *The Standsted 15: On Trial* (Eastwest Pictures 2019) <https://www.imdb.com/title/tt12771066/>; Damien Gayle, 'Stansted 15: No Jail for Activists Convicted of Terror-Related Offences' *The Guardian* (6 February 2019) <https://www.theguardian.com/global/2019/feb/06/stansted-15-rights-campaigners-urge-judge-to-show-leniency?share=email>.

91 Valsamis Mitsilegas, 'Contested Sovereignty in Preventive Border Control: Civil Society, the "Hostile Environment", and the Rule of Law' in Mary Bosworth and Lucia Zedner (eds), *Privatising Border Control: Law at the Limits of the Sovereign State* (OUP 2022).
92 Cusumano and Villa (n 88); International Organization for Migration (n 2).
93 Mitsilegas (n 62).
94 Decreto-Legge "*Disposizioni Urgenti in Materia di Protezione Internazionale e Immigrazione, Sicurezza Pubblica, nonché misure per la funzionalità del Ministero dell'Interno e l'Organizzazione e il funzionamento dell'agenzia nazionale per l'amministrazione e la destinazione dei beni sequestrati e confiscati alla criminalità organizzata*". (4 October 2018, n 113)
95 These permits were granted to those not eligible for international protection but whose return to the country of origin would have constituted a breach of constitutional and international obligations.
96 Vianelli (n 4).
97 Yara Nardi, 'Italy's Lampedusa Pleads for Help After Thousands of Migrant Arrivals' *Reuters* (14 September 2023) <https://www.reuters.com/world/europe/italys-lampedusa-at-point-no-return-with-migrants-mayor-says-2023-09-14/>.
98 Luigi Ferrajoli, 'Il Populismo Penale Nell'Età Dei Populismi Politici' (*Questione Giustizia*, 6 March 2019) <https://www.questionegiustizia.it/rivista/articolo/il-populismo-penale-nell-eta-dei-populismi-politici_627.php>; Minetti (n 9).
99 Luigi Ferrajoli, 'The New Populism Is Responsible for the Massacres in the Mediterranean' (*Verfassungsblog*, 13 March 2023) <https://verfassungsblog.de/the-new-populism-is-responsible-for-the-massacres-in-the-mediterranean/>.
100 Nadia Urbinati, 'The Populist Phenomenon' (2013) 51 Raisons Politiques 137; Nicola Lacey, 'Populism and the Rule of Law' (2019) 15 Annual Review of Law and Social Science 79; Muller (n 6).
101 Luigi Ferrajoli, 'Democrazia e Populismo' (2018) 3 Rivista Associazione Italiana dei Costituzionalisti 515 <https://www.rivistaaic.it/it/rivista/ultimi-contributi-pubblicati/luigi-ferrajoli/democrazia-e-populismo>.
102 Garland (n 31) 271.
103 Luigi Ferrajoli, 'Prove Giudiziarie' (15 September 2018) <https://www.youtube.com/watch?v=_wwqIzU6jT4>.
104 Declaration of Human and Civil Rights 1789, article 16.
105 Robinson and Darley (n 83).
106 Robinson and Darley (n 83).
107 Ferrajoli (n 99).

Bibliography

Alagna F, 'The Continuation of Criminalization by Other Means: The Role of Judicial Agency in the Italian Policing of Humanitarian Assistance at Sea' (2022) 29 Mediterranean Politics 235.

Aliverti A, 'Making People Criminal: The Role of the Criminal Law in Immigration Enforcement' (2012) 16 Theoretical Criminology 417.

Ashworth A and Zedner L, 'Preventive Orders: A Problem of Undercriminalization?' in Duff A and others (eds), *The Boundaries of Criminal Law* (OUP 2010).

Ashworth A and Zedner L, *Preventive Justice* (OUP 2014).

Beccaria C, *On Crimes and Punishment* (1764 Livorno).

Bingham T, *The Rule of Law* (Penguin 2011).

Borjas G, 'The Economic Benefits from Immigration' (1995) 9 Journal of Economic Perspectives 3.

Bosworth M, 'Border Control and the Limits of the Sovereign State' (2008) 17 Social and Legal Studies 199.

Bugaric B, 'The Two Faces of Populism: Between Authoritarian and Democratic Populism' (2019) 20 German Law Journal 390.
Carrera S and others, *Policing Humanitarianism: EU Policies Against Human Smuggling and Their Impact on Civil Society* (Hart 2019).
Cebulak P and Lippert F, *Shocks to the System. Lessons from Geert Wilders' Victory in the Dutch Elections* (KEW Publishing 2024).
Cornelli R, 'Contro Il Panpopulismo: Una Proposta Di Definizione Del Populismo Penale' (2019) 4 Diritto Penale Contemporaneo—Rivista Trimestrale 128.
Cusumano E and Villa M, 'From "Angels" to "Vice Smugglers": The Criminalization of Sea Rescue NGOs in Italy' (2021) 27 European Journal on Criminal Policy and Research 23.
Durkheim É, 'The Division of Labour in Society' in Lukes S (ed), *Durkheim: The Division of Labour in Society* (2nd edn, Bloomsbury Academic 2013).
Elholm T and Colson R, 'The Symbolic Purpose of EU Criminal Law' in Colson R and Field S (eds), *EU Criminal Justice and the Challenges of Diversity: Legal Cultures in the Area of Freedom, Security and Justice* (CUP 2016).
Funke M, Schularick M and Trebesch C, 'Going to Extremes: Politics After Financial Crises, 1870–2014' (2016) 88 European Economic Review 227.
Garland D, *The Culture of Control: Crime and Social Order in Contemporary Society* (OUP 2002).
Garland D, 'What's Wrong with Penal Populism? Politics, the Public, and Criminological Expertise' (2021) 16 Asian Journal of Criminology 257.
Gennari L, 'Navi in Porto, Naufragi Nel Mediterraneo: La Dimensione Amministrativa Del Contrasto Alle Operazioni Di Soccorso' (2021) 21 Diritto e Questioni Pubbliche 83.
Harcourt B, 'Beccaria's "On Crimes and Punishments": A Mirror on the History of the Foundations of Modern Criminal Law' in Dubber M (ed), *Foundational Texts in Modern Criminal Law* (OUP 2014).
Herring J, 'Inchoate Offences' in Herring J (ed), *Criminal Law: Text, Cases, and Materials* (10th edn, OUP 2022).
Horder J, 'Criminal Attempt, the Rule of Law, and Accountability in Criminal Law' in Zedner L and Roberts J (eds), *Principles and Values in Criminal Law and Criminal Justice: Essays in Honour of Andrew Ashworth* (OUP 2012).
Husak D, *Overcriminalization: The Limits of the Criminal Law* (OUP 2007).
Lamour C and Varga R, 'The Border as a Resource in Right-Wing Populist Discourse: Viktor Orbán and the Diasporas in a Multi-Scalar Europe' (2017) 35 Journal of Borderlands Studies 335.
Macklin A, 'Borderline Security' in Macklin A (ed), *The Security of Freedom: Essays on Canada's Anti-Terrorism Bill* (University of Toronto Press 2001).
Martufi A, 'The Paths of Offender Rehabilitation and the European Dimension of Punishment: New Challenges for an Old Ideal?' (2018) 25 Maastricht Journal of European and Comparative Law 672.
Minetti M, 'The Facilitators Package, Penal Populism and the Rule of Law: Lessons from Italy' (2020) 11 New Journal of European Criminal Law 335.
Minetti M, 'International Legal Principles, Penal Populism and Criminalisation of "Unwanted Migration". An Italian Cautionary Tale' (2022) 24 International Community Law Review 358.
Mitsilegas V, 'The Changing Landscape of the Criminalisation of Migration in Europe: The Protective Function of European Union Law' in Guia MJ, Van der Woude M and Van der Leun J (eds), *Social Control and Justice: Crimmigration in an Age of Fear* (Eleven International Publishing 2013).
Mitsilegas V, *EU Criminal Law After Lisbon* (Hart Publishing 2018).
Mitsilegas V, 'The Normative Foundations of the Criminalization of Human Smuggling: Exploring the Fault Lines Between European and International Law' (2019) 10 New Journal of European Criminal Law 68.

Mitsilegas V, 'Contested Sovereignty in Preventive Border Control: Civil Society, the "Hostile Environment", and the Rule of Law' in Bosworth M and Zedner L (eds), *Privatising Border Control: Law at the Limits of the Sovereign State* (OUP 2022).
Mitsilegas V, 'The EU External Border as a Site of Preventive (in)Justice' (2022) 28 European Law Journal 263.
Mitsilegas V and Billis E, 'Article 49—Principles of Legality and Proportionality of Criminal Offences and Penalties' in Peers S and others (eds), *The EU Charter of Fundamental Rights—a Commentary* (2nd edn, Hart 2022).
Moreno-Lax V, 'The Architecture of Functional Jurisdiction: Unpacking Contactless Control—On Public Powers, S.S. and Others v. Italy, and the "Operational Model"' (2020) 21 German Law Journal 385.
Moreno-Lax V and Lemberg-Pedersen M, 'Border-Induced Displacement: The Ethical and Legal Implications of Distance-Creation Through Externalization' (2019) 56 Questions of International Law 5.
Moreno-Lax V and others, 'The EU Approach on Migration in the Mediterranean' (Study Requested by the LIBE Committee, European Parliament 2021).
Muller J, *What Is Populism* (University of Pennsylvania Press 2017).
Munz R and others, *The Costs and Benefits of European Immigration* (Hamburg Institute of International Economics 2006).
Ormerod D and Child J, 'General Inchoare Offences' in Ormerod D and Child J (eds), *Smith, Hogan and Ormerod's Essentials of Criminal Law* (5th edn, OUP 2023).
Pratt J, *Penal Populism* (Routledge 2007).
Reviglio M, 'Externalizing Migration Management through Soft Law: The Case of the Memorandum of Understanding Between Libya and Italy' (2019) 20 Global Jurist 1.
Ricci MC, 'Criminalising Solidarity? Smugglers, Migrants and Rescuers in the Reform of the "Facilitators' Package"' in Mitsilegas V, Moreno-Lax V and Vavoula N (eds), *Securitising Asylum Flows* (Brill | Nijhoff 2020).
Robinson P and Darley J, 'The Role of Deterrence in the Formulation of Criminal Law Rules: At its Worst When Doing its Best' (2003) 91 The Georgetown Law Journal 949.
Rousseau J, *The Social Contract* (Amsterdam 1762).
Spalding A, 'The Treatment of Immigrants in European Court of Human Rights: Moving Beyond Criminalisation' (2024) 26 European Journal of Migration and Law 137.
Stumpf J, 'The Crimmigration Crisis: Immigrants, Crime, and Sovereign Power' (2006) 56 American University Law Review 367.
Taggart P and Pirro A, 'European Populism Before the Pandemic: Ideology, Euroscepticism, Electoral Performance, and Government Participation of 63 Parties in 30 Countries' (2021) 51 Italian Political Science Review 281.
Tronconi F, *Beppe Grillo's Five Star Movement* (Routledge 2015).
Vavoula N, *Immigration and Privacy in the Law of the European Union* (Brill | Nijhoff 2022).
Waldron J, 'The Concept and the Rule of Law' (2008) 43 Georgia Law Review 1.
Zedner L and Ashworth A, 'The Rise and Restraint of the Preventive State' (2019) 2 Annual Review of Criminology 429.
Zirulia S, 'Non c'é Smuggling Senza Ingiusto Profitto: Profili Di Illegittimitá Nella Normativa Italiana Ed Europea in Materia Di Favoreggiamento Irregolare' (2020) 3 Diritto Penale Contemporaneo—Rivista Trimestrale 143.
Zirulia S and Martinico G, 'Criminalising Migrants and Securitising Borders—the Italian "No Way" Model in the Age of Populism' in Stoyanova V and Smet S (eds), *Migrants' Rights, Populism and Legal Resilience in Europe* (CUP 2022).

10 The Criminalisation of Migration as Preventive (In)Justice

Valsamis Mitsilegas

10.1 Introduction

The past three decades have witnessed the growing use of criminal law for immigration control purposes, leading thus to the normalisation of the use of criminal law to regulate what essentially an administrative process. Criminalisation in this context blurs the boundaries between administrative and criminal law, and resorts to the disproportionate use of criminal law to fulfil administrative objectives. It is based on the creation of criminal offences which are too broad, built on shaky normative foundations, and whose justification is unclear from the perspective of the harm principle—raising the prospect of over-criminalisation. Such (over)criminalisation is inextricably linked with the dominance of a preventive agenda in immigration control, viewing migrants as unwanted or dangerous.[1] This preventive agenda reflects developments analysed from the theoretical framework of "preventive justice": The term has been used in the domestic context to refer to a phenomenon extending the scope of criminal law to gradually remove the link between criminalisation and prosecution on the one hand and the commission of concrete acts on the other.[2]

For the purpose of this contribution, the concept of preventive justice will be applied at the level of EU law. It is understood more broadly as the exercise of state power in order to prevent future acts which are deemed to constitute security threats.[3] The preventive justice paradigm is thus forward-rather than backward-looking; it is justified by states and EU institutions as aiming at preventing potential threats rather than punishing past acts; and in this manner, it introduces a system of control based on the creation of suspects or undesirable individuals on the basis of ongoing risk assessment.[4] While in the field of criminal law the preventive justice paradigm focuses primarily on the pre-emption of the commission of future criminal offences, in the field of immigration law the paradigm aims at preventing access of migrants to the territorial borders of states, and the external border of the European Union, and ultimately preventing access to law.[5] In closing this volume, this contribution will track the application of this paradigm of preventive justice, or rather preventive injustice, in the field of immigration control, by focusing

DOI: 10.4324/9781003378440-10

on three instances of criminalisation: The criminalisation of the facilitation of entry; the facilitation of entry as such; and the growing use of detention as a means of preventive criminalisation.

10.2 Criminalising the Facilitation of Entry

EU law has introduced a broad criminalisation of the facilitation of unauthorised entry. The relevant EU legal framework is set out by the Facilitators' Package, consisting of a (then) first-pillar Directive on the facilitation of unauthorised entry, transit, and residence,[6] accompanied by a (then) third-pillar Framework Decision on the strengthening of the penal framework to prevent the facilitation of unauthorised entry, transit, and residence, confirming that the conduct defined as facilitation in the Directive will be treated as a criminal offence by EU Member States.[7] Both instruments of what is rather old law by EU standards predate by far the entry into force of the Lisbon Treaty and, having being proposed not by the Commission but by a Member State (the French Government), were negotiated and adopted with minimal scrutiny and debate.[8]

The criminalisation of facilitation in EU law is very broad. Criminal sanctions will be imposed on any person who intentionally assists a person who is not a national of a Member State to enter, or transit across, the territory of a Member State in breach of the laws of the state concerned on the entry or transit of aliens.[9] The Facilitators' Package thus goes further than the relevant international law in the field. Unlike the Smuggling Protocol of the UN Palermo Convention,[10] EU law dispenses with the condition of obtaining a financial or other material benefit for the facilitation offence to be established.[11] The Directive does attempt to address this issue by granting Member States the discretion not to impose sanctions for facilitation and instead apply their national law and practice for cases where the aim of the behaviour is to provide humanitarian assistance to the person concerned.[12] However, this provision is discretionary, and its value in redressing the imbalance set out by the broad definition and criminalisation of facilitation under EU law is questionable. According to a 2017 Commission Report, only seven Member States specifically include in domestic law an exemption from punishment for facilitation for humanitarian assistance.[13]

It is clear from the above that the scope of criminalisation at the EU level is very broad, as it can cover any form of assistance to enter or transit the territory of an EU Member State in breach of what is essentially administrative law (such as cases where the migrant is traveling without travel documents). The preventive objective of this approach is evident: The key objective of EU law is not to fight organised crime (as per the aim of international law), but to prevent entry into EU territory, as it targets not only the smugglers but also the smuggled.[14] Spena makes an insightful point in legal semiotics by drawing our attention to the terminological differences between international law, which defines smuggling as procuring irregular entry, and EU law, which focuses on assistance. Spena notes that "while assisting denotes an ancillary action, which entails that the principal action is performed by the person who is assisted, "procuring" denotes instead a stand-alone action, with a meaning of its own".[15]

The over-criminalisation of facilitation of entry in EU law on the basis of a preventive paradigm has allowed Member States to use domestic criminal law to prosecute a wide range of elements of assistance to migrants, which are not motivated by, and do not involve, any financial benefit. Facilitation offences have been used to prosecute NGOs who are addressing state inaction in saving lives at sea,[16] as part of a broader strategy of generating a hostile environment targeting civil society.[17]

In addition to targeting of civil society, the over-criminalisation of the facilitation of unauthorised entry has further led to the prosecution of citizens assisting migrants.[18] It has also resulted in the prosecution of migrants for assisting other migrants,[19] a practice which is contrary to international law and which is currently subject to litigation before the Court of Justice of the European Union (CJEU).[20] Moreover, the criminalisation of facilitation has been combined with prosecution under different offences, such as organised crime,[21] and by the use of preventive measures such as boat seizures and entry bans, imposed on legally questionable grounds of organised crime and illegal waste disposal. These prosecutions place NGOs on the defensive and have a direct negative impact on rescue operations by suspending the work of NGOs or putting a stop to it altogether,[22] with the dismantling of humanitarian NGOs constituting the ultimate preventive tool employed by the states.[23]

In spite of the concerns raised regarding the over-criminalisation of facilitation in EU law and its negative impact on humanitarian assistance, the Commission initially appeared reluctant to revise the outdated pre-Lisbon EU legislative framework in the field. In an evaluation conducted in 2017, the Commission declined to take up the opportunity to reform the Facilitators' Package. The evaluation defended resolutely the status quo.[24] The Commission stated that "there is no sufficient evidence to draw firm conclusions about the need for a revision of the Facilitators' Package at this point in time".[25] The Commission changed its approach more recently. It tabled, in November 2023, a new Directive[26] aimed at replacing the Facilitators' Package.[27] The Directive introduces the following criminal offences:

- intentionally assisting a third-country national to enter, transit across, or stay within the territory of any Member State in breach of relevant Union law or the laws of the Member State concerned on the entry, transit and stay of third-country nationals where the person who carries out the conduct requests, receives or accepts, directly or indirectly, a financial or material benefit, or a promise thereof, or carries out the conduct in order to obtain such a benefit;[28]

- intentionally assisting a third-country national to enter, or transit across, or stay within the territory of any Member State in breach of relevant Union law or the laws of the Member State concerned on the entry, transit and stay of third-country nationals where there is a high likelihood of causing serious harm to a person;[29]
- publicly instigating third-country nationals to enter, transit across, or stay within the territory of any Member State in breach of relevant Union law or the laws of the Member State concerned on the entry, transit and stay of third-country nationals.[30]

The preventive aims of the proposal are clear throughout the text. The very title of the proposal refers to the prevention of facilitation, while the Preamble states that preventing and countering facilitation offences remain a priority for the Union.[31] Preventive aims are also used to justify the extension of criminalisation beyond the existence of a link with an actual or promised financial or material benefit—according to the Preamble, it is necessary to establish a criminal offence in order to discourage the *modus operandi* of persons who publicly instigate, for instance, through the internet, third-country nationals to enter, transit, or stay in the Union without authorisation.[32] Third-country nationals who have committed facilitation offences should also be subject to entry bans.[33]

The proposed Directive does little to address current concerns regarding the over-criminalisation of the facilitation of entry in EU law.[34] Criminal law continues to be used to address what could be dealt with under administrative law, and criminalisation is framed from a perspective of breach of regulations: Facilitation is defined as intentionally assisting a third-country national to enter, or transit across, or stay within the territory of any Member State *in breach of relevant Union law or the laws of the Member State concerned.* The scope of the Directive is broader than international law, in continuing to disassociate between facilitation from organised crime—as the new Directive criminalises not only facilitation for financial gain, but also facilitation where there is a high likelihood of causing serious harm to a person. In spite of claims of addressing the criminalisation of humanitarianism, it is notable that the Commission proposal does not include an express, unequivocal humanitarian exception to the criminalisation of the facilitation of unauthorised entry in the operative part of the text.[35]

The criminalisation of facilitation, where there is a high likelihood of causing serious harm to a person, risks maintaining the current paradigm of over-criminalisation and perpetuating the hostile environment against those who assist migrants, in particular through search and rescue (SAR) operations. Moreover, the definition of facilitation where there is a high likelihood of causing serious harm to a person does not meet the requirement of legal certainty; it is not clear how Member States will implement this provision, which, in essence, may serve to perpetuate the criminalisation of humanitarianism resulting from the current Facilitators' Package.

The potential introduction of the offence of the criminalisation of facilitation where there is a high likelihood of causing serious harm to a person to exacerbate the hostile environment against humanitarian assistance is also clear from the high level of penalties envisaged for this offence, including attempts to commit it—both are punishable by a maximum term of imprisonment of at least 15 years.[36] Finally, mitigating circumstances are strictly limited to cooperation with state authorities, maintaining thus a securitised emphasis on criminalisation and disregarding humanitarian motives.

Litigation before the CJEU presented a first-class opportunity to reform EU criminal law on facilitation of entry. This is the result of a reference for a preliminary ruling to the CJEU by the Tribunale di Bologna in Italy. In the *Kinshasa* reference[37] (now renamed as *Kinsa*), lodged on 21 July 2023, the referring court has asked the CJEU whether the criminalisation of the facilitation of unauthorised entry in EU law and in national law, even where the conduct is carried out on a non-profit-making basis, without providing, at the same time, an obligation on Member States to exclude from criminalisation conduct facilitating unauthorised entry aimed at providing humanitarian assistance is compatible with the Charter. The facts in *Kinsa* lay bare the shaky normative foundations and adverse effects of over-criminalisation of facilitation of unauthorised entry in EU and Italian law.[38] They involve the prosecution of a Congolese woman arriving at the air border of Bologna for the facilitation of the unauthorised entry of her minor daughter and niece.[39]

The reference has already been a game changer in EU law, leading arguably to the change of stance by the Commission and its decision to table new legislation on facilitation.[40] The court would have the opportunity to examine the compatibility of the Facilitators' Package with EU law, in particular with the Charter. It was a first-class opportunity for the court to reflect on the current paradigm of preventive over-criminalisation, and to assess this from the perspective of EU constitutional law, including the principle of legality (including achieving legal certainty and foreseeability in criminal law), the principle of effectiveness (focusing on the effective functioning of the EU asylum system based on ensuring effective access to asylum), and taking into account international law (aligning the EU criminalisation objectives with those of the Palermo Convention and interpreting EU law in conformity with international refugee law and international law of the seas, in particular SAR obligations).[41]

The Court eventually delivered its ruling on *Kinsa* on 3 June 2025.[42] The Court held, sitting in Grand Chamber, that Article 1(1)(a) of Directive 2002/90, read in the light of Articles 7 and 24 and Article 52(1) of the Charter, must be interpreted as meaning that, first, the conduct of a person who, in breach of the rules governing the movement of persons across borders, brings into the territory of a Member State minors who are third-country nationals and are accompanying him or her, and over whom he or she exercises actual care, does not fall within the scope of the general offence of facilitation of unauthorised entry, and, second, those articles preclude national legislation criminalising such conduct.[43] The Court based its reasoning not only on the basis of Articles 7 and 24 and Article 52(1) of the Charter, but also on Article 18 of the Charter on the right to asylum and on the requirement to interpret EU law in the light of international law, including both international refugee law and the Palermo Convention on transnational organised crime.

Kinsa will generate much discussion. For those who view the glass as half empty, the Court's ruling in *Kinsa* is a missed opportunity to examine the compatibility of the criminalisation of humanitarian assistance with fundamental rights. The narrow focus of the Court to the facts of the case perpetuates legal uncertainty regarding the position of those providing humanitarian assistance to migrants, including civil society organisations subject to a sustained establishment of a hostile environment, and means that the impact of the ruling on the current negotiations of a new Directive on facilitation may be more limited than hoped for. On the other hand, those who view the glass as half full, will hail Kinsa as a significant step forward: the Court relied expressly on an array of fundamental rights and Article 52(1) of the Charter to interpret EU criminal law on facilitation, leading to a degree of decriminalisation at EU and at national level. In addition to family life and the rights of children, the Court examined specifically the impact of criminalisation on the right to asylum, in a significant finding that irregular entry leading to the submission of an asylum application, and until the issuance of a first instance decision, is not to be treated as a criminal offence. This finding, along with the Court's express reliance on international law not only in terms of refugee law, but also in terms of the Palermo Convention,[44] can open the door towards the decriminalisation of humanitarian assistance, if the latter is linked to enabling the exercise of the right to asylum.

10.3 Criminalising Entry

A further instance of over-criminalisation in the field of immigration control involves the criminalisation of entry. Irregular entry and stay are not criminalised as such in international or in EU law.[45] Yet, they are treated as criminal offences in the legal systems of a number of EU Member States.[46] The criminalisation of irregular migration along these lines has been characterised as "precautionary criminalisation", with irregular entry viewed as a wrong of a public kind (*malum in se*).[47] The use of criminal law in this manner is, however, problematic. It is unclear what criminal law is designed to achieve, where the harm in the criminalised conduct lies, and what the legal interest to be protected consists of.[48] Prevention is key in the criminalisation of irregular entry and stay, with criminal offences being designed in order to prevent the presence of undesirable individuals within the territory of the state. Criminal law is used here in addition to administrative immigration law, although the arrangements of the latter would suffice to legally regulate migration flows.

Spena highlights in this context the stigmatisation of migrants by criminal law, which moves from targeting unlawful conduct to targeting undesirable individuals in a logic of pre-emption, where "crimes should be averted by directly selecting and picking out those persons who, because of their matching a given actor stereotype (*Tätertyp*), can be assumed/presumed to be dangerous, deviant, disloyal, and so on".[49] Instead of addressing a concrete harm which has been committed, criminal law is used here to prevent, and to send a strong symbolic message against specific categories of individuals and their undesirable conduct. In this manner, the concept of harm is stretched beyond its limits: Criminal law is being used to punish conduct that can be regulated by administrative law, and thus becomes symbolic criminal law in sending a signal on the undesirability and dangerousness of the migrant. As Aliverti has eloquently noted:

> [W]e should resist that expansive conception of harm, which runs the risk of turning it in a meaningless principle because the conducts that can be criminalised under it are too far removed from the causation of actual harm . . . that diluted version of the harm principle can espouse, buttress and legitimise bigoted and prejudiced interests and demands for criminalisation that are motivated by genuine or fabricated social anxieties and fears about suspicious other . . . embracing of subjective security.[50]

Limits to the criminalisation of entry have been set out by the CJEU, highlighting the protective function of EU law in this context.[51] In its key rulings in *El Dridi*[52] and *Achughbabian*,[53] the CJEU has limited national criminalisation of irregular entry and stay on the grounds of upholding effectiveness and proportionality in EU law. In setting limits to the blanket criminalisation of irregular entry and stay by EU Member States, the CJEU highlighted the protective function of EU law, all the more remarkable because protection against criminalisation has emerged from an EU Directive focusing primarily on enforcement.[54] The CJEU has not been as protective to migrants in cases of re-entry, of the criminalisation by Member States of breaches of entry bans—setting up an artificial distinction between first entry and re-entry.[55] Entry bans are intended to supplement a return order by prohibiting the person concerned, for a specified period of time following his return, thus after leaving the territory of the Member States, from again entering or staying in that territory.[56]

The difference in the CJEU approach between the criminalisation of entry and the re-entry is questionable and highlights the willingness of the court to assign a greater moral culpability to migrants who have defied the system of immigration enforcement that the EU and Member States have put in place, although the distinctiveness in the interests protected by national law criminalising re-entry or the harm in re-entry is difficult to pin down unless re-entry is viewed as an additional affront to state sovereignty as translated into its capacity to guard the border effectively.[57] However, the effectiveness and proportionality standards set out by the court in *El Dridi* and *Achughbabian* constitute good law and limit the criminalisation of entry at the national level.

10.4 Detention as Criminalisation

A further element of criminalisation in immigration control is immigration detention. The criminalisation of migration through immigration detention is based on a strong preventive rationale, underpinned by the view of the migrant as a risk. As Campesi has noted, immigration detention is an inherently punitive measure having a powerful stigmatising effect, strengthening the public perception that irregular migration is tied to crime and disorder, and depends on the characterisation of migrants not just as unwanted outsiders but also as potentially dangerous subjects.[58] Campesi adds eloquently that

> immigration detention that can be related to the symbolic dimension of penalties . . . clearly belongs to the family of preventive measures, given that in its implementation it follows the logic of a control model in which the exercise of coercive powers is not justified on account of "individual responsibility" and "culpability", but rather is based on the construction of abstract typologies of "dangerous individuals" identified as presenting risks to society . . . according to this argument, migrants placed in detention are never considered to be full legal subjects but are taken into custody precisely because they are deemed irresponsible and untrustworthy.[59]

This preventive character of immigration detention based on the perception of the migrant as a risk is reflected in EU immigration and asylum law, which contains a number of provisions allowing immigration detention in the territory.[60] A key justification for detention is the perception that migrants present a "risk of absconding"—with the criminal law undertones of such terminology noted by authors.[61] An express example of detention as criminalisation consists of Member States detaining migrants under the Return Directive not in immigration detention centres, but in prisons. The Court of Justice initially resisted such blurring of boundaries in detention,[62] but worryingly reverted its case law more recently. In a marked U-turn from earlier case law, the CJEU interpreted Article 16 para 1 of Directive 2008/115 as not precluding national legislation which allows an illegally staying third-country national to be detained in prison accommodation for the purpose of removal, separated from ordinary prisoners, on the ground that they pose a genuine, present, and sufficiently serious threat affecting one of the fundamental interests of society or the internal or external security of the Member State concerned.[63] The court required an individualised assessment of threat, but this requirement cannot mask the acceptance of the logic of risk assessment by the state of a third-country national who is not subject to a criminal conviction but is imprisoned on grounds of their "dangerousness". In this way, the severity of criminal punishment is introduced directly in what is essentially an administrative process. This approach is also contrary to the court's approach in *El Dridi*, where the court limited the use of criminal law, emphasising the effectiveness of the administrative return procedure.

Further concerns regarding the overuse of detention arise in the context of the normalisation of detention in asylum procedures, following the adoption of the EU Migration Pact.[64] Legality concerns arise in terms of the imposition of detention as a rule, and not as an exception; the imposition of detention for long periods of time and on a wide range of grounds, many of which focus on dangerousness; and the deterioration of detention conditions, with a normalisation of the "hotspots" approach at the border, which renders detention conditions akin to imprisonment.[65]

10.5 Rethinking the Criminal Law of Migration

In a volume that highlights the interconnections between criminal law and immigration control, the present contribution aims to constitute a double reminder: A reminder of the fact that the use of criminal law for the purposes of immigration control is largely unjustified and disproportionate; and a reminder that the (over)criminalisation of migration is based on a preventive agenda, consisting of efforts by states and EU institutions and agencies to prevent migrants from accessing the territory, the jurisdiction, and the law of the Union and its Member States. By focusing on three key elements of criminalisation, the criminalisation of the facilitation of entry, the facilitation of entry, and immigration detention, the present contribution highlighted not only the negative effect that such criminalisation has on the rights of migrants, but also, crucially, the incompatibility of the criminalisation of migration in EU law with the rule of law and with fundamental principles of criminal law, including the need to justify the adoption of criminal law, which should only be adopted as *ultima ratio*. In the current climate with legislative and judicial possibilities for reform, it is hoped that this volume, and particularly the present chapter, will prove to be helpful contributions in the pressing theoretical and practical debate on rethinking the criminalisation of migration in EU and in national law.

Notes

1 See Chapter 5 in this volume.
2 Andrew Ashworth and Lucia Zedner, *Preventive Justice* (OUP 2014).
3 Valsamis Mitsilegas, 'The Security Union as a Paradigm of Preventive Justice: Challenges for Citizenship, Fundamental Rights and the Rule of Law' in Valsamis Mitsilegas and Sergio Carrera (eds), *Constitutionalising the Security Union. Effectiveness, Rule of Law and Rights in Countering Terrorism and Crime* (CEPS 2017) 2.

4 Valsamis Mitsilegas, *EU Criminal Law After Lisbon* (Hart Publishing 2016) ch 9.
5 Valsamis Mitsilegas, 'The EU External Border as a Site of Preventive (In)justice' (2022) 28 European Law Journal 263–80.
6 Council Directive 2002/90/EC of 28 November 2002 defining the facilitation of unauthorised entry, transit and residence [2002] OJ L328/4 (hereinafter, in the Chapter, Facilitation Directive).
7 Council Framework Decision 2002/946/JHA of 28 November 2002 on the strengthening of the penal framework to prevent the facilitation of unauthorised entry, transit and residence [2002] OJ L328/1 (hereinafter, in the Chapter, Facilitation Framework Decision).
8 For a background, see Valsamis Mitsilegas, Jörg Monar and Wyn Rees, *The European Union and Internal Security* (Palgrave/Macmillan 2003) 106–8.
9 Article 1 para 1(a) of the Facilitation Directive combined with article 1 para 1 of the Facilitation Framework Decision.
10 For a comparison see Valsamis Mitsilegas, 'The Normative Foundations of the Criminalisation of Human Smuggling. Exploring the Fault Lines Between European and International Law' (2019) 10 New Journal of European Criminal Law 68–85.
11 Article 1 para 1 (a) of the Facilitation Directive.
12 Article 1 para 2 of the Facilitation Directive.
13 European Commission, 'Staff Working Document—REFIT Evaluation of the EU Legal Framework Against Facilitation of Unauthorised Entry, Transit and Residence' COM (2017) 117 final, 14.
14 On the justification of criminalisation as a migration management tool in national jurisdictions, see Chapter 2 in this volume.
15 Alessandro Spena, 'Human Smuggling and Irregular Immigration in the EU: From Complicity to Exploitation?' in Sergio Carrera and Elspeth Guild (eds), *Irregular Migration, Trafficking and Smuggling of Human Beings* (CEPS 2016) 37.
16 For an overview, see Sergio Carrera and others, *Policing Humanitarianism. EU Policies Against Human Smuggling and Their Impact on Civil Society* (Hart Publishing 2020) ch 4 and 5.
17 Valsamis Mitsilegas, 'Contested Sovereignty in Preventive Border Control: Civil Society, the 'Hostile Environment' and the Rule of Law' in Mary Bosworth and Lucia Zedner (eds), *Privatising Border Control: Law at the Limits of the Sovereign State* (OUP 2022) 36–56.
18 See in Greece, see Nikolaos Chatzinikolaou, 'Crimmigration in Greece: A Study of Exceptional Derogations from the Rule of Law Within a Permanent Situation of Emergency' in Gian Luigi Gatta, Valsamis Mitsilegas and Stefano Zirulia (eds), *Controlling Immigration Through Criminal Law. European and Comparative Perspectives on "Crimmigration"* (Hart Publishing 2021) 165–92.
19 Flavia Patanè and others, 'Asylum-Seekers Prosecuted for Human Smuggling: A Case Study of Scafisti in Italy' (2020) 39 Refugee Survey Quarterly 123. On migrants being coerced by smugglers, see Chapter 6 in this volume.
20 See the Kinsa litigation (n 37).
21 See Chapter 9 in this volume.
22 See Chapter 3 in this volume.
23 Mitsilegas (n 17).
24 European Commission (n 13).
25 European Commission (n 13) 35; Valsamis Mitsilegas 'The Criminalisation of Migration in the Law of the European Union. Challenging the Preventive Paradigm' in Gatta, Mitsilegas and Zirulia (eds) (n 18).
26 European Commission, 'Proposal for a Directive of the European Parliament and of the Council laying down minimum rules to prevent and counter the facilitation of unauthorised entry, transit and stay in the Union, and replacing Council

Directive 2002/90/EC and Council Framework Decision 2002/946 JHA' COM (18 November 2023) 755 final.

27 European Commission (n 26) article 18. For an analysis see Valsamis Mitsilegas 'Reforming EU Criminal Law on the Facilitation of Unauthorised Entry: The New Commission Proposal in the Light of the Kinshasa Litigation' (2024) 15 New Journal of European Criminal Law 3.

28 European Commission (n 26) Article 3 para 1(a).

29 European Commission (n 26) article 3 para 1(b).

30 European Commission (n 26) article 3 para 2.

31 European Commission (n 26) Recital 1.

32 European Commission (n 26) Recital 6.

33 European Commission (n 26) Recital 11.

34 Mitsilegas (n 27).

35 European Commission (n 26) Recital 7.

36 European Commission (n 26) article 6.4.

37 Case C-460/23 *Kinsa* [2023] ECLI:EU:C:2023:784. The case was formerly named as "Kinshasa".

38 Mitsilegas (n 27).

39 Mitsilegas (n 27) paras 1–5.

40 Mitsilegas (n 27).

41 For further details see Valsamis Mitsilegas, 'Reforming the 'Facilitators' Package' Through the *Kinsa* Litigation: Legality, Effectiveness and Taking International Law into Account' (2024) 3 Eurojus 155.

42 C-460/23, Kinsa, ECLI:EU:C:2025:392.

43 Para. 73.

44 The Court's interpretation is supported by the Palermo Protocol against the Smuggling of Migrants, in the light of which that directive must be read-indeed, in accordance with Article 2 of that protocol, the purpose of the protocol is to criminalise the smuggling of migrants, while protecting the rights of the migrants themselves, para. 66.

45 Valsamis Mitsilegas, *The Criminalisation of Migration in Europe. Challenges for Human Rights and the Rule of Law* (Springer 2015).

46 See European Union Agency for Fundamental Rights, *Criminalisation of Migrants in an Irregular Situation and of Persons Engaging with Them* (Self-Published 2014).

47 Alessandro Spena, '*Iniuria Migrandi*: Criminalization of Immigrants and the Basic Principles of the Criminal Law' (2014) 8 *Criminal Law and Philosophy* 635.

48 Mitsilegas (n 25).

49 Spena (n 44) 646.

50 Ana Aliverti, 'The Wrongs of Unlawful Immigration' (2017) 11 Criminal Law and Philosophy 375, 386.

51 Valsamis Mitsilegas, 'The Changing Landscape of the Criminalisation of Migration in Europe: The Protective Function of European Union Law' in Maria Joao Guia, Maartje Van der Woude and Joanne Van der Leun (eds), *Social Control and Justice: Crimmigration in an Age of Fear* (Eleven International Publishing 2012).

52 Case C-61/11 PPU *Hassen El Dridi, alias Karim Soufi* [2011] ECLI:EU:C:2011:268.

53 Case C-329/11 *Alexandre Achughbabian v Préfet du Val-de-Marne* [2011] ECLI:EU:C:2011:807.

54 Mitsilegas (n 48).

55 Case C-290/14, *Skerdjan Celaj* [2015] ECLI:EU:C:2015:640. By contrast, see the Opinion of AG Szpunar who applied the CJEU's logic in Case C-61/11 PPU *El Dridi* (n 49) and in Case C-329/11 *Achughbabian* (n 50).

56 Case C-225/16, *Mossa Ouhrami* [2017] ECLI:EU:C:2017:590, para 51.

57 Mitsilegas (n 10).

58 Giuseppe Campesi, 'Genealogies of Immigration Detention: Migration Control and the Shifting Boundaries Between the "Penal" and the "Preventive" State' (2020) 29 Social and Legal Studies 528.
59 Campesi (n 55) 541.
60 Mitsilegas (n 5).
61 Majcher notes that the concept of absconding embraces penal law logic. See Izabella Majcher, 'Creeping Crimmigration in CEAS Reform: Detention of Asylum-Seekers and Restrictions on Their Movement under EU Law' (2021) 40 Refugee Survey Quarterly 82, 97. Costello and Mouzourakis note that the term is usually invoked in the criminal law context when individuals against whom there is a reasonable suspicion of having committed a crime flee in order to evade prosecution. See Cathyrin Costello and Minos Mouzourakis, 'EU Law and the Detainability of Asylum Seekers' (2016) 35 Refugee Studies Quarterly 47.
62 Case C-474/13, *Thi Ly Pham*, ECLI:EU:C:2014:2096; Joined Cases C-473/13 and C-514/13, *Bero and Bouzamate*, ECLI:EU:C:2014:2095; Mitsilegas (n 42).
63 Case C-294/16 PPU *JZ v Prokuratura Rejonowa Łódź—Śródmieście* ECLI:EU:C:2016:610, para 48.
64 Mitsilegas (n 5).
65 Amnesty International, 'Samos: "We Feel in Prison on the Island". Unlawful Detention and Sub-Standard Conditions in an EU-Funded Refugee Centre' Research Briefing, EUR 25/8356/2024 (July 2024) <https://www.amnesty.org/en/documents/eur25/8356/2024/en/>. Last access 20 September 2024.

Bibliography

Aliverti A, 'The Wrongs of Unlawful Immigration' (2017) 11 Criminal Law and Philosophy 375.

Amnesty International, *Samos: "We Feel in Prison on the Island". Unlawful Detention and Sub-Standard Conditions in an EU-Funded Refugee Centre* (Self-published, 2024).

Ashworth A and Zedner L, *Preventive Justice* (OUP 2014).

Campesi G, 'Genealogies of Immigration Detention: Migration Control and the Shifting Boundaries Between the "Penal" and the "Preventive" State' (2020) 29 Social and Legal Studies 528.

Carrera S and others, *Policing Humanitarianism: EU Policies Against Human Smuggling and Their Impact on Civil Society* (Hart 2019).

Chatzinikolaou N, 'Crimmigration in Greece: A Study of Exceptional Derogations from the Rule of Law Within a Permanent Situation of Emergency' in Gatta GL, Mitsilegas V and Zirulia S (eds), *Controlling Immigration Through Criminal Law. European and Comparative Perspectives on "Crimmigration"* (Hart 2021).

Costello C and Mouzourakis M, 'EU Law and the Detainability of Asylum Seekers' (2016) 35 Refugee Studies Quarterly 47.

European Union Agency for Fundamental Rights, *Criminalisation of Migrants in an Irregular Situation and of Persons Engaging with Them* (Self-Published 2014).

Majcher I, 'Creeping Crimmigration in CEAS Reform: Detention of Asylum-Seekers and Restrictions on Their Movement under EU Law' (2021) 40 Refugee Survey Quarterly 82.

Mitsilegas V, 'The Changing Landscape of the Criminalisation of Migration in Europe: The Protective Function of European Union Law' in Guia MJ, Van der Woude M and Van der Leun J (eds), *Social Control and Justice: Crimmigration in an Age of Fear* (Eleven International Publishing 2012).

Mitsilegas V, *The Criminalisation of Migration in Europe. Challenges for Human Rights and the Rule of Law* (Springer 2015).

Mitsilegas V, *EU Criminal Law After Lisbon* (Hart 2016).

Mitsilegas V, 'The Security Union as a Paradigm of Preventive Justice: Challenges for Citizenship, Fundamental Rights and the Rule of Law' in Mitsilegas V and Carrera S (eds), *Constitutionalising the Security Union. Effectiveness, Rule of Law and Rights in Countering Terrorism and Crime* (CEPS 2017).

Mitsilegas V, 'The Normative Foundations of the Criminalisation of Human Smuggling. Exploring the Fault Lines Between European and International Law' (2019) 10 New Journal of European Criminal Law.

Mitsilegas V, 'The Criminalisation of Migration in the Law of the European Union. Challenging the Preventive Paradigm' in Gatta GL, Mitsilegas V and Zirulia S (eds), *Controlling Immigration Through Criminal Law. European and Comparative Perspectives on "Crimmigration"* (Hart 2021).

Mitsilegas V, 'Contested Sovereignty in Preventive Border Control: Civil Society, the "Hostile Environment" and the Rule of Law' in Bosworth M and Zedner L (eds), *Privatising Border Control: Law at the Limits of the Sovereign State* (OUP 2022).

Mitsilegas V, 'The EU External Border as a Site of Preventive (In)justice' (2022) 28 European Law Journal 263.

Mitsilegas V, 'Reforming EU Criminal Law on the Facilitation of Unauthorised Entry: The New Commission Proposal in the Light of the Kinshasa Litigation' (2024) 15 New Journal of European Criminal Law 3.

Mitsilegas V, 'Reforming the "Facilitators' Package" Through the *Kinsa* Litigation: Legality, Effectiveness and Taking International Law into Account' (2024) 3 Eurojus 155.

Mitsilegas V, Monar J and Rees W, *The European Union and Internal Security* (Palgrave/Macmillan 2003).

Patanè F and others, 'Asylum-Seekers Prosecuted for Human Smuggling: A Case Study of Scafisti in Italy' (2020) 39 Refugee Survey Quarterly 123.

Spena A, '*Iniuria Migrandi*: Criminalization of Immigrants and the Basic Principles of the Criminal Law' (2014) 8 Criminal Law and Philosophy 635.

Spena A, 'Human Smuggling and Irregular Immigration in the EU: From Complicity to Exploitation?' in Carrera S and Guild E (eds), *Irregular Migration, Trafficking and Smuggling of Human Beings* (CEPS 2016).

Index

Note: Page locators in *italic* indicate a figure.

FSC
www.fsc.org
MIX
Papier | Fördert gute Waldnutzung
FSC® C083411

Kolibri 360 GmbH
Ferdinand-Jühlke-Straße 7
99095 Erfurt, Deutschland
produktsicherheit@kolibri360.de